PROMOT...   ...ERSITY

...s Guide

PROMOTING EQUALITY AND DIVERSITY

A Practitioner's Guide

Henrietta Hill and Richard Kenyon

OXFORD

UNIVERSITY PRESS

OXFORD
UNIVERSITY PRESS

Great Clarendon Street, Oxford OX2 6DP

Oxford University Press is a department of the University of Oxford.
It furthers the University's objective of excellence in research, scholarship,
and education by publishing worldwide in

Oxford New York

Auckland Cape Town Dar es Salaam Hong Kong Karachi
Kuala Lumpur Madrid Melbourne Mexico City Nairobi
New Delhi Shanghai Taipei Toronto

With offices in

Argentina Austria Brazil Chile Czech Republic France Greece
Guatemala Hungary Italy Japan Poland Portugal Singapore
South Korea Switzerland Thailand Turkey Ukraine Vietnam

Oxford is a registered trade mark of Oxford University Press
in the UK and in certain other countries

Published in the United States
by Oxford University Press Inc., New York

© Henrietta Hill and Richard Kenyon 2008

The moral rights of the author have been asserted
Database right Oxford University Press (maker)

Crown copyright material is reproduced under Class Licence
Number C01P0000148 with the permission of OPSI
and the Queen's Printer for Scotland

First published 2008

British Library Cataloguing in Publication Data

Data available

Library of Congress Cataloging in Publication Data

Data available

Typeset by RefineCatch Limited, Bungay, Suffolk
Printed in Great Britain
on acid-free paper by
Biddles Ltd, King's Lynn
ISBN 978–0–19–923545–2

1 3 5 7 9 10 8 6 4 2

For Dadie

FOREWORD

ANTHONY LESTER[1]

This book is a timely contribution towards shaping the equality and diversity agenda in the UK. The birth of the Equality and Human Rights Commission presents an exciting opportunity to shape discrimination law for the decades to come, as does the recently published Discrimination Law Review Green Paper, *A Framework for Fairness: Proposals for a Single Equality Bill for Great Britain*. If we are to eliminate unlawful discrimination and promote equality regardless of sex, race, colour, ethnic or national origin, religion or belief, disability, age, sexual orientation or other status, we must all adopt the practical approach espoused by this book.

Henrietta Hill and Richard Kenyon have written a well-constructed and practical guide to promoting equality and diversity in employment. The authors give clear and readable advice to employers and others about how to adopt good practice so as to avoid litigation and achieve equality and diversity outcomes.

During the forty years since the first anti-discrimination legislation in the UK (the Race Relations Act 1965), the various strands of our anti-discrimination law have become a tangled, complex web. The authors take a functional and versatile approach to guide the reader through this web, organising chapters around practical aspects of the workplace, for example recruitment and promotion, resolving grievances and medical issues. The chapters are supplemented with helpful 'in brief' summaries, suggested checklists and sample policies, which bring the subject matter alive and dispel the myth that equality and diversity are concerned with bureaucratic measurements, rather than providing sensible tools for better business and employment practices. The authors recognise that in order to secure genuine equality of opportunity and treatment, there must be less emphasis on procedures, and more emphasis on outcomes. This also marks the book out from other, more academic publications in the

---

[1] Lord Lester of Herne Hill QC is a practising barrister at Blackstone Chambers and a Liberal Democrat peer. He introduced a Civil Partnership Bill and an Equality Bill in the House of Lords. As Special Adviser to the Home Secretary (Roy Jenkins) between 1974 and 1976, he developed policy on what became the Sex Discrimination Act 1975 and the Race Relations Act 1976.

discrimination field: all have their place, but this work will easily find its way to non-legal readers.

Attention is also given to topical issues such as religious practice, dress codes and freedom of expression in the workplace. Detailed analysis of the law is supplemented by brief case summaries and recommendations of best practice. There is also a useful chapter on the new Equality and Human Rights Commission, which will play a key role in advancing and monitoring best practice in promoting equality and eliminating unlawful discrimination.

As the authors recognise, the Commission will only be effective if, instead of the tangled and incoherent mess of existing equality laws, we have a comprehensive, coherent, and user-friendly Single Equality Act. There are several key points which must be followed if we are to achieve effective equality legislation. First, there must be no levelling down of existing protection. Second, there must be effective individual remedies and scope for enforcement. Third, there must be less emphasis on procedures, and more emphasis on outcomes.

A Single Equality Act must contain clear, consistent and easily intelligible standards which state the whole of the law, including EU law implementation, as far as possible. It must set out an effective, efficient and equitable regulatory framework, aimed at encouraging personal responsibility and self-generating efforts to promote equality—aims which this book will assist employers and individuals to achieve. Individuals should be free to seek redress for the harm they have suffered as a result of unlawful discrimination, through procedures which are fair, inexpensive and expeditious, and the remedies should be effective.

Meanwhile this book provides useful guidance for lawyers and non-lawyers alike. It deserves a wide readership.

CONTENTS—SUMMARY

CONTENTS

TABLE OF CASES

TABLE OF LEGISLATION

EUROPEAN LEGISLATION

Directives

TABLE OF TREATIES AND CONVENTIONS

GLOSSARY AND ABBREVIATIONS

AAL	Additional Adoption Leave
ACAS	Advisory, Conciliation and Arbitration Service
ADR	Alternative Dispute Resolution
AML	Additional Maternity Leave
APL	Additional Paternity Leave
AR	Employment Equality (Age) Regulations 2006
AR Notes	The DTI Notes on the AR
ASPP	Additional Statutory Paternity Pay
BERR	The Department for Business Enterprise and Regulatory Reform
CA	Court of Appeal
CCT	Compulsory Competitive Tendering
CEDR	The Centre for Effective Dispute Resolution
CEHR	Commission for Equality and Human Rights (from October 2007 the Equality and Human Rights Commission – see 'EHRC')
CIPD	The Chartered Institute of Personnel and Development
CPR	Civil Procedure Rules
CRE	Commission for Racial Equality
CRE Code 2005	CRE Code of Practice on Racial Equality in Employment 2005
Cty Ct	County Court
Ct Sess	Court of Session
DDA Duties Regulations 2005	Disability Discrimination (Public Authorities) (Statutory Duties) Regulations 2005
DDA	Disability Discrimination Act 1995
DES	Disability Equality Scheme
DLR consultation paper	*Discrimination Law Review: A Framework for Fairness: Proposals for a Single Equality Bill for Great Britain*
DPA	Data Protection Act 1998

DRC	Disability Rights Commission
DRC Code 2004	DRC Code of Practice on Employment and Occupation 2004
Disability Duty Code	DRC, The Duty to Promote Disability Equality, Statutory Code of Practice (England and Wales), 2005
DRC Practical Guide	DRC Practical Guide to the Law and Best Practice for Employers
DTI	Department of Trade and Industry (now the Department for Business, Enterprise and Regulatory Reform)
EA	Equality Act 2006
EAT	Employment Appeal Tribunal
ECHR	European Convention on Human Rights
ECJ	European Court of Justice
ECommHR	European Commission of Human Rights
ECtHR	European Court of Human Rights
EHRC	Equality and Human Rights Commission (formerly the CEHR)
EOC	Equal Opportunities Commission
EOC Code 1985	EOC Code of Practice for the Elimination of Discrimination on the Grounds of Sex and Marriage and the Promotion of Equality of Opportunity in Employment 1985
EqPA	Equal Pay Act 1970
ERA	Employment Rights Act 1996
ET	Employment Tribunal
ET Rules	The Employment Tribunals Rules of Procedure 2004
EWC	Expected Week of Childbirth
FOIA	Freedom of Information Act 2000
Gender Duty Code	EOC Gender Equality Duty Code of Practice, 2007
GES	Gender Equality Scheme
GOQ	Genuine Occupational Qualification
GOR	Genuine Occupational Requirement
HC	High Court
HL	House of Lords
HMRC	Her Majesty's Revenue and Customs
HR	Human Resources
HRA	Human Rights Act 1998

IDR	Intended Date of Retirement
IT	Industrial Tribunal
ITT	Invitation to Tender
JES	Job Evaluation Study
JM	Judicial Mediation
KIT day	Keeping in Touch day
LGB	Lesbian, Gay and Bisexual
MHSWR	Management of Health and Safety at Work Regulations 1999
MPLR	Maternity and Parental Leave etc Regulations 1999
MPS	Metropolitan Police Service
NDPB	Non-Departmental Public Bodies
NMW	National Minimum Wage
NMWA	National Minimum Wage Act 1998
OAL	Ordinary Adoption Leave
OGC	Office of Government Commerce
OJEU	Official Journal of the European Union
OML	Ordinary Maternity Leave
PALR	Paternity and Adoption Leave Regulations 2002
PCP	Provision, Criterion or Practice
PCR 2006	Public Contracts Regulations 2006
PFI	Private Finance Initiative
PHA	Protection from Harassment Act 1997
PPP	Public Private Partnership
PQQ	Pre-Qualification Questionnaire
Quango	Quasi-autonomous non-governmental organisation
Race Duty Code	CRE Code of Practice on the Duty to Promote Race Equality, 2002
RBR	Employment Equality (Religion or Belief) Regulations 2003
RES	Race Equality Scheme
RRA	Race Relations Act 1976
RRA Duties Order 2001	Race Relations Act 1976 (Statutory Duties) Order 2001
RRAA	Race Relations (Amendment) Act 2000
SAP	Statutory Adoption Pay
SDA	Sex Discrimination Act 1975

SDA Duties Order 2006	Sex Discrimination Act 1975 (Public Authorities) (Statutory Duties) Order 2006
SME	Small and Medium-sized Enterprises
SMP	Statutory Maternity Pay
SOR	Employment Equality (Sexual Orientation) Regulations 2003
SOSR	Some Other Substantial Reason (for dismissal)
SPP	Statutory Paternity Pay
TUPE	Transfer of Undertakings (Protection of Employment) Regulations 2006
UCR 2006	Utilities Contracts Regulations 2006

1

INTRODUCTION

The greatest revolution of our generation is the discovery that human beings, by changing the inner attitudes of their minds, can change the outer aspects of their lives.

(William James, American psychologist and philosopher, 1842–1910)

A. The Objective of this Book

Books on discrimination tend to tell you what the law says. They either relate **1.01** to one of the six 'strands' of discrimination (sex, race, disability, sexual orientation, religion or belief and age) or alternatively cover discrimination more generally but with chapters on each strand of discrimination. We have aimed to make the approach of this book different in three respects:

- first, we take a practical task-based approach with pragmatic guidance, checklists and examples. By taking a task-based approach, we are able to explain, for example, how to carry out a recruitment process from advertising the post, through selection and interview to appointment, ensuring that the process is compliant with *all* discrimination legislation and best practice. It is the practical application of the law that we take as our starting point rather than the law itself;

- secondly, we explain the new proactive approach to promoting equality and diversity emerging in the legislation in respect of which race has been the pioneer, but where positive duties in respect of sex and disability discrimination are now in place. We again aim to take a practical approach to explaining how to carry out impact assessments and monitoring, how to prepare equality schemes and their role; and

- thirdly, we have aimed to make this book readable beginning to end, rather than a traditional text book from which the reader takes what they need from page 241 and then returns it to the library.

1

1.02 Barely a day goes past without some aspect of equality hitting the headlines, whether it is the 200-year anniversary of the abolition of the slave trade; an attack on immigration policy or on asylum seekers or on economic migrants; a Tribunal case involving a teaching assistant who wishes to wear a veil at work or an employee who wants to wear a cross in conflict with a 'no jewellery' policy; reports from the Equalities or Discrimination Law Reviews; press releases from the Equality and Human Rights Commission ('EHRC') or the Commission on Integration and Cohesion; harassment of Muslims in response to the threat of terrorist attacks or clashes between Church and State over sexual orientation and religious belief.

1.03 The subject of equality and diversity is all pervading, covering not only employment but also housing, education, the provision of goods, facilities and services and all functions of public authorities. Our focus is on only one of these areas of concern: the workplace. But it is within the context of employment that the law of discrimination has been mostly developed. We hope that we can make at least some contribution to demystifying the subject and promoting a better run and more inclusive workplace for the benefit of both employers and employees.

The Aspiration

To give ourselves a sense of direction in our objectives for this book, we can do no better than quote from a Government consultation paper relating to the implementation of the European directives that brought unlawful discrimination on the grounds of sexual orientation and religion or belief to our legislation in December 2003. The Government wants to see:

> An equal, inclusive society where everyone is treated with respect and where there is opportunity for all. Everyone must be able to play their full part in social and economic life. We need to tackle barriers to participation and change culture so that equal opportunities and equal treatment become a priority for all. We want to see a Britain where there is increasing empowerment of all groups, with economic empowerment a key goal; where attitudes and biases that hinder the progress of individuals and groups are tackled; where cultural, racial, and social diversity is respected and celebrated; where communities live together in mutual respect and tolerance; and where discrimination against individuals is tackled robustly.[1]

---

[1] *Equality and Diversity: Making It Happen* (Office of the Deputy Prime Minister, October 2002), Part 1.

The title of this book poses three immediate questions: what is equality; what is **1.04** diversity; and why promote them?

B. Defining Equality

The concept of equality is hardly new. In its broadest sense it means having **1.05** identical privileges, rights and status and being treated in the same way as other people regardless of individual difference.

The principle that 'all men are created equal' is sometimes suggested to have a **1.06** Biblical root. Despite our reasonable endeavours (well at least a Google search!) we have been unable to find this quote. The best we could do is the following from Paul's Letter to the Galatians, Chapter 3, verse 28 which gives a 2000-year-old view of a form of equality: 'There is neither Jew nor Greek, there is neither slave nor free, there is neither male nor female; for you are all one in Christ Jesus.'

However, the preamble to the Declaration of Independence of the thirteen **1.07** united States of America drafted by Thomas Jefferson in 1776 does begin: 'We hold these truths to be self-evident: that all men are created equal, that they are endowed by their Creator with certain unalienable rights, that among these are life, liberty and the pursuit of happiness.' At least then, in late-eighteenth-century America, equality between men was seen as self-evident—or at least equality between some men, given that slavery was not finally abolished until the 13th Amendment of the Constitution in 1865—and there was no explicit mention of women!

A few years later in France 'Liberté, égalité, fraternité' was the cry of the **1.08** revolution, where 'égalité' referred to equality of all citizens before the law without preference for birth or status. That concept now also finds form in our democratic traditions and, for example, within the European Convention for the Protection of Human Rights and Fundamental Freedoms,[2] commonly known as the 'European Convention on Human Rights', where Convention rights are secured without discrimination on any ground such as sex, race, colour, language, religion, political or other opinion, national or social origin, association with a national minority, property, birth or other status.[3]

In the UK, equality has, in some contexts, been seen as a class struggle for social **1.09** mobility. In his 1987 speech to the Welsh Labour Party Neil Kinnock asked:

---

[2] Agreed by the Council of Europe at Rome on 4 November 1950.   [3] Article 14.

Why am I the first Kinnock in a thousand generations to be able to get to university? Why is Glenys the first woman in her family in a thousand generations to be able to get to university? Was it because our predecessors were thick? Does anybody really think that they didn't get what we had because they didn't have the talent or the strength or the endurance or the commitment? Of course not. It was because there was no platform upon which they could stand.

1.10 Twenty years later the types of issue raised by Neil Kinnock find voice not as a class struggle but as a struggle for equality of treatment for a range of disadvantaged groups on grounds of sex, race, disability, sexual orientation, religion or belief and age.

1.11 The Equalities Review, which reported in February 2007,[4] examined the question of what we mean by equality. In particular the Review compared and contrasted different academic approaches to equality:

- *equality of process*: ensuring that everyone is treated in the same manner in any given situation;
- *equality of worth*: ensuring each individual is accorded equal respect;
- *equality of outcome*: aiming to ensure that despite substantive differences everyone ends up with the same outcome measured in terms of, for example, income or attainment;
- *equality of opportunity*: whether in terms of ensuring that opportunities depend only on a person's talents and the efforts s/he makes or going further to ensure that everyone has the opportunity to acquire the relevant skills, competencies and qualifications to compete.

1.12 The Equalities Review team did not seek to settle these differences of approach once and for all. Rather, they focused, in accordance with their terms of reference, on outcomes—'what will reduce the gap between those who enjoy the best life chances and those who suffer the worst'. The Review produced a definition of an equal society (see boxed text) and an 'Equality Scorecard' based on ten areas or 'dimensions' in which we as a society think it is most important to achieve greater equality. Interestingly, not one of those dimensions is directly related to the workplace other than that current inequalities in physical security, health, education and standard of living, for example, are often related to income.

---

[4] *Fairness and Freedom: The Final Report of the Equalities Review* (Communities and Local Government publications, 2007), <www.theequalitiesreview.org.uk>.

> ## The Equalities Review definition of an equal society
>
> An equal society protects and promotes equal, real freedom and substantive opportunity to live in the ways people value and would choose, so that everyone can flourish. An equal society recognises people's different needs, situations and goals and removes the barriers that limit what people can do and can be.[5]

The current legal framework, which we summarise in Chapter 2, already takes **1.13** different approaches to equality. The predominant approach, that has been with us at least since the Sex Discrimination Act 1975 and the Race Relations Act 1976, is one of equality of treatment. Each person must be treated the same way regardless of their sex or their racial origin. To treat people differently on these grounds would amount to direct discrimination for which there is no legal justification or excuse.

It has, however, long been recognised that equality of treatment may not lead to **1.14** equality of outcome. The concept of indirect discrimination captures a provision, criterion or practice which is applied (in the context of the workplace, applied by the employer) equally and consistently to all people (or employees in the workplace) but nevertheless causes particular disadvantage to one group when compared to another. This is still, however, primarily about equality of treatment since the offending provision, criterion or practice will not be unlawful if it is a proportionate means of achieving a legitimate aim. In other words, the unequal outcome can be disregarded if there is equality of treatment based on a legitimate objective.

The law does focus on equality of outcome in the case of disability. Uniquely in **1.15** discrimination law, there is a duty to make 'reasonable adjustments' to help overcome the disadvantages of disability and achieve equality. There is therefore an obligation to treat the disabled differently in order to overcome disadvantage. There is also, to a degree, legal recognition of the unique status of pregnant women that is not simply addressed by ensuring equality of treatment with men.

It is worth mentioning only in passing that the legal definition of 'equality' in **1.16** section 8(2) of the Equality Act 2006 is 'equality between individuals'. That definition does not really take us very much further.

---

[5] *Fairness and Freedom: The Final Report of the Equalities Review* (Communities and Local Government Publications, 1 June 2007, Product Code 06DL0440/a, <www.theequalitiesreview.org.uk>), p 6.

1.17 As lawyers we naturally gravitate towards a legal approach. For our purposes, when we refer to 'promoting equality' we are referring to the active steps that an employer can take towards the eradication of unlawful discrimination and such other steps as are permitted within the law to remove barriers and encourage all employees to achieve their full potential.

1.18 Finally, we can at least place 'Equality' on the map. It is a village in Gallatin County, Illinois, USA with a population of 721 at the time of the 2000 census. Somewhat ironically, the racial make-up of Equality is 99.17 per cent white!

C. Defining Diversity

1.19 Prior to the Equality Act 2006, the word 'diversity' had no legal definition. It is now defined by section 8(2) of that Act to mean 'the fact that individuals are different'. Importing that definition into the duties of the new EHRC that mention 'diversity', set out in section 8(1), the EHRC is required to:

- exercise its powers to promote understanding of the importance of the fact that individuals are different;
- exercise its powers to encourage good practice in relation to the fact that individuals are different; and
- exercise its functions with a view to encouraging and supporting the development of a society in which there is mutual respect between groups based on understanding and valuing of the fact that individuals are different.

1.20 Providing at least a basic definition for diversity may help to elevate the term beyond being a rather woolly and trendy concept which carries the risk of confusion. The Morris Inquiry, established by the Metropolitan Police Authority to examine the approach of the Metropolitan Police Service towards resolving workplace conflicts, reported on 14 December 2004 that:

> We have heard much about the approach of the Metropolitan Police Service to 'diversity.' Indeed it dominated the evidence we received. We appreciate that extensive work has been undertaken in developing the policies of the MPS in this area and in trying to implement them across the organisation. However, we were left with concern that there is no common understanding of diversity within the organisation and that it is not embedded in the culture of the MPS. We fear that it remains, at worse, a source of fear and anxiety and, at best, a process of ticking boxes.[6]

---

[6] *The Case for Change: The Report of the Morris Inquiry*, 14 December 2004, <www.mpa.gov.uk/downloads/issues/morris/morris-report.pdf>.

The final report of the Equalities Review neatly summarises the distinction **1.21** between equality and diversity when it says at page 16:

> equality does not mean sameness, nor should an equal society try to force every- one into the same mould. On the contrary, the pursuit of equality is about empowering people to live their dreams, to be themselves and to be different, if they wish.

For our purposes, when we refer to 'promoting diversity' we are referring to **1.22** the active steps that an employer can take to prevent harassment of individuals because they are different, thereby promoting a working environment that is accepting and tolerant of difference. Diversity is also the natural outcome of promoting equality.

D. Are Equality and Diversity Conflicting Concepts?

Although we have described above how equality and diversity are comple- **1.23** mentary concepts, the latter being the positive outcome of the former, there are also potential tensions. These are particularly evident where we stray into talk- ing about the 'value' of having a diverse workforce and try to make the busi- ness case for diversity. This argument works on the basis that if an employer employs more gay employees or those from ethnic minorities or with different belief systems, it will potentially have routes into the new markets that those individuals 'represent' or be better able to deliver client or customer needs to those groups.

This concept of diversity trades on difference. It assumes that one racial group **1.24** is different from another, men are different from women, gay people different from straight people, older people different from younger people and that these differences should be celebrated and exploited for the good of the employer. The logical extension of this attitude is that the employer should actively recruit people on the basis of their race, sex or religious belief. In other words, actively (and, as it happens, unlawfully) discriminate.

However, as Michael Rubenstein, Editor of the *Equal Opportunities Review* **1.25** puts it:

> . . . presumptions about people because of their race, gender, sexual orientation etc are stereotypes and should be avoided. Indeed acting on such stereotypes is unlawful. There are good reasons for this. Aside from the fact generalisations are not true of all members of the group, one person's positive stereotype is another's negative attribute. If women are more consensual decision makers does that allow an organisation looking for someone 'assertive' to prefer a man? If the business case for diversity tells us that the composition of retail staff should resemble the customer base in multicultural areas, what of the financial sector firm whose

middle-aged white male customers would much prefer to deal with people just like themselves? If women judges will decide cases differently from men, where does that leave our system of justice: and if they will not, why do we need more women judges? Diversity, in this sense of reifying difference, is a dangerous road to take.[7]

1.26 There is much talk, particularly within the public sector where positive equality duties apply, of equality and diversity outcomes. In our target-driven working lives there is a logic to applying metrics to the promotion of equality and diversity. However, there is a fine line between monitoring the workforce by gender and ethnicity as a method of testing whether individuals are being treated equally, for example, in recruitment and promotion and setting quotas for the composition of the workforce.

1.27 An organisation that sets itself the target of increasing the percentage of women managers from, say, 16 per cent to 25 per cent within three years may have a laudable objective and a clear measure of whether that objective has succeeded. The same organisation must, however, be careful not to stray into unlawful positive discrimination in favour of women in order to achieve that target. Promotion choices between men and women must still be made on the basis of merit only.

E. Why Promote Equality and Diversity?

(a) The Economic Argument

1.28 Having somewhat rubbished the economic case for diversity above, the economic argument does remain the one argument that is most eye-catching to the average employer. It is undoubtedly the case that the more diverse an employer's workforce, the greater the employer's reservoir of knowledge and experience of the diverse world in which it operates. The more knowledge and experience, the more opportunity to have and to exploit a competitive edge.

1.29 There is merit in the economic argument. However, if the economic argument was that compelling, in the highly competitive capitalist world within which we live, why have equality and diversity not happened naturally? There is also the danger, identified above, of there being a very fine line between actively wanting to encourage diversity as being good for business and positively and unlawfully discriminating by targeting the recruitment of groups of people to exploit certain markets. In Chapter 6 we deal with the circumstances in which, for

---

[7] Issue 162, March 2007, p 26.

example, being of a particular sex or race is a genuine occupational qualification or requirement, but they are limited circumstances.

(b) The Moral Argument

In its simplest terms, we suggest, the moral argument claims that promoting equality and diversity is the 'right' thing to do. It sits comfortably alongside the 'broader less technical idea of *fairness*' which the Final Report of the Equalities Review suggested at page 15 is 'so precious to our society'.

1.30

(c) The Social Cohesion Argument

It is a stock phrase of politicians that immigration has greatly enriched our society. In her speech launching the Commission on Integration and Cohesion on 24 August 2006, then Communities Secretary Ruth Kelly said:

1.31

> Immigration has helped enrich our cultural life, with the capital's diversity now commonly acknowledged to be one of its key attractions. A weekend spent at the Notting Hill Carnival or exploring Brick Lane are attracting tourists and residents alike.

But enriching our society must mean more than an increase in the range of eating out options for the majority white population or a white middle class recreating a colonial class structure in the UK, with Brazilian cleaners and Polish nannies. Some first generation immigrants may naturally gravitate to 'entry professions' like running restaurants and takeaways, cleaning or security. They may do so out of choice or because of language issues or a lack of training or education that would fit them for other work. Whatever the reason, the life choices of their children and their children's children cannot be stereotyped and restricted if we are to maintain social cohesion.

1.32

A report in 2001 into social cohesion in Bradford[8] was commissioned to examine why the community was fragmenting along social, cultural, ethnic and religious lines, and to recommend ways of promoting race relations and equal opportunities. It reported only days after major social disturbances in the summer of that year. Rather than seeing the emergence of a confident multicultural district, where people were respectful and had understanding and tolerance for differences, the report found that attitudes appeared to be hardening and intolerance towards differences was growing. This situation was hindering people's understanding of each other and preventing positive contact between people from different cultural communities.

1.33

---

[8] *Community Pride not Prejudice, Making Diversity Work in Bradford*, Presented to Bradford Vision by Sir Herman Ousley, July 2001.

1.34 There were a number of reasons for this: misinformation about and mis-management of diverse community relations had fuelled white people's resentment about a perceived dominant presence of visible minorities with strong religious affiliation. Simultaneously, a fast-growing Muslim community was, to an extent, resentful of perceived as well as actual unfair and unequal treatment. The Muslim community therefore tended to draw on the comfort and security derived from staying together, retaining its strong culture, religious affiliation and identity, to live in self-contained communities and maintain strong links with Pakistan.

1.35 Other smaller minority communities such as Polish, Italian, Black Caribbean, African, Ukrainian, Sikh, Hindu, Bangladeshi and refugee communities were squeezed into either integrated self-contained entities, or lived in isolated and vulnerable situations and were marginal to the wider, more dominant culture clashes and divisions. For instance, the small Black African/Caribbean communities complained specifically of being squeezed out of areas of previous occupation, while the Ukrainian community claimed to be harassed, attacked and overlooked.

1.36 The Bradford report criticised, in particular, the role that single-faith schools played in reinforcing difference. Education is beyond our remit. Employment, however, also presents a great field of opportunity to bring different groups together, to break down barriers and social divisions and to increase respect for each other notwithstanding our differences.

(d) Legal Compliance

1.37 If an employer is unimpressed by the arguments that have gone before, most employers will nevertheless understand very well the importance of complying with the law. We try throughout this book to go beyond merely setting out the minimum requirements of the law, but those minimum requirements do at least set a standard against which all employers will be measured.

1.38 In Chapter 14 we deal with handling litigation. The days of the informal half-day Tribunal hearing are now long gone. Cynically speaking, every initiative to streamline and shorten the process seems to have had entirely the opposite effect! For claims involving discrimination it is now more usual to consider three days as being around the minimum time needed to hear a case with a short case management discussion in addition and a remedies hearing if the employer is unsuccessful in defending the claim.

1.39 Legal compliance should significantly reduce the number of claims that an employer will have to face and the success rate of those cases. This is where we come full circle back to the economic argument.

F. Backlash

To paraphrase Sir Isaac Newton, 'every action has an equal and opposite reac- **1.40**
tion'.[9] And so it is with promoting equality and diversity. It is no accident that
the public race equality duty (described below) on the one hand requires public
authorities to promote race equality and on the other to promote good relations
between persons of different racial groups. The positive promotion of equality
and diversity can be significantly undermined if equal effort is not expended in
training and educating employees.

The Morris Inquiry found, in its summary and recommendations: **1.41**

> We fear that some of the efforts the MPS has made to promote the message
> of diversity across the organisation have been counterproductive and that the
> organisation may now be seeing the beginnings of a backlash. This would be
> catastrophic. The policy is right, it is the approach and application which we
> believe needs to be reviewed and this is essentially what we are recommending.[10]

It seems counterintuitive to have a backlash from white officers to diversity **1.42**
training when the essential finding of the Morris Inquiry was that 'The statistics indicate clear disproportionality in the way black and minority ethnic
officers are treated in relation to the management of their conduct.'[11]

One area that has felt this backlash is translation. Many public authorities, **1.43**
conscious of the general duty to promote equality, have undertaken programmes to translate their published materials into the first languages of the
communities they serve. The logic of translation is that it encourages individuals in marginalised communities who do not read English to use public
services and therefore take a step closer to integration. However, the final report
of the Commission for Integration and Cohesion states:

> English is both an important part of our shared heritage, and a key access factor
> for new communities to the labour market and wider society. It binds us together
> as a single group in a way that a multiplicity of community languages cannot—
> hence our proposal in Annex E that translation into those community languages
> should not always be the first approach.[12]

To be fair, the report itself takes a rather more balanced approach than some of **1.44**
the more sensationalist reporting following a BBC study in December 2006
which suggested that £100,000,000 of public money was spent on translation
services in the UK in 2006.[13]

---

[9] Newton's third law from *Philosophiae Naturalis Principia Mathematica* (1687).
[10] *The Case for Change: The Report of the Morris Inquiry*, 14 December 2004,
<www.mpa.gov.uk/downloads/issues/morris/morris-report.pdf>, para 1.22.
[11] Paragraph 1.23.   [12] *Our Shared Future* (June 2007), para 5.36.
[13] <news.bbc.co.uk>, 12 December 2006.

1.45 There has also been something of backlash to the whole concept of 'multi-culturalism'. This became national news when the then Chair of the Commission for Racial Equality ('CRE'), Trevor Phillips (now Chair of the EHRC) called for the concept to be 'killed off' in his interview with the Times newspaper on 3 April 2004. 'Multiculturalism suggests separateness' said Phillips, 'the word is not useful, it means the wrong things . . . what we should be talking about is how we reach an integrated society, one in which people are equal under the law, where there are some common values—democracy rather than violence, the common currency of the English language, honouring the culture of these islands like Shakespeare and Dickens.'

1.46 However, multiculturalism is a fact and not necessarily incompatible with an integrated, cohesive society. Mutual respect for different cultures is probably much more likely to bring us all together than any attempt to enforce or engineer assimilation.

G. Words and Phrases

1.47 Much diversity training focuses on cultural awareness and language. Language has always been important in discrimination law. The language that we use is a window on our thoughts, feelings, conceptions, preconceptions and prejudices. By changing language it may be possible to change attitude. That is the objective of what is, somewhat disparagingly referred to as, politically correct language: 'chair' or 'chairperson' rather than 'chairman', for example.

1.48 Inappropriate use of language can also cause offence and in itself constitute discrimination. For example, the Disability Rights Commission on its website used to provide guidance on expressions that are likely to offend disabled people because they suggest that the disabled person is dependent or helpless such as 'wheelchair bound' rather than 'wheelchair user' or 'deaf and dumb' rather than 'deaf and without speech.'

1.49 But there is a danger in trying to tackle negative stereotyping perpetuated by language, that this merely degenerates into linguistic fashion where individuals are branded, for example, 'racist' for referring to 'coloured' rather than 'black', 'mixed race' rather than 'dual heritage' or 'Afro-Caribbean' rather than 'African and Caribbean.' Two extreme examples of politically correct language at its most ludicrous are:

- in 2002 Home Office minister John Denham was criticised by the police for using the phrase 'nitty gritty' during a debate at the Police Federation conference. He was told that police officers could face disciplinary charges for saying 'nitty gritty' because it was derived from the era of slavery. This was news to Mr Denham, to the Chair of the CRE and to the vast majority of linguistic experts; and

- President Clinton similarly had a run-in with the Welsh community of America when in 1995 he referred publicly to 'welching on a debt' having no idea that there was any connection between the etymology of 'welching' and the Welsh.

A survey by Vision Twentyone[14] found that it was apparent from comments by those attending their focus groups that there is a lot of fear surrounding the 'language of disability'. This was associated with a desire to be politically correct and not wishing to cause offence. This in itself was seen as a major barrier to employing disabled people. **1.50**

Of course, there are also plenty of examples of inappropriate use of language which causes genuine offence where the perpetrators really have no excuse and frequently pay the price of unemployment. Dishonourable mentions go to the following: **1.51**

- Congleton MP Ann Winterton was sacked as shadow rural affairs minister in 2002 after telling a rugby club dinner a 'joke' about an Englishman throwing a Pakistani out of a railway carriage coach because, the Englishman said, they were 'ten a penny' in this country. Mrs Winterton also had the party whip withdrawn in 2004 after making another 'joke' about Chinese cockle pickers at a Whitehall dinner to improve Anglo-Danish relations. Undeterred, in 2005 she wrote a piece in the *Congleton Guardian* sympathising with the victims of the London bomb attacks. In it, she wrote: 'We live in times of tremendous change but the United Kingdom is still, thankfully, a predominantly white, Christian country.'
- In 2002 comedian Jim Bowen resigned from his job at Lancashire radio after referring, on air, to a black female training officer as a 'nig-nog'.
- Racially derogatory comments in 2004 by football pundit Ron Atkinson about black Chelsea player Marcel Desailly, which were caught by a microphone Atkinson thought was turned off, led to his resignation from ITV and from the *Guardian*.

It is, however, these overtly discriminatory phrases, perhaps used deliberately or perhaps carelessly or thoughtlessly, that can create a hostile environment within the workplace. The fact that the perpetrator 'was only joking' is no defence if the person on the receiving end is intimidated or offended. **1.52**

---

[14] *Employers and Barriers to Employing Disabled People*, April 2007.

1.53 Four months before he died in June 2007, the Daily Mail asked Bernard Manning to write his own obituary:

> I don't think the Commission for Racial Equality will be holding a wake for me . . . Nor will the lesbian and gay rights lot or the feminists . . . I was an equal opportunities comedian. Unlike them [the po-faced, politically correct brigade] with all their little checklists and taboos and easy targets, I never discriminated against anyone or anything. I was quite happy to get a laugh out of any situation . . . I told gags about everyone . . . Racist? Rubbish. Do these self righteous critics know that Clive Lloyd, the great West Indian cricket captain, asked me to perform a part of his testimonial? Or that I did fundraising events for the Lancashire and India wicket keep Farokh Engineer, and the black boxing champion John Conteh? I was multiracial myself, a descendent of Jewish immigrants from Sevastopol.

1.54 By common consent it seems, Bernard Manning was a skilled comedian but right to the end he appears not to have understood why it was that many people found him offensive. In the section of his self-penned obituary quoted above he sets out the three most hackneyed and lame defences to any allegation of racist behaviour:

- I don't discriminate because I pick on everyone;
- I'm not racist because I have associated with black people; and
- I can't be racist because I'm descended from immigrants.

1.55 'Sticks and stones may break my bones but names will never hurt me' goes the school yard anti-bullying rhyme. However, the reality is that offensive words and phrases have huge potential to cause harm by damaging employee relations, undermining individuals, and, in extreme cases, damaging mental health and resulting in litigation. For that reason, it is important that anti-harassment training and cultural awareness are included in any drive to promote equality and diversity. However, such training should be put in context and part of a programme of more specific training on recruitment and promotion, performance management, handling grievances and disciplinary hearings, etc. If not, those in charge of promoting equality and diversity run the risk of being regarded as nothing more than the politically correct 'thought police'.

H. The Traditional Approach

(a) Rights-based Legislation

1.56 The traditional approach to tackling discrimination has been to create legal rights that individual victims of discrimination can enforce through the Employment Tribunal and court systems. As we set out in Chapter 2, UK equality legislation has a good deal in common across the strands. In broad terms, it outlaws four types of behaviour: direct discrimination, indirect discrimination, harassment and victimisation:

- *Direct discrimination*—is where a person is treated differently because of, for example, their sex or race.
- *Indirect discrimination*—happens where a provision, criterion or practice applies to everyone but causes disadvantage to a certain group and cannot be shown to be a proportionate means of achieving a legitimate aim.
- *Harassment*—previously fell within the concept of direct discrimination but has recently been separately defined as unwanted conduct which has the effect of violating a person's dignity or creating an intimidating, hostile, degrading, humiliating or offensive environment.
- *Victimisation*—happens when a person is treated less favourably because they have been involved in making a complaint about discrimination.

There is a slightly different approach for disability discrimination with concepts **1.57** of discrimination on the grounds of disability, for a reason related to disability and the added concept of 'reasonable adjustments', accommodating a person's disability by, for example, altering their duties or working environment.

(b) Equal Opportunities Policies

Commitment to compliance with this legislation has traditionally been stated **1.58** in an employer's Equal Opportunities Policy. Such policies are not mandatory. They are, however, recommended by the Codes of Practice issued by the three former Commissions:

- The Commission for Racial Equality Code of Practice on Racial Equality in Employment (2005) which came into effect on the 6 April 2006 replacing the 1983 version (the 'CRE Code 2005').
- The Equal Opportunities Commission: Code of Practice on Sex Discrimination; Equal Opportunity Policies, Procedures and Practices in Employment (1985) which came into effect on 30 April 1985 (the 'EOC Code 1985').
- The Disability Rights Commission Code of Practice: Employment and Occupation (2004) which came into effect on 1 October 2004 (the 'DRC Code 2004').

Although those Codes of Practice do not impose any legal obligations they can **1.59** be used in evidence in legal proceedings and must be taken into account by Courts and Tribunals to the extent they are relevant to the issues in those proceedings. The CRE Code 2005 has, at Appendix 2, a sample equal opportunities policy and a sample anti-harassment policy.

Most organisations will want to take an integrated cross-strand approach to **1.60** their policies: they will want one policy covering all six strands rather than six separate policies, one for each strand—if only for brevity and a more integrated approach to equality and diversity issues. For that reason the sample policies in the CRE Code 2005 are a helpful starting point only, because they refer only to race.

1.61 Paragraph 3.11 of the CRE Code 2005 does have a brief summary of the content of an equal opportunities policy which is not race specific. It suggests including:

- the employer's commitment to the principle of equality;
- the organisation's ethos and values;
- how the policy applies to the organisation's procedures and practice;
- how to use the organisation's complaints procedure to raise any concerns or complaints that workers might have about discrimination or harassment;
- the rights and responsibilities of all; and
- how the organisation will deal with any breaches of the policy.

1.62 The CRE Code 2005 recommends[15] that the equal opportunities policy should cover all aspects of employment from the recruitment stage through to treatment after the employment has ended, including terms of employment, training, performance, promotion, grievance and discipline. It also recommends[16] that as far as possible the policy should be drawn up in consultation with the workforce and their representatives.

1.63 The Codes go on to discuss the implementation of equal opportunity policies: see for example paragraph 2.12 of the DRC Code 2004, paragraphs 33 to 40 of the EOC Code 1985 and paragraphs 3.16 to 3.47 of the CRE Code 2005. For example, the EOC Code 1985 states at paragraph 35 that 'An equal opportunities policy must be seen to have the active support of management at the highest level' and all three Codes highlight the need to train staff on equal opportunities.

(c) Enforceability

1.64 There appears to be some judicial uncertainty as to whether equal opportunities policies can become incorporated into contracts of employment—in other words whether they are merely policy documents that are not legally enforceable or whether they are part of the terms of employment. The distinction is significant: a failure to comply with a policy creates no legal risk (other than perhaps a breach of the implied term of mutual trust and confidence in every

---

[15] Paragraph 3.12.   [16] Paragraph 3.13.

employment relationship) whereas a failure to comply with a contractual term could lead to remedies for breach of contract.

An example of this in the context of a disciplinary procedure is *Gunton v* **1.65**
The Mayor, Aldermen and Burgesses of the London Borough of Richmond-upon-Thames[17] where the employer's purported dismissal of Mr Gunton was held to be unlawful because the employer had bypassed the introductory steps prescribed by what turned out to be a contractual disciplinary procedure.

In *Grant v South-West Trains Ltd*[18] Ms Grant attempted to argue that she was **1.66**
entitled to a travel concession for her partner on the basis of her employer's equal opportunities policy, which committed them to 'ensuring that all individuals are treated fairly and are valued irrespective of disability, race, gender, health, social class, *sexual preference*, marital status, nationality, religion, employment status, age or membership or non-membership of a trade union'. Her application was dismissed on grounds that the equal opportunities policy was not incorporated into the contract of employment. It was a statement of policy in 'very general, even idealistic, terms'.

However, in *Taylor v Secretary of State for Scotland*,[19] the House of Lords, **1.67**
without considering the *Grant* case, appeared to have no difficulty with the proposition that the equal opportunities policy, negotiated with trade union representatives and then notified to employees by means of a circular, formed part of the individual contract of employment despite its aspirational character. Although their Lordships concluded that the introduction of the policy could not have been intended to remove the employer's right to terminate the contract when staff reached the minimum retirement age, or to remove the employer's discretion regarding retention beyond the minimum retirement age. Their ruling nevertheless makes it feasible for employees to enforce rights not to be discriminated against as part of their contract of employment. As the facts of the *Taylor* case showed, this may extend to grounds for discrimination not currently the subject of statutory protection (at the time of the decision, age discrimination was not prohibited).

(d) Limited Success

Although there has traditionally been some emphasis on promoting equality **1.68**
and diversity through Equal Opportunities Policies and use of permissible positive action (described in Chapter 6) there has probably been more emphasis on a litigation-based approach. This has produced some significant successes

---

[17] [1980] 3 WLR 714, CA.   [18] [1998] IRLR 188, QBD.
[19] [2000] IRLR 502, HL.

for individual claimants on a micro level. For example, the following were the highest awards made by Employment Tribunals in the 2005/2006 financial year:

- race discrimination—£984,465;
- sex discrimination—£217,961; and
- disability discrimination—£138,650.[20]

1.69 However, the current system has largely failed to achieve equality on a macro level. Despite over thirty years of equality legislation in relation to equal pay, gender and race:

- The EOC's final report[21] estimates that the 'power gap' for women in Parliament will take almost 200 years to close and it will take up to 65 years to have a more equitable balance of women at the top of FTSE 100 companies; the 'pensions gap' will take 45 years to equalise: retired women's income is currently 40 per cent less than men's; the 'part-time pay gap' will take 25 years to close (women working part-time earn 38 per cent less per hour than men working full time); and the 'full-time pay gap' twenty years (full-time female employees earn 17 per cent less per hour than men).

- In 2004 Pakistani women had the highest unemployment rates in Great Britain, at 20 per cent. The next highest female rates were among women from the Black African or Mixed ethnic groups (each 12 per cent). These rates were around three times the rates for White British and White Irish women (4 per cent). The unemployment rates for Black Caribbean (9 per cent), Indian (8 per cent) and Chinese (7 per cent) women were around twice the rates for White British and White Irish women. Among men, those from Black Caribbean, Black African, Bangladeshi and Mixed ethnic groups had the highest unemployment rates (between 13 and 14 per cent). These rates were around three times the rates for White British and White Irish men (5 per cent in each case). The unemployment rates for Pakistani and Chinese men, 11 and 10 per cent, were around twice the rates for White British men or White Irish men.[22]

1.70 The more recent 'strands' of discrimination legislation in relation to disability, sexual orientation, religion and belief and age, are only just beginning to address the issues of discrimination in these areas. For example, according to the DRC[23] 1,300,000 disabled people without a job, want to work.

---

[20] Employment Tribunal Service Annual Report 2005/2006.
[21] *Completing the Revolution* (EOC, 24 July 2007).
[22] Labour Market Statistics, Office of National Statistics, 21 February 2006, <www.statistics.gov.uk>.
[23] Disability Briefing, May 2007.

I. A New Approach

A fundamental change is developing in the method of achieving equality both **1.71** in employment and in access to goods and services. The limited success of the traditional litigation-based approach is therefore being supplemented by a proactive approach aimed at pushing for institutional change by promoting equality and diversity. This is partly driven by new legislation and partly by other factors such as profit motives and peer pressure.

The most dramatic catalyst for change was the murder of Stephen Lawrence **1.72** and the subsequent campaign for justice by his family. Stephen Lawrence was murdered in 1993 in an unprovoked attack in a South London street. Both he and the friend who was with him were black, his murderers were white. The subsequent police investigation failed to result in a prosecution.

The Macpherson Inquiry examined the matters arising from Stephen Lawrence's **1.73** death, focusing in particular on the lessons to be learned for the investigation of racially motivated crimes. The Macpherson Report deals with racism in one of the country's main public services (the Metropolitan Police) and, in particular, the issue of 'institutional racism' which the report described as:

> The collective failure of an organisation to provide an appropriate and professional service to people because of their colour, culture, or ethnic origin. It can be seen or detected in processes, attitudes and behaviour which amount to discrimination through unwitting prejudice, ignorance, thoughtlessness and racist stereotyping which disadvantage minority ethnic people.

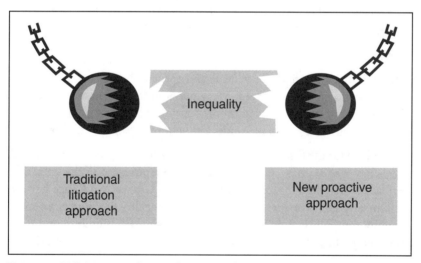

Figure 1.1 Differing approaches to achieving equality

19

1.74 The Race Relations (Amendment) Act 2000 ('RRAA') arose out of the Macpherson Report. Like much of the discrimination legislation that preceded it, the RRAA created individual legal rights. It did so by extending the concept of unlawful race discrimination into functions of public authorities not previously covered, opening up new possibilities for individuals to bring County Court claims of race discrimination against public authorities.

(a) General and Specific Duties

1.75 However, the RRAA also marked a radical shift in emphasis by introducing a 'general duty' on a long list of public authorities to have due regard to the need to eliminate unlawful race discrimination, promote equality of opportunity and promote good relations between persons of different racial groups. Subordinate legislation then introduced 'specific duties' on certain public authorities setting out practical steps for them to take towards compliance with the general duty. The central, specific duty was the duty to prepare and publish a 'Race Equality Scheme'—an action plan for race equality.

1.76 General and specific duties were also subsequently introduced for disability (December 2006) and gender (April 2007). They differ from the race duties, reflecting both the lack of a coordinated approach to equality law across the strands and also a process of developing and improving upon the race duties through experience.

1.77 We describe in Chapters 3, 4 and 5 the profound changes these duties have introduced. Jenny Watson former Chair of the EOC wrote in her foreword to the Gender Equality Duty Code of Practice in November 2006 that:

> The gender equality duty . . . is the biggest change in sex equality legislation in thirty years, since the introduction of the Sex Discrimination Act itself.

(b) Equality Scheme Surveys

1.78 Early indications are that the general and specific duties have not been as successful as they might have been. Many public authorities have seen Equality Schemes as being an end in themselves and have produced enormous, colourful documents which are big on platitudes but light on tangible commitments.

1.79 The deadline for the first tranche of public authorities to produce Race Equality Schemes was 31 May 2002. Two surveys were produced in the immediate aftermath of that deadline, our own published in Croners Workplace Equality and Diversity News in March 2003, and a Schneider–Ross survey commissioned by the CRE in July 2003. Disappointingly, both studies found widespread failures by public authorities to comply with the terms of the legislation.

1.80 Our survey looked at a hundred randomly selected Race Equality Schemes across several sectors and found that 96 per cent failed to comply with the basic requirements of the legislation. The Schneider–Ross survey avoided this stark statistic but basically came to the same conclusion.

The disability and gender specific duties have been drafted to be more out-   **1.81** come focused rather than process driven. The race specific duties had been drafted to help public authorities take a more structured approach to equality and diversity but progress has seemed somewhat mired in bureaucracy. If the public duties are to make a difference, somehow we need to get across the message that what is needed is a legally compliant and structured approach with an emphasis on brevity in document production.

J. The Future

Tucked away as the penultimate paragraph of the Labour Party's 2005 Mani-   **1.82** festo, was a commitment that: 'In the next Parliament we will establish a Commission on Equality and Human Rights to promote equality for all and tackle discrimination, and introduce a Single Equality Act to modernise and simplify equality legislation.' Never accuse the Government of failing to deliver on its promises. As this book goes to press the EHRC is beginning its life as the overarching equality Commission and consultation has closed on the Government's proposals for a Single Equality Bill for Great Britain. Chapter 15 looks to the future that these developments hope to bring. We have done our best to state the law as it is at 1 October 2007.

Acknowledgements

For contributions, comments and support: Louise Fernandes; Ruth Maloney; Terri Robinson; Sarah Youatt; Marcus Turle; David Gallagher; David Gollancz; Neil Johnston; Sara Khoja; Andy Lucas; Hannah Cunningham; Catherine Jordan; Georgie Heatley; Anne King; Ted Maloney; Anisa Niaz; Paul Friend; Melanie Stephenson; Arsineh Gaspariance; Fiona McKenzie and Chetna Varia.

For early career opportunities: Paul Honnigman; Peter Hayes; Howard Coffell; Tony Fisher and Steve Lorber.

For lifelong support: our respective families.

2

THE LEGAL FRAMEWORK

The Universal Declaration of Human Rights 1948 provided in article 2 that
'Everyone is entitled to all the rights and freedoms set forth in this Declaration,
without distinction of any kind, such as race, colour, sex, language, religion, political or other opinion, national or social origin, property, birth or other status'. Since
1948 steps have been taken, in this country and the European Community, to give
legal effect, in part, to this general objective of non-discriminatory treatment . . .

(Lord Bingham, *St Helens MBC v Derbyshire*[1])

A. Introduction

The aspirational legal promise of equality and the enjoyment of rights without **2.01**
discrimination can be traced back, at least, to the Universal Declaration of
Human Rights 1948. However, the attempts to give legal effect in the British
workplace to the general objective of non-discriminatory treatment have been
faltering, and, at times, confused. The structure of discrimination law in Britain
is—at least until the much-anticipated Single Equality Bill becomes a reality—
not so much a clear framework as a rambling patchwork. This means that
practitioners need to have at their fingertips a large range of primary and
secondary legislation, some with common concepts, but some with anomalies
unique to a particular kind of discrimination.

In this chapter we provide an overview of this mass of legislation in order to **2.02**
give a legal context for the chapters that follow, where we seek to apply this law
to particular themes and issues likely to arise in the workplace. Here, we explain
the different *strands* of discrimination where the law provides protection, and
the different *types* of discrimination that the law prohibits within each strand.
Throughout we highlight some of the anomalies and pitfalls in the law. At the
end of the chapter we discuss the distinct but important role of the Human

---

[1] [2007] ICR 841, HL.

Rights Act 1998 (the 'HRA') in the creation of substantive equality and a respect for diversity in the workplace.

B. The 'Strands' of Protected Discrimination

(a) Overview

2.03 Although it is hoped that in the future a Single Equality Act will provide a general prohibition on discrimination, with consistent concepts across all the discrimination strands, at present there is no such provision. This means that each strand of discrimination is protected by a discrete legal source, principally:

- Sex, pregnancy/maternity leave, married status, civil partnership status and gender reassignment—by the Sex Discrimination Act 1975 (the 'SDA') and the Equal Pay Act 1970 (the 'EqPA').
- Race—by the Race Relations Act 1976 (the 'RRA').
- Disability—by the Disability Discrimination Act 1995 (the 'DDA').
- Religion and belief—by the Employment Equality (Religion or Belief) Regulations 2003 (the 'RBR').[2]
- Sexual orientation—by the Employment Equality (Sexual Orientation) Regulations 2003 (the 'SOR').[3]
- Age—by the Employment Equality (Age) Regulations 2006 (the 'AR').[4]

2.04 All these sources, now defined collectively by the Equality Act 2006 ('EA') as 'the equality enactments',[5] prohibit discrimination in the employment sphere, and some (principally the statutes) extend to other spheres such as education, the provision of goods, facilities and services, housing, planning and the actions of public authorities in the exercise of their public functions.[6] These various sources are all derived in part from a range of Articles of the EC Treaty[7] and a number of EC Directives[8] relevant to discrimination law.

---

[2] SI 2003/1660.   [3] SI 2003/1661.   [4] SI 2006/752.   [5] EA, s 33(1).

[6] Discrimination beyond the employment context is outside the scope of this book, but is covered in full in C Palmer et al, *Discrimination Law Handbook* (2nd edn, LAG, 2007).

[7] These are principally: Art 12 (which prohibits discrimination on the grounds of nationality); Art 13 (which gives the European Council wide powers to legislate in relation to discrimination on grounds of sex, race or ethnic origin, religion or belief, age or sexual orientation, and which provided the legal basis for the Race and Employment Directives referred to below); Art 39 (which provides for freedom of movement of workers who are EC nationals); and Art 141 (which establishes the principle of equal treatment for equal work).

[8] These are principally: the Equal Pay Directive (Council Directive 75/117/EEC); the Equal Treatment Directive (Council Directive 76/207/EEC); the Burden of Proof Directive (Council Directive 97/80/EC); the Parental Leave Directive (Council Directive 96/34/EC); the Part-Time Workers Directive (Council Directive 97/81/EC as amended by Council Directive 98/23/EC); the Race Directive (Council Directive 2000/43/EC); and the Employment Directive (Council Directive 2000/78/EC).

There are various other legislative provisions which seek to achieve substantive **2.05** equality (such as those creating additional rights for parents and those who wish to work flexibly) which we address throughout the book as and when they become relevant. Here, we consider the core discrimination strands and types of discrimination in further detail.

(b) Sex, Pregnancy/Maternity, Married or Civil Partnership Status and Gender Reassignment Discrimination

Under the SDA it is currently unlawful for an employer to discriminate on the **2.06** grounds of sex,[9] pregnancy or maternity leave,[10] married status[11] or civil partnership status.[12] Unlike the RRA, RBR and SOR, the SDA only applies to prohibit discrimination on the ground of the sex or other status *of the complainant*, because the wording of the SDA specifically refers to discrimination on 'the ground of *her* sex'[13] etc. This means that there is no ability to argue under the SDA that, for example, discrimination on the ground of association with another's sex or other status within the SDA is covered.[14] However, the law in this area is undergoing change as far as the specific kind of discrimination referred to as harassment[15] is concerned, which we discuss further in Chapter 11. The Government is also considering removing the prohibition on discrimination against people on grounds of their married or civil partner status.[16]

The SDA also prohibits direct discrimination on the grounds that the com- **2.07** plainant intends to undergo gender reassignment, is undergoing gender reassignment, or has undergone gender reassignment.[17] Again the SDA currently only extends to prohibiting discrimination on grounds of the claimant's actual gender reassignment status, but the Government is considering amending the law to prohibit discrimination on the basis of association with transsexual people. The Government is, however, not currently persuaded that it should extend the law to prohibit discrimination against someone because of their perceived transsexual status.[18]

---

[9] SDA, s 1. [10] SDA, s 3A. [11] SDA, s 3. [12] SDA, s 3.
[13] SDA, ss 1 and 4A.
[14] See below for a description of the different position under the RRA, RBR and SOR, where we give some examples of how this may work in practice.
[15] SDA, s 4A.
[16] *Discrimination Law Review: A Framework for Fairness: Proposals for a Single Equality Bill for Great Britain* (Department for Communities and Local Government, June 2007) (the 'DLR consultation paper'), paras 8.21–8.22.
[17] SDA, s 2A.
[18] DLR consultation paper, para 1.24.

2.08 A transperson is to be regarded as having the sexual identity of the gender to which he or she has been reassigned.[19] In any event, since the coming into force of the Gender Recognition Act 2004, transpersons are given legal recognition of their acquired gender, provided that they have been granted a gender recognition certificate by a Gender Recognition Panel. This means that, for example, a male-to-female transperson who obtains such a certificate will be legally recognised as a woman, will be free to marry a man and will be entitled to the state retirement pension and other benefits appropriate to her new status as a female. As far as employers are concerned, this means that they must ensure that the person is treated as if he or she is of the acquired gender, and is not treated less favourably on grounds of the acquired gender, or because he or she has had gender reassignment in the past.

2.09 Under the SDA, employers must not discriminate against applicants on the prohibited grounds in the arrangements they make for determining who should be offered employment, in the terms on which employment is offered, or by refusing or deliberately omitting to offer the employment;[20] nor must they discriminate in the way in which employees are afforded access to opportunities for promotion, transfer or training, or to any other benefits, facilities or services, or by refusing or deliberately omitting to afford such access, or by dismissing an employee or subjecting him or her to any other detriment on the prohibited grounds.[21]

2.10 Contract workers who are supplied to an employer under contract from another business (which will include a range of agency staff and consultants) are also protected: employers must ensure that they do not discriminate on grounds of sex in the terms of which the contract worker is allowed to do the work, by not allowing the contract worker to do or continue to do the work, in the way the contract worker is afforded access to benefits, facilities and services, or by subjecting the contract worker to any other detriment.[22]

2.11 Similar provisions apply to office holders, partnerships, trade unions, bodies that confer professional authorisations or qualifications, bodies concerned with vocational training, employment agencies and the training commissions.[23] There are specific provisions relating to the police, prison officers, ministers of religion and midwives.[24]

2.12 Discrimination on the prohibited grounds remains unlawful even after the

---

[19] *A v Chief Constable of West Yorkshire* [2005] AC 51, HL.
[20] Sections 6(1)(a), (b) and (c).   [21] Sections 6(2)(a) and (b).   [22] Section 9(2).
[23] Sections 10A–16.   [24] Sections 17–20.

employment relationship has come to an end, if the discrimination complained of arises out of and is closely connected to the employment relationship.[25]

There are certain exceptions where sex is a genuine occupational qualification,[26] **2.13** which we consider further in Chapter 6 where we specifically address genuine occupational qualifications and requirements across all the strands.

Domestic sex discrimination law has (at least historically) been more driven **2.14** by European law requirements than the law relating to other strands—the SDA gives effect to the Equal Treatment Directive,[27] as amended by Directive 2002/73. This requires that men and women are treated equally with regard to access to employment, vocational training, promotion and working conditions, and that states outlaw direct and indirect discrimination and harassment. The mandatory parts of the Equal Treatment Directive—along with the other EC Directives referred to in this chapter—are directly effective in domestic law and so can be directly relied on by individuals, against the state and emanations of the state, in certain circumstances. The wording of the Equal Treatment Directive prohibits all discrimination 'on grounds of sex either directly or indirectly by reference in particular to marital or family status'. If this should be read as embracing single people, lone parents and unmarried couples, then there is a gap in domestic law provision, as these groups are not currently protected by the SDA (although discrimination against lone parents may constitute indirect discrimination against women who are more frequently lone parents than men). The fact that discrimination is only unlawful if it is on grounds of the complainant's sex, etc (see above) may be another area in which the SDA does not fully implement the Directive.

The EqPA, and not the SDA, addresses discrimination on grounds of sex in **2.15** relation to pay or other contractual terms and pensions. The EqPA dictates, by implying an equality clause into contracts of employment, that a male and female employee working for the same employer must receive the same pay and be subject to the same contract terms if they do:

- like work, ie if they are doing the same or a broadly similar job;
- work rated as equivalent, ie that an analytical job evaluation scheme has reached this conclusion; or
- work of equal value, ie work that is different but nonetheless broadly of the same value in terms of effort, skill and decision, etc.[28]

---

[25] Sections 17–20.   [26] Sections 7 and 9(3B).   [27] Council Directive 76/207/EEC.
[28] Sections 1(1) and 1(2)(a), (b) and (c).

An employer can defend an equal pay claim by showing that there is a 'material factor' other than the difference in sex that differentiates the male and female employee's work.[29] The EqPA is the domestic implementation of Article 141 of the EC Treaty and the Equal Pay Directive,[30] which require Member States to ensure that men and women receive equal pay for equal work. However, it is the SDA and not the EqPA that regulates discrimination in pay and other contractual terms in connection with gender reassignment.[31]

2.16 In 1985 the Equal Opportunities Commission (the 'EOC'[32]) published a statutory Code of Practice for the Elimination of Discrimination on the Grounds of Sex and Marriage and the Promotion of Equality of Opportunity in Employment (the 'EOC Code 1985'). The Code is relevant to employers not only for the practical guidance it provides, but because a failure by an employer to observe the Code is admissible as evidence before an Employment Tribunal ('ET'), and may be probative of discrimination (albeit that a breach of the Code is not itself unlawful).[33] There is a separate EOC Code of Practice on Equal Pay, published in 2003, which is similarly admissible in proceedings. The EOC has also recently published a Code of Practice on the new gender equality duty, which we discuss further in Chapter 3.

2.17 The EOC was replaced by the Equality and Human Rights Commission (the 'EHRC', which we discuss further in Chapter 15) with effect from October 2007, but the above guidance is likely to continue to prove instructive to employers and managers until such time as the EHRC issues its own codes of practice using its powers under section 14 of the EA, for which the Government expects it to have 'primary responsibility'.[34]

2.18 The UK Parliamentary Forum on Transexualism has produced a Code of Practice Regarding Discrimination on Grounds of Transexualism,[35] and the Women and Equality Unit has published its own guide, *Gender and Reassignment—A Guide for Employers*.[36] Both make a number of recommendations about how employers should develop good employment practice with regard to transsexual employees, covering issues such as updating personnel records to reflect workers' current names, titles and sex, and agreeing in advance the process and procedures to be adopted during a worker's gender reassignment.

---

[29] Section 1(3).   [30] Council Directive 75/117/EEC.   [31] SDA, s 6(8).
[32] <www.eoc.org.uk>.   [33] SDA, s 56A.
[34] *Discrimination Law Review: A Framework for Fairness: Proposals for a Single Equality Bill for Great Britain* (Department for Communities and Local Government, June 2007), para 1.2.
[35] Published by Press for Change, December 1998.
[36] Women and Equality Unit, January 2005.

(c) Race Discrimination

The RRA prohibits direct discrimination 'on racial grounds'.[37] The signifi-   **2.19**
cance of this wording is that, unlike the SDA, it is not limited to the particular
characteristic of the complainant—rather, 'on racial grounds' has been given a
wide interpretation, covering any action based on the real or *perceived* race of
the complainant, the complainant's *association* with another of a particular
race, or where the complainant has been less favourably treated because of their
failure to follow *instructions to discriminate* on grounds of race.[38]

This broad interpretative approach was invoked by the claimant in *Redfearn v*   **2.20**
Serco Ltd,[39] where a British National Party councillor had been dismissed from
his job of driving predominantly Asian people in Bradford, because his membership of the BNP was thought to pose a health and safety risk to the company. He argued that he had been dismissed on racial grounds. The Court of
Appeal held that although the circumstances in which the decision to dismiss
was made included racial considerations, this did not mean that it was taken
'on racial grounds'. The Court had to take into account 'the anti-
discrimination purposes for which the legislation was enacted'. The Court
dismissed the claim, because any other result would have been incompatible
with those purposes.

'Racial grounds' within the direct discrimination definition means 'colour,   **2.21**
race, nationality or ethnic or national origins'; and 'racial group' within the
indirect discrimination definition means 'a group of persons defined by reference to colour, race, nationality or ethnic or national origins'.[40] The fact that
a racial group comprises two or more distinct racial groups does not prevent
it from constituting a particular racial group for the purposes of the RRA,[41]
and references to a person's racial group refer to 'any racial group into which
he falls'.[42] In *Orphanos v Queen Mary College*,[43] for example, the House of
Lords accepted that the claimant fell into three racial groups—Cypriot,
non-British and non-EEC—in concluding that the respondent college's
requirement that students who had not been ordinarily resident in the
EEC area for three years pay higher fees than EEC residents was indirectly
discriminatory contrary to the RRA. The *Orphanos* case also illustrates the
principle that a racial group can be defined negatively, such as 'not being of
UK origin'.

---

[37] RRA, s 1(1)(a).
[38] *Showboat Entertainment Centre Ltd v Owens* [1984] 1 All ER 836, EAT and *Weathersfield Ltd
v Sargent* [1999] ICR 425, CA.
[39] [2006] IRLR 623, CA.   [40] RRA, s 3(1).   [41] RRA, s 3(2).   [42] RRA, s 3(1).
[43] [1985] AC 761, HL.

2.22 Discrimination on grounds of *colour* should be fairly straightforward to identify and has been found, for example, where an employee was repeatedly harassed
on the grounds that they were black,[44] or where an advertisement required that
applicants be from the 'black community'.[45]

2.23 *Race* allegedly denotes the possession of particular biological characteristics and
is based on the outdated assumption that certain groups do indeed possess such
characteristics different from other groups. In *Mandla v Dowell Lee*,[46] Lord
Fraser observed that '. . . within the human race, there are very few, if any,
distinctions which are scientifically recognised as racial'.

2.24 Of greater relevance is probably the concept of *ethnic origins*, the main issue
in the *Mandla* case. The House of Lords concluded that the term 'ethnic' in
section 3 of the RRA was to be construed relatively widely in a broad cultural
and historic sense. For a group to constitute an 'ethnic group' for the purposes
of the RRA it had to regard itself, and be regarded by others, as a distinct
community by virtue of certain characteristics, two of which were essential.
First it had to have a long shared history, of which the group was conscious
as distinguishing it from other groups, and the memory of which it kept alive,
and second it had to have a cultural tradition of its own, including family
and social customs and manners, often but not necessarily associated with
religious observance. In addition, the following characteristics could also be
relevant:

- a common geographical origin or descent from a small number of common
  ancestors;
- a common language, which did not necessarily have to be peculiar to the
  group;
- a common literature peculiar to the group;
- a common religion different from that of neighbouring groups or from the
  general community surrounding it; and
- the characteristic of being a minority or being an oppressed or a dominant
  group within a larger community.

A group defined by reference to enough of these characteristics would be capable
of including converts to the group.

2.25 Applying those characteristics to the facts of the *Mandla* case itself, Sikhs were
held to be a group defined by reference to 'ethnic origins' for the purpose of

---

[44] eg *HM Prison Service v Johnson* [1997] ICR 275, EAT.
[45] *Lambeth LBC v Commission for Racial Equality* [1990] ICR 768, CA.
[46] [1983] 2 AC 548, HL at 561.

the RRA, even though they were not racially distinguishable from other people living in the Punjab. Jews,[47] Romany Gypsies,[48] European Roma[49] and Irish Travellers[50] have all been held to be ethnic groups for the purposes of the RRA.

However, Rastafarians and Muslims have been held to fall outside the defin- **2.26** ition, the former because although Rastafarians as a group possess certain iden- tifiable characteristics, the Court of Appeal concluded that they did not meet the definition of an ethnic group, in part at least because their shared history (then around 60 years) was not sufficiently long to satisfy the tests set out in the *Mandla* case;[51] and the latter because of the wide geographical spread of the Muslim religion.[52] Discrimination against these groups may, nevertheless, constitute indirect discrimination connected with national origins or race. Moreover, the exclusion of Rastafarians and Muslims from the RRA is of less practical significance now that these groups can claim the specific protection against direct and indirect religious discrimination under the RBR.

The Scots and the English are not distinct racial groups defined by reference to **2.27** ethnicity under the RRA;[53] however, they do constitute distinct racial groups by reference to national origins (see below). It is unlikely that language alone will be sufficient to define an 'ethnic group'.[54]

There is a legal distinction between *nationality* and *national origins*. In *Ealing* **2.28** *LBC v Race Relations Board*,[55] the House of Lords had to consider the issue in the context of a claim under the Race Relations Act 1968 (the forerunner to the RRA). It was a condition of access to a local authority housing list that the applicant be a 'British subject within the meaning of the British National- ity Act 1948'. A Polish national challenged this as discriminatory on national origins grounds. The House of Lords concluded that 'national origins' described a person's connection by birth with a group of people who could be described as a 'nation' and did not mean the same as 'nationality' in the sense of citizenship of a particular state.

Accordingly, English people were held to be a distinct racial group by national **2.29** origins (albeit not nationality, that being British) in *National Joint Police Board*

---

[47] *Seide v Gillette Industries Ltd* [1980] IRLR 427, EAT.
[48] *Commission for Racial Equality v Dutton* [1989] QB 783, CA.
[49] *R (European Roma Rights Centre) v Immigration Officer at Prague Airport* [2005] 2 AC 1, HL.
[50] *O'Leary v Allied Domecq Inns Ltd* (Central London County Court, CL/950275, July 2000), Cty Ct.
[51] *Dawkins v Department of the Environment* [1993] ICR 517, CA.
[52] *Nyazi v Rymans Ltd* EAT/6/8 (Race Discrimination Law Reports, Commission for Racial Equality, 85), EAT.
[53] *Boyce v British Airways Plc* EAT 385/97, EAT.
[54] *Gwynedd CC v Jones* [1986] ICR 833, EAT.   [55] [1972] AC 342, HL.

31

v Power[56]—a claim by an English man that he was discriminated against on racial grounds when he was not short-listed for the post of Chief Constable of the Scottish Highland Council Joint Police Board. Scottish, Welsh and Irish people would be similarly defined as a racial group by national origins.

2.30 Although in many cases the alleged grounds of discrimination will overlap, it is important to note that discrimination on the grounds of colour and nationality are more narrowly protected (as these grounds fall outside the scope of the Race Directive[57] which compelled certain changes to the RRA) than those on the other grounds. We explain this further when considering the different types of discrimination prohibited. However, what it does mean is that it may be beneficial to a complainant to cast their allegation of discrimination on grounds other than colour or nationality, in order to benefit from the more generous legal protection given to the other grounds.

2.31 Otherwise, the RRA provides virtually identical protection for employees, contract workers and other groups as the SDA. There are also similar provisions relating to general occupational requirements and general occupational qualifications,[58] which again we consider further in Chapter 6.

2.32 There is, however, no equivalent to the EqPA for race discrimination, and the RRA itself embraces discrimination with regard to pay, contractual terms and pensions. The RRA as amended gives effect to the EC Race Directive,[59] which enshrines the principle of equal treatment between persons irrespective of racial or ethnic origin (but not nationality or colour).

2.33 The CRE[60] produced a Statutory Code of Practice on Racial Equality in Employment, which came into force on 6 April 2006 (the 'CRE Code 2005', replacing the 1983 Code). The Code contains a set of recommendations and guidance on how to avoid unlawful racial discrimination and harassment in employment. It 'outlines employers' legal obligations under the RRA and contains general advice on the policies they will need to safeguard against discrimination and harassment, as well as more detailed recommendations on the procedures and practice that will help ensure fair and equal treatment for everyone'. The Code is also admissible in proceedings before the Tribunal under the RRA.[61] The CRE also provided detailed guidance on the general race equality duty and the employment duty, which we discuss further in Chapter 3. The CRE was also subsumed into the EHRC from October 2007.

---

[56] [1997] IRLR 610, EAT.   [57] Council Directive 2000/43/EC.
[58] RRA, ss 4A and 5.   [59] Council Directive 2000/43/EC.
[60] <www.cre.gov.uk>.   [61] RRA, s 47.

(d) Disability Discrimination

The DDA applies to all those persons who have a disability as defined by **2.34** section 1(1) of the Act, namely 'a physical or mental impairment which has a substantial and long-term adverse effect on his ability to carry out normal day-to-day activities'. This definition is amplified by Schedules 1 and 2 of the DDA, Regulations[62] and Guidance issued by the Secretary of State under section 3 of the DDA.[63]

An impairment is to be given its ordinary and natural meaning.[64] It is not **2.35** necessary to establish an impairment by reference to an illness, because there is no 'rigid distinction' between 'an underlying fault, shortcoming or defect of or in the body on the one hand and evidence of the manifestations or effect thereof on the other'.[65] Several examples of impairment are listed at paragraph A6 of the Guidance, namely:

- sensory impairments, such as those affecting sight or hearing;
- impairments with fluctuating or recurring effects such as rheumatoid arthritis, myalgic encephalitis (ME)/chronic fatigue syndrome (CFS), fibromyalgia, depression and epilepsy;
- progressive impairments, such as motor neurone disease, muscular dystrophy, forms of dementia and lupus (systemic lupus erythematosus—SLE);
- organ specific impairments, including respiratory conditions, such as asthma, and cardiovascular diseases, including thrombosis, stroke and heart disease;
- developmental impairments, such as autistic spectrum disorders (ASD), dyslexia and dyspraxia and other learning difficulties;
- mental health conditions and mental illnesses, such as depression, schizophrenia, eating disorders, bipolar affective disorders, obsessive compulsive disorders, as well as personality disorders and some self-harming behaviour; and
- impairments produced by injury to the body or brain.

Certain behaviours are specifically excluded from being considered as impair- **2.36** ments for the purposes of the DDA, namely dependency on alcohol, nicotine or non-medically prescribed substances, a tendency to set fires, a tendency to steal, a tendency to physical or sexual abuse of other persons, voyeurism,

---

[62] The Disability Discrimination (Meaning of Disability) Regs 1996 (SI 1996/1455).
[63] Guidance on Matters to be Taken into Account in Determining Questions Relating to the Definition of Disability (most recently published on 1 May 2006).
[64] *McNicol v Balfour Beatty Rail Maintenance* [2002] ICR 1498, CA.
[65] *College of Ripon and York St John v Hobbs* [2002] IRLR 185, EAT.

exhibitionism, and seasonal allergic rhinitis (hay fever) except where it aggravates the effect of another condition.[66]

2.37 Where a person has more than one impairment (whether mental or physical or both) each should be identified so that the combined effect of the various conditions can be considered.

2.38 The DDA provides that an impairment is to be treated as affecting a person's ability to carry out normal day-to-day activities if and only if it affects one or more of the following list of 'capacities':

- mobility;
- manual dexterity;
- physical coordination;
- continence;
- the ability to lift, carry or otherwise move everyday objects;
- speech, hearing or eyesight;
- memory or ability to concentrate, learn or understand; and
- the perception of the risk of physical danger.[67]

Section D of the Guidance provides a range of useful examples of normal day-to-day activities by reference to the list of capacities and examples of circumstances that it would be reasonable to regard as having a substantial adverse effect.

2.39 Regard should also be had to the fact that those with a disability will often seek to minimise the effect of their disability or develop coping mechanisms to enable them to carry out day-to-day activities. The focus of the DDA remains on whether their ability to carry out those activities is substantially adversely affected by their impairment, even if they do, in fact, manage to carry out the activities in question.[68] The effect of the impairment is to be judged at the time of the alleged discrimination.[69]

2.40 The Government is currently considering removing the requirement that a complainant prove their disability by reference to this list of capabilities.[70]

2.41 The effect on a person's day-to-day activities must be a substantial adverse effect. A 'substantial' effect is one which is more than insubstantial.[71] The

---

[66] The Disability Discrimination (Meaning of Disability) Regs 1996 (SI 1996/1455), regs 3 and 4.
[67] DDA, sch 1, para 4.   [68] *Goodwin v Patent Office* [1999] ICR 302, EAT.
[69] *Cruickshank v Vaw Motorcast Ltd* [2002] ICR 729, EAT.
[70] DLR consultation paper, paras 8.3–8.6.
[71] *Ekpe v Metropolitan Police Commissioner* [2001] IRLR 605, EAT.

concept of 'substantial' reflects the general understanding of disability as a limitation going beyond the normal differences in ability which may exist among people. Section B of the Guidance addresses the issue of substantiality, by reference to the time taken to carry out the activity, the way in which the activity is carried out, the cumulative effects of an impairment on different activities, coping strategies, environmental factors and the effect of treatment (which is broadly to be disregarded[72]). As far as coping strategies are concerned, in *Vicary v British Telecommunications Plc*[73] the Employment Appeal Tribunal (the 'EAT') cautioned employers and Tribunals about having unrealistic expectations of how disabled people can or should modify their behaviour to minimise the effects of their disability. There are also particular provisions that deem an impairment which consists of a severe disfigurement as having a substantial adverse effect on day-to-day activities regardless of its actual effect.[74]

The substantial and adverse effects of the impairment must also be long term to enable the person to fall within the DDA. An effect is defined by the DDA as being long term if it has lasted for at least twelve months, it is likely to last for at least 12 months or it is likely to last for the rest of the affected person's life.[75] If an impairment has had a substantial adverse effect which has ceased, but is likely to recur, then that substantial effect is to be treated as continuing.[76]   **2.42**

The definition of disability was amended with effect from 5 December 2005, to deem those with HIV, multiple sclerosis and cancer to be disabled, and to remove the requirement that a person with mental illness prove that they have a 'clinic-ally well-recognised' mental illness in order to fall within the DDA.[77] This means that, for example, those suffering from stress and anxiety-related mental health illnesses will simply need to satisfy the Tribunal that they suffer from an impairment which is severe enough in its effects to fall within section 1(1) of the DDA, not that the illness from which they suffer is clinically well recognised.   **2.43**

The employment provisions of the DDA apply equally to a person who had, but no longer has, a disability within the meaning of the Act.[78] This means that, for example, it could be unlawful to refuse to promote an employee to a managerial position simply because he or she previously had a depressive illness which at the time satisfied the definition of disability under the DDA but in respect of which there has been no recurrence.   **2.44**

The DDA adopts a rather different approach to the kinds of discrimination prohibited than the SDA and RRA, which we discuss further below.   **2.45**

---

[72] DDA, sch 1, para 6(1).   [73] [1999] IRLR 680, EAT.   [74] DDA, sch 1, para 3.
[75] DDA, sch 1, para 2(1).
[76] DDA, sch 1, para 2(2); *Swift v Chief Constable of Wiltshire* [2004] ICR 909, EAT.
[77] Disability Discrimination Act 2005, s 18.   [78] DDA, s 2 and sch 2.

2.46 The DDA, as significantly amended by the Disability Discrimination Act 1995 (Amendment) Regulations 2003,[79] gives effect to the parts of the Employment Directive[80] which relate to disability.

2.47 The Disability Rights Commission (the 'DRC'[81]) published a Code of Practice on Employment and Occupation in 2004 (the 'DRC Code 2004'), which is again admissible in Tribunal proceedings.[82] It also issued a Code of Practice on the disability equality duty, which we discuss further in Chapter 3. The EHRC also took over the work of the DRC in October 2007.

(e) Religion and Belief Discrimination; Sexual Orientation Discrimination and Age Discrimination

2.48 The RBR, SOR and AR—all of which have been enacted to give effect to the corresponding parts of the Employment Directive[83]—prohibit discrimination in the employment sphere to an extent very similar to that of the SDA and RRA.

2.49 The RBR came into force on 2 December 2003. The original definition of 'religion or belief' set out in regulation 2 of the RBR was amended by sections 44 and 77 of the EA on 30 April 2007. Accordingly 'religion' is defined to mean any religion and 'belief' means any religious or philosophical belief; and any reference to religion or belief includes a reference to a lack of religion or belief. The Explanatory Note to the relevant sections of the EA makes clear that the new definitions are intended to be broad and to mirror that guaranteed by Article 9 of the European Convention on Human Rights (the 'ECHR').[84] The Notes state that 'the main limitation on what constitutes a religion for the purposes of Article 9 is that it must have a clear structure and belief system',[85] so that it will embrace the following:

- Religions widely recognised such as Christianity, Islam, Hinduism, Judaism, Buddhism, Sikhism, Rastafarianism, Bahai'ism, Zoroastrianism and Jainism;
- Branches or sects within a religion, such as Catholics or Protestants within the Christian Church;
- Collective religions such as Druidism, the Church of Scientology, Seventh Day Adventism and the Divine Light Zentrum; and
- Belief founded on a religion if they attain a certain level of cogency, serious-

---

[79] SI 2003/1673. [80] Council Directive 2000/78/EC. [81] <www.drc.gov.uk>.
[82] DDA, s 53A. [83] Council Directive 2000/78/EC.
[84] The right to freedom of thought, conscience and religion.
[85] Paragraph 170 of the Explanatory Notes.

ness, cohesion and importance, provided the beliefs are worthy of respect in a democratic society and are not incompatible with human dignity.[86]

The guidance to the RBR produced by the Advisory, Conciliation and Arbitration Service ('ACAS') has a useful Appendix which sets out all the main religions and beliefs in Britain together with their main customs, needs and festivals.[87] However, as is clear from the above, the RBR extend beyond these religions and beliefs and are likely to cover fringe religions such as Druidism, Scientology and Seventh Day Adventism.

The new definition also means that there is no longer a requirement for a 'philosophical belief' to be *similar* to a 'religious belief'. It remains to be seen whether this will lead to a rush of claims that those with certain political beliefs should be able to benefit from the protection of the RBR, and we discuss this further in Chapter 10 when considering free expression issues generally. **2.50**

The SOR came into force on 1 December 2003. 'Sexual orientation' is defined as orientation towards persons of the same sex, orientation towards persons of the opposite sex and orientation towards persons of the same sex and the opposite sex.[88] Accordingly, the Regulations protect those who are homosexual, heterosexual and bisexual from discrimination based on their sexual orientation. 'On the grounds of sexual orientation' includes treatment based on a characteristic related to sexual orientation such as sexual behaviour.[89] In December 2005 the SOR were amended to ensure that civil partnerships and marriage are treated in the same way—so that the fact that one person is in a civil partnership while another is married cannot be regarded as a material difference between their respective circumstances, when assessing whether there has been unlawful sexual orientation discrimination under regulation 3(1) and (2).[90] **2.51**

The AR came into force in April 2007. 'Age' is not defined as such. The AR contain specific provisions in relation to retirement ages (permitting discretionary retirement ages in certain circumstances), and permitting direct discrimination to be justified in certain circumstances (a provision unique to age). We discuss this further at paragraph 2.64 below. **2.52**

All three sets of Regulations cover discrimination based on the complainant's **2.53**

---

[86] *Campbell and Cosans v UK* (1982) 4 EHRR 293, ECtHR at 304.

[87] *Religion or Belief and the Workplace* (ACAS, 2005), available at <www.acas.org.uk/media/pdf/f/l/religion_1.pdf>.

[88] SOR, reg 2.

[89] *R (Amicus—MSF section) v Secretary of State for Trade and Industry* [2004] IRLR 430, QBD (Admin), para 119.

[90] SOR, reg 3(3) as amended by the Civil Partnerships Act 2004.

actual or *perceived* sexual orientation, religion or age, even if the same is based on an incorrect assumption. It is also unlawful to treat less favourably a complainant who refuses to carry out an *instruction* to discriminate against a person on grounds of their religion, sexual orientation or age.

2.54 However, only the RBR and SOR also cover discrimination based on the complainant's *association* with a person of a particular sexual orientation or religion. Thus homophobic comments to a man who is not in fact gay but perceived to be gay would be unlawful; as would disparaging remarks made to a woman about her brother who has converted to Islam. The Government is currently not persuaded that it should extend this protection to the age strand, by outlawing discrimination on the grounds of the age of those with whom a person associates.[91]

2.55 There were no dedicated statutory commissions akin to the EOC, CRE or DRC addressing discrimination on the grounds of religion or belief, sexual orientation or age when the Regulations covering these strands came into force. However, it is clearly intended that the work of the new EHRC will include these strands, as the EHRC's powers and duties extend to all the equality enactments. We discuss the likely work of the EHRC further in Chapter 15.

C. The Kinds of Discrimination Prohibited

2.56 In this section, we explain the four kinds of discrimination common to all the strands: direct discrimination, indirect discrimination, victimisation and harassment. We deal with the kinds of prohibited discrimination in this way because where the common definitions apply, cases decided under one strand are relevant to the others.[92] We then go on to look at the additional ways in which discrimination on the grounds of disability is prohibited.

(a) Direct Discrimination

2.57 Direct discrimination for the purposes of the employment provisions in the SDA, RRA, DDA, RBR, SOR and AR is broadly defined as 'less favourable treatment' of the complainant on the protected ground in question.[93]

2.58 In order to show that s/he has been treated less favourably, the complainant

---

[91] DLR consultation paper, para 1.25.
[92] eg the comments to this effect by Lord Nicholls in *Shamoon v Chief Constable of Royal Ulster Constabulary* [2003] 2 All ER 26, HL at para 3.
[93] SDA, s 1 (sex, married status or civil partnership status) and s 2 (gender reassignment); RRA, s 1; DDA, s 3A(5); RBR, reg 3; SOR, reg 3 and AR, reg 3.

must show that s/he has been, or would have been, treated differently from a person of a different sex, race, religion, etc. In conducting this comparative exercise, the complainant must be compared with how another employee was or would have been treated in similar circumstances: like must be compared with like. The relevant circumstances in which the comparison is carried out must not themselves be discriminatory, so that it is necessary to remove the characteristic in dispute (sex, race, etc) from the comparison process.[94] If an actual comparator cannot be found, a complainant is entitled to rely on a hypothetical comparator, so that the Tribunal will have to determine how someone in an analogous position would have been treated if they existed.[95] A Tribunal is also entitled to look at actual non-identical but similar cases.

There are two important caveats to this approach: first, in DDA cases, the comparison is to be drawn with a person who does not have the disability in question but whose abilities are the same or similar;[96] and second, the comparison approach does not apply at all in pregnancy/maternity cases, where it is well established from European case law that no comparator is needed.[97] **2.59**

The law applies a low threshold to the question of whether or not the different treatment is less favourable. The complainant is not required to show, for example, that s/he has suffered any physical harm or economic loss by the treatment. A failure to shortlist for a post, denial of an opportunity to go on a training course, a failure to appoint or promote, disparaging remarks or the refusal to provide a reference could all constitute less favourable treatment. Less favourable treatment is often equated with the concept of detriment.[98] Segregation on racial grounds is specifically deemed to be less favourable treatment.[99] **2.60**

Often a simple causation test helps to determine whether an employee has been discriminated against—would s/he have been treated less favourably 'but for' the prohibited ground? Another approach, favoured by the House of Lords in *Shamoon v Chief Constable of Royal Ulster Constabulary*,[100] and later followed in *Macdonald v Advocate General for Scotland; Pearce v Mayfield Secondary School* **2.61**

---

[94] *James v Eastleigh BC* [1990] 2 AC 751, HL and *Showboat Entertainment Centre Ltd v Owens* [1984] 1 All ER 836, EAT.

[95] *Balamoody v UK Central Council for Nursing, Midwifery and Health Visiting* [2002] ICR 646, CA.

[96] DDA, s 3A(5). Direct discrimination on grounds of disability overlaps with disability-related discrimination, which we discuss further below.

[97] For a recent domestic restatement of the principle, see *Fletcher v Blackpool Fylde and Wyre Hospitals NHS Trust* [2005] IRLR 689, EAT.

[98] eg the comments to this effect by Lord Hoffman in *Chief Constable of West Yorkshire v Khan* [2001] 4 All ER 834, HL at para 53.

[99] RRA, s 1(2).

[100] [2003] 2 All ER 26, HL.

Governing Body,[101] is to ask the 'reason why' the complainant was treated less favourably compared to how another employee was or would have been treated, and then assess whether it was one of the prohibited strands of discrimination or another reason. This approach may be particularly appropriate where the identity of the comparator is in dispute.

2.62 Some discrimination is deliberate and motivated by prejudice, but such cases of overt discrimination are less common. Most discrimination is unconscious and is therefore not acknowledged or admitted by the perpetrator. It may be based on misguided assumptions about whether someone will 'fit in' and/or unfair stereotypes of the group to which the person belongs—in *Coleman v Skyrail Oceanic Ltd,*[102] for example, the dismissal of a woman because it was assumed that she would be less likely than a man to be the primary supporter of a family was held to be discriminatory. Similarly, an employer may discriminate for genuine business reasons, but this is no defence either—for example, in *R v Commission for Racial Equality, ex p Westminster CC*[103] the withdrawal of a job offer to a black road sweeper because the manager in question feared a racially motivated strike was held to be discriminatory.

2.63 Put simply, the law dictates that motive and intention are largely irrelevant to allegations of direct discrimination, save that an overtly hostile motive may well be probative of discrimination. Moreover, the prohibited ground need not be the only cause for the less favourable treatment for discrimination to be made out—it is sufficient if it is an important factor or effective cause of the treatment.[104]

2.64 Direct discrimination cannot be justified in the employment context except in cases of age discrimination, but only then if the action in question is 'a proportionate means of achieving a legitimate aim'.[105] Establishing a legitimate aim for the employer's actions will, therefore, be the first step in the justification process. In its 2005 *Coming of Age* consultation document, the then Department for Trade and Industry ('the DTI') explained that:

> A wide variety of aims may be considered as legitimate. The aim must correspond with a real need on the part of the employer . . . Economic factors such as business needs and considerations of efficiency may also be legitimate aims.

---

[101] [2004] 1 All ER 339, HL   [102] [1981] IRLR 398, CA.
[103] [1985] ICR 827, CA.
[104] *Owen and Briggs v James* [1982] ICR 618, CA; *Nagarajan v London Regional Transport* [2000] 1 AC 501, HL.
[105] AR, reg 3(1).

> However, discrimination will not be justified merely because it may be more
> expensive not to discriminate . . .[106]

However, the DTI had given the following examples of potential legitimate
aims in its 2003 *Age Matters* consultation on the regulations:

- health, welfare and safety;
- facilitation of employment planning;
- particular training requirements;
- encouraging and rewarding loyalty;
- the need for a reasonable period of employment before retirement; and
- recruiting or retaining older people.[107]

Once a legitimate aim is shown, the employer will then have to show that the
action taken was nevertheless a proportionate means of meeting that aim. It is
likely that in interpreting this, Tribunals will take a similar approach to the
proportionality element of the justification defence in indirect discrimination
claims, which we consider further at paragraph 2.71 below.

(b) Indirect Discrimination

The prohibition on indirect discrimination broadly seeks to challenge practices **2.65**
which on their face are neutral and apply to all, but which in reality have a
disparate impact on a particular sex, race, religion etc. In the employment
context, the most widely used definition of indirect discrimination states that
the same is made out by:

- the application of a provision, criterion or practice;
- which puts or would put someone in a prohibited group at a particular
  disadvantage compared with someone not of that prohibited group;
- which is such that it does or would put the complainant at a particular
  disadvantage; and
- which cannot be shown to be a proportionate means of achieving a legitimate aim (justified).

This definition is found throughout the SDA, RRA, RBR, SOR and AOR,[108]
save in relation to gender reassignment (where indirect discrimination is not yet

---

[106] *Equality and Diversity: Coming of Age: Consultation on the draft Employment Equality (Age)
Regulations 2006* (DTI, 2005), <www.dti.gov.uk/files/file16397.pdf>, at para 4.1.16.
[107] *Equality and Diversity: Age Matters: Age Consultation 2003* (DTI, 2003), available at
<www.dti.gov.uk/files/file24331.pdf>, at para 3.15.
[108] SDA, s 1(2) (sex, married status or civil partnership status); RRA, s 1A RBR, reg 3; SOR,
reg 3 and AR, reg 3.

prohibited at all, although there are proposals to change this[109]) and claims under the RRA based on colour or nationality discrimination (where an older definition of indirect discrimination continues to be used[110]).

2.66 A *provision* means a condition or requirement, such as those set out in contracts of employment, or workplace rules. A *criterion* implies something such as a desirable attribute in an applicant for a post: in this regard it is notably wider than the old definition, which only applied to conditions or requirements, effectively 'musts' for such posts.[111] *Practice* is given its normal everyday meaning and so can cover a wide range of informal practices and procedures.

2.67 It is not necessary to show that the provision, criterion or practice has in fact been applied to anyone else. In *British Airways plc v Starmer*,[112] for example, the airline had said that it would accommodate a female co-pilot's childcare needs by permitting her to work 75 per cent of the full-time hours (she had asked for 50 per cent). Although this 75 per cent requirement was not applied to anyone else, the EAT upheld the Tribunal's finding that it was a provision for the purposes of the complainant's indirect discrimination claim (and upheld the claimant's claim overall).

2.68 In order to establish whether the provision, criterion or practice does in fact put the group into which the complainant falls at a particular disadvantage an appropriate pool for comparison must be selected, and the percentages of those within the comparison groups who are placed at a particular disadvantage and those who are not established. Consistent with the approach to direct discrimination, the relevant circumstances between the comparator groups must be the same or not materially different, so that there is a like for like comparison. Pools can be drawn from, for example, all employees in the particular workplace, all those in a particular geographical location, all those with a particular qualification or all those in the UK: in *London Underground Ltd v Edwards (No 2)*[113] it was held that the Tribunal is entitled to have regard to the wider sociological picture and use its 'general knowledge and expertise' by looking at national statistics. The choice of pool must not be limited by the very discriminatory factors which give rise to the complainant's inability to

---

[109] DLR consultation paper, para 1.33.
[110] The old definition is set out in RRA, s 1(1). This is made out, instead, by (i) the application of a condition or requirement; (ii) with which a considerably smaller proportion of the relevant group than of others can comply; (iii) which is to the complainant's detriment because s/he cannot comply with it; and (iv) which cannot be justified.
[111] *Perera v Civil Service Commission (No 2)* [1983] ICR 428, CA.
[112] [2005] IRLR 863, EAT.   [113] [1999] ICR 494, CA.

comply with the requirement.[114] In some cases it can be helpful to use a mathematical prediction approach, as discussed in *Jones v Chief Adjudication Officer*,[115] to assess whether there is a disparate impact. The new definition of indirect discrimination makes clear that it applies to provisions, criteria or practices that have not yet had a disparate impact on a particular group, or the complainant, but *would* do. This would cover, for example, contract clauses which have yet to take effect.

The third element of the definition requires the complainant to show that the **2.69** provision, criterion or practice either does in fact put him or her at a particular disadvantage, or again, that it *would* do so.

The final issue in an indirect discrimination claim is whether or not, assuming **2.70** discrimination is made out, the employer can provide a justification for it. Justification in this context is a European law concept, as set out by the European Court of Justice (the 'ECJ') in *Bilka-Kaufhaus GmbH v Weber von Hartz*.[116]

Under this approach, in order to show justification the employer must show **2.71** that the provision, criterion or practice was imposed other than to discriminate on protected grounds; that the means selected by the employer to achieve the chosen aim corresponded to a real need; that the means selected were appropriate to meet that aim; and that they were necessary in order to achieve that end. This approach was applied to domestic discrimination legislation by the House of Lords in *Hampson v Department of Education and Science*.[117] A Tribunal must apply a 'proportionality' approach, which broadly means that it must conduct a balancing exercise, taking into account all the surrounding circumstances, and giving due emphasis to the degree of discrimination caused, against the object or aim to be pursued. The Tribunal will not merely consider whether or not the employer's views were within the range of reasonable responses, but will make its own judgment as to whether justification is made out.[118] Again, the intention of the employer is largely irrelevant, and indirect discrimination can easily be found even if that is not what the employer intends.

Applying this definition, requirements to work anti-social hours may indirectly **2.72** discriminate against women; language criteria may indirectly discriminate against certain racial groups; dress codes may indirectly discriminate against certain religious groups; a requirement that a certain post can only be filled by a married couple may indirectly discriminate against same-sex couples; and certain length of service requirements may discriminate on grounds of age.

---

[114] *R v Secretary of State for Education, ex p Schaffter* [1987] IRLR 53, EAT.
[115] [1990] IRLR 533, CA.   [116] [1986] IRLR 317, ECJ.   [117] [1991] 1 AC 171, HL.
[118] *Hardys and Hansons plc v Lax* [2005] IRLR 726, CA.

2.73 The DDA does not regulate indirect discrimination as such, although the other forms of discrimination prohibited under the DDA (which we discuss further below) are intended to embrace many of the situations that would otherwise be covered by the indirect discrimination definition.

(c) Harassment

2.74 By section 3A of the RRA, it is unlawful to engage in unwanted conduct which has the purpose or effect of violating another person's dignity, or creating an intimidating, hostile, degrading, humiliating or offensive environment for an individual. Conduct is regarded as having this effect only if, having regard to all the circumstances, including, in particular, the perception of that other person, it should reasonably be considered as having that effect. This provision in the RRA only applies to harassment on grounds of race or ethnic or national origins and not colour or nationality. There are broadly comparable provisions in the employment provisions of the SDA, DDA, RBR, SOR and AR,[119] although the SDA also specifically prohibits the less favourable treatment of a woman on grounds that she has rejected or submitted to harassment.[120]

2.75 Historically, allegations of harassment were framed as complaints of direct discrimination, and this will continue to be the case in the context of alleged racial harassment on the grounds of colour or nationality. In such circumstances the requirement in a direct discrimination complaint to provide a comparator would remain,[121] although there is no such requirement in a statutory harassment complaint. Rather, the wording focuses on whether or not the unwanted conduct has occurred in the complainant's case, and whether the conduct in question had the specified purpose or effect.

2.76 As the definition makes clear, the Tribunal will apply a reasonableness test, and so will only conclude that the conduct in question had the effect of violating the complainant's dignity, or creating an intimidating, hostile, degrading, humiliating or offensive environment for them, if it concludes that it would be reasonable to reach that conclusion.

2.77 Harassment can include deliberate abuse or insults, ridicule, embarrassing remarks or jokes, unwelcome comments about matters of a personal nature (such as appearance, dress or sexuality), offensive emails, action intended to isolate the complainant in their work, unwanted physical attention or demands for sexual activity, and in the most serious cases, physical or sexual assaults.

---

[119] SDA, s 4A; DDA, s 3B; RBR, reg 5; SOR, reg 5 and AR, reg 6.
[120] SDA, s 4A(1)(c).
[121] *Macdonald v Advocate General for Scotland; Pearce v Mayfield Secondary School Governing Body* [2004] 1 All ER 339, HL.

As with other forms of discrimination, the intention and motive of the alleged **2.78** harasser are largely irrelevant, save, that if the *purpose* of the treatment is to violate the complainant's dignity, or create an intimidating, hostile, degrading, humiliating or offensive environment for them, then harassment will be made out.

Harassment may give rise to other legal issues in criminal and civil law, which **2.79** we discuss further in Chapter 11, when considering the issues raised by harassment in the workplace generally in more detail.

(d) Victimisation

Victimisation occurs when a person treats another person less favourably than **2.80** he treats or would treat another person because, put simply, that person has sought to exercise their rights under the discrimination provisions, or assisted someone else to do so. The victimisation provisions are broadly common across the SDA, RRA, DDA, RBR, SOR and AR,[122] although the DDA provision has some slight differences:[123] one such difference is that the wording of section 2(a)(iii) refers to a protected act being one done 'under' the DDA rather than 'by reference' to it (the wording in the parallel provisions), which may be significant because in *Kirby v Manpower Services Commission*,[124] it was held that the wording 'under' required the complainant to have done something under a specific provision of the statute in question.

The first issue is whether the complainant has done a 'protected act', or **2.81** whether the employer knows or suspects that the complainant has done or is intending to do such an act. A protected act is defined as bringing proceedings for discrimination, giving evidence or information in connection with discrimination proceedings (including those brought by others), alleging that the discriminator or any other person has done an act of discrimination (for example, by lodging an internal grievance or questionnaire alleging discrimination), or by doing anything else under or by reference to the equality enactments (for example, by disseminating information to others about their rights under them). Although the complaint need not include a statement that an act of discrimination contrary to one of the equality enactments had occurred, it must be such that, if proved, the complaint would amount to unlawful discrimination under the relevant legal strand.[125] An employer also has a defence to a victimisation claim if it is proved that the complaint was false and not

---

[122] SDA, s 5(1)(a); RRA, s 2(1)(a); RBR, reg 4; SOR, reg 4; and AR, para 4.
[123] [1980] 3 All ER 334, EAT.   [124] [1980] 3 All ER 334, EAT.
[125] For an example of where the claim failed on this ground, see *Waters v Metropolitan Police Commissioner* [1997] ICR 1073, CA.

made in good faith. This would only really apply where the employer could prove that the complainant knowingly and maliciously made a false allegation of discrimination, for improper motives.

2.82 The second issue is whether the complainant has been treated less favourably by reason of his or her protected act. This issue is approached in a similar way to the same question in direct discrimination cases. *Chief Constable of West Yorkshire Police v Khan*[126] makes clear that what is needed is a simple comparison between the treatment afforded to the complainant who has done a protected act and the treatment that was or would be afforded to other employees who have not done the protected act. The sex, race, religion, etc of the complainant and the comparator are irrelevant, as the distinguishing feature in victimisation complaints is the doing of the protected act. The circumstances of the complainant and the comparator must otherwise be the same. Again, the Tribunal is entitled to have regard to the treatment that would have been afforded to a hypothetical comparator, and in carrying out that assessment, can consider how the employer has treated others who have not done protected acts, in different but not dissimilar circumstances.

2.83 Victimisation, like the other kinds of discrimination, does not require any conscious motive on the part of the victimiser. Again, the victimised person does not need to show any financial or material loss in order to show less favourable treatment, provided he or she has suffered a detriment.

2.84 A recent example of this kind of discrimination was *St Helens MBC v Derbyshire*[127] where the House of Lords held that sending intimidating letters to 39 equal pay claimants, pointing out that they might be responsible for the loss of their colleagues' jobs if they won their claims, and sending similar letters to their colleagues, amounted to victimisation.

(e) Disability-related Discrimination

2.85 The DDA also prohibits disability-related discrimination. This provides that it is unlawful if, for a reason that relates to the disabled person's disability, an employer treats a disabled person less favourably than he treats or would treat others to whom that reason does not apply, and he cannot show that the treatment is justified.[128]

2.86 Although there is clearly an overlap between disability-related discrimination and direct discrimination (so that, for example, a decision not to promote someone on grounds of their disability is likely to constitute both forms of

---

[126] [2001] 4 All ER 834, HL, per Lord Nicholls at para 27.
[127] [2007] ICR 841, HL.   [128] DDA, s 3A(1).

discrimination), the phrase 'relates to' in the disability-related discrimination definition is much wider than 'on the grounds of' in the direct discrimination definition, as it relates to both the fact of and the effects of a disability. This means that disability-related discrimination embraces the sort of issues that might be considered as indirect discrimination under the other equality enactments.

Another key distinction is that disability-related discrimination is capable of **2.87** justification by an employer. By section 3A(3), treatment is only justified if the reason for it is both material to the circumstances of the particular case and substantial. However, this test affords considerable leeway to employers, and the Tribunal will not substitute its own view of what is reasonable: rather the issue will be whether the employer's actions fell within the range of reasonable responses.[129]

However, by section 3A(6) if an employer is under a duty to make reasonable **2.88** adjustments and has failed to do so, disability-related discrimination cannot be justified unless it would have been justified even if he had complied with that duty—so, for example, an employer would not be justified in rejecting an applicant for a post on the basis that her typing speed is too slow, if this was due to her arthritis, and this could have been remedied by the provision of an adapted keyboard.[130]

Although an employer need not know of an employee's disability in order to **2.89** subject him to disability-related discrimination, the disability-related *reason* must affect the employer's mind either consciously or subconsciously—so, for example, an employee disciplined for being unduly slow in completing his work, where the reason for this was a disability of which the employer was unaware, would have been subjected to disability-related discrimination.

(f) The Duty to Make Reasonable Adjustments for Those with a Disability

Finally, sections 3A(2) and 4A of the DDA place positive duties on employers **2.90** to make reasonable adjustments to any provisions, criteria or practices (which includes any arrangements made by the employer) or physical features of their premises if they place disabled people at a substantial disadvantage, so as to prevent the provision, criterion, practice, arrangement or feature from having that effect. A proper risk assessment by the employer will often be needed in order to assess what adjustments it might be reasonable to make. However, the duty does not apply where the employer does not know and could not reasonably be expected to know that the person is disabled and likely to be disadvantaged.[131]

---

[129] *Jones v Post Office* [2001] IRLR 384, CA.   [130] DRC Code 2004, paras 6.5 and 6.6.
[131] DDA, s 4A(3)(b).

2.91 The word 'arrangements' is given a wide meaning in this context, and will embrace, for example, the arrangements made for determining to whom employment should be offered, and the terms and conditions on which employment, promotions, transfers, training or other benefits are offered to employees.[132] An employer may, therefore, for example, have to alter the conditions of an interview for a disabled person,[133] allocate some of a disabled person's duties to another person, assign him a different place of work or training, or provide him with modified instructions or equipment.[134]

2.92 In assessing the reasonableness of any adjustments made, the Tribunal will have regard to issues such as the extent to which the taking of the step would prevent the effect in question, the extent to which it is practicable for the employer to take that step, the financial and other costs of taking the step and the extent of any disruption, the extent of the employer's financial and other resources, the availability of financial or other assistance, the size of the employer and the nature of its activities and (in the case of private households only) the extent of the disruption and disturbance that would be caused by the adjustment.[135] Unlike the approach to disability-related discrimination, the Tribunal's assessment of what was or might have been a reasonable adjustment is purely objective: it is concerned not with the reasonableness of the employer's belief, but with the objective reasonableness of what the employer did or did not do. Throughout the chapters that follow we consider the sort of adjustments that might be reasonable at each stage of the employment process.

(g) The Burden of Proof in Discrimination Claims

2.93 In cases of employment discrimination on any of the prohibited grounds, except colour or nationality, there is a statutory regime that provides for a potential shift in the burden of proof. If the complainant proves facts from which the Tribunal could conclude that s/he has been discriminated against, the burden of proof will shift to the employer to show that there has been no discrimination. A step-by-step approach to the reversal of the burden of proof was set out in *Barton v Investec*,[136] which approach was amended by the Court of Appeal in *Igen and others v Wong and others*,[137] and considered further in *Madarassy v Nomura International Plc*.[138] In carrying out this approach, the Tribunal will be very conscious of the case law which recognises that it is

---

132 DRC Code 2004, para 5.8.   133 *Ridout v TC Group* [1998] IRLR 628, EAT.
134 DDA, s 18B(2).   135 DDA, s 18B(1).   136 [2003] ICR 1205, CA.
137 [2005] 3 All ER 812, CA.   138 [2007] IRLR 246, CA.

increasingly unusual to find direct evidence of discrimination, and that instead discrimination is more likely a matter of inference.[139]

If the complainant is alleging discrimination on grounds of colour or national-   **2.94**
ity, then there is no statutory reversal of the burden of proof. However, the common law effects a similar process of looking to the employer for an explan-ation for any less favourable treatment proven, and assessing the quality of that explanation before deciding whether discrimination can be inferred.[140]

Moreover, the EAT has recently held, 'with some degree of hesitation and   **2.95**
disquiet', that the provisions relating to the reversal of the burden of proof do not apply to allegations of *victimisation* under the race strand;[141] although they do apply in the same way with regard to victimisation complaints under the other strands.

We consider the step-by-step approach derived from *Igen and others v Wong and*   **2.96**
others, and the practical and evidential consequences of the burden of proof regime, further in Chapter 14, when looking at litigation issues in more detail.

D. The Human Rights Act 1998, Equality and Diversity

The HRA enshrines in domestic law most of the rights set out in the ECHR,   **2.97**
and provides individuals with certain remedies under domestic law for breaches of those rights. Although these operate in a different way from the other strands of discrimination law, they have a potentially important role to play in the creation of substantive equality and respect for diversity in the workplace.

(a) Substantive ECHR Rights

Although there is no ECHR right to employment, or to acceptable conditions   **2.98**
of employment, the following ECHR rights can all be relevant to the creation of an equality and diversity friendly workplace:

• Article 3—the right to protection from inhuman or degrading treatment. The ECommHR has recognised that severe race discrimination can, in certain circumstances constitute degrading treatment within Article 3.[142] Importantly, an interference with the rights under Article 3, unlike those

---

[139] *King v Great Britain China Centre* [1992] ICR 516, CA; *Glasgow City Council v Zafar* [1998] 2 All ER 953, HL; and *Anya v University of Oxford* [2001] ICR 847, CA.
[140] *King v Great Britain China Centre* [1992] ICR 516, CA; *Glasgow City Council v Zafar* [1998] 2 All ER 953, HL; and *Anya v University of Oxford* [2001] ICR 847, CA.
[141] *Oyarce v Cheshire County Council* UKEAT/0557/06/DA, 13 June 2007 (this decision is currently being appealed).
[142] *East African Asians v UK* (1973) 3 EHRR 76, ECommHR.

protected by Articles 8 to 11 and 14, may not be justified on any grounds by the state.

- Article 6—the right to a fair hearing. This applies to discrimination litigation, and requires that all parties have a fair and public hearing within a reasonable time by an independent and impartial tribunal established by law. The Article 6 standards therefore apply to all the courts that determine employment disputes, including the ET and EAT. Article 6 can raise issues regarding unjustified procedural or substantive limitations which preclude people from having access to a tribunal (such as, potentially, the denial of Public Funding even in complex discrimination cases[143]); can compel the Tribunal to take steps to ensure that there is 'equality of arms' between the parties (for example, by ensuring that there has been full disclosure, or that the burden of preparing for a Tribunal hearing is appropriately shared between the parties); and has been used to challenge the composition of the ET itself.[144]

- Article 8—the right to respect for private and family life, home and correspondence. This embraces the right of an individual to develop his or her own personality and develop relationships with others,[145] including his or her sexual activities. An interference with an Article 8 right can only be justified if it is in accordance with law, and is proportionate and necessary in a democratic society in the interests of national security, public safety, for the economic well-being of the country, for the prevention of disorder or crime, for the protection of health or morals, or for the protection of the rights and freedoms of others. In the employment sphere Article 8 may be engaged by issues such as telephone and email surveillance,[146] dress codes[147] and the use of medical records in court. Historically, there have also been several cases under Article 8 relating to the rights of homosexuals[148] and transsexuals[149] at work (although these groups now have specific legal protection under the SOR and SDA, as explained above).

- Article 9—the right to freedom of thought, conscience and religion. Article 9 protects against unjustified infringements with 'manifestations' of the right to religion, which the ECtHR has defined as worship, teaching, practice and observance of religion. This applies to not only the major world religions, but

---

[143] *Airey v Ireland* (1979–1980) 2 EHRR 305, ECtHR.
[144] *Scanfuture UK Ltd v Secretary of State for Trade and Industry* [2001] ICR 1096, EAT.
[145] *Niemietz v Germany* (1992) 16 EHRR 97, ECtHR.
[146] eg *Halford v UK* (1997) 24 EHRR 523, ECtHR and *Copland v UK* (2007) The Times, 24 April, ECtHR.
[147] eg *Kara v UK* (1996) 24 EHRR 205, ECtHR.
[148] *Smith and Grady v UK* (2000) 29 EHRR 493, ECtHR.
[149] *Goodwin v UK* (2002) 35 EHRR 18, ECtHR.

also a number of less mainstream beliefs such as the Krishna Consciousness movement,[150] the Divine Light Zentrum,[151] the Church of Scientology,[152] Druids,[153] the Moon Sect,[154] pacifism[155] and veganism.[156] An interference with an Article 9 right can only be justified if it is in accordance with law, and is necessary and proportionate in a democratic society in the interests of public safety, for the protection of public order, health or morals, or for the protection of the rights and freedoms of others. In the employment context this can raise issues such as time off work for religious observance and dress codes at work.

- Article 10—the right to freedom of expression. Article 10 protects the right to hold opinions and to receive and impart information and ideas without interference by public authorities. Article 10 rights can only be restricted to the extent that the same is in accordance with law, and is necessary and proportionate in a democratic society in the interests of national security, territorial integrity or public safety, for the prevention of disorder or crime, for the protection of health or morals, for the protection of the reputation or the rights of others, for preventing the disclosure of information received in confidence, or for maintaining the authority and impartiality of the judiciary. In the employment context Article 10 can again raise issues relating to dress codes, access to information and the expression of political opinions in the workplace.

- Article 11—the right to freedom of association. This protects the right to freedom of peaceful assembly and to freedom of association with others; including the right to form and to join trade unions. Restrictions can only be placed on Article 11 rights insofar as they are prescribed by law and are necessary and proportionate in a democratic society in the interests of national security or public safety, for the prevention of disorder or crime, for the protection of health or morals or for the protection of the rights and freedoms of others. The text of Article 11 makes clear that nothing therein prevents the imposition of lawful restrictions on the exercise of Article 11 rights by members of the armed forces, the police or the administration of the state.

---

[150] *Iskcon v UK* (1994) 76A DR 90, ECommHR.
[151] *Omkarananda and the Divine Light Zentrum v Switzerland* (1981) 25 DR 105, ECommHR.
[152] *X and Church of Scientology v Sweden* (1979) 16 DR 68, ECommHR.
[153] *ARM Chappell v UK* (1987) 53 DR 241, ECommHR.
[154] *X v Austria* (1981) 26 DR 89, ECommHR.
[155] *Arrowsmith v UK* (1978) 8 DR 123, ECommHR.
[156] *W v UK*, Application 18187/91, 10 February 1993, ECommHR.

We discuss the interaction between the Article 8, 9 and 10 rights and the workplace further in Chapter 10, when considering religious practice, dress codes and freedom of expression in the workplace in further detail.

(b) Article 14: The Prohibition of Discrimination under the ECHR

2.99 Article 14 of the HRA prohibits discrimination in the enjoyment of ECHR rights on 'any ground', such as (but not limited to) sex, race, colour, language, religion, political or other opinion, national or social origin, association with a national minority, property, birth or other status.

2.100 In *Michalak v London Borough of Wandsworth*,[157] at paragraph 20, Lord Justice Brooke set out a step-by-step approach to deciding Article 14 issues, by posing the following questions:

> (i) Do the facts fall within the ambit of one or more of the substantive ECHR provisions?;
> (ii) If so, was there different treatment as respects that right between the complainant on the one hand and other persons put forward for comparison on the other, on a ground within Article 14?;
> (iii) Were the chosen comparators in an analogous situation to the complainant's situation?; and
> (iv) If so, did the difference in treatment have an objective and reasonable justification: in other words, did it pursue a legitimate aim and did the differential treatment bear a reasonable relationship of proportionality to the aim sought to be achieved?

Lord Justice Brooke's approach was adopted by Baroness Hale in *Ghaidan v Godin-Mendoza*,[158] and although a less structured approach was preferred by the House of Lords in *Carson v Secretary of State for Work and Pensions*,[159] we still think that Lord Justice Brooke's approach is a helpful checklist for practitioners assessing a potential Article 14 issue.

2.101 Element (i) of Lord Justice Brooke's approach reflects the fact that Article 14 does not provide a free-standing protection from discrimination.[160] This means that in order to invoke its protections, an individual must show that s/he was seeking to enjoy another of their ECHR rights (or strictly, was acting within the 'ambit' of that right), and was discriminated against while so doing. The 'ambit' test has generally been given a wide meaning, but something more than a mere 'tenuous link' is required, so there must be some meaningful

---

[157] [2003] 1 WLR 617, CA.   [158] [2004] 2 AC 557, HL at para 133.
[159] [2006] 1 AC 173, HL.
[160] The new Protocol 12 to the ECHR does provide such a free-standing right to protection from discrimination, but the same has yet to be ratified by the Government (and indeed it indicates that it has no plans to do so), let alone incorporated into the HRA.

connection between the facts complained of and one of the substantive ECHR rights.[161] In practical terms what this means is that, for example, an employee could not complain under Article 14 that s/he was not promoted because s/he was black (as there is no other ECHR right to promotion) but s/he could complain under Article 14, read with Article 8, that his emails were only being monitored at work because he was black (because this would fall within the 'ambit' of the Article 8 right to respect for correspondence, and s/he was complaining of discrimination in the exercise of that right).

Elements (ii) and (iii) reflect the requirement, common to all allegations of **2.102** direct discrimination in domestic law, that the complainant has been subjected to a difference in treatment when compared to others in the same or an analogous situation. In *Van der Mussele v Belgium*[162] a trainee barrister alleged a breach of Article 4 (forced labour) in conjunction with Article 14 on the grounds that, unlike apprentices in other professions, he was obliged to complete a certain amount of voluntary legal work in order to qualify. The Court rejected his claim on the basis that as there were significant differences between the different professions he was not comparing 'like with like' and therefore discrimination was not made out.

Element (ii) also reflects the fact that, as is again the case in domestic direct **2.103** discrimination law, the complainant must show that he or she has been treated differently from others by reason of the ground in issue. Under Article 14 this can be one of the protected grounds listed, or another ground classified as 'other status', which has been interpreted to include discrimination on the grounds of sexual orientation,[163] illegitimacy,[164] marital status,[165] trade union status,[166] poverty,[167] military status, conscientious objection to military service, professional status and imprisonment.[168]

Element (iv) in Lord Justice Brooke's approach reflects the fact that Article 14 **2.104** does not prohibit all kinds of discrimination. The jurisprudence of the ECHR recognises that differential action may be appropriate but distinctions have to be soundly and objectively based.[169] Whether there is such justification depends

---

[161] *M v Secretary of State for Work and Pensions* [2006] 2 AC 91, HL per Lord Bingham at para 4 and Lord Walker at para 60.
[162] (1984) 6 EHRR 163, ECtHR.
[163] eg *Sutherland v UK* (2001) The Times, 17 April, ECtHR.
[164] eg *Marckx v Belgium* (1979–1980) 2 EHRR 330, ECtHR.
[165] eg *Rasmussen v Denmark* (1985) 7 EHRR 371, ECtHR.
[166] eg *National Union of Belgian Police v Belgium* (1975) 1 EHRR 578, ECtHR.
[167] eg *Airey v Ireland* (1979–1980) 2 EHRR 305, ECtHR.
[168] D Harris, M O'Boyle and C Warbrick, *Law of the European Convention on Human Rights* (Butterworths, 1995) at p 470.
[169] *Belgian Linguistics (No 2)* (1986) 1 EHRR 252, ECtHR.

on the aim and effect of the measure and whether there is a reasonable relationship of proportionality between the means employed and the aim sought to be realised. The burden of proof is on the individual to show a difference in treatment—it then shifts to the state authority in question to justify the difference. The level of justification required depends on the protected ground in issue, because Article 14 jurisprudence has generated a hierarchy within the protected grounds. Where the differential treatment is on grounds such as sex, race, religion, illegitimacy or nationality, 'very weighty' reasons would have to be put forward before the justification defence is made out;[170] whereas where the differential treatment is on another ground such as membership of a trade union, or landowning status, it will breach Article 14 only if it has no objective and reasonable justification.[171]

2.105   Issues of discrimination may arise under Article 14 even in areas where states are not obliged to provide specific protection. Where a state chooses to provide a greater protection than is necessary to 'secure' the right in question, Article 14 applies to all aspects of the right in question. So, for example, breaches of Article 14 have been found where Belgium chose to provide a state education system,[172] and where the UK chose an immigration scheme which permitted wives to join their husbands,[173] albeit that neither of these practices were compelled by the ECHR, but where the Member State had operated the practice in a discriminatory manner.

2.106   Moreover, the ECtHR confirmed in *Thlimmenos v Greece*[174] that Article 14 prohibits both direct and indirect discrimination. This was an employment-related case, where a Jehovah's Witness had been refused appointment as an accountant because he had a conviction for a felony. However, his conviction arose out of his refusal to enlist in the army at a time of general mobilisation, on the grounds that he was a conscientious objector. The ECtHR concluded that the facts of which he complained fell within the ambit of the Article 9 right to freedom of religion, and that there had been a breach of Article 14 because the state had failed to 'treat differently persons whose situations [were] significantly different'. This form of discrimination has long been recognised by the ECJ.[175]

---

[170]   eg *Abdulazis, Cabales and Balkandali v UK* (1985) 7 EHRR 471, ECtHR; *Marckx v Belgium* (1979–1980) 2 EHRR 330, ECtHR and *Gaygusuz v Austria* (1997) 23 EHRR 364, ECtHR.

[171]   eg *National Union of Belgian Police v Belgium* (1975) 1 EHRR 578, ECtHR; *Swedish Engine Drivers v Sweden* (1976) 1 EHRR 632, ECtHR and *Chassagnou v France* (1999) 29 EHRR 615, ECtHR.

[172]   *Belgian Linguistics (No 2)* (1986) 1 EHRR 252, ECtHR.

[173]   *Abdulaziz, Cabales and Balkandali v UK* (1985) 7 EHRR 471, ECtHR.

[174]   (2000) 31 EHRR 15, ECtHR.

[175]   eg Case 203/86, *Kingdom of Spain v Council of the European Communities* [1988] ECR 4563, ECJ.

(c) Litigating Employment-related Human Rights Issues

The HRA enables individuals within the UK to litigate human rights issues in the domestic courts, rather than having to go to the ECtHR. It does so by: **2.107**

- Incorporating almost all of the ECHR rights (including all those listed above) into domestic law.[176]
- Requiring all public bodies, and those private bodies performing public functions, to ensure that they do not act incompatibly with human rights.[177]
- Enabling individuals to bring 'free-standing' claims alleging breaches of their human rights in certain specified courts, for which they can recover damages if the same is necessary to give them 'just satisfaction'.[178]
- Enabling individuals to rely on human rights arguments in all other causes of action.[179]
- Requiring all courts and tribunals where appropriate to have regard to the case law of the ECommHR and ECtHR.[180]   •
- Requiring all courts and tribunals to 'read and give effect' to all legislation 'in a way which is compatible with the Convention rights'.[181]
- Permitting the higher courts to make a declaration that legislation is incompatible with Convention rights.[182]

In practical terms what this means for employment law is that: **2.108**

- All public bodies must be conscious of the need to act compatibly with the incorporated ECHR rights at all times.
- Public sector employees can bring 'free-standing' claims under the HRA alleging breaches of their human rights in the County Court.[183]
- All employees bringing employment-related claims can argue human rights points in their cases (so, for example, a private sector employee could argue that she was unfairly dismissed in breach of her Article 8 rights).
- All courts and tribunals considering human rights issues must have regard to the ECommHR and ECtHR case law, and interpret legislation in a way that is compatible with human rights.
- The higher courts but not the ET or EAT[184] can declare a piece of employment legislation incompatible with the incorporated ECHR rights.

---

[176] HRA, sch 1.   [177] HRA, s 6(1).   [178] HRA, ss 7(1)(a) and 8.
[179] HRA, s 7(1)(b).   [180] HRA, s 2.   [181] HRA, s 3.   [182] HRA, s 4.
[183] The ET is not a specified court under the Civil Procedure Rules for hearing HRA claims.
[184] *Whittaker v P & D Watson (t/a P & M Watson Haulage)* (2002) The Times, 26 March, EAT.

The Legal Framework: In Brief

- Domestic law in Britain does not currently incorporate a single right not to be discriminated against, although it is hoped that there will soon be a Single Equality Bill which will do this.
- At present, different 'strands' of discrimination are protected by discrete legal sources. The key legal provisions are:
  - The Sex Discrimination Act 1975 (which prohibits discrimination on grounds of pregnancy or maternity leave, married status, civil partnership status and gender reassignment as well as sex);
  - The Equal Pay Act 1970;
  - The Race Relations Act 1976;
  - The Disability Discrimination Act 1995;
  - The Employment Equality (Religion or Belief) Regulations 2003;
  - The Employment Equality (Sexual Orientation) Regulations 2003; and
  - The Employment Equality (Age) Regulations 2006.
- There are also a range of European treaty Articles and directives relevant to discrimination law.
- Employers must not discriminate on the prohibited grounds against applicants in the arrangements they make for determining who should be offered employment, in the terms on which employment is offered, or by refusing or deliberately omitting to offer the employment; nor must they discriminate in the way in which employees are afforded access to opportunities for promotion, transfer or training, or to any other benefits, facilities or services, or by refusing or deliberately omitting to afford such access, or by dismissing an employee or subjecting him or her to any other detriment.
- There are four types of discrimination common to all the strands: direct discrimination, indirect discrimination, harassment and victimisation. In addition the Disability Discrimination Act 1995 (as amended) prohibits disability-related discrimination and requires employers to make reasonable adjustments for those with a disability.
- Discrimination on the prohibited grounds remains unlawful even after the employment relationship has come to an end, if the dis-

crimination complained of arises out of and is closely connected to the employment relationship.

- There are certain exceptions where a particular sex, race, religion/belief, etc is a genuine occupational qualification or requirement for a particular job.

- There is a range of statutory guidance on discrimination issues published by the Equal Opportunities Commission, the Commission for Racial Equality and the Disability Rights Commission. These bodies were replaced by the Equality and Human Rights Commission with effect from October 2007.

- The Human Rights Act 1998 incorporates many of the rights set out in the European Convention on Human Rights into domestic law. Several of these rights are relevant to the creation of substantive equality and respect for diversity in the workplace.

- Public sector employees can bring specific claims against their employers under the Human Rights Act 1998 alleging breaches of their human rights. There are other ways in which private sector employees can rely on alleged breaches of their human rights in litigation.

3

THE PUBLIC DUTY TO
PROMOTE EQUALITY

By helping public authorities to embed equality considerations throughout their activities, public sector equality duties support the design and delivery of personalised and responsive public services. The duties are intended to help bring about a culture change so that promoting equality becomes part and parcel of public authorities core business.[1]

A. Introduction

The underlying theme of this book is the promotion of equality and diversity as best practice. For some employers, however, promoting equality is not just best practice, it is mandatory. To date, those duties extend only to the race, disability and sex strands but there is a possibility that the duties might be extended to the other strands in the future.   **3.01**

The duties apply *directly* only to public authorities. This includes not only what we would traditionally understand as the public sector (central and local Government) and what would once have been described disparagingly as 'quangos' (for example, executive agencies and Non-Departmental Public Bodies or 'NDPBs'), but also in some cases private or voluntary sector bodies carrying out public functions through contracts with the public sector.   **3.02**

The duties may also apply *indirectly* to private and voluntary sector employers contracting with the public sector through the procurement process and the terms of those contracts. There may also be some knock-on good practice effect even for private sector employers who have nothing to do with the public sector.   **3.03**

---

[1] DLR consultation paper, paras 5.2–5.3.

59

3.04 The public duties to promote equality apply to all the functions of those public authorities covered by the legislation. This would include everything that the public sector does from running hospitals to collecting rubbish. We are primarily concerned, however, with functions that relate to employment.

B. Public Duties to Promote Equality

3.05 Recent legislation, beginning with the Race Relations (Amendment) Act 2000, has introduced obligations on public authorities to take positive steps to promote equality. In broad terms there are now two approaches to achieving equality:

- the *traditional* individual rights-based approach, which makes discrimination unlawful and provides a legal remedy to the victims of discrimination; and
- the *new* approach, which places public authorities under positive duties to promote equality.

3.06 Given the historical lack of a coordinated approach to equality law, the new public duties have evolved into different forms and are at different stages of development for each strand. There is, however, a common approach in that they break down into:

- a *general duty* that provides a high level equality objective rather like an organisation's mission statement; and
- *specific duties* that are a set of more clearly defined tasks for the public authority to carry out, which tasks are aimed at assisting that authority to comply with the general duty.

3.07 Currently there are general and specific duties for race, disability and sex but not for sexual orientation, religion or belief or age (see Appendix 3.1). However, some legislation does create a broad cross-strand obligation for specific public authorities—for example, section 404 of the Greater London Authority Act 1999 imposes upon the Greater London Authority, the Metropolitan Police Authority and the London Fire and Emergency Planning Authority a duty, when exercising their functions, to have regard to the need:

- to promote equality of opportunity for all persons irrespective of their race, sex, disability, age, sexual orientation or religion;
- to eliminate unlawful discrimination; and
- to promote good relations between persons of different racial groups, religious beliefs and sexual orientation.

Strand	General duty?	Specific duties?
Race	√	√
Disability	√	√
Sex	√	√
Sexual orientation	X	X
Religion of belief	X	X
Age	X	X

C. The General Duties

(a) Origins of the General Duties

Although we have described the public duties to promote equality as being **3.08** 'new' their origins are older. The original section 71 of the Race Relations Act 1976 imposed a duty on all local authorities:

> . . . to make appropriate arrangements with a view to securing that their various functions are carried out with due regard to the need:
>
> • to eliminate unlawful racial discrimination; and
> • to promote equality of opportunity and good relations between persons of different racial groups . . . .

This duty was not enforceable and as a result compliance with it was extremely **3.09** uneven and inconsistent. In the aftermath of the February 1999 Macpherson Report (the Stephen Lawrence Inquiry), section 2 of the Race Relations (Amendment) Act 2000, which came into effect on 2 April 2001, provided a new section 71, stating that a public authority bound by the duty must '. . . in carrying out its functions . . . have due regard to the need—(a) to eliminate unlawful racial discrimination; and (b) to promote equality of opportunity and good relations between persons of different racial groups'. This is the new race general duty.

The new race general duty is different from the one under the original **3.10** section 71 because it applies to a large number of listed public authorities (not merely to local authorities), and because it is a much clearer, stronger duty. Rather than being obliged to 'make appropriate arrangements with a view to securing that their various functions are carried out' with due regard to the elimination of discrimination and the promotion of equality, public authorities are now directed to carry out their functions with that purpose.

Disability was the next strand after race to incorporate a general duty, **3.11** which came into effect on 4 December 2006,[2] shortly followed by the gender duty coming into effect on 6 April 2007.[3] We set out the terms of the disability and gender general duties in Appendix 3.2, at the end of this chapter.

(b) Public Authorities Covered by the General Duties

3.12 A peculiarity of the race legislation is that only those public authorities listed in Schedule 1A of the RRA are covered by the general duty. Schedule 1A is an extensive but not exhaustive list of public authorities that has been amended on a number of occasions since it was first introduced. For example, the Civil Nuclear Police Authority was added to the list by the Energy Act 2004 and The Olympic Delivery Authority were added by the London Olympic Games and Paralympic Games Act 2006. Maintaining an accurate and up-to-date list in a world of ever changing quangos must be a major undertaking.

3.13 Section 49A of the DDA and section 76A of the SDA eschewed the list approach and instead provide simply that the disability and gender general duties apply to 'public authorities'. There is a further inconsistency in the respective definitions of 'public authority' in that:

- section 49B of the DDA defines a public authority as including 'any person certain of whose functions are functions of a public nature'; and
- section 76A(2) of the SDA defines one as including 'any person who has functions of a public nature'.

3.14 In both cases certain bodies are then excluded, for example, the House of Commons and the Secret Intelligence Service, although the exclusions are not identical. For example, the General Synod of the Church of England is excluded from the gender general duty but not the disability general duty.

3.15 Under section 49B(2) of the DDA a person is not a public authority in relation to a particular act if the nature of the act is private. There is no equivalent wording in the race or sex legislation as far as the general duty is concerned.

3.16 These inconsistencies are unhelpful, because the overall approach of the disability and sex legislation is to rely on the definition of 'public authority' from the HRA, and that definition has been the subject of confusing and at times inconsistent case law.

(i) The HRA Approach to Public Authorities

3.17 Under the HRA a threefold classification is generally used to determine whether a body is a public authority. This approach groups bodies into:

---

[2] DDA, s 49A.   [3] SDA, s 76A.

- pure public bodies;
- pure private bodies; and
- hybrid bodies.

As far as pure public bodies are concerned, during the passage of the equivalent **3.18** provisions in the HRA through the House of Lords, the then Lord Chancellor commented that:

> In many cases it will be obvious to the courts that they are dealing with a public authority. In respect of Government departments, for example, or police officers, or prison officers, or immigration officers, or local authorities, there can be no doubt that the body in question is a public authority. Any clear case of that kind comes in under [s.6(1)] . . .[4]

Pure private bodies are bodies with no public functions that are not caught **3.19** by the HRA or the disability and gender general duties. It is possible, however, that the public duties will set a benchmark for behaviour in the private sector and influence the actions of 'pure' private bodies, as the CRE Code 2005 observes at paragraph 1.9: '. . . it should be emphasised that much of the guidance and good practice associated with these duties is relevant to all employers'.

It is the classification of 'hybrid' bodies which causes the most difficulty. The **3.20** section 49B DDA definition of public authorities including 'certain of whose functions are functions of a public nature', is a concept taken directly from section 6(3)(b) of the HRA. The aim of the latter section was described by the Lord Chancellor as including '. . . bodies which are not manifestly public authorities but some of whose functions only are functions of a public nature'. The definition therefore captures bodies that have some public functions and some private functions.

In the Parliamentary debates on the HRA, the then Lord Chancellor, Lord **3.21** Irvine, said:

> When we were drawing up the Bill, we noted that the Convention had its origins in a desire to protect the individual against the abuse of power by the state, rather than to protect one individual against the actions of another . . . we wanted a realistic and modern definition of the state so as to provide a correspondingly wide protection against the abuse of human rights.

He said that the drafting of the relevant provisions was designed to '. . . provide as much protection as possible for the rights of the individual against the misuse of power by the State'.[5]

---

[4] Hansard HL, 24 November 1997, col 811.   [5] HL Deb, 24 November 1997, col 808.

3.22   He and the then Home Secretary made clear that privatised or contracted-out public services were intended to be brought within the scope of the HRA by the 'public function' provision. The specific examples given were: Railtrack when it was engaged in public functions (as opposed to commercial property development), GPs seeing NHS patients (as opposed to private ones) and Group 4 when managing contracted-out prisons (as opposed to guarding commercial premises).[6]

3.23   However, the courts have not been consistent in replicating the wide-ranging approach to the definition of a hybrid authority envisaged in the Parliamentary debates, holding that the fully privatised utilities such as the water companies in their delivery of public services,[7] a housing association providing rented accommodation on behalf of a local authority,[8] a private provider of mental health care[9] and a private company which ran farmers' markets[10] were hybrid bodies, whereas a Parochial Church Council,[11] Railtrack while acting as infrastructure controller of the national railway network[12] and a private charitable organisation running a care home[13] were not.

3.24   The most recent decision of the House of Lords on this point, in *R (Johnson) v LB Havering and others*,[14] appears to indicate (albeit with heavy dissenting judgments from Lord Bingham and Baroness Hale) a particularly restrictive approach to the applicability of section 6(3)(b) to hybrid bodies.

3.25   By mirroring the approach of the HRA, the application of the disability and gender general duties does go beyond the narrow category of central and local Government and the police, namely the organisations that represent the minimalist view of what constitutes the state. However, the use of this approach does—as the case law under the HRA illustrates—bring with it a substantial area of uncertainty as to which bodies are in fact rightly classified as hybrid bodies, and so bound by the general duties.

---

[6] Home Secretary, HL Deb, 17 June 1998, cols 409–410; Lord Chancellor, HL Deb, 24 November 1997, col 811.

[7] *Marcic v Thames Water* [2002] 2 WLR 932, CA.

[8] *Poplar Housing and Regeneration Community Association v Donoghue* [2001] 4 All ER 464, CA.

[9] *R (A) v Partnerships in Care Ltd* [2002] 1 WLR 2610, QBD (Admin).

[10] *R (Beer) v Hampshire Farmers Market* [2004] 1 WLR 233, CA.

[11] *Aston Cantlow and Wilmcote with Billesley Parochial Church Council v Wallbank* [2004] 1 AC 546, HL.

[12] *R (Cameron) and others v Network Rail Infrastructure* [2007] 1 WLR 163, QBD.

[13] *R (Heather) v Leonard Cheshire Foundation* [2002] 2 All ER 936, CA.

[14] [2007] 3 WLR 112, HL.

(ii) What the Codes of Practice Say

Additional confusion is then caused by the commentary in the DRC's statutory **3.26** Code of Practice on the disability duty[15] and the equivalent statutory EOC Code of Practice on the gender duty[16] on this issue.

The Disability Duty Code and the Gender Duty Code state that where a **3.27** private or voluntary sector body carries out public functions on behalf of a public authority, that body is itself a 'public authority' to the extent that it carries out those public functions. As such, it is a 'hybrid' or 'functional' public body and is covered by the general duties when carrying out its public functions.

The Disability Duty Code provides that a body will be exercising a 'public **3.28** function' where it is in effect exercising a function that would be otherwise exercised by the state—and where individuals have to rely upon that person for the exercise of the governmental function. Examples given in the Code are:[17]

- a private company contracted at the Home Office to run a prison establishment; and
- where the Secretary of State appoints a private company to run a failing state school.

The Disability Duty Code continues by saying that ultimately, whether or not a **3.29** private or voluntary body is exercising a public function and is therefore covered by the general duty will be a matter for the courts. However, paragraph 5.5 of the Disability Duty Code suggests that a private body is likely to be held to be performing public functions if:

- its structures and work are closely linked with the delegating or contracting-out state body; or
- it is exercising powers of a public nature directly assigned to it by statute; or
- it is exercising coercive powers devolved from the state.

It continues by saying that additional factors that may be relevant in determin- **3.30** ing whether or not an authority is carrying out a function of a public nature include:

- the fact of delegation from a state body;
- the fact of supervision by a state regulatory body;
- public funding;

---

[15] DRC, *The Duty to Promote Disability Equality, Statutory Code of Practice (England and Wales), 2005* (the 'Disability Duty Code').

[16] EOC, *Gender Equality Duty Code of Practice, 2007* (the 'Gender Duty Code').

[17] Paragraph 5.4.

- the public interest in the functions being performed; or
- motivation of serving the public interest, rather than profit.

3.31 In relation to a particular act a person is not a public authority if the nature of the act is private (for example, the private company running the prison will not be covered by the duty in relation to its private activities such as providing security guards for supermarkets).[18]

3.32 The Gender Duty Code states that the gender general duty applies to private and voluntary bodies which are carrying out public functions but only in respect of those functions.[19]

3.33 Appendix A of the Gender Duty Code expands on this: an organisation will be exercising a public function where it is in effect exercising a function which would otherwise be exercised by the state—and where individuals have to rely upon that person for the exercise of that function.

3.34 A similar list of factors to that in the Disability Duty Code is included in Appendix A. The examples given of 'functional public bodies' are (i) privatised utilities, (ii) private security firms managing contracted-out prisons and (iii) GPs when providing services under contract to a Primary Care Trust.

3.35 Appendix A also goes on to say that where a 'pure' public authority contracts out a function to a private or voluntary body, both bodies will be subject to the gender duty in their own right. Responsibility for any breach of the general duty could rest with either body depending upon the circumstances.

3.36 The practical advice from the Gender Duty Code for bodies unsure if they are functional public authorities, is to assume that they are and comply with the general duty. In light of the lack of clarity in the HRA case law, this must be sensible advice.

(c) Nature of the General Duties

3.37 The race, disability and gender general duties are all different in terms of content (see Appendix 3.2). A little more consistency would probably help those charged with responsibility for implementing the legislation and there is some hope that the forthcoming Single Equality Act may deliver that consistency.

3.38 The Code of Practice on the race duty published by the CRE[20] sets out four guiding principles which might equally apply to the disability and gender general duties. These principles are:

---

[18] Paragraph 5.7.   [19] Paragraph 1.11.

[20] CRE, *Code of Practice on the Duty to Promote Race Equality, 2002* (the 'Race Duty Code').

- Obligatory: that the promotion of race equality is obligatory for those public authorities covered by the legislation.
- Relevant: that public authorities must meet the duty to promote race equality in all relevant functions.
- Proportionate: the weight given to race equality should be proportionate to its relevance.
- Complementary: the elements of the duty are complementary and are therefore all necessary to meet the general duty.

The purpose of the general duties is to bring equality thinking to the forefront **3.39** of the public authority's activities—a process which is often referred to as 'mainstreaming'. Where the authority is developing policies or proposals or carrying out its functions those responsible should be actively considering the general duties. That means all the authority's functions although for the purposes of this book, our primary concern is with employment.

Each of the general duties requires a public authority to have 'due regard'. This **3.40** wording in effect recognises that the authority will need to work out its equality priorities and allocate resources towards its functions in a way that is proportionate to the relevance equality has to those functions. However, given that the duty is mandatory, a lack of resources is no excuse for non-compliance.

D. The Specific Duties to Produce 'Equality Schemes'

In order to ensure better performance by public authorities of their general **3.41** duties, the Secretary of State, or where relevant, Scottish Ministers have power to impose specific duties under:

- section 71(2) of the RRA;
- section 49D of the DDA; and
- sections 76B and 76C of the SDA.

Specific duties have so far been introduced in respect of race, disability and **3.42** gender. Under each of these strands there is an obligation on those public authorities listed in the respective legislation to produce Equality Schemes. Many public authorities covered by the legislation are now moving towards having integrated equality schemes rather than one for each strand. The fact that the requirements for each strand are different is an obstacle to this integrated approach. Whilst there is much to be said for integration, it is important that the separate strands remain distinct within the overall scheme so it is clear that all the legal requirements are properly covered.

Appendix 3.3 provides a single equality scheme framework with distinct **3.43** sections for race, disability and gender. What follows is an analysis by strand of the requirements for the respective equality schemes.

(a) Race Equality Schemes

3.44 The first specific duties were introduced by the Race Relations Act 1976 (Statutory Duties) Order 2001[21] (the 'RRA Duties Order 2001'). Further Orders in 2003, 2004 and 2006 brought more public authorities within the scope of the same specific duties. The 2001 Order introduced two related requirements on certain listed public authorities:

- to produce a Race Equality Scheme ('RES') by 31 May 2002; and
- to carry out and publish ethnic monitoring in relation to employment.

3.45 The aim of an RES is to make a public authority set out in a publicly available document how it intends to fulfil its general duty. The mandatory content of an RES is set out in Appendix 3.3. If any of that information is missing the document is non-compliant with the requirements of the Order. We have set out the required content of an RES below, for ease of references, as a series of chapters.

(i) Chapter 1—List of Functions, Policies and Proposed Policies

3.46 An RES must list the functions, policies and proposed policies of the authority, which the authority has assessed as relevant to the performance of the general duty.[22]

3.47 This part of the specific duty requires a public authority to look at three separate things (i) its functions; (ii) its policies; and (iii) its proposed policies. The purpose of this exercise is to help the public authority work out whether what it does is relevant to race equality and to enable it to assess how relevant. This will enable the authority later to work out its priorities when drawing up an action plan. In the jargon of the public duty the following expressions have the following meanings:

- 'Functions' (as defined in the Race Duty Code) means: 'the full range of a public authority's duties and powers'.
- 'Policies' means: 'The formal and informal decisions about how a public authority carries out its duties and uses its powers' (as defined in the Race Duty Code); 'The sets of principles or criteria that define the different ways in which an organisation carries out its role or functions and meets its duties. Policies also include formal and informal decisions made in the course of their implementation' (as defined in the CRE Guide to Impact Assessments).

---

[21] SI 2001/3458.   [22] RRA Duties Order 2001, art 2(2)(a).

The non-statutory CRE guide for public authorities on the duty to promote **3.48**
race equality also contains the following comments:

> The term 'policies' has a wide meaning. Ideally, your policies should be clearly
> and plainly written. However, in reality, some policies are built into everyday
> procedures and customs. As a result, not all policy has been open to inspection
> and review . . . You should take 'policies' to mean the full range of formal and
> informal decisions you make in carrying out your duties, and all the ways in which
> you use your powers—or decide not to. You should therefore include in any
> assessment of a policy an examination of long-standing 'custom and practice'
> and management decisions, as well as your formal written policy.[23]

In summary therefore, 'policies' has a much broader meaning than simply **3.49**
written documents labelled 'policies' such as an 'Equal Opportunities Policy'.
Rather, it means all the ways in which a public authority carries out its
functions.

Functions, Policies and Proposed Policies

The success of an RES lies in getting into the detail of the way an
organisation operates. Simply observing that, for example, employment
is one of our functions and is relevant to race equality, takes the organisation no further forward. Instead the authority should break down the
elements of the employment function into, for example, (i) recruitment
(ii) terms and conditions (iii) appraisals (iv) performance management
(v) discipline (vi) training (vii) promotion and (viii) termination. Then
break down those sub-functions into policies and proposed policies, for
example, in relation to recruitment:

- How we draw up job
  descriptions
- On what basis we filter
  applications
- How the interview panel is
  selected
- How we handle offers and
  rejections
- How we draw up person
  specifications

- Where we place adverts for
  jobs
- Which agencies do we use
- Procedures for arranging
  interviews
- On what criteria is selection
  made
- What terms we offer

---

[23] *The Duty To Promote Race Equality: A Guide for Public Authorities* (CRE, 2002), at pp 24–25.

3.50 Each of the public authority's functions, policies and proposed policies should be assessed for their relevance to each of the three elements of the general duty (i) the elimination of unlawful racial discrimination; (ii) the promotion of equality of opportunity; and (iii) the promotion of good relations between persons of different racial groups.

3.51 In order to carry out the assessment a public authority first needs to produce a comprehensive list of functions. Against each of those functions the authority can then identify its policies and proposed policies.

3.52 Once the authority has its comprehensive list of functions, policies and proposed policies it will then need to carry out an '*impact assessment*' (see Chapter 4) of each to establish systematically whether each function, policy or proposed policy is relevant to—in other words has an impact upon—the performance of the general duty. In many cases this is likely to involve asking whether different racial groups are affected differently by the ways in which the public authority carries out its operations.

3.53 Ultimately, the objective is to produce a list of functions, policies and proposed policies that are relevant to race equality. The legislation requires that the RES must contain a list of those functions and policies or proposed policies identified by the assessment as being relevant to one or more of the three limbs of the race general duty. The assessment must be reviewed at least every three years (beginning 31 May 2002 in the case of the 2001 RRA Duties Order[24]) and the list in the RES updated.

Questions to Ask When Assessing Relevance to Race Equality

- Does the function, policy or proposed policy apply to (i) the elimination of unlawful racial discrimination (ii) the promotion of equality of opportunity or (iii) the promotion of good relations between persons of different racial groups?
- Which racial groups are affected?
- Is there a reason to believe that some racial groups could be differently affected?
- Is there any public concern that the function or policy is being carried out in a discriminatory way?

---

[24] Article 2(3) thereof.

70

(ii) Chapter 2—Arrangements for Impact Assessing Proposed Policies

An RES must set out the authority's arrangements for assessing and consulting **3.54** on the likely impact of proposed policies on the promotion of race equality.[25]

In this part of the RES the public authority is required to set out its arrange- **3.55** ments, ie what it will do, when developing new policies to (i) assess and (ii) con- sult, on the likely impact of those proposed policies on the general duty. The express legal requirement is to set out in the RES the public authority's *arrange- ments* for carrying out those assessments and consultation. In other words, the authority must have standing arrangements built into its policy development process and must set out in its RES the details of those arrangements.

The fact that a public authority must have in place standing arrangements for **3.56** assessing and consulting on new policies, means by implication that a public authority should when developing a policy:

- assess how a proposed policy may affect people from different racial groups;
- consult those people who are likely to be affected by the proposed policy; and
- review and revise the proposed policy in light of assessment and consultation if an adverse impact on some racial groups is likely.

If during the policy development process a likely adverse impact on certain **3.57** racial groups is identified, it is sensible to consider whether the proposed policy can be altered in some way or replaced, so as to eliminate or reduce the adverse effect on the racial groups in question whilst achieving the same policy goals. An initial assessment may also assist in the development of a number of policy options on which consultation could be based.

A public authority may wish to consider the following factors when deciding **3.58** whether to introduce a policy:

- the aims of the policy;
- the results of the race equality impact assessment;
- the results of consultation; and
- the relative merits of alternative policies.

(iii) Chapter 3—Arrangements for Monitoring Policies

The RES must set out the authority's arrangements for monitoring its policies **3.59** for any adverse impact on the promotion of race equality.[26]

Again, this means that the authority must have standing monitoring arrange- **3.60** ments. As with many elements of the legislation, public authorities are

---

[25] RRA Duties Order 2001, art 2(2)(b)(i).   [26] RRA Duties Order 2001, art 2(2)(b)(ii).

given a great deal of flexibility over how they choose to comply. The Race Duty Code recognises that the arrangements put in place will differ and should be relevant to the size of the authority and the nature of the policy being monitored. However, the RES must record the standing arrangements that the authority has in place even if there are a number of different arrangements.

3.61 The Race Duty Code refers to a number of different monitoring methods such as:

- statistical analysis of ethnic monitoring data;
- satisfaction surveys (that also gather ethnic monitoring data);
- random or targeted surveys; and
- feedback in meetings and focus groups.

3.62 As with a number of the other steps, whilst the specific duty is to record the public authority's monitoring arrangements in the RES, it is implicit in the requirements of the Order and in the general duty, that the authority should be carrying out that monitoring and taking steps to remedy any adverse impact identified.

(iv) Chapter 4—Arrangements for Publishing Results

3.63 The RES must set out the authority's arrangements for publishing the results of those assessments, consultation and monitoring.[27] In other words, the RES must set out the arrangements for publishing the results of:

- the assessments it has carried out (RES chapter 2) on its proposed policies;
- the consultation it has carried out (RES chapter 2) on its proposed policies; and
- the monitoring it has carried out on its policies (RES chapter 3).

3.64 Once again, the mandatory duty is to record the *arrangements* in the RES: in order to do this the authority must have standing arrangements in place and should by implication publish information in accordance with those arrangements. A compliant RES might simply state where the information will be published although it might be better practice also to indicate what type of information will be published.

3.65 The most cost effective method of publishing is likely to be on an authority's website. However, it is important to ensure that the information is available to people in all affected racial groups and not everyone will have Internet access. It may be necessary to use other methods of publishing including using free local

---

[27] RRA Duties Order 2001, art 2(2)(b)(iii).

newspapers, possibly directing people to libraries or other free or low cost Internet access points.

There is little point in publishing just in English if English is not widely spoken **3.66** in the racial group the public authority is particularly concerned to target. That does not mean that every document needs to be translated into every possible language spoken within the population served by the authority. However, translation of some information into some languages may assist the authority to comply with the general duty.

(v) Chapter 5—Arrangements for Ensuring Public Access

The RES must set out the authority's arrangements for ensuring public access **3.67** to the information and services that it provides.[28] In other words, an RES must record the arrangements that the authority has in place for ensuring that everyone, whatever their racial group, can access the information that the authority provides and its services. So far as information is concerned, the wording of the Order does not appear to require the provision of more information. Rather, where information is provided, it must be accessible to everyone.

The Race Duty Code, however, approaches information and services in a more **3.68** connected way: in that people from ethnic minorities might be unaware of a service, or lack the confidence to use the service or meet barriers when they try to use a service, if they have insufficient information about the services provided. The Code therefore directs public authorities to ask themselves whether enough information about their services is being provided at the right time and in the right way (which might involve translation) and whether improvements need to be made.

(vi) Chapter 6—Arrangements for Training Staff

The RES must set out the authority's arrangements for training staff in connec- **3.69** tion with the general and specific duties.[29] Once again, the specific duty is to record the arrangements that the authority has put in place for training staff. Many public authorities provide equality and diversity training to staff but it is important to note that this requirement is specifically for training in relation to the race general and specific duties.

(viii) Chapter 7—Arrangements for Employment Monitoring

The RES must set out the authority's arrangements for meeting its employment **3.70** duty. Although not specifically listed in article 2(2) of the Order, the requirement to include in an RES how the public authority intends to fulfil the

---

[28] RRA Duties Order 2001, art 2(2)(b)(iv). [29] RRA Duties Order 2001, art 2(2)(b)(v).

requirements of the employment duty are captured by article 2(1). Article 2(1) states that an RES is a scheme showing how the authority 'intends to fulfil its duties under section 71(1) of the Race Relations Act and this Order.' The reference to 'and this Order' captures the employment duty, although the Race Duty Code and the CRE guidance are confusing on this point.

3.71   It is the authority's *arrangements* for carrying out the required employment monitoring that must be included in the RES.

(b) Disability Equality Schemes

3.72   The next 'strand' to develop a set of general and specific duties was disability. The specific duties under the Disability Discrimination (Public Authorities) (Statutory Duties) Regulations 2005[30] (the 'DDA Duties Regulations 2005') require authorities listed in the Regulations to produce a Disability Equality Scheme ('DES') with the first tranche of public authorities having to do so by 4 December 2006. The requirements for a DES are different from an RES. We have set out the required content of a DES below as a series of chapters.

(i) Chapter 1—Involvement of Disabled Persons

3.73   A DES must set out the ways in which disabled people have been involved in its development.[31]

3.74   The Race Duty Code approached consultation with different racial groups as being good practice. The disability specific duty takes that a step further. Regulation 2(2) of the DDA Duties Regulations 2005 makes it mandatory for a public authority to 'involve' in the development of its DES disabled people who appear to have an interest in the way the authority carries out its functions.

3.75   The Disability Duty Code says of involvement that:

> Public authorities will be unable to identify and prioritise equality initiatives effectively unless disabled people . . . have been involved in that identification and prioritisation.[32]

Disabled people generally are under-represented in policy determining positions within public authorities so ensuring their involvement in the development and implementation of a DES is particularly important.

3.76   The DRC produced a separate guidance document entitled 'Guidance for Public Authorities on How to Effectively Involve Disabled People'. That made

---

[30] SI 2005/2966.   [31] DDA Duties Regulations 2005, reg 2(3)(a).
[32] Paragraph 2.52.

it clear that 'involvement' requires more active engagement than 'consultation'. It also stressed the involvement of disabled people, not merely people who represent the interests of disabled people but who are not themselves disabled, and continued by saying that 'It is important for public authorities not to create a shopping list of people with different impairments for inclusion on a review group'.[33]

It is not necessary for a public authority to gather together disabled persons **3.77** representing as many kinds of disability as it can think of! Of course, involving a spread of people with different disabilities including both physical and mental impairments can only help in providing experience and guidance to the public authority. Overall, though, the purpose of involving disabled people is to harness their general awareness of barriers that disabled people encounter which does not necessarily require an impairment specific approach.

The Guidance suggests various methods of involving disabled people, including: **3.78**

- review groups;
- citizen juries;
- focus groups;
- involving people online; and
- using representative groups.

Whatever method the public authority decides to use to involve disabled **3.79** people, the first step in drafting a DES is to record the ways in which disabled people have been involved in its development.

(ii) Chapter 2—Methods for Carrying Out Impact Assessments

The DES must set out the authority's methods for assessing the impact of its **3.80** policies and practices, or the likely impact of its proposed policies and practices on equality for disabled persons.[34]

Unlike the corresponding race duty which uses the expression 'functions, pol- **3.81** icies and proposed policies' the architects of the disability duty have referred to 'policies and practices'. The disability legislation also refers to 'methods' rather than 'arrangements' under the race legislation. The wording is different but the substance is the same. According to the Disability Duty Code, the expression 'policies and practices' covers 'all the proposed and current activities which the authority carries out'.[35]

---

[33] Page 31.   [34] DDA Duties Regulations 2005, reg 2(3)(b).
[35] Disability Duty Code, para 3.29.

3.82 In a reference to the other strands, the Disability Duty Code states[36] that authorities may consider that the most effective way to conduct impact assessments is to consider all the possible equality impacts of an activity at once. The Code is not very prescriptive on the method used to carry out those impact assessments. It suggests[37] that approaches are likely to vary depending upon the nature of the public authority and the degree of relevance of the function for disabled people. More information on impact assessments is contained in Chapter 4 of this book.

(iii) Chapter 3—Steps to Fulfil the General Duty

3.83 The DES must set out the steps which the authority proposes to take towards the fulfilment of the general duty.[38] In the parlance of the Disability Duty Code, this means having an 'action plan'.

3.84 The Code suggests that an action plan should take full account of the needs of disabled people who are potentially employees or service users, as well as those disabled people who are already employees and service users. Those areas that the Code describes as being ones to include in a 'highly effective' DES[39] have been included in the disability action plan at Appendix 3.3.

3.85 The action plan should include any measures necessary to strengthen the capacity of the authority to work towards disability equality such as training staff, human resources policies and harassment policies.

3.86 Over-enthusiastic authorities should beware that regulation 3(a) of the DDA Duties Regulations 2005 requires authorities, within three years, to action their action plans! Action plans should therefore be realistic rather than aspirational.

(iv) Chapter 4—Arrangements for Gathering Information

3.87 The DES must[40] include the authority's arrangements for gathering information on the effect of its policies and practices on disabled persons and in particular its arrangements for gathering information on:

- their effect on the recruitment, development and retention of its disabled employees;
- (in the case of educational bodies) their effect on the educational opportunities available to and the achievements of disabled pupils and students; and
- (in the case of the other listed bodies) the extent to which the services it

---

[36] Paragraph 3.34.   [37] Paragraph 3.35.
[38] DDA Duties Regulations 2005, reg 2(3)(c).   [39] Disability Duty Code, para 3.46.
[40] DDA Duties Regulations 2005, reg 2(3)(d).

provides and those other functions it performs take account of the needs of disabled persons.

Many key activities of a public authority will already be monitored although **3.88** adjustments may be needed to gather disability related data. In addition to any quantitative information, authorities often also use more qualitative information including:

- staff surveys;
- customer surveys;
- feedback from staff network groups;
- analysis of complaints; and
- research.

Of course, people with different impairments are likely to experience different **3.89** barriers. It may be necessary to gather information according to different impairments. There may, however, be some resistance to information gathering. Many disabled employees and job applicants fear that if they reveal a disability this information will be used against them. These individuals may need convincing that any information supplied will be used to improve the authority's practices.

As with the action plan, authorities should ensure that their arrangements **3.90** are realistic because regulation 3(b)(i) of the DDA Duties Regulations 2005 requires authorities to put those arrangements into effect.

(v) Chapter 5—Arrangements for Using Information

The DES must[41] contain details of the authority's arrangements for making use **3.91** of the information it gathers to assist it in the performance of the general duty and, in particular, its arrangements for:

- reviewing on a regular basis the effectiveness of the steps which the authority proposes to take towards fulfilment of the general duty; and
- preparing subsequent DESs.

Again, authorities should ensure that their arrangements are realistic because **3.92** they are required not only to have arrangements but to put them into effect ie use the information they gather.[42]

(vi) Chapter 6—Other Duties

The DES is required to show not only how the authority will fulfil its general **3.93** duty but also its duties under the 2005 Regulations as a whole.[43] That is broad

---

[41] DDA Duties Regulations 2005, reg 2(3)(e).
[42] DDA Duties Regulations 2005, reg 3(b)(ii).
[43] DDA Duties Regulations 2005, reg 2(1).

enough to capture details of how the authority will implement the DES (regulation 3), how the authority will carry out its annual reporting (regulation 4) and, where the authority is listed in Schedule 2 of the Regulations (broadly, central Government) how the authority will prepare and publish its policy sector report.

(c) Gender Equality Schemes

3.94 General[44] and specific duties[45] for gender quickly followed those for disability. These are supported by the Gender Duty Code, a statutory Code of Practice produced by the EOC.[46] At paragraph 2.12 of the Gender Duty Code there is an explanation that the term 'sex' is used to describe biological differences between women and men whereas the term 'gender' refers to the wider social roles and relationships which structure men's and women's lives. The purpose of the gender duties are 'not to establish processes but to make visible and faster progress towards gender equality'.

3.95 The specific duties require authorities listed in the Regulations to produce a Gender Equality Scheme ('GES') with the first tranche of public authorities having to do so by 30 April 2007. The GES must be reviewed and revised at least every three years. The requirements for a GES are, unhelpfully, different from those of either an RES or a DES.

3.96 As with an RES and a DES, a GES must show how the authority intends to fulfil its general duty and its duties under the Order. Article 1(2) of the Order requires an authority to 'consult' its employees, service users and others (including trade unions) who appear to it to have an interest in the way it carries out its functions. There is no equivalent provision in race, and in disability the requirement is to involve disabled people in the production of the scheme not merely consult them.

3.97 In preparing its GES, an authority shall take into account any information it has gathered on the effect of its policies and practices on men and women, in particular (i) the extent to which they promote equality between its male and female staff (ii) the extent to which the services it provides and the functions it performs take account of the needs of men and women; and (iii) and any other information it considers to be relevant to the performance of its general and specific duties.

---

[44] SDA, s 76A—inserted by the Equality Act 2006, s 84(1).
[45] Sex Discrimination Act 1975 (Public Authorities) (Statutory Duties) Order 2006 (the 'SDA Duties Order 2006').
[46] In Scotland, the Sex Discrimination (Public Authorities) (Statutory Duties) (Scotland) Order 2007 applies along with a separate Code of Practice.

We have again set out the required content of a GES below as a series of **3.98** chapters.

(i) Chapter 1—Overall Objectives

The authority must set out in its GES the overall objectives which it has **3.99** identified as being necessary for it to perform its general and specific duties.[47] When formulating its objectives the authority must consider the need to have objectives that address the causes of any differences between the pay of men and women that are related to their sex.[48] The Gender Duty Code[49] recommends that the GES should also contain a rationale for its choice of objectives.

(ii) Chapter 2—Actions to Gather Information

The GES must set out the actions which the authority has taken or intends **3.100** to take to gather information on the effect of its policies and practices on men and women and in particular (i) the extent to which they promote equality between its male and female staff, and (ii) the extent to which the services it provides and the functions it performs take account of the needs of men and women.[50]

Employment related examples given in the Gender Duty Code[51] of areas where **3.101** an authority might consider gathering information, are:

- the gender profile of staff including analysis of patterns for part-time staff and those with caring responsibilities;
- the extent and causes of the gender pay gap;
- the prevalence of harassment and sexual harassment of staff;
- return rates of women from maternity leave and whether they are returning to jobs at the same level of responsibility and pay; and
- issues and barriers affecting transsexual staff and potential staff.

(iii) Chapter 3—Actions to Use Information

The GES must set out the actions which the authority has taken or intends to **3.102** take to make use of the information it has gathered and any other information the authority considers to be relevant, to assist it in the performance of its general and specific duties and in particular its regular review of:

- the effectiveness of the actions identified to achieve the authority's overall objectives; and
- its arrangements for the preparation of subsequent GESs.[52]

---

[47] SDA Duties Order 2006, art 1(4).   [48] SDA Duties Order 2006, art 1(5).
[49] Paragraph 3.9.   [50] SDA Duties Order 2006, art 1(6)(a).   [51] Paragraph 3.19.
[52] SDA Duties Order 2006, art 1(6)(b).

(iv) Chapter 4—Actions to Assess Impact

3.103 The GES must set out the actions which the authority has taken or intends to take to assess the impact of its policies and practices, or the likely impact of its proposed policies and practices, on equality between women and men.[53]

3.104 An impact assessment should be used to (i) ensure that neither sex is disadvantaged by the authority's policies and practices, and (ii) to identify opportunities to promote equality between men and women.

(v) Chapter 5—Actions to Consult

3.105 The GES must set out the actions which the authority has taken or intends to take to consult relevant employees, service users and others (including trade unions).[54] Consultation is particularly important where one sex is underrepresented in the formal decision-making processes of the authority. Special efforts may be needed to encourage participation from both sexes in consultation where one sex has been under-represented or disadvantaged, for example, men may not have previously been involved in discussions about childcare services.

(vi) Chapter 6—Actions to Achieve Objectives

3.106 The GES must set out the actions which the authority has taken or intends to take to achieve the fulfilment of its overall objectives.[55] In other words, as with a DES, there must be an action plan.

(vii) Chapter 7—Other Duties

3.107 The GES is required to show not only how the authority will fulfil its general duty but also its duties under the 2006 Order as a whole.[56] That is broad enough to capture details of how the authority will implement the GES (article 3) and how the authority will carry out its annual reporting (article 6).

E. Other Specific Duties

3.108 In addition to Equality Schemes, there are also several other specific duties. These differ from strand to strand.

(a) Race—Employment Monitoring

3.109 The specific duty on employment in articles 5(1), 5(2) and 5(3) of the RRA Duties Order 2001 applies to most of the public authorities to which the

---

[53] SDA Duties Order 2006, art 1(6)(c).   [54] SDA Duties Order 2006, art 1(6)(d).
[55] SDA Duties Order 2006, art 1(6)(e).   [56] SDA Duties Order 2006, art 1(1).

general duty applies—which is a larger number of the public authorities than those required to produce an RES. The duty is to monitor, by reference to the racial groups to which they belong, the numbers of:

- employees; and
- applicants for (i) employment; (ii) training; and (iii) promotion.

Where the public authority has 150 or more full time staff, it must in addition **3.110** monitor, by reference to the racial groups to which they belong, the numbers of employees who:

- receive training;
- benefit as a result of its performance assessment procedures;
- suffer detriment as a result of its performance assessment procedures;
- are involved in grievance procedures;
- are the subject of disciplinary procedures; or
- cease employment.

The public authority is obliged to publish the results of this monitoring **3.111** annually.

(b) Disability—Annual Reports

Those authorities covered by Schedule 1 of the DDA Duties Regulations **3.112** 2005 are required by regulation 4 to publish an annual report containing a summary of:

- the steps it has taken in its action plan;
- the results of its information gathering exercises; and
- the use it has made of the information gathered.

The first report must be published within a year of the publication of the **3.113** authority's DES and each subsequent report must be published within a year of the last.

(c) Disability—Policy Sector Reports

This specific duty falls upon 'reporting authorities'—certain Secretaries of State **3.114** and the National Assembly for Wales listed in Schedule 2 to the DDA Duties Regulations 2005. The reporting authorities are required by regulation 5 to publish a report in their respective policy sectors which:

- gives an overview of progress towards equality of opportunity, between disabled persons and other persons, made by public authorities operating in the policy sector; and
- sets out the reporting authority's proposals for the coordination of action by

public authorities operating in that policy sector which will bring about further progress towards equality of opportunity between disabled persons and other persons.

3.115 The first reports must be published on or before 1 December 2008 and every three years thereafter. The manner of publication is not specified. However, it is important that it accessible to all and that might include publishing in various formats such as on the Internet, in hard copy, in large print or audiotape.

3.116 This specific duty therefore draws together public authorities into various policy sectors such as: culture, media and sport; transport; environment, food and rural affairs and heath. Each policy sector is then led by a Secretary of State. The Disability Duty Code describes the purpose of this specific duty as being '. . . to prompt leadership on disability equality across key elements of the public sector. The object is to ensure that a strategic view is taken, by identifying gaps in provision or particular trends, and opportunities for public authorities to work more effectively in partnership with each other to deliver highly effective services.'

(d) Gender—Annual Reports

3.117 Article 6 of the SDA Duties Order 2006 requires the authorities required to publish a GES also to take such steps as are reasonably practicable to publish an annual report summarising the actions taken towards achievement of the authority's overall objectives.

G. Enforcement

(a) Individual Claims for Discrimination

3.118 As part of the package of legal changes affecting public authorities described above, public authorities are now liable to claims by individuals alleging that they have been discriminated against on the grounds of race,[57] disability[58] and gender,[59] when carrying out any of their functions. Such claims are made in the County Court. Given that the definition of public authority extends beyond pure public bodies to those who carry functions of a public nature, this opens up the possibility of private bodies contracted to carry out public functions being sued by members of the public. In the employment context, however, this is all rather academic as although employment is a function of public authorities, the appropriate legal framework is the employment provisions of the RRA, DDA and SDA, which are determined in the ET.

---

[57] RRA, s 19B.   [58] DDA, s 21B.   [59] SDA, s 21A.

(b) General Duties

Any body or person affected by a public authority's failure to comply with the **3.119** general duty may take action through judicial review proceedings.

An individual may also rely on an alleged breach of the general duty to support **3.120** a judicial review claim of public law unreasonableness or irrationality. In *R (Elias) v Secretary of State for Defence*,[60] for example, the claimant succeeded in arguing that in deciding to limit payment of compensation for 'British' civilians who were internees of the Japanese during the Second World War to those with a blood link to the United Kingdom, the Secretary of State for Defence had breached his section 71 duty. Similarly, in *R (BAPIO) v Secretary of State for the Home Department and others*,[61] it was held that the Home Office had not produced sufficient evidence to establish that it had complied with its duty under section 71 before making changes to the Immigration Rules applying to foreign postgraduate doctors and dentists and very recently, in *Eisai Ltd v The National Institute for Health and Clinical Excellence (NICE)*,[62] it was successfully argued that guidance that had been issued relating to the Alzheimer's medication was flawed as no proper consideration had been given to the disability general duty.

In addition, there is a new power in section 31 of the EA for the EHRC to **3.121** assess the extent to which a public authority has complied with its general duties. This is intended to provide a flexible means for the EHRC to work with public authorities to secure improvement. However, given the broad nature of the general duties it will be difficult for the EHRC to measure compliance without a detailed assessment of the actions that the public authority has taken towards compliance with its general duties. This creates an obvious resource issue.

Where the EHRC thinks that a public authority has failed to comply with its **3.122** general duties, it can issue a compliance notice under section 32(2) of the EA. Any such compliance notice can be enforced through the courts if an authority fails to take adequate steps to comply. Compliance notices relating to the general duties are enforced through the High Court (or Court of Session in Scotland) whereas compliance notices for breaches of specific duties are enforced through the County Court (or Sheriff's Court in Scotland).

The reasons given for this in the Discrimination Law Review consultation on **3.123** the Single Equality Bill are that 'the High Court is better placed to undertake

---

[60] [2005] IRLR 788, CA.   [61] [2007] EWHC 199, QBD (Admin).
[62] [2007] EWHC 1941, QBD (Admin).

the nuanced balancing judgement that is required in considering whether a public authority has given due regard to the general duty'.[63]

3.124 The reference to 'nuanced balancing judgement' neatly summarises the difficulties that public authorities have in identifying precisely when they have complied with their general duties. However, given resource constraints it is highly unlikely that the EHRC will be taking any public authority to the High Court unless that authority has spectacularly failed to comply with (i) the general duties (ii) any informal guidance from the EHRC and (iii) with the compliance notice. That is, however, in no way meant to suggest that public authorities should take a minimalist approach to the general duties.

(c) Specific duties

3.125 Enforcement of the specific duties is the responsibility of the EHRC under section 32 of the EA. The process tends to start with the threat of a compliance notice, followed by the compliance notice itself and then a court order requiring compliance if the failure to comply with the specific duty is not remedied. We discuss this process further in Chapter 15 when considering the powers of the EHRC generally.

3.126 Under the race legislation, at present, there is no requirement for most public authorities to do anything more than publish their RES. There is no obligation in the Orders actually to follow through with the 'arrangements' an authority has said it has made. This is where the general duty kicks in, but because the Orders stop short of requiring that the arrangements are carried out, the CRE's enforcement powers were limited to the sufficiency of the RES document rather than the implementation of those arrangements in practice.

3.127 That said, in 2005, the CRE made a high profile challenge to various police forces and police authorities threatening to issue compliance notices for failure to produce legally compliant RESs. Ultimately compliance was achieved without the need for further action.

3.128 The situation is different for educational bodies required by article 3 of the RRA Duties Order 2001 to produce race equality policies, where there is a duty not only to produce a policy document but also to assess and monitor policy impact. This lacuna has been addressed by the later disability and gender legislation where the specific duties include an implementation obligation[64] in addition to an obligation to draft a scheme.

---

[63] DLR consultation paper, para 5.82.
[64] DDA Duties Regulations 2005, reg 3; SDA Duties Order 2006, art 3.

H. The Future

The Discrimination Law Review consultation ran from 12 June 2007 to 4 **3.129**
September 2007. It contained an entire section on the public sector equality
duties (chapter 5). The key areas of the consultation were as follows.

(a) A Single Equality Duty

The Government would like to replace the race, disability and gender equality **3.130**
duties with a single duty covering all three strands. There seemed rather less
enthusiasm for extending the public sector duties to the other strands (sexual
orientation, religion or belief and age). This caution may be because the Government is mindful of possible adverse media coverage misrepresenting such
duties as, for example, 'promoting homosexuality' or 'banning Christmas'!

There seems little logic to excluding those strands and creating inequality **3.131**
between strands within equality legislation especially where other legislation
and practice within the public sector already covers those strands—for example,
the Greater London Authority Act 1999 and the Equality Standard for Local
Government. Exclusion of the remaining strands would also be at odds with
the recommendation of the Equalities Review[65] for a 'strong, integrated public
sector duty covering all equality groups'.

(b) Key Principles

The specific duties may be replaced by four key principles (i) consultation and **3.132**
involvement; (ii) use of evidence; (iii) transparency, and (iv) capability. This
would appear to make the law more intangible and, potentially, severely weaken
the enforcement powers of the EHRC, because it is much easier to enforce a
tangible specific duty than an intangible key principle. Of course, equality is
never going to be achieved simply by following processes. Ethnic monitoring,
for example, is not an end in itself. What is needed is a combination of tasks and
principles. We are concerned that reliance simply on principles risks a major
step backwards for the public duties.

(c) Statement of Purpose

The consultation floated the idea of an integrated general duty for race, dis- **3.133**
ability and gender being supported by a 'statement of purpose' with four
dimensions (i) addressing disadvantage; (ii) promoting respect for the equal
worth of different groups and fostering good relations within and between

---

[65] *Fairness and Freedom: The Final Report of the Equalities Review* (Communities and Local
Government publications, 2007), <www.theequalitiesreview.org.uk>, p 115.

85

groups; (iii) meeting different needs while promoting shared values, and (iv) promoting equal participation.

3.134 It is easy to see how public authorities struggle with the distinction between permissible positive action and unlawful positive discrimination when even a proposed clarifying statement of purpose talks in terms of 'taking steps to counter the effects of disadvantage so as to place people on an equal footing with others' (ie treating people differently in order to achieve equality). This is recognisable in terms of the provision of reasonable adjustments for the disabled, rather less so in relation to race and sex, and we are concerned that this provision would lead to additional confusion.

(d) Priority Areas

3.135 The consultation also asked consultees to consider whether the public duties would be more effective if they required public authorities to focus action on a limited number of priority areas. Were such a model to be adopted, public authorities would need to decide on their priority equality objectives in the context of local and national priorities. The obvious advantage of focusing time and resources on specific areas needs to be balanced against the potential damage to the concept of 'mainstreaming' equality into everything the authority does. Those areas that are not a priority could therefore be ignored. However, current equality duties require authorities to have 'due regard' to the need to promote equality which in itself suggests that some areas would be more of a priority than others.

3.136 There does not appear to be any current intention to extend the general and specific duties to the private sector.

The Public Duty to Promote Equality: In Brief

- Whilst promoting equality is best practice for some employers, for those public authorities caught by the general equality duties, it is mandatory.

- There are public equality duties in relation to the race, disability and sex strands but not in relation to sexual orientation, religion or belief or age.

- For each strand there is a general duty that acts like an equality mission statement and specific duties that require a limited number of listed authorities to produce Equality Schemes and carry out other activities towards compliance with the general duties.

- The race general duty applies only to listed public authorities. The disability and gender general duties, however, apply to bodies carrying out public functions which may extend to private and voluntary bodies contracting with public bodies to carry out public functions.

- Breach of the general duties can lead to judicial review proceedings or an assessment and compliance notice from the EHRC, ultimately enforceable in the High Court (Court of Session in Scotland). Breach of the specific duties can lead to enforcement action from the EHRC in the County Court (Sheriff's Court in Scotland).

- The general and specific duties may be substantially altered in a more harmonised Single Equality Act.

APPENDIX 3.1

General and Specific Duties

Strand	General duty	Specific duties
Race	s71 Race Relations Act	• Race Relations Act 1976 (Statutory Duties) Order 2001 • Race Relations Act 1976 (Statutory Duties) (Scotland) Order 2002 • Race Relations Act 1976 (Statutory Duties) Order 2003 • Race Relations Act 1976 (Statutory Duties) Order 2004 • Race Relations Act 1976 (Statutory Duties) Order 2006
Disability	s49A Disability Discrimination Act 1995	• Disability Discrimination (Public Authorities)(Statutory Duties) Regulations 2005 • Disability Discrimination (Public Authorities)(Statutory Duties) (Scotland) Regulations 2005
Sex	s76A Sex Discrimination Act 1975	• The Sex Discrimination Act 1975 (Public Authorities)(Statutory Duties) Order 2006
Sexual orientation	Currently no legislation	• Currently no legislation
Religion or belief	Currently no legislation	• Currently no legislation
Age	Currently no legislation	• Currently no legislation

APPENDIX 3.2

The General Duties

Strand	General duty
Race: s 71 Race Relations Act 1976	Every body or other person specified in Schedule 1A or of a description falling within that Schedule shall, in carrying out its functions, have due regard to the need to: • eliminate unlawful racial discrimination; • promote equality of opportunity; and • promote good relations between persons of different racial groups.
Disability: s 49A Disability Discrimination Act 1995	Every public authority shall in carrying out its functions have due regard to the need to: • eliminate discrimination that is unlawful under this Act; • eliminate harassment of disabled persons that is related to their disabilities; • promote equality of opportunity between disabled persons and other persons; • take steps to take account of disabled persons' disabilities, even where that involves treating disabled persons more favourably than other persons; • promote positive attitudes towards disabled persons; and • encourage participation by disabled persons in public life.
Sex: s 76A Sex Discrimination Act 1975	A public authority shall in carrying out its functions have due regard to the need to: • eliminate unlawful discrimination; • eliminate harassment; and • promote equality of opportunity between men and women.

Framework of a Single Equality Scheme

Introduction
Our role as a public authority is: [*insert details of role*] Our broad values in respect of equality are: [*insert details of values*] Our objectives for equality are: [*insert objectives*] Signed by Chief Executive or equivalent
Race
We are a public authority listed in Schedule 1A of the Race Relations Act 1976 as being subject to the general statutory duty in relation to race. That general duty is set out in Section 71 of the Race Relations Act 1976. It requires us in carrying out our functions to have due regard to the need to: • eliminate unlawful racial discrimination; • promote equality of opportunity; and • promote good relations between persons of different racial groups. Functions, policies and proposed policies * Our functions, policies and proposed policies that we have assessed as relevant to our performance of the general duty, are listed at Annex 1. The list must be reviewed at least every three years. The next review will take place on or before [*insert date*]. Arrangements for assessing and consulting * Our arrangements for assessing and consulting on the likely impact of proposed policies on the promotion of race equality are: [*insert details of those arrangements*] Arrangements for monitoring policies * Our arrangements for monitoring our policies for any adverse impact on the promotion of race equality are: [*insert details of those arrangements*] Arrangements for publishing results * Our arrangements for publishing the results of those assessments, consultation and monitoring are: [*insert details of those arrangements*]

Arrangements for ensuring public access

* Our arrangements for ensuring public access to the information and services that we provide are: [*insert details of those arrangements*]

Arrangements for training staff

* Our arrangements for training staff in connection with the general and specific duties are: [*insert details of those arrangements*]

Arrangements for meeting the employment duty

* Our arrangements for meeting the employment duty are: [*insert details of those arrangements*]

Disability

Involvement of disabled persons

* Disabled people have been involved in development of this Scheme in the following ways: [*insert details*]

Methods for carrying out impact assessments

* Our methods for assessing the impact of our policies and practices, or the likely impact of our proposed policies and practices on equality for disabled people are: [*insert details*]

Steps to fulfil the general duty

* The steps which we propose to take towards the fulfilment of the general duty are set out in our action plan at Annex 2.

Arrangements for gathering information

* Our arrangements for gathering information on the effect of our policies and practices on disabled persons generally are: [*insert details*]

* Our arrangements for gathering information on the effect of our policies and practices on the recruitment, development and retention of our disabled employees are: [*insert details*]

* (in the case of educational bodies) our arrangements for gathering information on the effect of our policies and practices on the educational opportunities available to and the achievements of disabled pupils and students are: [*insert details*]

* (In the case of the other listed bodies) our arrangements for gathering information on the effect of our policies and practices on the extent to which the services we provide and those other functions we perform take account of the needs of disabled persons: [*insert details*]

Arrangements for using information

* Our arrangements for making use of information to assist us in the performance of the general duty are: [*insert details*]

* Our arrangements for reviewing on a regular basis the effectiveness of the steps which we propose to take towards fulfilment of the general duty are: [*insert details*]

* Our arrangements for preparing the disability elements of future Equality Schemes are: [*insert details*]

Other duties

* We will implement the disability elements of this Equality Scheme by: [*insert details*]

* We will carry out our annual reporting obligation by: [*insert details*]

* Our arrangements for [contributing to][preparing and publishing] policy sector reports are: [*insert details*]

Gender

Overall objectives

* The overall objectives which we have identified as being necessary for us to perform the general and specific duties are: [*insert details*]

Actions to gather information

* The actions we have taken or intend to take to gather information on the effect of our policies and practices on men and women generally are set out in our action plan at Annex 2.

* The actions we have taken or intend to take to gather information on the extent to which our policies and practices promote equality between our male and female staff; are set out in our action plan at Annex 2.

* The actions we have taken or intend to take to gather information on the extent to which the services we provide and functions we perform take account of the needs of men and women are set out in our action plan at Annex 2.

Actions to use information

* The actions which we have taken or intend to take to make use of information gathered and any other information we consider to be relevant to assist us in the performance of the general and specific duties generally, are set out in our action plan at Annex 2.

* The actions which we have taken or intend to take to make use of information gathered and any other information we consider to be relevant to assist us in our regular review of the effectiveness of the actions identified for the purposes of fulfilling our overall objectives, are set out in our action plan at Annex 2.

* The actions which we have taken or intend to take to make use of information gathered and any other information we consider to be relevant to assist us in the preparation of the gender elements of future Equality Schemes, are set out in our action plan at Annex 2.

Actions to assess impact

* The actions which we have taken or intend to take to assess the impact of our polices and practices or the likely impact of our proposed policies and practices on equality between women and men, are set out in our action plan at Annex 2.

Actions to consult

* The actions which we have taken or intend to take to consult relevant employees, service users and others (including trade unions) are set out in our action plan at Annex 2.

Actions to achieve objectives

* The actions which we have taken or intend to take to achieve the fulfilment of our overall objectives are set out in our action plan at Annex 2.

Other duties

* We will implement the gender elements of this Equality Scheme by: [*insert details*]

* We will carry out our annual reporting obligation by: [*insert details*]

Sexual orientation
There are no mandatory rules so we recommend that authorities follow the lead of the gender duty which is focused on identifying objectives and drawing up an action plan.

Religion or belief
There are no mandatory rules so we recommend that authorities follow the lead of the gender duty which is focused on identifying objectives and drawing up an action plan.

Age
There are no mandatory rules so we recommend that authorities follow the lead of the gender duty which is focused on identifying objectives and drawing up an action plan.

Annex 1—Relevant functions, policies and proposed policies
Race

* We have identified the following functions as being relevant to the race general duty: [*insert list*]

We have identified the following policies as being relevant to the race general duty: [*insert list*]

We have identified the following proposed policies as being relevant to the race general duty: [*insert list*]

Other strands

NB—this approach is not mandatory for the other strands but we recommend that public authorities adopt the same approach and include separate lists for each strand.

Annex 2—Action plan

Disability

It is mandatory to have an action plan but its terms are a matter for each authority.

This list is taken from the Disability Duty Code paragraph 3.46.

- [*insert the priorities of the disabled people as elicited through involvement*];
- [*insert the strategic priorities of the authority including business milestones and major projects to be implemented over the timescale of the scheme*];
- [*insert evidence of where the problems and priorities lie*];
- [*insert specific outcomes which the authority wishes to achieve to promote disability equality set out against a realistic timetable*];
- [*insert measurable indicators of progress towards those outcomes*];
- [*insert lines of accountability*].

Gender

- * [*insert actions to gather information that have been taken*]
- * [*insert actions to gather information that will be taken*]
- * [*insert actions to use information that have been taken*]
- * [*insert actions to use information that will be taken*]
- * [*insert actions to assess impact that have been taken*]
- * [*insert actions to assess impact that will be taken*]
- * [*insert actions to consult that have been taken*]
- * [*insert actions to consult that will be taken*]
- * [*insert actions to achieve objectives that have been taken*]
- * [*insert actions to achieve objectives that will be taken*]

Other strands

Action plans are not mandatory for the other strands but they are recommended.

* Mandatory information for those public authorities listed in the respective Orders and Regulations dealing with the specific duties to produce RESs, DESs and GESs.

4

AUDITS, MONITORING AND
IMPACT ASSESSMENTS

To have an equality policy without ethnic monitoring is like aiming for good
financial management without keeping financial records.[1]

A. Introduction

The vast majority of employers are familiar to some degree with management   **4.01**
practices that analyse performance and set direction. These practices will vary
from employer to employer and many will depend upon size, sophistication and
resources. But it would be an unusual employer that did not draw up long-
and short-term business plans, carry out some form of analysis of its operation
and design metrics to monitor its performance.

The purpose of this chapter is to look at the way those general business con-   **4.02**
cepts of planning, implementing and analysing can be imported into the promotion of equality and diversity. We begin by looking at auditing, a snapshot
analysis of the employer's existing equality framework. Then we look at monitoring which will generally be a rolling process of analysing the make-up of the
employer's workforce and the effect of its policies and practices on different
groups. Finally, we cover the issue of carrying out an impact assessment, which
looks at the likely and actual impact of a new policy on different groups. There
is some overlap between each of these three areas. What they share in common
are those business concepts of planning, implementing and analysing with the
ultimate aim of improving equality performance.

---

[1] *Ethnic Monitoring: A guide for public authorities* (CRE, July 2002).

B. Audits

(a) General Audits

4.03 A good starting point is to carry out a general audit of the systems and processes adopted by an employer to establish what has been put in place to deal with equality, whether that is to avoid discriminating or to promote equality and diversity in a more proactive way. A simple checklist is set out at Appendix 4.1 against which an employer can benchmark its performance to date.

(b) Equal Pay Audits

4.04 There is nothing more likely to strike fear into the heart of a Human Resources officer than the thought of an equal pay audit—except perhaps, an equal pay claim! Superficially, equal pay audits have a simple three-stage process:

- compare the pay of men and women doing equal work;
- look for an explanation for any equal pay gaps;
- close those pay gaps that cannot satisfactorily be explained on grounds other than sex.

4.05 There are, of course, technical issues around what qualifies as equal work. However, what creates the real resistance to conducting thorough equal pay audits is that where unequal pay is discovered, those affected (typically women) can claim arrears of pay back over the previous six years. Where the claims are for 'work of equal value' involving large groups of one type of employee claiming equal pay with another type of employee of the opposite gender, the value of the claims can be enormous.

4.06 The EOC in its Submission to the Discrimination Law Review Green Paper[2] suggested a 'protected period' during which employers could carry out equal pay audits and remove any pay gaps whilst at the same time being protected from legal challenge. Of course, there are those who will point out that the introduction of the Equal Pay Act 1970 was delayed for five years to provide just such protection for employers and that had pay systems been properly audited years ago we would not be in the difficult position we are currently in. They will also no doubt ask why women who have been systematically under-paid should be deprived of a remedy against the very employer that has been operating a discriminatory pay system. We do, however, have a great deal of sympathy with the idea of a 'protected period' and we suspect that without it,

---

[2] April 2006, para 32.

employers will remain reluctant to carry out equal pay audits thorough enough to bring about a closing of the gender pay gap.

The EOC developed an 'Equal Pay Review Kit' to help employers carry out **4.07** equal pay audits. It is a five step process.

(i) Step 1—Decide the Scope of the Review

The EOC recommended including all groups of employees to avoid a partial **4.08** exercise and including other comparisons such as ethnicity, disability and age to produce a comprehensive equality pay review. The project is likely to require a team with skills in payroll and personnel systems and an understanding of how the existing pay scales came about and the reasons for any differences in pay. Outside help may be needed from, for example, ACAS. The EOC also recommended involving any recognised trade union—naturally an employer would need to consider how this could best be managed given that the object- ives of the union as representatives of their members are not necessarily always fully aligned with the interests of the employer.

(ii) Step 2—Determine where Men and Women are Doing Equal Work

As set out in Chapter 2, there are three limbs to equal pay: **4.09**

- *like work*:[3] this is where men and women are doing work which is the same or broadly similar. Job titles are a guide but not nearly so important as the work that the employees actually do. This need only be broadly similar so minor differences can be ignored;

- *work rated as equivalent*:[4] this is relevant where men and women have had their jobs rated as equivalent under an analytical job evaluation scheme. Men and women are likely to be doing work rated as equivalent where their job evaluation scores are similar and they are in the same grade although jobs either side of grade boundaries can be rated as equivalent; and

- *work of equal value*:[5] is work that is different but where the demands made on the employee in a job, for example in terms of effort, skill and decision making, are equal to those of another job done by someone of the opposite sex. An analytical job evaluation scheme is needed to assess whether work is of equal value. These types of claim, when they come before the Employ- ment Tribunal, are frequently very complex and require independent experts to resolve.

Where there is an existing job evaluation study ('JES') which meets the **4.10** requirements of section 1(5) of the EqPA, and which rates the claimant's work

---

[3] EqPA, s 1(2)(a).   [4] EqPA, s 1(2)(b).   [5] EqPA, s 1(2)(c).

lower than that of the comparator the Tribunal has no jurisdiction to proceed further. However, the JES can still be challenged on the basis that it is flawed, in that its method of evaluating is tainted by sex discrimination or it is otherwise unsuitable to be relied upon.[6] Nevertheless, having carried out and implemented a JES an employer does potentially have a powerful defence to an equal pay claim—or to put that in more positive terms, an employer that has carried out and implemented a JES is much less likely to be discriminating in its pay structures on the grounds of sex.

4.11 To meet the requirements of section 1(5) the JES must:

- be analytical;
- have objectively assessed the value to be placed on the work performed;
- have analysed both the claimant and the comparator's jobs; and
- have been carried out at the undertaking at which the claimant is employed.

(iii) Step 3—Collecting and Comparing Pay Data

4.12 The purpose of this step is to identify any significant pay gaps. If there is a genuine material factor other than sex that explains the difference in pay there is no equal pay issue.[7] Equal pay is only about differences in sex; it is not about 'fair' pay generally. If, however, there is no genuine material factor other than sex to explain the difference, women and men should be paid the same rate for the work.

4.13 The EOC suggests general percentage guidelines that might help to identify problems for further investigation:

- a difference of five per cent or more between the basic pay or total earnings of men and women employed in equal work; or
- a difference of three per cent or more between women and men generally at most or all grades or levels of the employer's organisation.

4.14 For each element of pay received by women and men doing equal work, an employer should work out:

- whether women and men have differential access to each element—what is the proportion of women and men who receive this element; and
- whether women and men receive unequal pay in respect of each element— what is the average amount of each pay element received by women and men.

(iv) Step 4—Establishing the Causes

4.15 In this step the employer should establish, if there are significant pay gaps, why that has occurred. What aspects of the pay system are contributing to the gaps

---

[6] EqPA, s 2A(2A).   [7] EqPA, s 1(3).

between the pay of women and men? The natural tendency for an employer in this position is to be defensive and look to justify the differences in pay. Unfortunately, what amounts to a satisfactory explanation (a genuine material factor defence) is a complex area that requires an analysis of the individual circumstances and equal pay case law.

(v) Step 5—Developing an Equal Pay Action Plan

An organisation that comes through an equal pay audit without discovering **4.16** any equal pay issues should still set up a system for reviewing and monitoring to ensure indefensible unequal pay systems do not develop in the future. For those organisations that discover a problem the EOC Equal Pay Review Kit finishes somewhat abruptly in terms of guidance. Put simply, the employer has now created a document trail which is discoverable in any legal procedure and, if it has done so with the involvement of a recognised union, there will be transparency in the process. The employer is immediately vulnerable for equal pay claims going back six years and for any differences in pay going forward. Levelling up at the same time as trying to settle claims for back pay risks cash flow problems and attempting to level down risks constructive dismissal claims. The employer may well be reliant on the goodwill of the employees if it wishes to resolve the problem gradually or without meeting the full extent of its historic liabilities.

Finally, those public authorities covered by the Sex Discrimination Act 1975 **4.17** (Public Authorities)(Statutory Duties) Order 2006 should note that one of their specific duties is, when formulating objectives for compliance with the general duty, to consider the need to have objectives that address the causes of any differences between the pay of men and women that are related to their sex.[8]

The Order is slightly convoluted but the effect is that: **4.18**

- article 2(5): there is an obligation to consider the need to have an objective in relation to equal pay if there are apparent differences in pay between men and women;
- article 2(4): where an objective is identified it must be included in the Gender Equality Scheme—such an objective would presumably be to remove the difference;
- article 2(6)(e): the Scheme must set out the actions that will be taken to achieve the objective; and
- article 3(1)(c): within three years the action must be taken.

---

[8] Article 2(5).

4.19 All of this presupposes that there is an obvious difference in pay between men and women. That can often only be determined by an equal pay audit. There is no specific duty that says in terms that an equal pay audit must be carried out. However, the general duty does require the elimination of unlawful discrimination and that includes eliminating unequal pay.[9]

C. Monitoring

(a) What is Monitoring?

4.20 Monitoring is the collection and analysis of equality data with the ultimate aim of testing an employer's success in achieving equality and, where that is found to be lacking, developing new policy initiatives to address any underlying problems. Monitoring is a circular 6 stage process:

- *Stage 1: planning*—the employer works out what data it wishes to collect about its workforce and those applying for jobs and how this data will be collected. The data might relate to any of the six strands.

- *Stage 2: data collection*—the employer collects the data it has assessed as being relevant for its purposes.

- *Stage 3: data analysis*—the employer analyses the data it has collected. In doing so the employer might make a number of comparisons between, for example, the gender of successful and unsuccessful candidates for employment or promotion; the composition of its workforce by age when compared to industry-wide data; or, the composition of its workforce by ethnicity compared to the general population from which the employer recruits its employees. This analysis might highlight possible inequalities.

- *Stage 4: investigation*—the employer carries out further investigation where possible inequalities have been highlighted, looking for any underlying causes of inequality.

- *Stage 5: policy development*—the employer develops policies to target inequalities which might include, for example, training for staff where there is the possibility that discrimination, including subconscious discrimination, might be occurring; or, positive action initiatives to encourage or train individuals from certain groups to improve their prospects in recruitment or promotion.

- *Stage 6: policy implementation*—the employer implements those policy initiatives taking care to explain to the wider workforce the reasons why these

---

[9] SDA, s 76A(2)(c).

steps are being taken. This stage then overlaps with stage 1 as the employer will be planning what data it will need to collect in order to test whether its policy is delivering the results it wants or needs to see.

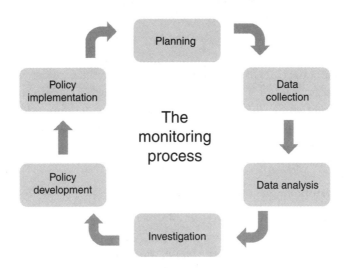

(b) Why Monitor?

There are a number of good practice reasons for monitoring which fall within the overall thrust of this book. They include ensuring that there are no barriers preventing persons from certain groups being recruited, appropriately rewarded or progressing within the employer's organisation. A by-product of such work can be an improved reputation for the employer within the market place, which might create a virtuous circle, attracting the best talent from the widest pool to the employer because of its enhanced reputation—in the process enhancing that reputation further. **4.21**

There are also good defensive reasons for monitoring. Monitoring will identify areas of potential risk, for example, where a recruitment process is sifting out members of a particular age group in greater proportions than those from other age groups. These areas of risk can lead to expensive Employment Tribunal claims draining the employer's resources in terms of non-recoverable legal fees, lost management time, compensation, wider staff morale issues and consequential recruitment and retention problems. **4.22**

It is important to be aware that monitoring can highlight hidden issues and in the process create documents that could be used against the employer in Employment Tribunal proceedings. For some employers that risk may lead to a reluctance to take any action—the old cliché of the ostrich sticking its head in **4.23** the sand. Taking any step in life tends to involve a balancing of the risks of various options. Without even considering the moral argument for monitoring and effecting any necessary change, the balance of risk between doing nothing and working out whether a problem exists will usually come out in favour of taking action.

(c) What to Monitor

4.24 A checklist of the types of things that an employer should consider monitoring is set out at Appendix 4.2. The checklist is not intended to be exhaustive. There may be other things that an employer may wish to monitor. However, an employer that adopts the checklist and collects, analyses and acts upon the results of that monitoring will be going a long way towards promoting equality and diversity.

(d) Mandatory Employment Monitoring

4.25 In most cases, for most employers, employment monitoring is not mandatory. However, in relation to race, there is a *specific duty* on certain public author-ities[10] to carry out monitoring in employment. The public equality duties are covered in more depth in Chapter 3. Strictly, the employment monitoring specific duty applies only to those public authorities listed in the legislation. However, the purpose of the specific duty is to provide direction on what authorities should do to comply with the general duty. Authorities covered by the general duty but not the specific duty, and indeed all employers in both the public and private sector who wish to promote equality and diversity, should consider whether the type of monitoring required by the specific duty will assist them to promote equality.

4.26 The specific duty is to *monitor*, by reference to the racial groups to which they belong, and *publish* on an annual basis the numbers of:

• employees; and
• applicants for employment, training and promotion.

4.27 Where the public authority has 150 or more full-time staff, it must in addition *monitor*, by reference to the racial groups to which they belong, and *publish* the numbers of employees who:

• receive training;
• benefit as a result of its performance assessment procedures;
• suffer detriment as a result of its performance assessment procedures;

---

[10] For example, Race Relations Act 1976 (Statutory Duties) Order 2001, SI 2001/3458, art 5.

- are involved in grievance procedures;
- are the subject of disciplinary procedures; or
- cease employment.

Many public authorities caught by this requirement carry out employment **4.28** monitoring but not to the full extent required by the legislation. Such authorities risk being embarrassed when responding to race relations questionnaires requesting the production of that data. Their senior employees also risk humiliation in cross-examination and adverse inferences of discrimination being drawn against them in Employment Tribunals, on the basis that they cannot take race equality seriously if they are not directing their authorities to comply with the basic requirements of the law.

Educational institutions also have specific monitoring duties in relation to race **4.29** which include employment related monitoring. Schools must access the impact of their policies on staff as well as on pupils and parents from different racial groups. Further and higher education institutions must assess the impact of their policies on staff as well as students including monitoring by racial group staff recruitment and career development.[11]

(e) Data Protection

The process of monitoring involves the collection, storage and analysis of **4.30** data about individuals. The Data Protection Act 1998 (DPA) protects the rights of those individuals and imposes obligations on employers processing monitoring data. Further guidance can be found in the Information Commissioner's Employment Practices Code available on the Commissioner's website, in particular paragraph 2.5 which has a small section on 'Equal Opportunities Monitoring'.

The DPA exists not to prevent the disclosure of data as such, but to set a **4.31** protective framework within which the necessary storage and use of data can be appropriately controlled. Before discussing how the DPA is relevant to monitoring, a short glossary of data protection jargon is needed:

- 'data subject' means an individual who is the subject of personal data which in our context will mean, typically, job applicants, employees and former employees;
- 'personal data' means data which on its own or when combined with other data in the possession of or likely to come into the possession of a data controller, identifies a living individual (the data subject);

---

[11] Race Relations Act 1976 (Statutory Duties) Order 2001 SI 2001/3458, art 3.

- 'sensitive personal data' means data that is in need of enhanced protection because of its sensitive nature. It includes the racial or ethnic origin of the data subject and his or her religious beliefs or beliefs of a similar nature, physical or mental health and sexual life. Therefore monitoring information relating to four strands (race, religion, disability and sexual orientation) is likely to be sensitive personal data;
- 'data controller' means a person who determines the purpose for which and the manner in which any personal data are processed. In our context this will inevitably be the employer;
- 'processing' means obtaining, recording, holding and carrying out any operation on the data. In the context of monitoring this includes collecting the monitoring data, storing and analysing it;
- 'data protection principles' means the eight broad principles set out in Schedule 1 of the DPA. These include requirements for fair and lawful processing (the 1st principle) and that the data must not be kept for longer than is necessary (the 5th principle);
- 'fair processing conditions' means those conditions listed in Schedules 2 and 3 of the DPA. For personal data to be processed fairly and lawfully in accordance with the 1st data protection principle in Schedule 1 of the DPA, at least one of the fair processing conditions in Schedule 2 must be satisfied. For sensitive personal data to be processed fairly and lawfully in accordance with the 1st data protection principle in Schedule 1, at least one of the fair processing conditions in Schedule 3 must be satisfied.

4.32 In broad terms the DPA creates rights for data subjects and imposes corresponding obligations on data controllers. In the context of employment monitoring the employer data controller must, when processing the monitoring data, comply with the eight data protection principles.

(i) The 1st Principle

4.33 Personal data must be processed fairly and lawfully. For personal data this means complying with the fair processing conditions in Schedule 2 which include:

- the data subject has explicitly consented to the processing;
- the processing is *necessary* for compliance with any legal obligation to which the data controller is subject, other than an obligation imposed by contract (this would include public authorities complying with the specific duty to monitor employment and arguably any public authority using monitoring as a means of complying with the public equality duties to which it is subject—see Chapter 3); and
- the processing is *necessary* for the purposes of legitimate interests pursued by

the data controller except where the processing is unwarranted in any particular case by reason of prejudice to the rights and freedoms or legitimate interests of the data subject (this condition would involve balancing the legitimate aims of an employer monitoring employment to promote equality with the rights of those being monitored).

For sensitive personal data there are more stringent fair processing conditions **4.34** with which the employer must comply. These are set out in Schedule 3 and include:

- the data subject has consented to the processing;
- the processing is *necessary* for the purposes of exercising or performing any right or obligation which is conferred or imposed by law on the data controller in connection with employment; and
- the processing is of data relating to racial or ethnic origin and is *necessary* for promoting equality and is carried out with appropriate safeguards for the rights and freedoms of the data subjects (there is therefore a specific provision allowing for ethnic monitoring in controlled circumstances).

Whilst obtaining the consent of data subjects is a fair processing condition for **4.35** both personal data and sensitive personal data, there may be issues in obtaining consent. Employers often include as a term in a contract of employment that the employee consents to data being processed by the employer for certain reasons. Given that this is but one of a number of essentially non-negotiable terms of a contract of employment, there may be legitimate arguments that consent has not been freely given. Where consent is requested but withheld, there is a danger that the monitoring data will be incomplete and therefore worthless.

In addition to ensuring that data is processed on a legitimate basis it must also **4.36** be collected fairly. The DPA makes clear[12] that processing will only be fair if the data subject:

- knows the identity of the data controller;
- knows why the data is being processed; and
- has any other information necessary for fairness (an employer collecting data from persons for whom English is not a first language should ensure that those persons understand fully who is collecting the data and for what purpose).

---

[12] DPA, Sch 1 Part II, para 2(1) and 2(3).

(ii) The 2nd Principle

4.37   Data controllers must only gather personal data for lawful and specified purposes and should not process that data further in ways that are incompatible
with the specified purposes. An employer should not therefore use data
collected for monitoring purposes to target certain groups with marketing
materials. Even using the data to target certain groups with information about
positive action (see Chapter 6) initiatives would potentially fall foul of this
principle if that purpose had not been specified by the employer when the data
was collected.

(iii)   The 3rd Principle

4.38   Personal data must be 'adequate, relevant and not excessive' for the purposes
for which the data is processed. An employer might breach this principle if it
gathers extensive monitoring data but then only analyses some of that data. The
data may not be 'adequate' ie 'fit for purpose' if a large percentage of the
workforce has refused to cooperate and has not provided data.

(iv)   The 4th Principle

4.39   Personal data should be accurate and, where necessary, kept up to date. An
employer can usually assume that data collected from the data subject is accurate and that monitoring data is unlikely to change over time to any major
degree. Nevertheless, occasional checks may be appropriate to give data subjects
the option of changing the data they have provided, for example, if they have
changed their religion or belief since providing the original data. Some organisations send an annual reminder to staff that they are processing personal data,
including monitoring data, and provide data subjects with a reminder of why
the data is being processed and an opportunity to check and amend that data.

(v)   The 5th Principle

4.40   Personal data must not be kept for longer than is necessary. Employers should
therefore review from time to time the monitoring data they have collected
to see whether they need to retain all or some of that data. For how long
should the employer retain monitoring data from unsuccessful job applicants
or from employees who have left the organisation? The answer may differ from
employer to employer depending upon the reasons why the employer is retaining the data. However, it is difficult to see in these two examples, why an
employer would need to keep data that could be linked back to an individual
for more than, say, a year after the respective recruitment or termination of
employment. General monitoring reports, which do not identify or link back
to individual data subjects, could in any event be retained for longer to show
trends in the employer's equality performance over time.

(vi) The 6th Principle

Personal data must be processed in accordance with the rights of data subjects **4.41** under the DPA. These rights include a right of access to personal data[13] and a right to prevent processing likely to cause damage or distress.[14]

(vii) The 7th Principle

Personal data must be guarded with appropriate security. Access to monitoring **4.42** data should be restricted. Where possible employers should use a system, whether paper or computer based, which uses anonymous data to analyse recruitment and progression of individuals but which is nevertheless linked back to the data subject through an identification code.

(viii) The 8th Principle

Personal data must not be transferred outside the EEA unless to a country or **4.43** territory that ensures an adequate level of protection for the rights and freedoms of data subjects in relation to the processing of personal data. This principle may be relevant, for example, if the employer is part of a group of companies with a head office outside the EEA and the monitoring data is emailed to HR staff at the head office. It may also be relevant if monitoring statistics are published on a website and then accessed by someone from outside the EEA. Argentina, Canada and Switzerland are examples of countries cleared by the European Commission as having adequate protection, Japan, China and India are not and the United States is cleared in only certain circumstances. Further information can be found on the Information Commissioner's website[15] and the website of the European Commission.[16]

(ix) Publishing Data

Public authorities covered by the race specific duty in relation to employment[17] **4.44** must publish monitoring data annually. For other employers in both the public and private sector publishing is mostly a question of choice and good practice.

There may be circumstances in which external pressure is brought to bear **4.45** on organisations to publish monitoring data. The then Department For Constitutional Affairs invited the top 100 law firms to publish monitoring data on their websites by 31 March 2006. Only 19 per cent of firms had complied with the request by the deadline[18] and only 40 per cent by the end of April 2007[19] leading the Parliamentary Under-Secretary of State at the Ministry

---

[13] DPA, s 7.   [14] DPA, s 10.   [15] <www.ico.gov.uk>.
[16] <www.ec.europa.eu>.
[17] Race Relations Act 1976 (Statutory Duties) Orders 2001, SI 2001/3458; 2003, SI 2003/ 3006; 2004, SI 2004/3125; 2006, SI 2006/2471 (different Orders apply in Scotland).
[18] The Lawyer, 22 May 2006.   [19] The Lawyer, 21 May 2007.

of Justice, Bridget Prentice MP, to brand the response from the legal profession 'disgraceful'.[20]

4.46 Data should not be published in any way that makes it possible for an individual to be identified, without that individual's permission.[21] In most circumstances it will not be difficult to publish anonymously. However, where certain functions are carried out by only a limited number of people, typically towards the top of a management pyramid, it will begin to become easier to link individuals to published monitoring data. Careful consideration should be given to how best to present the information to balance data protection considerations with publishing requirements, especially where publishing is mandatory. It may be, for example, that publishing all management information together rather than by management band, would resolve the dilemma.

(x) Objections

4.47 The DPA[22] gives data subjects a right to object to any processing that may cause them substantial and unwarranted damage or distress. The right does not apply if any of the conditions in paragraphs 1 to 4 of Schedule 2 are met. Paragraph 3 of Schedule 2 permits processing which is necessary for compliance with any legal obligation to which the data controller is subject other than one imposed by contract. Those public authorities subject to the general and specific duties to promote equality in respect of race, disability and gender (see Chapter 3) are likely to be able to argue that monitoring is a necessary part of them meeting those duties. In addition and for those employers who cannot satisfy the legal obligation condition, the 'substantial and unwarranted damage or distress' test is in any event likely to be high and difficult for an individual to meet—and it is difficult to see that this would have much relevance to a sensitively run monitoring process.

(f) Planning a Monitoring Exercise

4.48 Before launching into a monitoring exercise or developing an existing monitoring system, an employer needs to plan ahead. The types of issue that an employer will need to consider are:

- what data to collect and why it is to be collected;
- what steps to take to communicate the process to managers, employees and their representatives and to provide reassurance to ensure employee trust and therefore support;

---

[20] Speaking at the Lawyers Diversity Conference on 16 May 2007.
[21] As per the fair processing requirement for consent, noted above.   [22] DPA, s 10.

- how will the data be collected and stored, ensuring data security and confidentiality;
- who will be responsible for data collection, storage and analysis and will they require training;
- how will incomplete data be followed up;
- how will the data be presented (in charts, tables or written reports), to whom and with what frequency;
- who will be responsible for taking any steps identified as necessary through the monitoring process; and
- what data will be published and where will it be published.

(g) Collecting Monitoring Data

Different considerations apply to each of the different strands when data is **4.49** collected. A full explanation to job applicants and employees and reassurance about the use to which the data will be put are necessary for every strand. That said, some strands are likely to be more sensitive than others. There are unlikely to be too many issues with requesting data on gender and age; ethnic monitoring is a familiar concept to many but still can be a cause for suspicion or concern; disability tends to be less of an issue given that many disabled job applicants and employees need to be open about their disability when discussing with the employer what reasonable adjustments may be necessary; monitoring religion for many will be a relatively new concept and likely to be sensitive; and sexual orientation monitoring is likely to be particularly sensitive given the very personal nature of sexuality.

When gathering data in relation to race a decision needs to me made as to **4.50** which ethnic categories to use. The CRE were keen to encourage the use of the same ethnic categories as those used in the 2001 census, or categories that match them very closely.[23] If different categories are used it will be very difficult to use the census data, or other national surveys such as the annual Labour Force Survey, as a benchmark. The categories used in Appendix 4.3 reflect those used in the 2001 census.

The CRE Guide recommended ethnic categories that include subgroups, for **4.51** example, where the ethnic category is: 'Asian, Asian British, Asian English, Asian Scottish or Asian Welsh', the subgroups are:

- Indian
- Pakistani

---

[23] *Ethnic Monitoring: A Guide for Public Authorities* (CRE, July 2002), p 10.

- Bangladeshi
- Any other Asian background.

4.52 Using this approach, individuals are directed to an ethnic category but then asked to make their selection on the basis of the subgroups only ie there is no option to define one's self as 'Asian English'. Instead, a person who regards themselves as being Asian English is asked to go further and identify themselves as 'Indian, Pakistani, Bangladeshi or other Asian background'. The reasons for using subgroups are:

- to provide greater choice so people are more likely to respond;
- using broad headings may disguise important differences between, for example, Indians and Bangladeshis;
- more information provides greater flexibility when carrying out an analysis: it is easier to collate the subgroup data where required than to ask only for ethnic category data initially and then later decide that it is necessary to go back and collect subgroup data.

4.53 Employers may, if they wish, add additional ethnic groups to those used in the census. These should be added as additional sub-subgroups of the appropriate subgroup used in the census question. For example, 'Polish' might be a sub-subgroup of 'White other' if the employer is operating in an area such as Kent with a large Polish population where it might therefore be important to monitor the effect of the employer's policies on those of Polish origin. Similarly, 'Sri Lankan' might be a sub-subgroup of 'Any other Asian background' and Nigerian a sub-subgroup of 'Black African'. The main point is that using sub-subgroups still allows an employer to collate sub-subgroup data with the data from the rest of the census subgroup, thus allowing for comparisons with the results of the census.

4.54 The ethnic groupings used in the 2001 census were widely tested in advance of the census and the questions received a high response rate. However, the way people classify themselves is subject to linguistic fashion. Some groups are beginning to resent being referred to as 'black'. Job applicants are more likely to answer monitoring questions if the categories are acceptable to them. As time moves on it may become necessary to change the label put on the categories to avoid offence but hopefully this can be done without changing the categories themselves, therefore retaining the link with the census data.

4.55 When collecting monitoring information the CRE Guide recommended[24] that employers do not say anything that would encourage people not to complete the ethnic background question, for example, providing a 'rather not say'

---

[24] *Ethnic Monitoring: A guide for public authorities* (CRE, July 2002), p 14.

option or expressly stating the question is voluntary. That said, the Guide also says that an employer should not say or imply that the question is compulsory and staff who have to deal with enquiries about the question should make it clear, if asked, that answering the question is not compulsory. The CRE reasoning is that the data will be of much more use if it is complete rather than if a large number of people decline to state their ethnicity.

By contrast, the Stonewall Guide to monitoring sexual orientation in the workplace[25] specifically suggests including a 'prefer not to say' option which acknowledges an individual's right not to identify their sexual orientation. The best practice for phrasing a sexual orientation question, according to Stonewall's research, is included in the example monitoring form at Appendix 4.3. The Stonewall Guide suggests that some organisations who have monitored sexual orientation for a number of years have seen a decline in the number of individuals ticking the 'prefer not to say' option as employees see that the data is being kept confidentially and used for positive purposes. **4.56**

The Stonewall Guide also suggests a potential follow up question in some monitoring exercises that seeks to understand how open, or 'out', employees are about their sexual orientation. If a considerable number of employees are content to self-identify as LGB (lesbian, gay, bisexual) and are 'out' at home but not at 'work' that might suggest a fear of harassment or discrimination. **4.57**

Question about how 'out' an employee is: from the Stonewall Guide to monitoring

If you are lesbian, gay or bisexual, are you open about your sexual orientation:

	Yes	Partially	No
At home	☐	☐	☐
With colleagues	☐	☐	☐
With your manager	☐	☐	☐
At work generally	☐	☐	☐

The Stonewall Guide counsels employers against drawing an inference about an individual's sexual orientation where that individual has preferred not to disclose it. It is implicit that employers should resist the temptation to complete the monitoring form on the basis of what they perceive to be the employee's sexual orientation. **4.58**

By contrast, the CRE Guide states that where 'self-classification' does not deliver the minimum data an employer requires to monitor effectively, the employer should consider using 'other-classification' to top up the information. **4.59**

---

[25] <www.stonewall.org.uk/workplace>.

'Other-classification' involves someone other than the individual, typically a manager, making a judgement on that individual's ethnic origin. Various caveats are mentioned in the CRE Guide: self-classification should always be used wherever possible; high self-classification rates depend upon sound preparation; other-classification should be a last resort, used only where the individual has been given several opportunities to self-classify; the individual should be given an opportunity to confirm or correct the classification they have been given; and, the fact that someone else made the classification should be recorded.

4.60 Given the 'on grounds of' wording within the definition of direct discrimination under each of the strands (other than gender), less favourable treatment of employees on the basis of their perceived ethnicity, disability status, religion or belief, sexual orientation or age, can constitute direct discrimination. In other words, there is some risk of an aggrieved individual launching proceedings for direct discrimination if they are unhappy with the ethnicity, disability status, religion or belief, sexual orientation or age that they have been allocated through other-classification. Being direct discrimination, if the individual can show less favourable treatment the employer is not able to justify that treatment (other than in relation to age) however laudable the aim of ensuring a full quota of monitoring data.

4.61 We do not want to dissuade employers from following the CRE guidance on other-classification and, provided the various caveats are taken into account, the risk of a legal challenge may be small. It may be that ethnicity is a less contentious issue for other-classification than the other strands, particularly sexual orientation where it is likely to be seen as inappropriately intrusive. The starting point, however, must always be to have done sufficient preparation to generate the fullest possible response.

4.62 Another strand where monitoring might be seen as unnecessarily intrusive is religion or belief. The categories of religion used in Appendix 4.3 are taken from those used in the 2001 census by the Office of National Statistics which include a specific 'religion not stated' category which we have interpreted as a 'prefer not to say' category.

4.63 The Statutory Code of Practice on the Duty to Promote Disability Equality (2005) states that public authorities should, as a minimum, collect information on the basis of self-reporting against the question 'Do you consider yourself to be disabled?'[26] In many instances it will be helpful to collect more refined information broken down by impairment type. In Appendix 4.3 we have

---

[26] Paragraph 3.83.

provided space for additional information about the nature of the disability and what reasonable adjustments might be required. However, the collection of this type of data is only appropriate under the DPA when an organisation makes active use of the results.

Collecting monitoring data is not an end in itself. The data collected allows an **4.64** employer to see differences in outcome between groups at the analysis stage. This then feeds into the investigation stage and, where issues have been identified, the policy development and policy implementation stages to address those issues.

D. Impact Assessments

A cornerstone of the new public equality duties (described in Chapter 3) is the **4.65** concept of impact assessments, that is a systematic approach to identifying whether the way an organisation goes about its business has a negative impact on people because of, for example, their sex or race.

Impact assessments are effectively mandatory for those authorities covered by **4.66** the specific duty to produce a RES. For example, article 2(2)(b)(i) of the Race Relations Act 1976 (Statutory Duties) Order 2001 requires a specified public authority to include in its RES the authority's arrangements for assessing the likely impact of its proposed policies on the promotion of race equality. It is moot whether the enforcement powers under the legislation are limited only to requiring the authority to set out its arrangements or whether the authority could be required to put those arrangements into practice, but the carrying out of race equality impact assessments is essential to satisfying the general duty under section 71 of the Race Relations Act 1976.

Similarly, article 2(6)(c) of the Sex Discrimination Act 1975 (Public Authori- **4.67** ties)(Statutory Duties) Order 2006 requires specified authorities to include in their GES the actions which the authority has taken or intends to take to assess the impact of its policies and practices or the likely impact of its proposed policies and practices on equality between women and men.

Again, in regulation 2(3)(b) of the Disability Discrimination (Public Authori- **4.68** ties)(Statutory Duties) Regulations 2005 a DES must include a statement of the authority's arrangements for assessing the impact of its policies and practices or the likely impact of its proposed policies and practices on equality for disabled persons.

Although there are no legal requirements on private or voluntary sector **4.69** employers to carry out impact assessments, other than perhaps where such employers are contracting with the public sector (see Chapter 5), any organisation that is serious about promoting equality and diversity will want to assess the impact of its activities on equality across the strands of discrimination.

4.70 To date, impact assessments have not become a regular feature of litigation. However, it is only a matter of time. In cases involving challenges to policies, typically indirect discrimination claims or disability related discrimination, those representing claimants are becoming increasingly aware of the role that impact assessments should be playing in policy development. More and more claimants are requesting details of impact assessments in discrimination questionnaires (see Chapter 12). An authority can be caused severe embarrassment if it has developed and implemented a policy without having carried out an equality impact assessment or without giving that assessment sufficient consideration.

4.71 Only a few cases have so far come before the courts where there has been judicial criticism of the efforts made by public authorities to impact assess specific policies. We mention the three successful cases, *R (Elias) v Secretary of State for Defence*,[27] *R (BAPIO) v Secretary of State for the Home Department and others*,[28] and *Eisai Ltd v The National Institute for Health and Clinical Excellence (NICE)*,[29] in Chapter 3. In addition, the Government's proposals to reform legal aid contracts were challenged in the courts partly on the basis that the impact assessment that had been carried out had clearly identified a disproportionate impact of these proposals on businesses run by solicitors from ethnic minority backgrounds, but that had not deterred the Government from introducing the policy. The claim was unsuccessful.

4.72 There is no set way of carrying out an impact assessment. However, there is guidance available including on the websites of the three former Commissions (the CRE, EOC and the DRC). Of these, the CRE has the most comprehensive guidance.[30] Given that the law affects public authorities, we refer below to 'authorities' but the principles can be applied equally by private and voluntary sector employers.

4.73 The purpose of the public duties is to 'mainstream' equality considerations into policy development so consideration is given to the equality impact of policies before they are implemented. However, authorities will have a substantial backlog of existing policies which should also be impact assessed.

---

[27] [2005] IRLR 788, HC. Note, though, that although the case was appealed to the Court of Appeal this point was not.

[28] [2007] EWHC 199, QBD (Admin).   [29] [2007] EWHC 1941, QBD (Admin).

[30] How To Do A Race Equality Impact Assessment, <www.cre.gov.uk>.

Broadly, there are three levels of impact assessment: **4.74**

- an initial assessment or screening based on information that the authority already has in its possession;
- a partial impact assessment which builds upon the initial assessment and outlines risks and benefits and includes advice from experts and interested groups; and
- a full impact assessment that includes the results from external consultation, a final recommendation and arrangements for monitoring and evaluating its impact in practice.

It will not be necessary for an authority to undertake a full impact assessment of   **4.75**
every one of its functions, policies or proposed policies. Where assessments are undertaken they should be in proportion to the effect the function, policy or proposed policy is likely to have. Given that all authorities have resource constraints, it would be sensible to apply a simple preliminary sift to an authority's list of functions, policies and proposed policies. This preliminary sift might involve completion of a short assessment form asking the following types of question:

- Is the function, policy or proposed policy relevant to (ie does it have implications for) any of the three elements of the general duty?
- Which racial groups are affected?
- Is there evidence or reason to believe that some racial groups could be differently affected?
- How much evidence is there that the function, policy or proposed policy is relevant to any of the three elements of the general duty? The evidence might come from research, consultation, complaints or ethnic monitoring. The response might be graded, for example, as (1) none or a little; (2) some; and (3) substantial.
- Is there any public concern that the function, policy or proposed policy is being carried out in a discriminatory way? Again, evidence might come from research, consultation, or complaints. Again, this might be graded as (1) none or a little; (2) some; and (3) substantial.

The preliminary sift will hopefully screen out those functions, policies and proposed policies that are unlikely to be relevant to the performance of the general duty. A more detailed impact assessment may then follow on those remaining.   **4.76**

An obvious sign that a function, policy or proposed policy is relevant to the   **4.77**
performance of the general duty is where adverse impact has been detected. 'Adverse impact' in this context occurs where there are significant differences in patterns of representation or outcomes between different groups. We are

using 'groups' in this context in the same way as they are defined in section 10 of the Equality Act 2006: being, either a group or class of persons who share a common attribute in respect of the six strands of discrimination or a subgroup of one of those groups (such as black women or gay men).

4.78 Adverse impact is not a question merely of the numbers of people adversely affected but of the degree of the impact. A policy which has an extremely negative impact on a small number of people will be of greater relevance than one that has only a minor impact on a large number of people.

4.79 The general and specific duties cover all of a public body's functions not just its employment function. However, it is with employment that we are primarily concerned. Examples of adverse impact in the employment context are:

- a disproportionate representation of some groups in some areas of work or at certain grades, for example, managerial grades;
- higher levels of failure at interview for work or promotion in particular groups;
- higher levels of disciplinary action taken against persons of a particular group;
- higher turnover rates of staff from a particular group; and
- higher numbers of grievances from staff from a particular group.

4.80 A full assessment involves examining all aspects of a function, policy or proposed policy against the limbs of the general duty (where one exists for the strand in question), and analysing the effect (or in the case of proposed policies, forecasting the likely effect) on different groups.

4.81 The CRE guidance makes various recommendations for carrying out a full impact assessment on a policy which it summarises in the following eight steps:

- identifying the aims of your policy and how it will work;
- examining the data and research available;
- assessing the likely impact on race equality;
- considering other ways of achieving the same policy goals;
- consulting people who are likely to be affected by your policy;
- deciding whether to introduce your policy;
- making arrangements to monitor and review your policy and its impact; and
- publishing the results of the assessment.

4.82 An impact assessment may involve reviewing information that is already available such as research findings, population data, comparisons with similar policies in other public bodies, survey results, ethnic data, one-off gathering exercises, or specifically commissioning research.

4.83 It is important to remember that carrying out an equality impact assessment is not an end in itself, but a means of highlighting whether the way an authority conducts its business results in different outcomes for different groups and if so, doing something to prevent those outcomes.

Carrying out impact assessments will necessarily involve the generation of **4.84** documentation. We suggest that all documentation is retained so that the authority can demonstrate the steps that have been taken towards compliance with the legislation.

Audits, Monitoring and Impact Assessments: In Brief

- This chapter looks at the way general business concepts of planning, implementing and analysing can be imported into the promotion of equality and diversity.

- An employer should carry out a general audit to see what it is doing to promote equality and diversity.

- One area that employers often shy away from is the issue of equal pay audits. An employer should be confident that its pay scales do not discriminate on the grounds of sex. However, an audit needs to be carefully handled because of the potential risk of claims.

- Monitoring is also an important way in which the employer can evaluate its equality performance. Monitoring is not an end in itself but should instead be part of a process of continual analysis and improvement.

- In gathering monitoring information employers should ensure that data is kept confidential and processed in accordance with the data protection principles in the Data Protection Act 1998.

- Whilst there is a reasonable familiarity with ethnic monitoring, extending monitoring to other strands, particularly religion or belief and sexual orientation, needs careful handling. In time employers can gain the trust of employees but initially such monitoring may seem unnecessarily intrusive especially if the data is not obviously being put to good use.

- Where employees do not provide details of their ethnic origin, even after further encouragement, the CRE recommended that employers make their own assessment of the employee's ethnicity. This ensures that the data is as complete as possible. The principle should not be extended to religion or belief and sexual orientation given the private and sensitive nature of those issues.

- Some public sector organisations are required to carry out impact assessments to work out how their policies and practices affect or are likely to affect equality. Such a systematic approach is recommended for all authorities covered by the general duties not just those to which the specific duties apply. Impact assessments would also be good practice in the private and voluntary sectors.

General Equality Audit

Doing the basics
• Job advertisements contain equality statements • Managers have received equality and diversity training • Equal Opportunities Policy in place • Employee monitoring carried on in relation to sex and race • Reasonable adjustments in place as required
Making good progress
All of the above plus • Equality and diversity committee in place • Organisation makes efforts to encourage applicants from under-represented groups • Managers have regular equality and diversity training • Range of policies in place including Harassment Policy and Flexible Working • Equality practices extended beyond employment to service delivery
Promoting equality and diversity
All of the above plus • Equality Scheme or equivalent in place with clear action plan • Positive action schemes in place • Annual progress reports published • Commitment from the most senior managers in the organisation • Equality and diversity training for all • Targeted training for managers on recruitment, promotion and dispute resolution • Fully developed monitoring programme with results fed back into planning • Developed and integrated system for equality monitoring • Diversity statistics published on website • Support groups established • Senior managers involved in spreading good practice inside the organisation • Senior managers involved in spreading good practice outside the organisation

APPENDIX 4.2

Checklist of What to Monitor

Recruitment

- Sources of applications for employment
- Applicants for employment*
- Those successful or unsuccessful in being shortlisted
- Those successful or unsuccessful in any psychometric test
- Those successful or unsuccessful in any assessment centre
- Those successful or unsuccessful at interview

During employment

- Employees in post*
- Employees in post by grade and establishment
- Applicants for training*
- Employees who receive training**
- Applicants for promotion*
- Employees who are promoted—whether temporary or permanent
- Employees selected for particular career enhancing projects
- Time spent in a particular grade
- Employees who benefit as a result of performance assessment procedures**
- Employees who suffer detriment as a result of performance assessment procedures**
- Employees who are involved in grievance procedures**
- Employees who are the subject of disciplinary procedures**

Termination of employment

- Employees who cease employment**
- Dismissals for gross misconduct
- Dismissals for persistent misconduct
- Dismissals for poor performance
- Dismissals for sickness
- Redundancies
- Retirement
- Resignation
- Termination for other reasons

---

* Mandatory in respect of race for public authorities caught by the employment monitoring specific duty; and
** Mandatory in respect of race for public authorities with 150 or more employees caught by the employment monitoring specific duty.

APPENDIX 4.3

Sample Monitoring Form in a Recruitment Process

Introduction

[*Insert employer's name*] is committed to equality of opportunity in all areas of employment. To assist us in monitoring our equality performance during recruitment please complete all sections of this form and return it to us by email or post with your application form.

The data that you provide will be treated as confidential, retained separately from your application form and will not be seen by those responsible for making selection decisions at each stage of the recruitment process. The data will be seen only by a very limited number of people who will be responsible for monitoring the recruitment process.

Part 1: Questions about gender

Are you:

☐ Female
☐ Male

Part 2: Questions about your ethnic group

What is your ethnic group?

Choose *one* section from A to E, then tick the appropriate box only to indicate your cultural background:

A White

☐ British

    ☐ English
    ☐ Scottish
    ☐ Welsh
    ☐ Other . . . . .Please write in

☐ Irish
☐ Any other White background . . . . .Please write in

Now please go to Part 3: questions about disability

B Mixed

☐ White and Black Caribbean
☐ White and Black African
☐ White and Asian
☐ Any other Mixed background . . . . .Please write in

Now please go to Part 3: questions about disability

C Asian, Asian British, Asian English, Asian Scottish, or Asian Welsh

☐ Indian
☐ Pakistani
☐ Bangladeshi
☐ Any other Asian background . . . . .Please write in

Now please go to Part 3: questions about disability

D Black, Black British, Black English, Black Scottish, or Black Welsh

☐ Caribbean
☐ African
☐ Any other Black background . . . . .Please write in

Now please go to Part 3: questions about disability

E Chinese, Chinese British, Chinese English, Chinese Scottish, Chinese Welsh, or other ethnic group

☐ Chinese
☐ Any other background . . . . .Please write in

Now please go to Part 3: questions about disability

Part 3: Questions about disability

Do you consider yourself to be disabled?

☐ Yes
☐ No

If Yes, please describe your disability . . . .

What reasonable adjustments do you consider need to be made to assist you to carry out your work? . . . .

Part 4: Questions about your religion or belief

What is your religion or belief?

☐ Buddhist
☐ Christian
☐ Hindu
☐ Jewish
☐ Muslim
☐ No Religion/Belief
☐ Other Religion/Belief: please specify . . . .
☐ Prefer not to say
☐ Sikh

Part 5: Questions about your sexual orientation

What is your sexual orientation?

- ☐ Bisexual
- ☐ Gay man
- ☐ Gay woman/lesbian
- ☐ Heterosexual/straight
- ☐ Other
- ☐ Prefer not to say

Part 6: Questions about your age

What is your date of birth? . . . . .day . . . . .month . . . . .year

---

Part 7: Data protection

Thank you for completing this form. The data that you have provided to us is vital to helping us to promote equality and diversity. This form now contains your 'personal' and 'sensitive personal data'. This data will be treated as confidential and will be processed in accordance with the Data Protection Act 1998. It will be available only to a very limited number of our employees who will use it only for the purposes of monitoring our equality performance. If your application is successful this data will be retained for monitoring purposes throughout your employment. If your application is unsuccessful this data will be destroyed within 12 months. A summary of the data, which does not identify you as an individual, may be retained and aggregated with data from other individuals as part of a general report on our equality performance. This summary may be posted on our website or disclosed to third parties. Please sign below to authorise us to use your data in the ways described above.

Part 8: Signature

. . . . Date . . . .

5

PROCUREMENT AND OUTSOURCING

The Government has so far failed to do enough to ensure that an equalities
dimension is part of the public sector's procurement or commissioning decisions.
The public sector spends billions of pounds a year on procurement. Requiring
suppliers to follow sound equalities principles, and to adopt the provisions of
an updated public sector duty to promote equality, could have a profound
impact.

Fairness and Freedom: The Final Report of the Equalities Review[1]

A. Introduction

In this chapter we seek to examine the ways in which one organisation can **5.01**
influence the equality and diversity performance of other organisations, when
acting as a consumer of goods or services. That might occur where an organisation simply goes into the market as a purchaser. It might also occur when an
organisation outsources some of its support services to a private or voluntary
organisation or, having previously outsourced those services, decides to re-let
them to another service provider—also known as second, third, fourth, etc,
generation outsourcing.

An organisation that is itself committed to promoting equality and diversity **5.02**
will want to ensure that the organisations with which it does business are like
minded and will help to advance those objectives. Another way of looking at
this is that organisations should approach purchasing decisions on the basis that
they are buying goods or services *and* equality.

The broad principles of this chapter apply to the public, private and voluntary **5.03**
or third sectors. However, there are particular issues in the public sector (and by
extension with those organisations contracting with the public sector) where

---

[1] (Communities and Local Government publications, 2007), <www.theequalitiesreview.
org.uk>.

public authorities have duties to promote race, disability and gender equality when carrying out their functions, which include the function of buying goods and services.

5.04 The public sector spends £125 billion annually on procuring a wide range of goods and services.[2] Public authorities will want to ensure that they are not spending public money supporting organisations that operate with discriminatory practices but rather with those that promote equality and diversity.

5.05 These broad principles apply to all forms of purchasing by an organisation, from buying paper clips to major private finance initiative/public private partnership (PFI/PPP) projects. However, the bigger the procurement project, the more legal intervention there is in the process of selecting an appropriate provider. In this chapter we have therefore spent some time examining the domestic legal obligations on public authorities to promote equality and the relationship they have with the law of public procurement.

5.06 This book is about equality in the workplace. The general and specific duties described in Chapter 3 apply to all functions of public authorities, of which, employing people is just one. Much of our commentary relates to employment but there are wider issues of equality in relation, in particular, to public authority service delivery, which is outside the scope of this book.

B. Public Sector Equality Duties

(a) The General Duties

5.07 As we explained in Chapter 3, public authorities are under a *general duty* to promote equality in relation to race, disability and gender. In summary, those general duties provide that the public authority must, in carrying out its functions, have due regard to the need to:

- *Race*: eliminate unlawful racial discrimination; promote equality of opportunity; and promote good relations between persons of different racial groups.[3]
- *Disability*: eliminate unlawful discrimination; eliminate harassment of disabled persons that is related to their disabilities; promote equality of opportunity between disabled persons and other persons; take steps to take account of disabled persons' disabilities, even where that involves treating disabled persons more favourably than other persons; promote positive attitudes towards disabled persons; and encourage participation by disabled persons in public life.[4]

---

[2] *Transforming Government Procurement* (HM Treasury, January 2007), p 1.
[3] RRA, s 71.   [4] DDA, s 49A.

- *Gender*: eliminate unlawful discrimination and harassment; and promote equality of opportunity between men and women.[5]

Procurement is potentially relevant to these general duties in two areas: first, procurement is itself a 'function' of a public authority; and secondly, where functions are outsourced to a private or voluntary organisation, those functions may themselves be relevant to the general duties. In other words, both the process by which a contract is awarded and the way in which the goods or services are delivered during the life of the contract are potentially relevant to delivering the objectives of the *general duties*. **5.08**

(b) Procurement as a 'Function'

In carrying out the procurement function, a public authority will adopt existing policies or practices or will develop proposed policies or practices. 'Policy' in this context means the 'formal and informal decisions about how a public authority carries out its duties and uses its powers'[6] ie the way in which the authority carries out the procurement function. 'Practices', an expression used in the disability-[7] and gender-specific duties,[8] but not that relating to race, means much the same thing. **5.09**

Public authorities should, therefore, examine the stages of their procurement policies, against each of the elements of each of the general duties. So, for example, a public authority might ask itself the questions: for each stage of our procurement process, are the general duties relevant? And if they are relevant, how, or in what way, are they relevant? (See Appendix 5.1.) **5.10**

The point of this exercise is to see whether the way in which goods or services are bought or the criteria by which those bidding for contracts are selected has an impact on equality. Where potential impact is detected, the next stage will be to assess that impact, consult those affected, carry out any monitoring that might assist, publish the results and ultimately aim to change policy where necessary to ensure delivery of the objectives of the general duties. **5.11**

(c) Outsourcing

Where a public authority outsources work that has previously been done in-house, equality may be relevant in a number of ways: **5.12**

---

[5] SDA, s 76A.

[6] CRE Code of Practice on the Duty to Promote Race Equality (2002), Glossary.

[7] Disability Discrimination (Public Authorities) (Statutory Duties) Regulations 2005 (SI 2005/2966), reg 2(3).

[8] Sex Discrimination Act 1975 (Public Authorities) (Statutory Duties) Order 2006, art 2(6), SI 2006/2930.

- If there is a transfer of an economic entity that retains its identity or a service provision change such that, in either case, the Transfer of Undertakings (Protection of Employment) Regulations 2006 ('TUPE') apply, then there will be a statutory novation of any contractual rights related to equality enjoyed by the public authority employees before the outsourcing. Such rights will therefore be enforceable against the transferee. As we saw in Chapter 1, in some cases enforceable contractual rights might be created by equal opportunities policies which would transfer under TUPE.

- The public authority will remain responsible for complying with its public sector equality duties notwithstanding the outsourcing and will therefore want to include in the contract various terms requiring the supplier to deliver the same standard of equality as the authority itself would have been expected to deliver had the work not been outsourced.

- As we saw in Chapter 3, under the disability and gender legislation a public authority is a body that carries out public functions, suggesting that a private or voluntary sector body that contracts to provide functions previously provided by the public authority, will itself become a public authority when providing that function and therefore be covered by the disability and gender general duties. However, guidance to that effect from the DRC and the EOC needs to be read in the light of the later decision of *YL v Birmingham City Council*[9] a case where, by majority, the House of Lords found in the context of the HRA that a private care home providing accommodation under contract with a local authority, was not itself exercising a public function. This conclusion was reached notwithstanding the fact that the function was performed pursuant to a statutory arrangement, at public expense and in the public interest.

C. An Overview of Public Procurement

(a) Introduction

5.13 Public procurement is the contractual or other arrangements that a public authority makes to obtain goods, works or services from an outside organisation. Efficient public purchasing has a number of positive outcomes. It ensures value for money for the taxpayer; helps to eliminate corrupt practices of awarding contracts in return for bribes or through nepotism which can corrode confidence in Government; and it can promote growth and development by rewarding the most competitive 'economic operators' (ie contractors, suppliers

---

[9] [2007] 3 WLR, HL.

or services providers[10]). As we describe below, it can also be used to tackle social issues including those involving equality.

The regulation of procurement sees this function as comprising three separate and distinct activities: **5.14**

- *supplies*: the purchase of products such as office equipment and military hardware;
- *works*: the purchase of construction and engineering activities such as building roads, bridges, hospitals and schools; and
- *services*: the purchase of 'blue collar' services such as maintenance and 'white collar' services such as accountancy and law.

(b) Stakeholders

There are a number of key stakeholders in any procurement: (i) the people who fund the purchase; (ii) the people who benefit as 'users' from the supplies, works or services that are purchased; and (iii) the people who provide those supplies, works or services—whether as employees of the providers or as owners of provider businesses. In the case of public procurement, most adults will be contributing a proportion of their income, through the tax system, to fund the procurement activity. **5.15**

However, social exclusion might be preventing all of them from benefiting equally as citizens from the supplies, works and services purchased on their behalf and with their money. For the same reasons they may not be benefiting in the provision of those supplies, works or services because they are excluded from employment by the suppliers or work for businesses that are not getting a share of the procurement market. **5.16**

(c) In-house v Contracted Out

Obtaining quality supplies, works or services at a reasonable price is a prime concern of those involved in procurement on the purchasing side. A common issue is whether to buy from an 'in-house' team or by contracting out to another organisation. **5.17**

Within local Government, in more politically intrusive times, the concept of 'Compulsory Competitive Tendering' (CCT) sought to enforce a fair competition between in-house teams and external bidders. CCT has since been replaced by a more general framework which places on local authorities a legal duty to secure 'Best Value'—in carrying out its functions an authority must **5.18**

---

[10] The Public Contracts Regulations 2006 (SI 2006/05) ('PCR 2006'), reg 4(1).

make 'arrangements to secure continuous improvement in the way in which its functions are exercised having regard to a combination of economy, efficiency and effectiveness'.[11] Best value requires local authorities to consider contracting out as an option but does not mandate it if the authority can justify taking a different course of action.

5.19 Traditionally, individual Government departments, agencies and local authorities have carried out procurement activities independently, to meet their own individual needs. However, recent years have seen the development of a number of collective initiatives to take advantage of economies of scale and increased buying power muscle through joint purchasing arrangements. Local authorities and universities for example, have organised themselves into consortia to purchase, collectively, such services as Human Resources and Information Technology and products such as stationery and office equipment.

(d) Office of Government Commerce

5.20 Within central Government, the Treasury has overall responsibility for public procurement policy. The Office of Government Commerce ('OGC') sits within the Treasury and has responsibility for procurement strategy. OGC was established following the Gershon Review[12] to bring together various areas of procurement expertise that were previously scattered across Government. OGC's roles include developing procurement skills in Government personnel, issuing guidance and critically monitoring the progress of large procurement projects through the 'Gateway Review Process'.

5.21 An agency within OGC, OGC-Buying Solutions, provides specific advice and procurement services to central Government and the wider public sector including establishing framework agreements for procuring authorities to use. These include, by way of example, Catalist (formerly L-Cat), the OGC legal panels of private sector law firms.

(e) Treaty of Rome

5.22 The legislative framework for the award by contracting authorities and utilities of major contracts has been specifically adopted within Europe to prise open European markets to cross-border competition where there has been an historical tendency to look only to domestic providers.

5.23 It was at one time thought that the Treaty of Rome could affect *all* public procurements, however small the value of the purchase.[13] However, the

---

[11] Local Government Act 1999, s 3(1).
[12] *Review of Civil Procurement in Central Government* (April 1999).
[13] This principle is referred to in *Race Equality and Public Procurement*, CRE, July 2003, p 14.

Interpretive Communication on low value contracts[14] and the Advocate General's Opinion in Case C-195/04[15] make it reasonably clear that it is a matter not for the Treaty but rather for Member States to ensure that national law provides some transparency in the award of low value contracts. Very low value contracts are unlikely to be of interest to contractors based outside the contracting authority's Member State. Therefore, the award of the contract would have no impact on the functioning of the internal market and the obligations imposed by the Treaty should not apply to the award of the contract.

The Treaty directly affects public authorities as emanations of the state. It cannot be invoked in respect of private sector bodies so such bodies are free to carry out procurement exercises without having to take into account either the Treaty or the directives and Modernising Regulations mentioned below.   **5.24**

The key policy freedoms in the Treaty for procurement are the free movement of goods, freedom of establishment and freedom to provide services. There are also important principles derived from these freedoms which are relevant to ensuring fair and competitive public procurement: **5.25**

- *transparency*: procedures, criteria and all the elements of the decision-making process must be based on ascertainable facts and applied or carried out rationally and according to defined rules which are disclosed to all those with an interest;
- *objectivity and proportionality*: procedures and criteria must be objectively related to the stated aims of the public authority and must be proportionate in their effects; and
- *fairness and equal treatment*: procedures and criteria must be applied impartially and must not either amount to or be capable of enabling discrimination on grounds of nationality.

(f) The Modernising Regulations

Domestic procurement law is now contained in four sets of Regulations, which we have described as the 'Modernising Regulations':   **5.26**

- The PCR 2006;
- The Utilities Contracts Regulations 2006 ('UCR 2006');
- The Public Contracts (Scotland) Regulations 2006; and
- The Utilities Contracts (Scotland) Regulations 2006.

---

[14] *Commission Interpretative Communication on the Community law applicable to contract awards not or not fully subject to the provisions of the Public Procurement Directives, 23 June 2006.*

[15] *Commission v Republic of Finland,* Opinion of Advocate General Sharpston, 18 January 2007.

5.27 These Regulations were introduced on 31 January 2006, bringing UK procurement law into line with amendments to European legislation for (a) the public sector (Directive 2004/18/EC)—covering central and local Government and other public bodies; and (b) utilities (Directive 2004/17/EC)—covering certain operations in the water, energy and transport sectors.

5.28 The PCR 2006 apply where:

- a 'contracting authority' (defined in regulation 3 to cover central and local Government and a range of other public authorities);
- seeks offers in relation to various types of proposed contract (listed in regulation 5);
- where the value of the contract exceeds the relevant financial thresholds (set out in regulation 8).

5.29 The UCR 2006 apply where:

- a 'utility' (defined in regulation 3 and Schedule 1 as covering contracting authorities, other public bodies and private bodies involved in various activities to do with water, energy and transport);
- seeks offers in relation to various types of proposed contract (listed in regulation 5);
- where the value of the contract exceeds the relevant financial thresholds (set out in regulation 11).

5.30 Therefore, whilst the Treaty of Rome can (subject to our comments above about low value contracts) affect all public procurements, the procurement directives and the Modernising Regulations apply only to contracts above specified thresholds. The reason for this is that the cost of formal tendering processes can only be justified with large projects. In addition the thresholds are set to capture those contracts that are of sufficient size that they will potentially attract cross-border competitive bids.

(g) Procedures Leading to the Award of a Public Contract

5.31 Contracting authorities must award contracts covered by the PCR 2006 and the UCR 2006 using, broadly, one of four procedures:

- open procedure;
- restricted procedure;
- negotiated procedure;
- competitive dialogue procedure.

(i) Open Procedure

Under this procedure the contract is advertised and all interested providers can tender. A contracting authority using this procedure must comply with the following steps:[16]

5.32

- advertise the contract in the Supplement to the Official Journal of the European Union (the 'OJEU') through what is known as an 'OJEU notice';
- generally, allow at least 52 days for bidders to reply;
- evaluate their tenders without negotiation;
- award contract against the award criteria;
- publish award notice within 48 days and debrief losers.

(ii) Restricted Procedure

With this procedure the contract is advertised to invite providers to express an interest. The authority then selects a number of those providers and invites them to tender. A contracting authority using this procedure must comply with the following steps:[17]

5.33

- publish a contract notice in the OJEU;
- generally, allow at least 37 days (or 15 if urgent) for a reply;
- shortlist bidders (minimum number is five) as per objective and non-discriminatory criteria specified in the contract notice;
- invite the shortlist to tender (this is known as the Invitation to Tender or 'ITT') allowing at least 40 days (or 10 if urgent);
- evaluate their tenders without negotiation;
- award the contract against the award criteria;
- publish the award notice within 48 days and debrief losers.

(iii) Negotiated Procedure

This procedure has two elements, the *negotiated procedure with a contract notice* (the procedure is similar to the restricted procedure but with greater flexibility in relation to the negotiations) and the *negotiated procedure without a contract notice* (the authority selects one or more providers with whom to negotiate without any advertisement and usually without a competition). A contracting authority using the first of these procedures must comply with the following steps:[18]

5.34

- publish a contract notice in the OJEU;
- generally, allow at least 37 days (or 15 if urgent) for a reply;
- invite the shortlist to tender and issue draft contracts and other materials;

---

[16] PCR 2006, reg 15.   [17] PCR 2006, reg 16.   [18] PCR 2006, reg 17 SI 2006/5.

- conduct negotiation in accordance with the terms of the tender in as many stages as is necessary (no time limits apply);
- select a preferred bidder as per award criteria and finalise contract;
- publish the award notice within 48 days and debrief losers.

(iv) Competitive Dialogue Procedure

5.35 This new procedure introduced by regulation 18 of the PCR 2006 (not available under the UCR 2006) is for 'particularly complex contracts', where the contracting authority is not objectively able to define the technical means to satisfy its needs or objectives or specify in advance the legal and/or financial make-up of a project. The competitive dialogue procedure may be used for such contracts where the contracting authority does not consider that the use of the open or restricted procedure will allow the award of a contract.

5.36 This procedure provides for a greater degree of flexibility for the contracting authority to discuss its contractual needs with potential bidders. Under this procedure, the contracting authority is required to:

- publish a contract notice in the OJEU;
- allow 37 days for responses;
- select candidates from those who respond with whom it will open a dialogue, during which all aspects of the contract may be discussed. The aim of this is to identify and define the means best suited to meet the contracting authority's needs;
- when the appropriate solution(s) have been identified, conclude the dialogue and ask the candidates for the submission of bids on the basis of these solution(s);
- assess the submitted bids on the basis of the specified award procedure without further discussion or negotiation;
- publish the award notice within 48 days and debrief losers.

D. Incorporating Equality Issues into the Procurement Process

(a) Introduction

5.37 OGC has produced guidance on the way in which equality issues can be incorporated into public procurement.[19] This is in part based upon an Interpretative Communication from the European Commission.[20] Race, disability

---

[19] *Social Issues in Purchasing* (OGC, February 2006).
[20] *Community Law Applicable to Public Procurement and the Possibilities for Integrating Social Considerations into Public Procurement* (2001/C 333/08).

and gender equality sit within a broader category of 'social considerations' or 'social issues' which in turn sit within the concept of 'sustainable development' covering social, economic and environmental issues. These issues can be taken into account when the public sector buys goods, works and services. The key points to remember when looking to incorporate social issues are:

- They must be relevant to the subject of the contract.
- Actions must be consistent with the Government's procurement policy which is that all public procurement of goods, works and services is to be based at the *award* stage (the point of awarding the contract) on *value for money*, having due regard to propriety and regularity, where value for money means the optimum combination of whole-life cost and quality (or fitness for purpose) to meet the user's requirement.[21]
- Actions must be consistent with European and domestic legislation.
- Social issues can have implications in the shorter, medium and longer terms and therefore from the point of view of sustainable procurement those issues should be approached from a 'whole-life cost' perspective, meaning the cost to an organisation of a solution to a user's requirement over the full period that the requirement will exist.

(b) User Requirements

The purpose of procurement is to meet the user's requirement. The requirement, including any specific level of quality or standard of service must, however, be tested critically against the normal public expenditure tests of need, cost-effectiveness and affordability.[22] It is at this planning stage that consideration of social issues should first take place. **5.38**

Appendix 5.1 provides a checklist of the elements of the three public equality duties which can be used to begin the assessment of the relevance of the procurement to race, disability and gender equality. Where the public equality duties are relevant to the procurement this will form part of the 'need' element of the public expenditure tests. **5.39**

The other strands of discrimination, sexual orientation, religion or belief and age, can also be social issues worthy of consideration. However, for most public authorities there are currently no positive obligations to promote equality (as opposed to taking steps to avoid discrimination) for these strands. This should therefore be considered when assessing the 'need' element of the public expenditure test. **5.40**

---

[21] *Government Accounting 2000*, Chapter 22.
[22] *Government Accounting 2000*, Annex 22.1.

(c) Core Requirements

5.41 An authority should work out what are its core requirements (ie essential elements of what it is buying). There may be circumstances in which social issues are core requirements of a contract if they are central to the procurement and consistent with the tests of need, affordability and cost-effectiveness.

5.42 'Core requirement' is defined in the glossary to the CRE guide on race equality and procurement[23] as 'a requirement which the public authority has determined the contractor must meet, to provide effectively and efficiently the goods, works or services that are the subject of the contract'. For example, if the purpose of the contract is to provide services directly to the public, a supplier must be able to provide a service that meets everyone's needs. If equality is a core requirement it must:

- be reflected in the specification, dealt with in the provisions of the contract;
- considered at each stage of the procurement process; and
- considered in the arrangements for monitoring and managing the contract.

5.43 To determine whether equality is a core requirement, the authority should ask what is to be provided under the contract and whether the provision of the goods, works or services in question is likely to affect directly or indirectly the authority's ability to meet its duties to promote race, disability and gender equality. Is it *necessary* to include requirements for promoting equality in the contract to make sure the authority meets those duties and if so, what requirements are *appropriate* for the contract. By considering what is necessary and appropriate, the authority should be able to define core equality requirements that reflect the contract's relevance to promoting equality in proportion to the other essential elements of the contract.

5.44 Examples of contracts that are relevant to the promotion of race equality given in the CRE guide[24] and where race equality may therefore be a core requirement include:

- contracts for services which require interaction with the authority's staff and members of the public and might require, for example, awareness of different language, religious or cultural factors;
- a contract for the supply of uniforms for female staff which may require versions to take account of cultural dress codes; and
- a catering contract to supply meals to persons of different racial groups (there is also here an overlap with complying with religious requirements).

---

[23] *Race Equality and Public Procurement* (CRE, July 2003), p 10.
[24] *Race Equality and Public Procurement* (CRE, July 2003), part 3.

Even a contract for works, such as electrical installation, might involve the **5.45**
contractor's staff interacting with the authority's staff and members of the
public in circumstances where it would be necessary to ensure that they do not
discriminate or harass those persons. In such contracts the core requirements
are likely to be completion of the works to specified quality standards within a
specified timescale although equality may still be relevant to the contract.

The contractor's workforce should have enough people with the necessary skills **5.46**
and abilities, and should be highly motivated, suitably trained, supervised and
managed for the purpose of performing the contract to the required standard,
including any equality standards.

Given that the purpose of the public equality duties is to 'mainstream' race, **5.47**
disability and gender equality considerations into everything that a public
authority does, guidance from the CRE on what constitutes a core requirement
appears to suggest that race equality should be a core requirement of almost any
contract involving employees or interaction with the public.

(d) Small and Medium-sized Enterprises

Part of the Government's procurement agenda involves assisting small and **5.48**
medium-sized enterprises ('SME'). The expression is not legally defined but is
used by OGC to mean a business with less than 250 employees. At the beginning of 2004 there were estimated to be 4.3 million businesses in the UK of
which around 99 per cent had fewer than fifty employees and provided 47 per
cent of the UK's non-government employment and 37 per cent of turnover.[25]
Of particular interest for our purposes are the following sub-categories of SME:

- *Ethnic minority businesses*: a business 51 per cent or more of which is owned
  by members of one or more ethnic minority groups, or, if there are few
  owners, where at least 50 per cent of the owners are members of one or more
  ethnic minority groups—and for these purposes 'ethnic minority' means
  ethnic groups other than 'white British'.[26]

- *Social enterprises*: a business with primarily social objectives whose surpluses
  are principally reinvested for this purpose in the business or in the community, rather than being driven by the need to maximise profit for share-
  holders and owners.[27]

- *Voluntary and community organisations*: a voluntary organisation is neither a
  statutory organisation set up by law nor a commercial organisation run for

---

[25] *Social Issues in Purchasing* (OGC, February 2006), p 47.
[26] *Race Equality and Public Procurement* (CRE, July 2003), p 10.
[27] *Social Issues in Purchasing* (OGC, February 2006), p 47.

profit. Legal responsibility for the organisation rests with people who are not paid and who choose to be involved whether or not the organisation is staffed by volunteers or paid staff. There are over half a million such organisations in the UK working in a wide range of areas which benefit the public including health and social welfare, sport and recreation, environmental protection and the arts.[28]

- Businesses owned and/or run by women or disabled persons.

5.49 The Government's policy aim is to ensure that the SME sector has equal access to public sector contracts to encourage competition and to ensure that a valuable potential source of supply is not lost. SMEs can provide innovative, responsive and cost-effective solutions and may be well placed to deliver certain types of contract, such as services to deprived sections of the community.

5.50 Public authorities can support this agenda before procurements begin by assisting SMEs to compete for public contracts, for example, by training programmes aimed at helping SMEs to understand the procurement process and improve the quality of their tender documentation and by ensuring that SMEs are aware of procurements that are taking place.

5.51 There are various initiatives aimed at increasing awareness of what contracts are being procured including <www.supply2.gov.uk> which is a Government backed Internet portal designed specifically to give SMEs easy access to lower value contract opportunities. Suppliers can register to receive details of public sector contracts either in their chosen area free of charge or for the whole of England for £99. The portal also allows suppliers to register their own details so that potential buyers can contact them directly when looking for a product or service. The portal was launched in June 2006 and within its first year of operation 50,000 suppliers registered and 45,000 contract opportunities were advertised.

5.52 Public authorities should include the SME sector when testing market perspective, for example, in discussions with a range of suppliers on an authority's plans ahead of any particular procurement. Care should be taken in doing so that other suppliers are not disadvantaged.

(e) Drafting the Specification

5.53 The specification sets out what the authority wants to buy: in the parlance of procurement, it articulates the user requirement, in particular, the core requirements. The specification must be non-discriminatory in the sense that it must not discriminate against products or providers from other Member States of the European Union nor restrict competition.

---

[28] *Social Issues in Purchasing* (OGC, February 2006), p 49.

A specification can be expressed in terms of performance or functional requirements that include social aspects. For example, a requirement for a helpdesk to provide assistance to people with little proficiency in English might include requirements that this is staffed by people who have fluency in languages other than English. **5.54**

To achieve certain equality objectives, an authority may need to specify the processes it considers necessary. These could include: **5.55**

- consultation with potential service users;
- monitoring the change in use of the service by the ethnicity of service users; and
- training staff to be aware of the religious or cultural traditions of service users.

The specification will form the basis of the authority's notice advertising the contract including the notice in the OJEU where the contract is over the relevant thresholds or where the authority chooses to advertise in the OJEU even if the contract is below the thresholds. **5.56**

Under the procurement procedures other than the open procedure, interested parties who respond to the notice are generally then sent a 'pre-qualification questionnaire' ('PQQ') the purpose of which is to gather basic information that will allow the authority to conduct a preliminary screening process to reject interested parties who, for example, fail to meet minimum standards of technical or professional ability. **5.57**

An example of some equality-related questions in a PQQ is at Appendix 5.2. Before asking these questions you need to establish what standards you will apply to evaluating answers. The standards must be objective, but the authority may wish to allow suppliers to demonstrate their capacity in a variety of ways. What the authority should look for is evidence that suppliers have taken steps to achieve equality in their employment practice to an acceptable standard for the contract in question. **5.58**

(f) Selection

Although the next stage of the procurement process is referred to as 'selection',[29] that is something of a misnomer. This stage would be better labelled 'rejection', 'exclusion' or 'disqualification'. The criteria where an authority has the option to reject a bidder outright include circumstances in which the bidder has committed an act of grave misconduct in the course of its business **5.59**

---

[29] For example the heading to Part 4 of the PRC 2006.

or profession.[30] This might include breaches of the equality enactments[31] or equivalent provisions in other EU Member States revealed in the answers to the PQQ or from other sources.

5.60 In addition to findings of discrimination under the equality enactments or equivalent, an authority might choose to exclude a bidder convicted of employing child or forced labour or breaching International Labour Organisation conventions where ratified and implemented into law. Where relevant to the delivery of the contract, questions put to the bidder about its supply chain may also lead to exclusion in this context.

5.61 The decision to reject a bidder from the procurement process must be proportionate to the contract and the seriousness of the misconduct. Rejection for a minor offence many years ago is likely to be disproportionate. Unlike its general zero tolerance attitude to discrimination, the CRE in its procurement guidance took a rather more forgiving approach to findings of discrimination, suggesting that an authority should not automatically disqualify a bidder in a procurement process simply because it has a previous finding of discrimination against it. Instead the authority should consider whether the bidder has subsequently taken effective steps to avoid discrimination and promote race equality.[32]

5.62 Bidders can also be rejected or selected out on the basis that they do not meet any minimum standards of technical or professional ability required by the authority.[33] The authority can use the PQQ to establish the technical or professional ability of bidders. However, equality-related questions aimed at establishing technical or professional ability need to be relevant and tailored to each specific contract. A PQQ for a contract for the supply of stationery should not simply ask about bidders' equality policies as those policies will not affect the products being procured. On the other hand, equality policies may be relevant in a contract for training civil servants where the supplier's staff will be working alongside those civil servants.

(g) Invitation to tender

5.63 Once an authority has selected out unsuitable bidders, generally the next steps will be to issue an ITT to the remaining bidders. The ITT must set out the specific criteria that the authority will use to evaluate tenders including any relevant equality criteria. These should be listed in order of priority.

---

[30] PCR 2006, reg 23(4)(e) and UCR 2006, reg 26(5)(e).
[31] As defined in EA, s 33(1).
[32] *Race Equality and Public Procurement* (CRE, July 2003), p 50.
[33] PCR 2006, reg 25 and UCR 2006, reg 27.

If the contract specification includes promoting equality to certain standards, **5.64** the authority must make clear in its ITT what information it expects bidders to supply in evidence of their ability to meet those standards as well as the criteria the authority will use to evaluate it.

Annexed to the ITT will be the contract. It would be good practice for the ITT **5.65** to refer bidders to any clauses in the contract and conditions relating to equality and to ask bidders to confirm they will comply with these conditions if the contract is awarded to them.

(h) Tender Evaluation and Award

A contracting authority must award a public contract on the basis of the offer **5.66** which either:

• is the most economically advantageous from the point of view of the contracting authority; or
• offers the lowest price.

There are two exceptions: first, under the competitive dialogue procedure the **5.67** award can only be made to the most economically advantageous bid[34] and secondly, bids that are abnormally low may, subject to certain conditions, be rejected.[35] One of those conditions is that the authority must have made a written request for an explanation of the offer. The authority may request information about a number of issues including compliance by the bidder with employment protection provisions and working conditions in force at the place where the contract is to be performed.[36] 'Employment protection' and 'working conditions' are not defined but would probably cover not only general employment protections such as the national minimum wage but also equality legislation such as the EqPA, where the bidder can afford to make a low bid only because it is failing to comply with its legal obligations.

It is rarely appropriate for public authorities to award contracts on the basis of **5.68** 'lowest price'. This would not enable an authority to consider factors such as whole-life cost, quality and service delivery which are essential elements in value for money as defined in Government policy.

The purpose of the award stage is to allow the authority to compare tenders and **5.69** assess which tender best meets its needs. Criteria used to make this assessment must be justified by the subject of the contract. Using focused criteria ensures that tenders can be effectively and objectively compared. The example given in

---

[34] PCR 2006, reg 18(27).   [35] PCR 2006, reg 30(6), SI 2006/5.
[36] PCR 2006, reg 30(7)(d), SI 2006/5.

the OGC guidance[37] is the difficulty of objectively comparing one bidder who carries out equal pay audits with another that has an outstanding race equality policy.

5.70 Criteria suggested by the legislation include[38] quality, price, technical merit, aesthetic and functional characteristics, environmental characteristics, running costs, cost effectiveness, after sales service, technical assistance, delivery date and delivery period and period of completion. 'Social issues' are not one of the suggested criteria.

5.71 In the exceptional case where an authority had evaluated two or more tenders as being equally economically advantageous for the authority, bidders could be compared against a further equality factor such as the ability to provide equality training to the authority's employees. This could only be done if the additional criterion had been stated in the ITT or contract notice. Caution is also needed as it is extremely rare for bids to be exactly equal on value for money grounds.

E. Terms of the Contract and Contract Management

5.72 It is possible within the procurement legal framework to include positive social issue obligations on a successful bidder in the contract to achieve social policy objectives. To comply with EU law, any such obligations must not discriminate directly or indirectly on grounds of nationality and they must have been disclosed to bidders in advance with the tender documentation.[39]

5.73 Contract conditions should, however, be relevant to the contract and achievement of value for money for the taxpayer. Such conditions should not impose requirements that do not bring about a proportionate benefit, for example, because they act as a disincentive to SMEs bidding for the contract or add unnecessarily to the cost which may dissuade all bidders from bidding at all or at a sensible price. This is known as 'market flight'.

5.74 So far as the public equality duties are concerned, however, when a public authority contracts out one of its functions and that function is relevant to an equality duty, the public authority will need to ensure that its obligations under the duty continue to be met. This can only be achieved by passing on the obligation to the private or voluntary sector body through contractual terms and conditions.

---

[37] *Social Issues in Purchasing*, OGC, February 2006, p 26.
[38] PCR 2006, reg 30(2).   [39] PCR 2006, reg 39(2) and UCR 2006, reg 36(2).

For example, a public authority is obliged by specific duties to monitor its **5.75** workforce by ethnicity. It outsources one of its functions and its staff employed in the provision of the service TUPE transfer to the successful private sector bidder. Without a contractual term requiring the bidder to carry out the same level of ethnic monitoring as the authority, the outsourcing would result in a step backwards for race equality.

However, there is scope for debate around the extent of such a term. For **5.76** example, attempting to extend the monitoring beyond those employed in the provision of the services under the contract to the successful bidder's entire workforce would be laudable but potentially disproportionate. There may also be issues around extending monitoring obligations to the disability and gender duties where specific duties for those strands do not expressly require monitoring.

Given the importance of monitoring to the general duties, we have included a **5.77** monitoring obligation for race, disability and gender in the model contract clauses at Appendix 5.3.

Finally, the OGC guidance refers to other opportunities to work cooperatively **5.78** with suppliers to achieve social objectives[40] on a voluntary post-contract basis. There is some scope for cajoling suppliers into corporate social responsibility programmes outside the terms of a contract, particularly in the run up to a re-tender but these are always going to be more difficult to achieve than contractual obligations.

F. The Future

Procurement is one of the hottest issues in the field of equality and diversity. **5.79** Procurement was step eight in the 'ten steps to greater equality' recommended by the Equalities Review[41] which recommended a specific requirement on public authorities to use procurement as a tool for achieving greater equality in parallel with a single equality duty. The Review wants to see a standard rather than piecemeal approach to equality in procurement.

The Discrimination Law Review[42] is lukewarm on these proposals. Since pro- **5.80** curement is but one of a public authority's many functions, the Review suggests that having specific duties relating to procurement risks confusing authorities as

---

[40] *Social Issues in Purchasing* (OGC, February 2006), p 33.
[41] *Fairness and Freedom: The Final Report of the Equalities Review* (Communities and Local Government publications, 2007), <www.theequalitiesreview.org.uk>, p 118.
[42] DLR consultation paper, p 106.

to the weight they should give to procurement when compared to their other functions. It therefore rejects the idea without even including a question in the consultation as to whether respondents agree!

5.81 The Review notes that in Northern Ireland provisions have been introduced which allow for disqualification of bidders who have failed to comply with a statutory requirement to monitor and make an annual return to the Equality Commission on the religious composition of their workforce. However, the Review rejects the introduction of such a monitoring requirement on employers under British discrimination law. It describes mandatory disqualification as a blunt tool and points out, as we have above, that authorities can reject bidders for public contracts if they have committed a grave act of misconduct in the course of their business or profession—which might include a serious breach of discrimination law.

5.82 What is certain is that the debate around the use of procurement to achieve social objectives, balanced against the fear of market flight, within the context of complex EU single market rules, is likely to run and run.

Procurement and Outsourcing: In Brief

- Procurement (including outsourcing) provides an opportunity for the purchaser of goods and services to influence the equality and diversity performance of the supplier. This applies within the public, private and voluntary sectors although it has particular resonance in the public sector where duties to promote equality in respect of race, disability and gender apply.

- The public sector spends £125 billion annually on procuring a wide range of goods and services. Public authorities will want to ensure that they are not spending public money supporting organisations that operate with discriminatory practices but rather with those that promote equality and diversity.

- The rules of public procurement are largely derived from the Treaty of Rome and procurement directives dealing with public contracts and utilities contracts. These find form in domestic law as the 'Modernising Regulations'.

- The Modernising Regulations establish a set of procedures for advertising a contract and selecting a supplier. Equality issues can be relevant at each stage of the procurement process: in drafting the specification where equality is a core requirement; in excluding bidders who have breached the equality enactments or lack the technical ability to do the work and in the terms of the contract to be signed by the successful bidder.

- There is less scope for selecting a bidder simply because it has a fabulous equality record since contracts should be awarded on the basis of *value for money*, having due regard to propriety and regularity, where value for money means the optimum combination of whole-life cost and quality (or fitness for purpose) to meet the user's requirement.

- Procurement and equality also meet in the issue of enabling small businesses, many of which are run by people from disadvantaged groups, opportunities to compete for public contracts.

- Procurement was at the top of the agenda for both the Equalities and Discrimination Law Reviews so it is possible that there may be legal developments in the future.

APPENDIX 5.1

Procurement General Duty Checklist for a Public Authority			

Q1: For each stage of our procurement process, are the general duties relevant?

Q2: If we are contracting out a function, is that function relevant to the general duties?

General duty: race	Yes	No	If Yes, how is it relevant?
Duty to eliminate unlawful racial discrimination	☐	☐	. . . .
Duty to promote equality of opportunity	☐	☐	. . . .
Duty to promote good relations between persons of different racial groups	☐	☐	. . . .
General duty: disability			
Duty to eliminate unlawful discrimination	☐	☐	. . . .
Duty to eliminate harassment of disabled persons that is related to their disabilities	☐	☐	. . . .
Duty to promote equality of opportunity between disabled persons and other persons	☐	☐	. . . .
Duty to take steps to take account of disabled persons' disabilities, even where that involves treating disabled persons more favourably than other persons	☐	☐	. . . .
Duty to promote positive attitudes towards disabled persons	☐	☐	. . . .
Duty to encourage participation by disabled persons in public life	☐	☐	. . . .

General duty: gender

Duty to eliminate unlawful discrimination	☐ ☐	. . . .
Duty to eliminate harassment	☐ ☐	. . . .
Duty to promote equality of opportunity between men and women	☐ ☐	. . . .

APPENDIX 5.2

Model Pre-qualification Questionnaire Equality Questions[43]

[*Name of authority*] wishes to select firms to tender for a contract for [*brief description*]. The authority is required when carrying out its functions to have due regard:

- under section 71(1) of the RRA, to the need to eliminate unlawful discrimination and to promote equality of opportunity and good relations between persons of different racial groups;
- under section 49A of the DDA, to the need to eliminate unlawful discrimination; eliminate harassment of disabled persons that is related to their disabilities; promote equality of opportunity between disabled persons and other persons; take steps to take account of disabled persons' disabilities, even where that involves treating disabled persons more favourably than other persons; promote positive attitudes towards disabled persons; and encourage participation by disabled persons in public life; and
- under section 76A of the SDA, to the need to eliminate unlawful discrimination and harassment; and promote equality of opportunity between men and women.

In compliance with these legal obligations the authority seeks to ensure that external contractors from whom it purchases goods, works or services do not discriminate unlawfully, and can demonstrate that in terms of their employment policies and practice in relation to race, disability and gender equality they have the technical capacity to perform this contract.

The following questions are intended to give the authority information to evaluate your firm on its compliance with the non-discrimination provisions of the RRA, DDA, SDA, SOR, RBR and AR or equivalent legislation in another jurisdiction.

Please make sure you answer every question. Failure to provide the information requested may result in your firm being rejected. Please provide sufficient information to enable the authority to make a fair and accurate assessment of how you have dealt with race, disability and gender equality issues in employment.

(Note: Questions 5.01, 5.02 and 5.03 are designed to obtain necessary background information.)

5.01 What is the size of your organisation? Please state total number of employees (including all full-time and part-time employees, apprentices, and other trainees).

5.02 Of the total number of employees, how many are managers?

5.03 Is your firm part of a commercial group or a consortium? If it is, which of your employment policies are determined by you, and which ones apply to all firms within the group or consortium?

5.04 Is it your policy as an employer to comply with your statutory obligations under the RRA, DDA, SDA, SOR, RBR and AR which applies in Great Britain, or equivalent legislation that applies in the countries in which your firm employs staff?

---

[43] Adapted to include all discrimination strands, from *Race Equality and Public Procurement: A Guide for Public Authorities and Contractors* (CRE, July 2003), Chapter 7.

5.05 Do you observe, as far as possible, the provisions of:

(a) the Equal Opportunities Commission: Code of Practice on sex discrimination; equal opportunities policies, procedures and practices in employment (1985);

(b) the Disability Rights Commission Code of Practice: Employment and Occupation (2004);

(c) the Commission for Racial Equality's Code of Practice on racial equality in employment (2005); and/or

(d) any Codes of Practice introduced by the Equality and Human Rights Commission to replace or supplement the above Codes of Practice;

or comparable guidance under equivalent legislation in another Member State, which gives practical guidance to employers and others on the elimination of discrimination and the promotion of equality of opportunity in employment?

5.06 Do you:

(a) issue instructions on equality to those concerned with recruitment, selection, remuneration, training and promotion?

(b) Communicate your policy on equality to employees, recognised trade unions or other representative groups of employees?

(c) Advertise your commitment to equality in recruitment advertisements or other literature?

(d) Train staff with managerial responsibilities on equal opportunities?

(e) Have procedures in place to protect your employees from unlawful discrimination (including harassment)?

5.07 Please supply evidence to support your answers to questions 5.05 and 5.06. Such evidence may be examples or copies of documents, such as your equality or equal opportunities in employment policy, documents containing instructions to staff, or outlining arrangements for advertisements, recruitment, selection, access to training, opportunities for promotion, copies of recruitment advertisements, extracts from staff handbooks, copies of grievance and disciplinary procedures, or other materials that will enable the authority to make a fair and accurate assessment of your organisation's capacity to perform the contract.

5.08 In the last three years, has any finding of unlawful discrimination in the employment field been made against your organisation by any court or tribunal, or in comparable proceedings in any other jurisdiction?

5.09 In the last three years, has your organisation been the subject of formal investigation by the CRE, EOC, DRC or the EHRC, or a comparable body, on the grounds of alleged unlawful discrimination in the employment field?

5.10 If the answer to question 5.08 is yes or, in relation to question 5.09, the CRE, EOC, DRC or the EHRC or comparable body made a finding adverse to your organisation, what steps have you taken as a result of that finding?

APPENDIX 5.3

Model Contract Clauses [44]

5.01 The Contractor will not:

(a) unlawfully discriminate against any person, directly or indirectly, or by way of victimisation or harassment, on grounds of:
  (i) sex, gender reassignment, married or civil partner status, pregnancy or maternity leave;
  (ii) colour, race, nationality or ethnic or national origins;
  (iii) religion or belief;
  (iv) sexual orientation; and/or
  (v) age;
(b) unlawfully discriminate against any person, on the grounds of or for a reason related to disability, or victimise or harass any person on the grounds of disability or fail to make reasonable adjustments.

5.02 The Contractor will, for purposes of ensuring compliance with sub-clause 5.01 above, in relation to Contractor Staff [45] employed in the performance of the Agreement, observe as far as possible the provisions of:

(a) the Equal Opportunities Commission: Code of Practice on sex discrimination; equal opportunities policies, procedures and practices in employment (1985);
(b) the Disability Rights Commission Code of Practice: Employment and Occupation (2004);
(c) the Commission for Racial Equality's Code of Practice on racial equality in employment (2005); and/or
(d) any Codes of Practice introduced by the Equality and Human Rights Commission to replace or supplement the above Codes of Practice;

including, but not limited to, those provisions recommending the adoption, implementation, and monitoring of an equal opportunities policy.

5.03 The Contractor will in performing the contract comply with the provisions of:

(a) section 71(1) of the RRA as if the Contractor were a body within the meaning of Schedule 1A to the RRA;
(b) section 76A of the SDA whether or not the body is itself a public authority for the purposes of that section and this Agreement;
(c) section 49A of the DDA whether or not the body is itself a public authority for the purposes of that section and this Agreement; and
(d) any equivalent legislation introduced in relation to the promotion of equality on the grounds of sexual orientation, religion or belief and age.

---

[44] Adapted to include all discrimination strands, from *Race Equality and Public Procurement* published by the CRE, Chapter 6.

[45] 'Contractor Staff' should be defined as all persons employed by the contractor to perform the agreement.

5.04 Where in connection with this Agreement the Contractor, its agents or subcontractors, or the Contractor Staff are required to carry out work on the Authority's premises or alongside the Authority's employees on any other premises, the Contractor will comply with the Authority's own employment policy and codes of practice relating to discrimination and equal opportunities, copies of which are annexed at Schedule [ ].

5.05 The Contractor will monitor the representation among Contractor Staff of disabled persons and persons of different gender and different racial groups (which shall mean groups of persons classified as 'ethnic groups' in the most recent official census by the Office of National Statistics or successor body), having regard to the Authority's procedures for monitoring representation among its own employees.

5.06 Where it appears to the Contractor that the conditions for taking lawful positive action under any of the Equality Enactments[46] apply the Contractor will take such positive action as may be appropriate and reasonably practicable.

5.07 The Contractor will [12] months from the date of this Agreement and [annually] thereafter submit a report statement to the Authority demonstrating its compliance with Clauses 5.01 to 5.06 (inclusive).

5.08 In addition to the report statement referred to in Clause 5.07, the Contractor will provide such additional information as the Authority may reasonably require for the purpose of assessing the Contractor's compliance with Clauses 5.01 to 5.06 (inclusive).

5.09 Where the Contractor commits a breach of Clauses 5.01 to 5.06 (inclusive) which amounts to a failure to meet the Service Levels, the provisions of Clause [ ][47] will apply.

5.10 The Contractor will notify the [Authorised Officer] forthwith in writing as soon as it becomes aware of any investigation of or proceedings brought against the Contractor under the Equality Enactments.

5.11 Where any investigation is undertaken by a person or body empowered to conduct such investigation and/or proceedings are instituted in connection with any matter relating to the Contractor's performance of this Agreement being in contravention of the Equality Enactments, the Contractor will, free of charge:

(a) provide any information requested in the timescale allotted;

(b) attend any meetings as required and permit Contractor Staff to attend;

(c) promptly allow access to and investigation of any documents or data deemed to be relevant;

(d) allow itself and any Contractor Staff to appear as witness in any ensuing proceedings; and

(e) cooperate fully and promptly in every way required by the person or body conducting such investigation during the course of that investigation.

5.12 Where any investigation is conducted or proceedings are brought under the Equality Enactments which arise directly or indirectly out of any act or omission of the Contractor, its agents or subcontractors, or the Contractor Staff, and where there is a finding against the Contractor in such investigation or proceedings, the Contractor will indemnify the Authority with respect to all costs, charges and expenses (including legal and administrative expenses) arising out of or in connection with any such investigation or proceedings and

---

[46] As defined in EA, s 33(1).

[47] This sub-clause, which would not normally apply to contracts for goods, should refer to the relevant clause providing default mechanisms for failure to perform the contract in accordance with specified service levels.

such other financial redress to cover any payment the Authority may have been ordered or required to pay to a third party.

5.13 In the event that the Contractor enters into any Subcontract in connection with this Agreement, it will impose obligations on its Subcontractors in terms substantially similar to those imposed on it pursuant to this Clause 5.

6

POSITIVE ACTION AND OCCUPATIONAL REQUIREMENTS

It is true that some individuals from groups which have suffered discrimination and disadvantage have made it to the top. Yet in many spheres of society, and at senior levels, they remain under-represented. We still notice when a woman leads a FTSE company, or when a visibly disabled person becomes a Cabinet Minister, or when a Sikh becomes a judge. . . . Let us be clear. We do not want a situation where people get promoted just because people with whom they share a personal characteristic are under-represented in a particular sphere of activity—that is positive discrimination, and we do not believe it provides an answer to the persistent inequality experienced by some groups. However, we want to consider whether there is more we could allow business and other organisations to do to make more rapid progress towards greater diversity, because this is something which would benefit society as a whole. . . .[1]

A. Introduction

In Chapter 7 we look at the two decision-making processes of recruitment and promotion. This chapter is a precursor to Chapter 7. It deals with two preliminary considerations ahead of any recruitment or promotion exercise.   **6.01**

We begin with an examination of 'positive action', the legally permissible steps that an employer, wishing to promote equality and diversity, can take to encourage those from under-represented groups to apply for jobs and to better equip them for success at the selection stage in the recruitment and promotion processes.   **6.02**

Secondly, we look at the limited situations where the duties in a job description can only be properly fulfilled by a person with particular characteristics. In   **6.03**

---

[1] DLR consultation paper, paras 4.3–4.5.

the parlance of the equality enactments this is where having those characteristics is a 'genuine occupational qualification'[2] or 'genuine occupational
requirement'.[3]

B. Positive Action

6.04 The purpose of this book is to encourage employers not to limit their ambitions
to the avoidance of being sued for discrimination, but rather to promote
equality and diversity proactively. Lawful positive action provides opportunities
to achieve this goal.

6.05 The use of positive action can easily be misunderstood and unlawfully misap-
plied. Positive action is *not* the same as 'positive discrimination' (also sometimes referred to as 'affirmative action' or 'reverse discrimination'). Positive
action is lawful, positive discrimination is not.

6.06 Positive action allows an employer to take specific steps in terms of training or
encouraging applicants from certain groups to apply for positions. It is
intended to allow people from previously excluded groups to compete on equal
terms with other applicants, by positively addressing the accumulated effects of
past discrimination. However, *selection* of an applicant for a job must be based
on merit with all applicants treated equally.

6.07 If selection is based on, for example, racial or gender grounds that is unlawful
direct discrimination. The only exceptions to this are:

• disability, where the DDA does not make discrimination in favour of disabled
  people unlawful—which is subject, in turn, to limited exceptions;[4] and
• age, where direct discrimination can be justified, albeit that this is likely to be
  only in exceptional cases.

6.08 Although the action that can be taken is generally referred to as 'positive action'
it is phrased, with typically understated parliamentary drafting, in the double
negative: 'nothing in [the legislation] shall render unlawful. . . .'[5] The law does
not require employers to take positive action, but it provides parameters within
which positive action may be used to address apparent inequality. That is not to
say that an employer is not required to take positive steps such as: making

---

[2] SDA, s 7; RRA, s 5.
[3] RRA, s 4A; SOR, reg 7; RBR, reg 7; AR reg 8. Note there are no equivalent provisions in the
DDA.
[4] eg the Local Government and Housing Act 1989, s 7, which requires that every local
authority appointment be made on merit.
[5] eg RRA, s 38(1).

reasonable adjustments under the DDA; removing any provision, criterion or practice that has an unlawful, indirectly discriminatory effect; and preventing direct discrimination, harassment and victimisation in the workplace. However, 'positive action' is not in itself mandatory.

Given the patchwork legal framework which is described in more detail in **6.09** Chapter 2, it is impossible to provide a fully integrated cross-strand analysis of the legislation on positive action without missing subtle differences in the rules between strands. We have therefore grouped the rules so that we deal first with race, then sex and then take together religion or belief, sexual orientation and age where the legislation is identical. There are no equivalent positive action provisions in the DDA although employers are under a duty to make reasonable adjustments to accommodate the disabilities of employees and job applicants and positive discrimination in favour of those with disabilities is not unlawful.

(a) Race

Lawful positive action in relation to race requires an analysis of the employ- **6.10** ment prospects of a particular racial group, in particular work for an employer, at a particular establishment of that employer's business. The two types of positive action that an employer can take are:

- providing training to *employees* of a particular racial group, 'which would help fit them for' particular work;[6] and/or
- encouraging only *persons* of a particular racial group (whether they are employees or not) 'to take advantage of opportunities' for doing a particular type of work at the particular establishment.[7]

However, this action can only be taken where at any time within the preceding **6.11** 12 months either:

- there are no persons of that racial group among those doing that work at that establishment;[8] or
- the proportion of persons of that racial group among those doing that work at that establishment is small in comparison with the proportion of persons of that racial group either (i) among those employed generally by that employer at that establishment or (ii) among the population of the area from which the employer normally recruits persons for work at that establishment.[9]

Race is the only strand to have, worked into the rules on positive action, an **6.12** analysis by establishment. This recognises the fact that minority groups often

---

[6] RRA, s 38(1)(a).   [7] RRA, s 38(1)(b).   [8] RRA, s 38(2)(a).
[9] RRA, s 38(2)(b)(i) and (ii).

form communities within particular geographical locations. The statistical analysis is therefore carried out in relation to the particular establishment (eg the particular office, factory, shop or premises of the business) and its catchment area rather than have the figures distorted by taking into account the wider business or a wider geographical area.

6.13 Paragraph 3.10 of the CRE Code of Practice on Racial Equality in Employment 2005 deals with the aims of an equal opportunities policy. In broad terms these are the removal of direct discrimination and indirect discrimination and making sure that 'people from under-represented racial groups are given training and encouragement to take equal advantage of opportunities in the organisation'. In other words the CRE saw 'positive action' as being a key aim of the most fundamental document in an employer's equality package: something that has clearly failed to occur given the comparative rarity of positive action initiatives.

6.14 It is important for employers to remember that although positive action is lawful, it does exclude persons who are not members of the racial group targeted for training or encouragement. There is some scope for resentment to arise from those in racial groups that are excluded—this may be one of the reasons for the comparative rarity of positive action initiatives. For private sector employers this is a moral rather than a legal issue. For public sector employers covered by the race general duty (described in more detail in Chapter 3) there is a legal requirement to promote good relations between persons of different racial groups.[10] These are not reasons to avoid positive action but demonstrate that an employer should consider informing and consulting employees and their representatives in advance of taking any such action and emphasising the point that appointments will still be made on merit.

(b) Sex

6.15 Lawful positive action in relation to sex requires an analysis of the employment prospects of a particular gender in particular work for an employer. The two types of positive action that an employer can take are:

- providing training to *employees* of a particular gender, 'which would help fit them for' particular work;[11] and/or
- encouraging women only or men only (whether they are employees or not) 'to take advantage of opportunities' for doing particular work.[12]

6.16 However, this action can only be taken where at any time within the preceding 12 months either there were no persons of the gender in question among those

---

[10] RRA, s 71(1)(b).   [11] SDA, s 48(1)(a).   [12] SDA, s 48(1)(b).

doing that work or the number of persons of that gender doing the work was comparatively small.[13]

The EOC Code 1985[14] sets out some examples of positive action in practice: **6.17**

- training employees for work which is traditionally the preserve of one sex, for example training women for skilled manual or technical work;
- providing encouragement for women to apply for management posts;
- advertisements that encourage applications from the minority sex *but* which make it clear that selection will be on merit and not gender based; and
- notifying job agencies that the employer wishes to encourage applications from one sex—but men and women should both be told about the vacancies, with the under-represented gender told, in addition, that applications from them would be particularly welcome.

(c) Religion or Belief, Sexual Orientation, Age

There are a number of differences between the race and sex strands and, taken **6.18** together, religion or belief, sexual orientation and age; in particular:

- race is the only strand that incorporates the concept of the employer's 'establishment' into the requirements; and
- race and sex both require an analysis of the make-up of the employer's workforce over the previous 12 months whilst the other strands do not.

The two types of positive action that an employer can take in relation to **6.19** religion or belief, sexual orientation or age are:

- providing training to *persons* of a particular religion or belief,[15] sexual orientation[16] or age or age group,[17] 'which would help fit them for' a particular work; and/or
- encouraging *persons* of a particular religion or belief,[18] sexual orientation,[19] age or age group[20] 'to take advantage of opportunities' for doing particular work.

However, this action can only be taken where it reasonably appears to the **6.20** employer that it prevents or compensates for disadvantages linked to religion or belief, sexual orientation or age suffered by persons of that religion or belief, sexual orientation or age or age group doing that work or likely to take up that work.[21]

With age discrimination it is uniquely possible to justify direct discrimination.[22] **6.21**

---

[13] SDA, s 48(1). [14] Paragraph 42. [15] RBR, reg 25(1)(a).
[16] SOR, reg 26(1)(a). [17] AR, reg 29(1)(a). [18] RBR, reg 25(1)(b).
[19] SOR, reg 26(1)(b). [20] AR, reg 29(1)(b).
[21] RBR, reg 25(1), SOR, reg 26(1) and AR, reg 29(1). [22] AR, reg 3(1).

Where there are disadvantages linked to age suffered by persons of a particular age or age group it may be possible to justify taking positive action in respect of such persons (in other words justify discriminating directly against those of a different age or age group) beyond the narrow parameters of training and providing encouragement allowed for in AR, regulation 29(1).

Positive Action—Employer's Checklist

Race

In the last 12 months at one of our establishments has there been either:

- no one from a particular racial group doing particular work; or
- only a small proportion of persons of that racial group, among those doing that work, at that establishment when compared with the proportion of persons of that racial group either (i) within our workforce at that establishment or (ii) among the population of the area from which we normally recruit employees for work at that establishment?

Yes ☐ No ☐

Sex

In the last 12 months have there been no employees of one gender carrying out particular work or a comparatively small number of employees of that gender doing the work?

Yes ☐ No ☐

Religion or belief, sexual orientation and age

Does it appear to us, on reasonable grounds, that training and/or encouragement would prevent or compensate for disadvantages linked to religion or belief, sexual orientation or age suffered by persons of that religion or belief, sexual orientation or age or age group doing particular work for us or likely to take up that work?

Yes ☐ No ☐

If the answers to any of these questions are 'Yes'—consider taking lawful positive action.

(d) Other Lawful Positive Action

Both SDA, section 47 and RRA, section 37 allow for the provision of training **6.22** and encouragement 'by any person' to an under-represented gender or racial group in circumstances similar to those relevant to employers in SDA, section 48 and RRA, section 38 discussed above. As originally enacted SDA, section 47 and RRA, section 37 applied only to designated training bodies. As amended they apply to 'any person' which would include an employer and there is therefore an overlap with SDA, section 48 and RRA, section 38.

RRA, section 35 allows for discrimination in favour of a particular racial group **6.23** in access to facilities or services to meet their special needs in regard to their 'education, training or welfare or any ancillary benefits'.

SDA, section 47(3) permits any person to provide training for those in special **6.24** need because they have been discharging domestic or family responsibilities (more typically but not exclusively women) to help 'to fit them for employment'.

SDA, section 48 and RRA, section 38 apply, as well as to employers, to trade **6.25** organisations, trade unions and professional bodies; and SDA, section 49 allows the reserving of a minimum number of seats on the elected bodies of such organisations. We mention these provisions in passing although they are outside the scope of this book.

(e) Positive Action and Targets

A number of organisations, often those in the public sector seeking to comply **6.26** with the public duties to promote equality (Chapter 3), set targets, for example, for the ethnic composition of their workforces overall or by grade. Such targets are typically presented as 'outcomes' that will demonstrate the achievement of equality. It is often said by such authorities that the composition of their workforce needs to reflect the community which they serve. Targets can provide a useful measure but can equally suggest quotas—and that direct discrimin-ation has or will occur in order to achieve the quota. We reiterate that selection for employment or promotion must always be on merit and this should be strongly emphasised wherever an organisation sets targets.

Some confusion may have been caused in the minds of employers by the use by **6.27** political parties of 'all women shortlists' for candidate selection. The 'magic' by which this has been achieved is a specific legislative change.[23]

There has been a strong lobby for positive discrimination in relation to race, **6.28**

---

[23] SDA, s 42A—inserted by the Sex Discrimination (Election Candidates) Act 2002.

within the police service. No other organisation has been under more scrutiny in respect of its attitudes and policies in the field of race relations than the police, in particular following the findings of 'institutional racism' by the MacPherson Inquiry into the police investigation of the racist murder of black teenager Stephen Lawrence. The MacPherson Report recommended:

> That the Home Secretary and Police Authorities' policing plans should include targets for recruitment, progression and retention of minority ethnic staff. Police Authorities to report progress to the Home Secretary annually. Such reports to be published.[24]

6.29 However, achieving those targets has proved very difficult. Within the Metropolitan Police Service in 2002–2003, 9.8 per cent of recruits were from ethnic minorities, but by 2009 the Government target is 25.9 per cent.

6.30 Advocating a change in the law to allow for positive discrimination, the Metropolitan Police Service's Director of Human Resources, Martin Tiplady, said that the organisation did not 'stand a prospect of getting anywhere near the target' but that if the law was changed 'we would still require there to be a standard that is maintained, and then and only then would we at that point give discrimination or priority to the black candidate'.[25]

6.31 In response, however, the Select Committee on Home Affairs said that although many police forces remain unrepresentative of their wider communities,

> . . . it would be counterproductive to take action which led to a lowering of recruitment standards, or which created a widespread sense of unfairness on the part of white police officers. We believe that the best way forward is through a combination of:
>
> • increased effort put into 'positive action', that is, promotional and outreach activities aimed at encouraging more members of minority groups to apply to join the police; and
> • the prioritising in recruitment of certain abilities such as language skills and knowledge of cultural background, where relevant to policing needs in particular areas.[26]

6.32 Further initiatives followed. In July 2005 the 'Race Equality Programme for the Police Service' was published as part of the joint response of the Association of Chief Police Officers, the Association of Police Authorities and the Home Office to the CRE's formal investigation into the police service of England and Wales. This contains 14 recommendations/actions relating to positive action

---

[24] The Stephen Lawrence Inquiry Report, recommendation 64.
[25] <news.bbc.co.uk/2/hi/uk_news/3634085.stm>, 17 April 2004.
[26] *Select Committee on Home Affairs Fourth Special Report: Police Reform* (March 2005), para 146.

and employment targets. On 21 July 2005 the Home Office published 'Positive Action Events Toolkit', a good practice guide to conducting positive action events for police recruitment.

There have, however, still been controversies. In May 2005 there was some **6.33** adverse publicity around the Metropolitan Police Service's engineering of its groups of intakes sent for training. In order to make each intake more 'balanced' the Service was moving some women and ethnic minority recruits up the queue resulting in some white male recruits having to wait up to three years for the training. As Des Keenoy, the Metropolitan Police Federation's constables' chairman, put it: 'There is positive action which is legitimate, and positive discrimination which is not. The line between the two is getting very narrow indeed'.[27]

In September 2006, an ET heard that 108 potential recruits to Gloucestershire **6.34** Police had been rejected because they were white men in an unlawful attempt to boost the number of ethnic minority and women recruits. One of the rejected men, Matt Powell, took action against the Force, and was awarded £2,500 in compensation. The case came six months after Avon and Somerset Police admitted they had unlawfully rejected almost 200 applications from white men for the same reason.[28]

(f) The Future

Chapter 4 of the consultation paper on the Single Equality Bill[29] is devoted **6.35** to the issue of 'Balancing measures'. This is a slightly less intimidating description of positive action. Balancing measures are defined in paragraph 4.8 as being:

> . . . measures designed to address the under-representation of particular groups in a variety of roles and situations. This approach recognises that under-representation is usually a consequence of historical or entrenched disadvantage . . .

The consultation paper sets out the rationale for having balancing measures. In **6.36** particular it explains that outlawing discrimination (what we have previously referred to as the traditional human rights based approach to achieving equality) will not necessarily be enough by itself to ensure genuine equality in practice for everyone because not everyone is in the same position from the outset. Balancing measures are, according to the consultation paper, consistent with

---

[27] <news.bbc.co.uk/2/hi/uk_news/4526401.stm>, 8 May 2005.
[28] <www.channel4.com/news/articles/world/police%20admit%20positive%20 discrimination/169440>, 22 September 2006.
[29] DLR consultation paper, paras 4.1–4.58.

the principle of equal treatment which recognises that comparable situations are not to be treated differently and different situations are not to be treated alike.

6.37 Our legislation already contains a number of balancing measures, for example:

- the right to request flexible working helps to redress the disadvantage in the workplace to which parents of young or disabled children and carers of adults are exposed;
- reasonable adjustments in disability discrimination legislation helps to redress the disadvantage experienced by the disabled. Treating disabled and non-disabled persons the same would never achieve true equality because the two groups are not starting from the same position;
- existing positive action provisions;
- public sector general and specific duties to promote equality; and
- all women shortlists in relation to the selection of candidates by political parties.

6.38 As a general principle, the Government proposes that any balancing measures introduced should prevent or compensate for disadvantage or meet special needs linked to the particular strand and would always have to be (a) necessary, (b) proportionate, and (c) time-limited.

6.39 The Government are, however, shying away from two particular measures that have been mooted. First, they are not persuaded that the concept of 'reasonable adjustments' should be extended beyond disability law to other groups protected by equality legislation.

6.40 Secondly, they see a positive role for the EHRC in producing a Code of Practice and guidance on 'balancing measures' but do not see the EHRC's role as being to approve positive action schemes that employers would like to adopt. Unlike in certain tax-related situations, for example, where an employer can seek non-legally binding clearance from Her Majesty's Revenue and Customs, no such role is proposed for the EHRC. Although the EHRC will have plenty of work to do in its formative years, this is, potentially, an opportunity lost. One of the primary concerns of employers in adopting positive action measures is their legality. Legal advice provides some comfort but clearance from the EHRC (albeit non-legally binding) might provide that added seal of approval employers need to present positive action initiatives to their workforce and the wider community.

6.41 Although UK equality law is increasingly shaped and, therefore, in a sense, confined by European law, the positive action provisions in European law are framed more widely than their domestic equivalents. Article 141(4) of the Treaty of Rome states:

> With a view to ensuring full equality in practice between men and women in working life, the principle of equal treatment shall not prevent any Member State from maintaining or adopting measures providing for specific advantages in order to make it easier for the under-represented sex to pursue vocational activity or to prevent or compensate for disadvantages in professional careers.

6.42 This is carried through into Article 2(8) of the Equal Treatment Directive[30] which allows for the adoption of measures with a view to ensuring full equality in practice between men and women. Similarly, Article 5 of the Race Directive[31] allows for the adoption of measures to prevent or compensate for disadvantages linked to racial or ethnic origin, with a view to ensuring full equality in practice; and Article 7 of the Framework Directive[32] has equivalent provisions for sexual orientation, religion or belief, disability and age.

6.43 It would be unlawful under both domestic and European law to appoint a candidate from an under-represented group over a *better qualified* candidate (notwithstanding any good intention of redressing under-representation). However, the ECJ has held that it is not incompatible with European law for women to be given preference for promotion where they are (a) under-represented and (b) there is no automatic and unconditional preference but there is instead an objective assessment which takes account of individual circumstances.[33]

6.44 The point here is that there is scope for widening positive action measures in the UK within the existing parameters of European law. The example, suggested by the Government as a voluntary measure that employers could adopt, is fast-tracking members of under-represented groups through initial training. Such individuals must first have met all the entrance criteria, passed any relevant tests and been accepted for initial training. This could be a way of, for example, speeding up the achievement of a more representative police force.

6.45 The Government believes that it is important that public institutions such as the police and the Civil Service are representative of the communities that they serve.[34] However, the more positive action measures push towards positive discrimination and unspoken quotas, the more the risk of creating winners and losers and with it a corrosive sense of unfairness. The argument that one is simply overcoming historical disadvantage experienced by a particular group may work on a collective basis but it becomes harder to rationalise on an individual level.

---

[30] Council Directive 76/207/EEC.   [31] Council Directive 2000/43/EC.
[32] Council Directive 2000/78/EC.
[33] *Briheche v Ministre de L'Interieur* [2004] C–3109, ECJ.
[34] DLR consultation paper, para 4.11.

6.46 The broad assumption that underpins, for example, the provision of training only to Bangladeshi employees to help 'fit' them for management roles is that every other candidate who is not of Bangladeshi origin is automatically in a more advantageous position in a competitive promotion exercise and every Bangladeshi candidate is automatically in a more disadvantaged position, simply because of their respective races. Such assumptions overlook a multitude of individual circumstances. Positive action is a powerful tool for change and the circumstances in which it is used may be extended in the future. However, a combination of a very clear rationale and great sensitivity is needed wherever it is deployed.

C. Genuine Occupational Qualifications and Requirements

6.47 In certain limited circumstances an employer can discriminate in recruitment and promotion where being of a particular gender[35] or race[36] (so far as colour and nationality only are concerned) is a 'genuine occupational qualification' ('GOQ'); or being of a particular race[37] (so far as race or ethnic or national origins but not colour or nationality is concerned), religion or belief,[38] sexual orientation[39] or age[40] is a 'genuine occupational requirement' ('GOR'), of the job in question. There are no equivalent provisions in respect of disability under the DDA.

(a) Sex as a GOQ

6.48 Being of a particular gender is only a GOQ where:

- Physiology and authenticity: the essential nature of the job calls for a particular gender for reasons of physiology (other than physical strength or stamina) or in dramatic performances or other entertainment for reasons of authenticity, so that the essential nature of the job would be materially different if carried out by a person of the other gender.[41]

- Preservation of decency or privacy: the job needs to be held by a person of one gender to preserve decency or privacy because (i) the job is likely to involve physical contact with, for example, men where they might reasonably object to it being carried out by a woman or (ii) the job holder is likely to do the work in circumstances where, for example, women might reasonably object to the presence of a man because they are in a state of undress or are using sanitary facilities.[42]

---

[35] SDA, s 7.   [36] RRA, s 5.   [37] RRA, s 4A.   [38] RBR, reg 7.
[39] SOR, reg 7.   [40] AR, reg 8.   [41] SDA, s 7(2)(a).   [42] SDA, s 7(2)(b).

- Work in a private home: the job holder will be working or living in a private home where objection might reasonably be taken to allowing someone of the opposite gender the degree of physical or social contact with a person living in the home or the knowledge of intimate details of such a person's life.[43]

- Single sex accommodation: the nature or location of the job makes it impractical for the job holder to live anywhere other than in premises provided by the employer and the employer can only reasonably provide single sex accommodation and sanitary facilities.[44]

- Hospitals, prisons and establishments for special care: the nature of the establishment requires that the work is done by a person of one gender because it is a hospital, prison or other establishment for persons of one gender requiring special care, supervision or attention and it is reasonable given the 'essential character' of the establishment that the job holder be of that gender.[45]

- Personal services: the job holder provides individuals with personal services promoting their welfare or education, or similar personal services, and those services can most effectively be provided by someone of a particular gender.[46]

- Employment outside the UK: the job holder needs to be of a particular gender because the work is likely to involve performance of duties outside the UK in a country whose laws and customs are such that the duties could not, effectively, be performed by someone of the opposite gender.[47]

Each of the circumstances listed above applies where some only of the duties of the job fall within the exception as well as where all of them do.[48] However, where a female complainant was refused a job with a menswear shop on the grounds that she would have to measure the inside leg of male customers, a Tribunal rejected the GOQ argument partly on the ground that it was a limited part of the job and there were male assistants who could be called upon where necessary.[49] Other than where the work is in a private home, the GOQ argument cannot be deployed to refuse employment, for example, to a woman, when filling a vacancy if the employer already has male employees who could cover the duties without undue inconvenience.[50]   **6.49**

The GOQ argument can be deployed where the job is one of two to be held by a married couple, by a couple who are civil partners or by either a married couple or a couple who are civil partners.[51]   **6.50**

---

[43] SDA, s 7(2)(ba).   [44] SDA, s 7(2)(c).   [45] SDA, s 7(2)(d).
[46] SDA, s 7(2)(e).   [47] SDA, s 7(2)(g).   [48] SDA, s 7(3).
[49] *Wylie v Dee & Co (Menswear) Ltd* [1978] IRLR 103, IT; *Etam plc v Rowan* [1989] IRLR 150, EAT.
[50] SDA, s 7(4).   [51] SDA, s 7(2)(h).

6.51 SDA, sections 7A and 7B apply the sex GOQ to gender reassignment. These apply to dismissal as well as to recruitment or promotion, so that a person can be dismissed without such dismissal being discriminatory where the person complied with a GOQ but then ceased to do so because of gender reassignment. There are four additional GOQs connected to gender reassignment[52] although these cease to apply in relation to discrimination against a person whose gender has become the acquired gender under the Gender Recognition Act 2004.

(b) Race as a GOQ

6.52 Being of a particular racial group is only a GOQ where the GOR requirements do not apply and where:

- authenticity: the job involves participation in a dramatic performance or other entertainment[53] or as an artist's or photographic model[54] or in a place where food or drink is provided in a particular setting[55] for which a person of that racial group is required for reasons of authenticity; or

- personal services: the job holder provides individuals of that racial group with personal services promoting their welfare and those services can most effectively be provided by someone of that racial group.[56] This has been held to cover a playgroup advertising for an African-Caribbean worker where the personal services included maintaining cultural links with the children, dealing with their parents on such matters, reading and talking in dialect and skin and hair care[57] but not jobs which were managerial or administrative in nature with limited contact with the public.[58]

6.53 As with sex as a GOQ, the race GOQ can be deployed where not all of the duties of the job fall within one of the exceptions above[59] but the exceptions do not apply when filling a vacancy, where the employer already has employees of the racial group in question who could cover without undue inconvenience.[60]

(c) Race, Religion or Belief, Sexual Orientation and Age as GORs

6.54 It will not be discriminatory to recruit or promote on the grounds of race,[61] religion or belief,[62] sexual orientation[63] or age[64] where, having regard to the nature of the employment or the context in which it is carried out:

---

[52] SDA, s 7B(2)(a)–(d).   [53] RRA, s 5(2)(a).   [54] RRA, s 5(2)(b).
[55] RRA, s 5(2)(c).   [56] RRA, s 5(2)(d).
[57] *Tottenham Green Under Fives Centre v Marshall* [1989] ICR 214, EAT.
[58] *Lambeth LBC v CRE* [1990] ICR 768, CA.   [59] RRA, s 5(3).   [60] RRA, s 5(4).
[61] RRA, s 4A (for discrimination on the grounds of colour or nationality, however, see the section on GOQs above).
[62] RBR, reg 7.   [63] SOR, reg. 7.   [64] AR, reg 8.

- being of a particular race or of particular ethnic or national origins, religion or belief, sexual orientation or possessing a characteristic relating to age (as the case may be) is a genuine and determining occupational requirement;
- it is proportionate to apply that requirement in the particular case; and
- either (i) the person to whom that requirement is applied does not meet it; or (ii) it is reasonable for the employer not to be satisfied that he or she meets it.

6.55 In relation to religion or belief the GOR can apply even where the employer does not itself have an ethos based on religion or belief.[65] However, where the employer does have an ethos based on religion or belief there is an additional GOR[66] framed in very similar terms where, having regard to that ethos, being of a particular religion or belief is a 'genuine [note: does not have to be "determining"] occupational requirement.'

6.56 In relation to sexual orientation the GOR can apply whether or not the employment is for the purposes of an organised religion.[67] However, where the employment is for the *purposes* of an organised religion, the employer can apply a requirement related to sexual orientation (eg that applicants be 'straight') so as to comply with the doctrines of the religion or to avoid conflicting with the strongly held religious convictions of a significant number of the religion's followers.[68] This is an uncomfortable provision seeking as it does to walk the tightrope between competing rights in relation to sexual orientation and religion or belief. It is all the more uncomfortable for allowing the employer to reject a candidate if the employer is not satisfied on reasonable grounds that the candidate has been honest about his or her sexual orientation.[69]

6.57 As direct age discrimination can be justified as a proportionate means of achieving a legitimate aim, it is unlikely that employers will often rely on the age GOR. Examples might nevertheless be where an age-related characteristic is necessary in theatre, film or modelling.

(d) Distinction between GOQs/GORs and Positive Action

6.58 The idea that GOQs could be used as a form of positive action was rejected by Lord Justice Balcombe in *London Borough of Lambeth v Commission for Racial Equality*.[70] In that case, Lambeth had advertised for managerial positions in its housing department with positions restricted to those of Asian and African-Caribbean origin. The CRE brought proceedings under section 29 of the RRA and Lambeth sought to rely on the GOQ exception in section 5. The Court of

---

[65] RBR, reg 7(2).   [66] RBR, reg 7(3).   [67] SOR, reg 7(2).   [68] SOR, reg 7(3).
[69] SOR, reg 7(3)(c)(ii).   [70] [1990] ICR 768, CA.

Appeal applied a restrictive view of the 'personal services' envisaged in section 5(2)(d).

6.59 The wind of change is, however, blowing through equality law. The reports coming out of the Discrimination Law Review[71] and the Equalities Review[72] suggest an impatience for change and more of a focus on positive action. With GORs more broadly defined than GOQs there may be more scope than before to designate certain jobs as requiring candidates with characteristics, for example, defined by reference to race or gender.

6.60 We mentioned above the Select Committee on Home Affairs First Special Report: Police Reform (March 2005), which rejected positive discrimination to improve diversity in the Police Service but endorsed instead the prioritising in recruitment of certain abilities such as language skills and knowledge of cultural background, where relevant to policing needs in particular areas. In this example, being of a particular race or particular ethnic or national origin would still have to be a genuine and determining occupational requirement, but the approach does suggest a subtle shift towards using GORs as a form of positive action.

(e) The Future

6.61 In the consultation paper on the Single Equality Bill[73] the Government set out their proposal to introduce a GOR test for all strands of discrimination other than disability (where one is unnecessary because it is not unlawful to discriminate against persons who are not disabled). The Government has invited responses to the proposal and to the question of whether the new GOR should list specific examples, as is the case currently with GOQs.

---

[71] DLR consultation paper.
[72] *Fairness and Freedom: The Final Report of the Equalities Review* (HMSO, February 2007).
[73] DLR consultation paper, paras 1.64–1.70.

Positive Action and Occupational Requirements: In Brief

- Positive discrimination, also sometimes referred to as 'affirmative action', is unlawful with only limited exceptions in the case of disability and age (if that can be justified).

- Positive action, however, in the sense of providing training and encouragement to under-represented groups, is lawful within a narrow statutory framework. Selection must still always be on merit.

- Certain jobs can be reserved for candidates only from a specific group where being a member of that group is a genuine occupational qualification (GOQ) or, depending upon the strand, a genuine occupational requirement (GOR).

- The Single Equality Bill is likely to deal with both of these issues with a possible extension of the circumstances in which positive action may be used and a likely cross-strand harmonised GOR.

7

RECRUITMENT AND PROMOTION

Riddle: A father and son are involved in a car accident. The father dies. The son is taken to hospital for emergency surgery. The surgeon arrives to operate and says: 'I cannot operate on this boy because he is my son.' How can that be?

To the extent that this riddle still works at all, it demonstrates the power of job stereotyping. The fact that the surgeon is female, and therefore the boy's mother, may not be an obvious first thought to everyone!

A. Introduction

Both recruitment and promotion are essential to the promotion of equality and **7.01** diversity, dealing as they do, respectively, with entry and progress in employment and the rewards that follow. The equality enactments for each strand make it unlawful for an employer to discriminate against a person in the arrangements it makes for, amongst other things, recruitment and promotion.[1] We have chosen to put recruitment and promotion together into one chapter as they share many of the same characteristics, in particular the selection of an appropriate candidate to take a particular job.

In this chapter we examine the various steps in the recruitment and promotion **7.02** processes to which we have applied the principles of the equality enactments. An employer that follows these steps will have the comfort of a strong defence in the event that an unsuccessful candidate seeks to challenge the legality of the process on the basis of one of the strands of discrimination.

Returning to the central theme of this book however, we aim to look beyond **7.03** the actions of an employer that wishes merely to avoid being sued successfully

---

[1] SDA, s 6(1) and (2); RRA, s 4(1) and (2); DDA, s 4(1) and (2); RBR, reg 6(1) and (2); SOR, reg 6(1) and (2); and AR, reg 7(1) and (2).

for discrimination, to the employer that wishes, proactively, to promote equality and diversity. This chapter should therefore be read with Chapter 6 which examines 'positive action', the legally permissible steps that an employer, wishing to promote equality and diversity, can take to encourage those from under-represented groups to apply for jobs and to better equip them for success at the selection stage in the recruitment and promotion processes.

7.04 It is probably worth saying from the beginning that there is nothing to prevent an employer from deciding not to recruit or promote someone if they do not have the necessary skills or abilities to perform the job. Putting that more positively, employers can, of course, choose who to recruit or promote on the basis of merit. Objectors to the promotion of equality and diversity in recruitment and promotion frequently find a collective voice in allegations of 'dumbing down' or 'sacrificing quality on the altar of political correctness'.

7.05 This chapter and Chapter 6 aim, amongst other things, to emphasise that the object of the exercise is always to recruit or promote the best person for the job.[2] The promotion of equality and diversity is not about positive discrimination (which, with the limited exceptions of disability and justifiable age discrimination, would in any event be unlawful) but about ensuring that the pool of candidates for a particular post is widely drawn and not unreasonably or unlawfully restricted, prior to a lawful selection being made.

B. The Recruitment Process

7.06 In examining the recruitment process we have broken this down into five stages (a checklist is also provided at Appendix 7.1):

- Planning: preparing for the recruitment process by drawing up a job description, person specification and application form.
- Advertising: advertising the job to ensure a good number of responses from applicants capable of fulfilling the requirements of the job description.
- Selection: carrying out a selection process by applying criteria to the applicants for the job, which might include a preliminary screening to form a shortlist, selection tests and assessment centres and interviews.
- Offer: making the offer to the successful candidate and providing feedback to the unsuccessful candidates.
- Checking: pre-employment checks including taking up references and ensuring that the successful candidate is eligible to work in the UK.

---

[2] CRE Code 2005, para 4.16.

C. Planning

(a) Job Descriptions

It is recommended[3] that employers prepare a job description for any vacant **7.07** post they decide to fill. The purpose of a job description is to set out what the job entails and how it fits into the employer's organisational structure. This might simply be a list of the duties that are likely to form the basis of the role. Alternatively, this might be expressed as a list of the duties that the employee would be expected to carry out in a given period, for example, over the period of a day, week or month.

The list of duties in a job description is a list of 'criteria' in the context of **7.08** indirect discrimination. An employer should therefore take care only to include those duties that it can justify as being necessary without overstating the need for a particular duty or the responsibilities associated with it.

(b) Person Specifications

It is also recommended[4] that a person specification is drawn up to accompany **7.09** the job description. A person specification sets out, for example, the qualifications, experience, skills, knowledge, abilities and qualities that are considered necessary or desirable in the person selected and employed to do the job. Taking a methodical approach to the drafting of a person specification will help to remove irrelevant criteria from the selection process, some of which may be potentially discriminatory. In drawing up a person specification an employer should make sure, for example, that:

- The specification includes only the criteria needed to perform satisfactorily the duties in the job description. For example, stipulating that candidates must be 'active and energetic', when the job is a sedentary one introduces a requirement which is both irrelevant and potentially discriminatory in that it could unjustifiably exclude (or deter from applying) some people whose disabilities result, for example, in them getting more tired than others, or those who are less mobile.[5]

- The requirements are not overstated, for example, by calling for 'excellent knowledge of English' (or Welsh in Wales) when 'good understanding' is

---

[3] At para 4.5 of the CRE Code 2005, although the point applies to all strands.
[4] At para 4.8 of the CRE Code 2005, although again the point applies to all strands.
[5] DRC Code 2004, at para 7.7; The DRC 'Practical Guide to the Law and Best Practice for Employers' (the 'DRC Practical Guide', para 3.3).

more appropriate, or by asking for higher qualifications than are actually needed to do the job satisfactorily.[6]

- The specification is not too specific about how a task should be done but rather focuses on what the outcome needs to be. For example, stating that a person must be 'willing to travel' where a job requires travel is better than stating that the person 'must have a driving licence'. The former requirement would not exclude those applicants who could comply with the requirement by, for example, using public transport whereas the latter requirement would potentially exclude those who do not hold driving licences for disability related reasons.[7]

- The specification makes clear the relative importance placed on each criterion and whether it is necessary or desirable.[8] Similarly, the DRC recommend separating essential and minor criteria to assist employers to think about what aspects of the job could be reassigned to another person if that was a reasonable adjustment for a disabled person.[9]

- As far as possible, all the criteria are capable of being tested objectively. The CRE Code of Practice uses 'leadership' as an example, suggesting that such a requirement should be more objectively sub-divided into the skills and qualities that contribute to it such as 'fairness, knowledge, diplomacy, imagination and decisiveness'.[10]

- Where qualifications are required, the specification should state that qualifications obtained abroad of equivalent standard to those obtained in the UK, will be acceptable.[11] Care also needs to be taken in respect of the DDA that the qualification required is relevant and significant to the role. In some cases it may be a reasonable adjustment to assign those areas of the role to which the qualification relates to another person or to waive the requirement for the qualification if the particular applicant can demonstrate the competence required by other means.[12]

- The specification should avoid blanket exclusions. The DRC Code of Practice gives as an example, the exclusion of all persons with epilepsy from consideration for a driving job, when in fact the job requires only a standard licence and standard insurance cover, both of which some people with epilepsy can obtain.[13]

- The specification should avoid stating that a certain personal, medical or health related characteristic is essential or desirable where either it is not

---

[6] CRE Code 2005, para 4.9(b).
[7] DRC Practical Guide, para 3.3.
[8] CRE Code 2005, para 4.9(c).
[9] DRC Practical Guide, para 3.3.
[10] CRE Code 2005, para 4.9(d).
[11] CRE Code 2005, para 4.9(d).
[12] DRC Code 2004, para 7.10.
[13] DRC Code 2004, para 7.8.

necessary for the role at all or reasonable adjustments could be made where a disabled person is otherwise unable to comply with the requirement.

- The specification should not give the impression that the person sought is of one gender or the other, for example, by referring just to 'he' throughout rather than 'he or she'. Any such impression given could give rise to, or be used to support a claim for, direct sex discrimination. Similar considerations, although they are likely to be less common, arise in relation to the other strands of discrimination.

- References to age should not be included: using age as a criteria could amount to direct age discrimination. This is broader than merely avoiding references to 'young' and 'old'. References to number of years' experience should be avoided where possible as they are likely to discriminate against younger candidates on the grounds of their age. Similarly, a requirement for continuous experience is likely to indirectly discriminate against women who take maternity leave. The person specification should focus on the type of experience necessary for the job not the amount of time a person has worked in the area in question.

(c) Application forms

The use of a standard application form has a number of advantages for employ- **7.10** ers and for job applicants. An application form benefits employers as it ensures that all applications are in a standard format containing all the information necessary for selecting candidates against the requirements of the job. Applicants understand clearly what information is required from them and are given an opportunity to compete on equal terms.

Only information that is relevant to the job description and the person specifi- **7.11** cation should be requested in that part of the application form that will be used in the selection process. It is helpful, however, to include a tear-off 'personal details' section for monitoring purposes. We dealt with monitoring in more detail in Chapter 4. Applicants should not be asked to provide photographs unless a genuine occupational qualification or requirement applies.[14]

In the case of disability it is likely to be a reasonable adjustment to provide **7.12** application forms, on request, in formats that are accessible to a disabled applicant. Accessible formats include email, Braille, Easy Read, large print, audio tape and computer disc.[15] A potential applicant's requirements will depend upon his or her impairment. An employer does not need to anticipate what

---

[14] CRE Code 2005, para 4.13(e)—although the point potentially applies to all strands.
[15] DRC Code 2004, para 7.16.

disabilities potential applicants might have and cater for all of them. To do so is likely to lead to unnecessary expenditure which might be better used elsewhere, for example, in training those dealing with recruitment in how to respond to requests for application forms in different formats. However, where for example, a website with down-loadable job application forms can be made more accessible to people with particular disabilities (eg those with visual impairments) at relatively little additional cost, this should be encouraged as both an anticipatory adjustment which could benefit disabled people and as a positive demonstration of the employer's commitment to equal treatment.

7.13 Where an employer adopts a particular application form it may need to be flexible with candidates who ask, because of a disability, to submit an application in a different format, for example, on tape. It is likely to be a reasonable adjustment to allow this. That does not mean, necessarily, that a disabled candidate has an absolute right to submit an application in a format of his or her choosing. For example, a candidate may prefer to submit his or her application in Braille but may not be substantially disadvantaged by providing it in some other format (such as email) that the employer would find easier to access.[16]

D. Advertising

7.14 Some employers ask current staff to recommend family members or friends when vacancies arise. Typically, a financial bonus is offered if the person put forward is appointed and stays in the role for a given period. The advantages to an employer are that recruitment costs are saved and staff tend to recommend for employment people that they know and like, which can help to retain a good collegiate working environment. However, where a workforce is drawn largely from, for example, one racial group, such policies can lead to a self-perpetuation of that workforce profile. It is better to advertise the role more widely so the employer can select staff from a wider and more diverse pool.

7.15 Once the planning stage has been completed the employer can move on to advertising the job in the hope of attracting suitable candidates. The job advert will inevitably be based up the job description and person specification already prepared.

7.16 It is unlawful to publish or cause to be published a job advert which indicates, or might reasonably be understood as indicating, an intention to discriminate on the grounds of:

---

[16] DRC Code 2004, para 7.17.

- sex,[17] and for these purposes an advert that uses a job description implying gender, for example, 'waiter', 'salesgirl', 'postman' or 'stewardess' will be taken as indicating an intention to discriminate unless the advert contains an indication to the contrary;[18]
- race;[19] and
- disability.[20]

In this context a job advert has a wide definition capable of capturing all of an employer's internal and external publications.[21] The advert includes not only the text but also any illustration used to accompany the text. The following examples are drawn from the EOC website: **7.17**

- An advert for clerical work, a profession traditionally undertaken by women, uses a picture of a woman working at a computer. Although the advert does not say in terms that the role is for a woman, taken as a whole the advert could reasonably indicate an intention to discriminate by implying that the employer is looking to recruit women. In order to counterbalance the message portrayed by the illustration, the EOC recommended that the advertisement should contain a bold disclaimer saying that the posts are open to both men and women. Alternatively, the illustration should also depict a man, in equal prominence, doing the same work.
- In a similar example, a picture of a woman at a computer was again used to illustrate secretarial/administrative jobs; positions historically held by women. In addition, some of the language used in the text of the advert, such as 'smiley' and 'charming', could, the EOC suggested, further add to the inference that they are looking to employ women. The EOC suggested that in their view a statement in the text that 'we are an equal opportunities employer' would not suffice as a disclaimer to counterbalance the message being portrayed by the advertisement as a whole. Rather, the advert would need a bold disclaimer to indicate that the positions are open to both men and women, and/or an illustration depicting a man and a woman equally and the adjectives used should also be more gender neutral.
- An advert for a sales role showed a man holding a trophy for achieving high sales. The inference from the illustration could be that this competitive profession was looking for male employees. Although, the text of the advert stated that the company was looking for 'men and women' the EOC felt that such a disclaimer should be more prominent, for example, in bigger font, to counterbalance the inference given by the illustration used.

---

[17] SDA, s 38(1).   [18] SDA, s 38(3).   [19] RRA, s 29(1).   [20] DDA, s 16B(1).
[21] SDA, s 82(1); RRA, s 78(1); DDA, s 16B(4).

7.18 When using illustrations to advertise jobs it is better to use an illustration relating to the nature of the work and not to a person doing the job. For example, an advert for medical staff could portray a male or alternatively a female patient, of whatever age or ethnicity, without there being an inference that the employer is looking to employ employees from one gender over another or of a particular age or ethnicity, religion or sexual orientation.

7.19 In determining whether an advertisement shows an intention to discriminate unlawfully, the test is not what the employer intended the advert to convey but what an ordinary reasonable person, without any special knowledge, would find to be the natural and ordinary meaning of the words used. No evidence is admissible to show what meaning was intended by the advertiser.

(a) Complaints about Adverts

7.20 Anybody can complain to the advertiser or publisher about an advertisement but proceedings in respect of discriminatory adverts may only be brought by the EHRC and then only in relation to sex,[22] race[23] and disability.[24] There are no equivalent provisions in relation to the religion or belief,[25] sexual orientation or age strands. However, the different treatment of the strands is really only of academic interest since in the period 1 January 1999 to 1 June 2006 none of the former Commissions used their powers in respect of discriminatory adverts[26] and there is little to suggest that the EHRC will be any more proactive in this area.

7.21 There are therefore few recent cases to cite on this issue. Going back to 1980 in *Equal Opportunities Commission v Robertson*[27] the EOC brought proceedings against Mr Robertson, Chairman of various companies in the Trago Mills out of town shopping group, for a series of job adverts which the EOC alleged showed an intention to discriminate. The Industrial Tribunal (as it then was) made a number of findings against Mr Robertson including:

- Adverts using the words 'craftsmen' and 'handyman' without any further statement to indicate that the jobs advertised were open to both men and women, could reasonably be understood to indicate that a man was required for the job and they were therefore unlawful.

- Similarly, adverts that used the words 'ex-policeman or similar' might

---

[22] SDA, s 38(6).   [23] RRA, s 29(6).   [24] DDA, s 16B(5).

[25] EA, s 54 deals with discriminatory adverts in some areas but not employment.

[26] 'Teeth and Their Use—the Enforcement Action by the Three Equality Commissions' (Public Interest Research Unit, 2006, <www.piru.org.uk>), reported in 'Equality Bodies Failing to Enforce Discrimination Law', EOR (October 2006) 157, pp 2–3.

[27] [1980] IRLR 44, IT.

reasonably be understood as indicating that a man was required for the job. The argument that the words 'or similar' referred to a policewoman did not impress the Tribunal who found that if that was what Mr Robertson intended, he would have said 'ex-policeman or policewoman'.

- Mr Robertson also showed an intention to discriminate in placing an advertisement, the opening words of which read 'a good job opportunity for a good bloke (or blokess to satisfy fool legislators)'. This might reasonably be understood as indicating that the job was not really open to women but that 'or blokess' was inserted purely to satisfy the requirements of the EOC.

The SDA, RRA and DDA provide that generally, both the advertiser (the **7.22** employer) and its agents (recruitment agencies) and the publisher of the advertisement are liable if an advertisement is published which indicates an intention to discriminate. Publishers, including newspapers, magazines, television and radio stations, employment agencies, Jobcentres and advertising agencies are, however, not liable if they can show:[28]

- that they relied on a statement from the advertiser that the publication of a particular advertisement would not be unlawful; and
- that it was reasonable for them to rely on that statement.

A person who knowingly or recklessly makes such a statement, which is false or **7.23** misleading, commits an offence that is subject to a fine not exceeding level 5 on the standard scale (currently £5,000).[29]

A separate issue from the EHRC's enforcement powers in respect of adverts, is **7.24** that an advert suggesting an intention to discriminate in relation to any strand will be very good evidence that discrimination has occurred, for an unsuccessful candidate claiming discrimination in recruitment or promotion in relation to that strand. The DRC Code 2004[30] provides an example of an advert stating 'Sorry but gaining access to our building can be difficult for some people.' An applicant with mobility issues who applies but is turned down for the job could not bring proceedings in relation to the content of the advert but could ask an Employment Tribunal to take the content of the advert into account when deciding whether he did not get the job for a disability-related reason.

(b) Equality Statements

Of course, an employer wishing to promote equality and diversity would not **7.25** want to give any suggestion of an intention to discriminate. On the contrary,

---

[28] SDA, s 38(4); RRA, s 29(4); DDA, s 16B(2A).
[29] SDA, s 38(5); RRA, s 29(5); DDA, s 16B(2B).   [30] At para 7.15.

such an employer would aim to encourage applications from all areas of the community by promoting itself as an equal opportunities employer. One way of doing this is to add to all job adverts a statement to the effect that the employer is an equal opportunities employer. Here are some other examples taken from actual job advertisements:

- 'South Bank Employers' Group is an equal opportunities employer.' A simple statement but perhaps a little lacking in enough detail for potential applicants to understand fully what it means. In a similar vein, this example is taken from a advert for a post with Pembrokeshire County Council—'We welcome applications from all sections of the community'.

- 'We are actively working towards equality of opportunities and welcome applications from any individual regardless of ethnic origin, gender, disability, religious belief, sexual orientation or age.' This advert for a job with Guardian Newspapers contains not only a useful reference to each of the strands but also an endearing honesty, implied in the expression 'working towards equality', that equality of opportunity is a goal yet to be achieved but that recruitment for this post is part of the process.

- 'Merseyside Fire and Rescue Service are committed to equality of opportunity. All applications will be considered on their merits and selection will be made solely on the basis of the suitability of applicants when assessed against job criteria.' This statement refers not only to equality of opportunity but also usefully reiterates the point that selection will be made on 'merit'—a point that is often misunderstood when an organisation is promoting equality and diversity.

- 'We are working to actively improve the diversity of our staff.' This statement, in an advert for a post with the University of East London, makes implied reference to an 'outcome'—an improved diversity of staff. Without an appropriate emphasis on selection on merit, this type of approach can lead an employer down the path to unlawful positive discrimination or at least provide evidence that might support a claim for discrimination by an unsuccessful candidate whose selection would not have improved the diversity of staff.

- 'We are an equal opportunities employer and operate a no-smoking policy.' There is some danger with the approach adopted in this statement, contained in an advert for a post with the Consumer Council for Water, that equal opportunities are seen merely as a footnote to be lumped in with a rather less fundamentally important issue of whether staff can smoke at work.

180

> The CRE, in *Racial Equality and the Smaller Business* (Commission for Racial Equality, <www.cre.gov.uk/sineguide.pdf>), suggested the following simple but effective and all-encompassing wording:
>
>> Our aim is to be an equal opportunities employer. We welcome all applications, regardless of race, colour, nationality, ethnic or national origins, sex, disability, sexual orientation, age, or religion or belief. All applications will be considered solely on merit.

> This example is taken for the advert for the position of Chair of the EHRC:
>
>> The Government is committed to providing equal opportunities for all, irrespective of age, disability, gender, marital status, race, religion & belief, sexual orientation, transgender and working patterns and to the principle of public appointments based on merit with independent assessments, openness and transparency of process.

(c) Positive about Disabled People

7.26 Jobcentre Plus, an executive agency within the Department for Work and Pensions, grants the 'double tick' symbol to employers based in Great Britain who have agreed to take action on five commitments regarding the employment, retention, training and career development of disabled people. These commitments are:

- To interview all disabled applicants who meet the minimum criteria for a job vacancy and consider them on their abilities.[31]
- To ensure there is a mechanism in place to discuss, at any time, but at least once a year, with disabled employees what can be done to make sure they can develop and use their abilities.
- To make every effort when employees become disabled to make sure they stay in employment.
- To take action to ensure that all employees develop the appropriate level of disability awareness needed to make these commitments work.

---

[31] It is important always to remember that the disability strand is unique in that it permits discrimination in favour of disabled people. It would not be possible, lawfully, to commit in the same way to interviewing people of a certain gender, racial group, sexual orientation, religion or belief or age.

- Each year to review the five commitments and what has been achieved, plan ways to improve on them and let employees and Jobcentre Plus know about progress and future plans.

7.27 The commitments apply to all vacancies based in Great Britain where the employer has been awarded the Disability Symbol. Participating employers typically add the symbol to their job adverts to attract disabled candidates. The guaranteed interview promise also applies to internal vacancies. Disability Symbol-using employers are covered by the DDA in the same way as other employers. The actions that they take in accordance with the commitments under the Disability Symbol are in addition to the obligations placed on them by the DDA.

(d) Placing Adverts

7.28 When placing an advert, an employer wishing to promote equality and diversity should be aiming to reach as wide a pool of potential applicants as possible. Recruitment solely or primarily by word of mouth, or on the basis of recommendations by existing staff, can restrict the choice of applicants, particularly where, for example, a workplace consists predominantly of one sex or racial group.

7.29 The EOC Code 1985[32] recommends that advertising should encourage applications from both sexes, for example, by placing advertisements in publications likely to reach both sexes and should avoid presenting men and women in stereotyped roles. Such stereotyping 'tends to perpetuate sex segregation in jobs and can also lead people of the opposite sex to believe that they would be unsuccessful in applying for particular jobs'. Much the same is true of the other strands.

7.30 The CRE Code 2005[33] recommends that to avoid indirect discrimination, employers should not unjustifiably restrict job advertisements or information about vacant posts to areas, publications, recruitment agencies, job centres, careers offices and schools that would result in excluding or disproportionately reducing the number of applicants from a particular racial group (or groups). Again, the same is true of the other strands.

7.31 Conversely, an employer may wish to reach out to under-represented groups by placing adverts in publications which are themselves targeted at certain groups. However, this should not be seen as an alternative to a more broadly focused

---

[32] At para 19.   [33] At para 4.11.

advert in, for example, the national press or on the employer's website. An example given by ACAS[34] is an advert placed *only* in a magazine aimed at gay men and lesbians, which may indirectly discriminate against people who are heterosexual because they are less likely to subscribe to the magazine and therefore less likely to find out about the vacancy and apply.

The DRC Code 2004[35] suggests that an employer which recognises that suit- **7.32** ably qualified disabled people have not applied to work for it may want to take proactive steps to attract disabled applicants, for example, by contacting local employment services such as Jobcentre Plus and specialist disability employment services.

E. Selection

Moving forward in the recruitment process: the job advert has been placed, **7.33** applicants have responded and have been supplied with and completed job application forms. The next stage will usually be to carry out a preliminary screen or sift of all the applications to produce a more manageable shortlist of the most suitable candidates for interview.

(a) Records

Every selection decision from shortlisting through to the final decision of who **7.34** to appoint is important and employers should retain their notes and documents from each stage. There are good defensive reasons for keeping records in case a decision is challenged in the Employment Tribunal. Looking at this more positively however, records will help to demonstrate to managers monitoring the process that a fair and open process has been followed and may be needed to explain the decision to unsuccessful candidates.

(b) Shortlisting

The Codes of Practice of the former Commissions again provide a useful source **7.35** of good practice advice.[36] In shortlisting candidates employers should consider the following:

• Wherever possible more than one person should be involved in shortlisting

---

[34] ACAS guide, *Sexual Orientation and the Workplace*, available at <www.acas.org.uk/media/pdf/e/n/sexual_1.pdf>.
[35] At para 2.17.
[36] See, for example, the CRE Code 2005, para 4.21.

applications. This reduces the chances of one person's bias influencing who is shortlisted.

- The marking system should be agreed in advance and applied consistently to every application.
- Any weighting given in the person specification should not be changed midway through the process.
- Each person involved in the shortlisting exercise should mark the applications separately before meeting to agree a final mark.
- Selection should be based only on the information in the application form and no stereotypical assumptions should be made about candidates.

7.36 As mentioned above in relation to the Disability Symbol scheme, some employers operate a guaranteed interview scheme under which a candidate who is disabled will be shortlisted for interview automatically if his or her application demonstrates that he or she would meet the minimum criteria for the job. Notwithstanding that the DDA allows for discrimination in favour of disabled candidates, a policy like this needs careful managing. There are risks if the rationale for the policy is not properly explained at the start of the recruitment process and the minimum criteria not carefully drawn. In particular:

- Disabled applicants may feel patronised if they would have been shortlisted in any event.
- Disabled applicants who hit only the minimum criteria in a pool of candidates who exceed the criteria may have their expectations unnecessarily and unreasonably raised and their time wasted attending an interview for a job they are highly unlikely to get.
- Non-disabled candidates who meet the minimum requirements but who are not shortlisted may resent comparable candidates shortlisted merely because of their disability.
- Who decides which candidate is disabled? It seems likely that in most cases, candidates will self-assess themselves as disabled. This might be seen as an opportunity for some less scrupulous candidates to obtain an interview by inventing or exaggerating a physical or mental impairment and claiming to be disabled.

7.37 These may be seen as potential dilemmas to be managed, not reasons to abandon or refuse to entertain a guaranteed interview scheme for disabled candidates. However, providing that an employer is rigorous in its approach to ensuring that reasonable adjustments are made for disabled candidates (thus compensating for the substantial adverse effects of the disability), we can see no more reason for supporting affirmative action in disability than in any other strand.

Ability tests can be a useful method of predicting a candidate's performance in **7.38** a particular job provided they are well designed, properly administered and professionally validated as a reliable predictor of performance regardless of racial group.[37] Paragraph 4.25 of the CRE Code provided the following guidelines:

- tests should correspond to the job in question and measure the appropriate skills identified in the person specification;
- special care is needed where the test is taken by candidates for whom English (or Welsh in Wales) is not a first language;
- all candidates should take the same test; and
- all documents relating to the test should be retained for 12 months.

As with all stages of the recruitment process a duty to make reasonable adjust- **7.39** ments will arise where a provision criterion or practice of the employer or a physical feature of the employer's premises places a disabled candidate at a substantial disadvantage. In the case of testing candidates the DRC Code 2004[38] suggested that, depending upon the precise circumstances of the test and the disability, the following adjustments might be reasonable:

- allowing the disabled candidate more time to complete the test;
- permitting the disabled person the assistance of a reader or scribe;
- accepting a lower pass rate where the disability inhibits performance in the test.

(c) Interviews

The vast majority of recruitment exercises incorporate one or more interviews **7.40** with the opinions and impressions gained by the interviewer(s) being the deciding factor in who gets the job. It is at this stage however, that there is greatest room for decisions to be influenced by subjective impressions and stereotypical assumptions.

In *North West Thames Regional Health Authority v Noone*[39] the Court of Appeal **7.41** stressed that where interviewers fail to adopt detailed terms of reference but rely instead on 'gut feelings' or 'hunches', their subjectivity and the dangers of unconscious discriminatory assumptions may sway a tribunal towards the view that discrimination has occurred.

---

[37] CRE Code 2005, para 4.24. [38] At para 7.25. [39] [1988] ICR 813, CA.

7.42 The CRE Code 2005, paragraph 4.29 recommended that staff involved in interviews should be trained in interviewing techniques to help them:

- recognise when they are making stereotypical assumptions;
- apply a scoring method objectively;
- prepare questions based on the person specification and the information in the application form; and
- avoid questions about hobbies, social activities or religious or cultural beliefs or practices, unless relevant to the job.

7.43 Similarly, the EOC Code 1985[40] recommends that where it is necessary to assess whether personal circumstances will affect job performance (for example, where the job involves unsocial hours or extensive travel) this should be discussed objectively without detailed questions based on assumptions about marital status, children and domestic obligations. Questions about marriage plans or family intentions should not be asked—they could be construed as showing bias against women. Similarly, questions about energy levels and retirement plans, asked of a candidate in, say, his fifties, could be construed as showing bias on the basis of age.

7.44 When inviting candidates to interview, it is good practice to give candidates an opportunity to indicate any relevant effects of a disability and to suggest adjustments to the interview arrangements or the employer's premises to help overcome any disadvantage at interview.[41] However, an employer should not assume that no adjustments are needed simply because none of the candidates indicates a need for them. Strictly speaking, the DDA places no duty on the disabled person to specify what adjustments should or could be made—although one would hope that such person would take a more proactive approach and suggest adjustments for the employer to consider.

7.45 That said, whilst the DDA requires employers to react appropriately to that which they know or could reasonably be expected to know and that places a burden on employers to make reasonable enquiries based on the information given to them, it does not require them to make every possible enquiry, particularly where there was little or no basis for doing so. *Ridout v TC Group*[42] illustrates this point.

7.46 Ms Ridout declared on her application form that she suffered from photosensitive epilepsy. When she arrived for the interview she realised that the

---

[40] At para 23(c).   [41] DRC Code 2004, para 7.23.   [42] [1998] IRLR 628, EAT.

fluorescent lights in the interview room could trigger an epileptic attack and on entering the room she expressed some disquiet about the lighting. She had a pair of sunglasses around her neck and the employers took her remark to mean that she might need to use them. They proceeded with the interview. Ms Ridout did not use the sunglasses nor did she exhibit any symptoms of illness or tell the employers that she felt disadvantaged.

When she was not offered the job, however, she claimed that the company had **7.47** discriminated against her by their failure to make a reasonable adjustment to the premises. The employers told the tribunal that they had not realised that there was any need for them to make any adjustments. The EAT rejected Ms Ridout's suggestion that once she had mentioned the word 'epilepsy' the burden passed to the employers to do everything that needed to be done under the DDA.

> Suggested paragraph to be included in letter inviting a candidate to interview:
>
> If you have a disability that would put you at a substantial disadvantage at interview when compared to other candidates we will make reasonable adjustments in order to overcome that disadvantage. In order to help us to do so, please let me know in advance of the interview what adjustments might be needed to enable you to participate fully in the process.

Similarly, it is good practice to allow some flexibility around interview times so **7.48** as to avoid significant religious times, such as Friday afternoons. ACAS recommend both that individuals invited to attend an interview make it known to the employer if they have particular needs associated with their religion or belief, and employers specifically invite applicants to make any special needs known.[43] The types of issues that might be relevant include any catering arrangements and recruitment related social gatherings involving alcohol if the candidate's religion forbids association with alcohol.

As with any other stage of the recruitment process relevant notes and docu- **7.49** ments should be retained for monitoring purposes, in case the process needs to

---

[43] ACAS guide, *Religion or Belief and the Workplace*, available at <www.acas.org.uk/media/pdf/f/l/religion_1.pdf>, para 2.8.

be explained to an unsuccessful candidate or in the event that there is a legal challenge to the process. We would recommend that documents are retained, in accordance with a general document retention policy operated by the employer, for at least 12 months.

F. Offer

7.50 In an ideal world the job offer would be made once the checks described below had been completed. However, in practice, an employer will usually want to make an offer quickly to prevent a preferred candidate going to another employer, even if that offer is made subject to various pre-employment checks being made.

7.51 The DRC recommended[44] that wherever possible employers should give feedback to unsuccessful candidates as positive feedback can have a major impact on a person's confidence and perception of the employer. It should be explained to unsuccessful disabled candidates that the recruitment decision was made on skill or experience and not on the basis of disability. Although the DRC guidance does not make the point, the decision not to recruit might have been made for disability related reasons, after consideration of reasonable adjustments and for a reason which is justifiable—in which case, all this should be explained to the unsuccessful candidate.

G. Checking

7.52 An offer of employment will generally be made subject to certain pre-employment checks being made, typically:

- a check that the potential employee is entitled to work in the UK;
- a medical check; and
- taking up references.

(a) Checking Entitlement to Work in the UK

7.53 Under section 8 of the Asylum and Immigration Act 1996,[45] employers are obliged to verify that their employees are entitled to work in the UK. Employing an illegal worker is a criminal offence. Individuals working for a company

---

[44] DRC Practical Guide, para 3.16.
[45] Repealed by the Immigration, Asylum and Nationality Act 2006 from a day to be appointed.

involved in the employment of an illegal worker may be personally liable. Currently an employer can be fined up to £5,000 per illegal worker employed.[46]

The main groups who are not subject to immigration control in the UK, and who can be employed without restriction are:

7.54

- British citizens;
- Commonwealth citizens with the right of abode;
- nationals from the Common Travel Area (the UK, Channel Islands, the Isle of Man and Ireland);
- nationals from the European Economic Area (EEA) countries (subject to exceptions—see boxed section) and Switzerland; and
- family members of nationals from EEA countries and Switzerland, providing the EEA national is lawfully residing in the UK.

The Immigration (Restrictions on Employment) Order 2004 deals with the way in which documentary verification by employers of entitlement to work is carried out. The employer has a defence if, before the start of employment, it has checked and copied (either by photocopying or scanning onto a computer database) certain documents that confirm the prospective employee's right to work. The defence may still stand even if it later turns out that the employee was not entitled to work.[47] The employer may either check and copy one document from a 'top tier'[48] list, or two documents from a 'second tier'[49] list.

7.55

(i) Top Tier

The documents include:

7.56

- A passport which describes the holder as a British Citizen or as a citizen of the UK and Colonies having a right of abode in the UK.
- A passport which contains a Certificate of Entitlement issued by or on behalf of the UK Government certifying that the holder has a right of abode in the UK.
- A European Economic Area passport or an identity card which describes the holder as a national of a Member State of the European Economic Area.

---

[46] Asylum and Immigration Act 1999, s 8(4).
[47] Asylum and Immigration Act 1999, s 8(2)(a)—'. . . which appeared to him . . .'.
[48] The Immigration (Restrictions on Employment) Order 2004, art 4(2)(a).
[49] The Immigration (Restrictions on Employment) Order 2004, art 4(2)(b).

- A registration certificate or document certifying permanent residence.
- A residence card or permanent residence card.
- A passport or other travel document which is endorsed to show that the holder is exempt from immigration control, has indefinite leave to enter, or remain in, the UK.
- A passport or other travel document that is endorsed to show the holder has current leave to enter or remain in the UK and is permitted to take up the employment in question provided it does not require the issue of a work permit.
- A registration card which indicates the holder is entitled to work in the UK.[50]

(ii) Second Tier

7.57 The employer should check[51] a P45 or similar official document which contains the employee's National Insurance number and one of a list of other documents, including:

- a UK birth certificate, which specifies the names of the holder's parents;
- a birth certificate issued in the Channel Islands, the Isle of Man or Ireland;
- a certificate of registration or naturalisation as a British Citizen.

7.58 Alternatively, an employer can check that the individual has a work permit issued by Work Permits UK and either:

- a passport or other travel document showing leave to enter or remain in the UK, and entitlement to the work permit; or
- a letter from the Home Office, confirming this.

7.59 The Order gives employers more responsibility to check photos and dates of birth given in documents produced to them. So, if a prospective employee produces two documents from the second tier where the names are different, for example, because of marriage, the employer must check a third document that explains the difference.

7.60 Further information can be obtained from the Border and Immigration Agency Employers' Helpline on 0845 010 6677 or on the linked website <www.employingmigrantworkers.org.uk/index.html>.

---

[50] The Immigration (Restrictions on Employment) Order 2004, Schedule 1, Part 1.
[51] The Immigration (Restrictions on Employment) Order 2004, Schedule 1, Part 2.

Nationals from the following EEA countries may come to work freely in the UK:

Austria, Belgium, Cyprus, Denmark, Finland, France, Germany, Greece, Iceland, Ireland, Italy, Liechtenstein, Lithuania, Malta, Netherlands, Norway, Portugal, Spain and Sweden

Since 1 June 2002, nationals of Switzerland have had the same rights as EEA/EU citizens.

Nationals from the following EEA countries, often referred to as 'Accession States' or A8 countries, may come to work in the UK, but are required to register with the Home Office under the 'Worker Registration Scheme' (WRS) if they start work after 1 May 2004, unless they are exempt from the requirements of the WRS:

Czech Republic, Estonia, Hungary, Latvia, Lithuania, Poland, Slovakia and Slovenia

Once such an individual has been working legally in the UK for 12 months without a break he or she will have full rights of free movement, will no longer need to register on the WRS and can then get a residence permit confirming the right to live and work in the UK.

Nationals of Bulgaria and Romania must have authorisation to work in the UK during the 'accession period' (1 January 2007 to 31 December 2011). Although those countries joined the EU on 1 January 2007 the UK Government responded to media pressure about the number of Polish workers who had entered the UK following Poland's accession to the EU and the likely number of Bulgarian and Romanian nationals who might migrate. The Accession Treaty for Bulgaria and Romania (signed in Luxembourg on 25th April 2005) provides that existing Member States can, as a derogation from the usual position under European Community law, regulate access to their labour markets by Bulgarian and Romanian nationals. The restrictions on access to the UK labour market in the Accession (Immigration and Worker Authorisation) Regulations 2006 were imposed on the basis of that derogation.

(iii) Avoiding Race Discrimination in this Process

7.61 Section 8A(1) of the Asylum and Immigration Act 1996[52] requires the Secretary of State to issue a Code of Practice dealing with the measures employers are expected to take to ensure that whilst they do not commit an offence by employing an illegal worker they also avoid unlawful discrimination. This led to the Code of Practice: For all Employers on the Avoidance of Race Discrimination in Recruitment Practice While Seeking to Prevent Illegal Working (2001). Whilst the Code does not impose legal obligations it re-emphasises an employer's statutory duty to avoid race discrimination in recruitment and a failure to observe the Code is admissible evidence before an Employment Tribunal in a race discrimination claim. The main points covered in the Code are:

- a reminder that the UK is ethnically diverse. Most people from ethnic minorities are British citizens and most non-British citizens from ethnic minorities are entitled to work in the UK;

- assumptions about a person's right to work should not be made on the basis of their colour, race, nationality or ethnic or national origins or the length of time they have been in the UK;

- to avoid prosecution under the Asylum and Immigration Act 1996 the employer merely needs to check and copy the relevant document(s) before the employment begins. That document can be requested at a stage in the recruitment process that best suits the employer, for example, from everyone who attends the first interview, everyone who attends the second interview or just from the successful candidate. The only guiding principle is that the employer should request the relevant document(s) from all applicants being considered at the stage chosen; and

- each of the documents on the relevant lists is of equal status so an employer should not show preference for one type of document over another.

7.62 The CRE Code 2005, paragraph 4.13(c) suggests that the eligibility to work information which employers are required to obtain under the Asylum and Immigration Act 1996, should preferably be verified in the final stages of the selection process, to make sure the appointment is based on merit alone.

(iv) Future Developments

7.63 There is a recognition within Government that the current system for checking eligibility to work in the UK is too complicated for many employers to

---

[52] Repealed by the Immigration, Asylum and Nationality Act 2006 from a day to be appointed.

understand and in need of reform. In tackling this issue, it is hard not to see the influence of the media and a response to the not insignificant rise in the popular appeal of the British National Party in the rhetoric of the Government. The issue of illegal working has been conflated with terrorism, people trafficking and a basic exploitation of the British system. For example, in his foreword to the Home Office 'Strategy to Ensure and Enforce Compliance with Immigration Laws' (March 2007), Home Secretary, John Reid MP, stated:

> . . . the fact that many immigrants, at the end of their journey, end up in shadowy jobs in the grey economy undermines the terms and working conditions of British workers. That's not fair. It chips away at the social contract and fabric of our country. Resentment of it breeds discontent and racism. This is especially keenly felt among those who believe they are not getting the economic or social opportunities they should because others, who have flouted the rules and often the law, seem to be getting on ahead of them. That's not fair either. The public want people to play by the rules, and they don't like people who don't. Media stories about illegal immigrants getting access to housing, legal aid or NHS care may be exaggerated, but they do reflect an underlying concern that in the past we have not been tough enough in enforcing the rules.

7.64   The Immigration, Asylum and Nationality Act 2006 will repeal sections 8 and 8A of the Asylum and Immigration Act 1996 from a day to be determined. The 2006 Act:

- creates a power for the Secretary of State to apply a civil penalty, determined by a Code of Practice, to an employer of an adult subject to immigration control who has not been granted leave to enter or remain, whose leave is invalid, has ceased to have effect (whether by reason of curtailment, revocation, cancellation, passage of time or otherwise) or whose conditions of entry or stay prevent them from undertaking the employment. The provisions allow for objection and/or appeal by the employer against the imposition of a penalty and the amount. An employer who complies with requirements prescribed in an order of the Secretary of State is excused from paying a penalty;

- creates a new criminal offence of knowingly employing an adult who has not been granted leave to enter or remain, whose leave is invalid, has ceased to have effect (whether by reason of curtailment, revocation, cancellation, passage of time or otherwise) or whose conditions of entry or stay prevent them from undertaking the employment in question; and

- allows the Secretary of State to issue a code of practice to employers on how to avoid unlawful racial discrimination when applying these provisions.

7.65   The Border and Immigration Agency consulted on measures designed to prevent illegal working between May and August 2007. Under proposed regulations which were provided for by the Immigration, Nationality and Asylum Act 2006, an employer who employs illegal migrant workers as a result of negligent employment or recruitment practices will face civil penalties, while an employer who knowingly employs illegal migrant workers will commit a criminal offence punishable by up to two years' imprisonment.

(b) Medical Checks

7.66 The practice of requiring potential employees to undergo a medical check, or 'health screening', is less prevalent than it used to be since the introduction of the DDA. The DDA does not in itself prevent an employer from requiring employees to undergo a medical examination. However, requiring only disabled applicants to undergo an examination is likely to be discriminatory, as is refusing a candidate employment because of a negative medical report without first considering reasonable adjustments.

7.67 The DRC recommend[53] that any health screening takes place after the employer has gone through the selection process and decided who is the best person for the job (with or without reasonable adjustments). Waiting until you have identified a preferred candidate makes it far less likely, according to the DRC, that a decision on an individual's capability will be influenced by reasons related to disability without consideration of reasonable adjustments.

(c) References

7.68 A further consideration at this stage of the process will be the obtaining of satisfactory references in relation to a prospective employee. The law in this area, not least the common law requirements with regard to references, and the potential link between references and victimisation, has led to employers being increasingly cautious in the giving of references as we explain further in Chapter 13 when considering issues surrounding the ending of employment generally.

7.69 As far as the requesting of references is concerned, the CRE Code 2005[54] took a cautious approach, recommending that employers should avoid making them part of the selection process because of the risk that they might contain subjective judgements about a candidate. According to the CRE, the selection decision should be made first, on the basis of the application form, job description, person specification and any selection tests and interviews, before any reference is circulated to the selection panel.

7.70 The CRE Code 2005[55] also suggested that rather than asking for general

---

[53] DRC Practical Guide, para 3.15.   [54] Paragraph 4.34.   [55] Paragraph 4.35.

character references, the recruiting employer should send to the former employer copies of the job description and person specification and request evidence on his or her suitability for the specific requirements of the particular job.

H. Ethical Recruitment

A final pre-recruitment consideration is whether there are any ethical issues   **7.71** involved in the employer's recruitment policy. Within some sectors, principally so far within the health sector, there have been concerns for a number of years about ethical recruitment of candidates from the developing world. As John Hutton, Minister of State for Health, put it in the foreword to the revised Code of Practice for the international recruitment of healthcare professionals:

> The international mobility of healthcare professionals is a well established practice that has been going on for many years. More recent times have seen an increasingly large-scale, targeted international recruitment approach by many developed countries to address domestic shortages . . . concerns related to the impact this may have upon the healthcare systems of developing countries . . . need to be addressed.[56]

CNN reported that: **7.72**

> The British nursing register shows the number of nurses being certified from Botswana, Ghana, Malawi, Nigeria, Kenya, South Africa, Zambia and Zimbabwe —all former British colonies—has soared since 1999. As a result, more than 60 per cent of nursing positions remain unfilled in countries such as Ghana and Malawi.[57]

The three countries supplying the largest number of overseas nurses to the UK are the Philippines, India and South Africa. There is evidence that poorer countries, such as Malawi, are being denuded of their nursing workforce by UK and other Western recruitment.[58]

The Code of Practice for the international recruitment of healthcare profes-   **7.73** sionals is not mandatory but has been strengthened in its revised form and now includes as a best practice benchmark that 'no active recruitment will be undertaken in developing countries by UK commercial recruitment agencies, or by any overseas agency sub-contracted to that agency, or any healthcare organisation unless there exists a government-to-government agreement that healthcare professionals from that country may be targeted for employment'. Up-to-date

---

[56] Published 8 December 2004 by the Department of Health.
[57] <www.cnn.com/2004/WORLD/africa/08/03/nurses.uk/index.html>, 3 August 2004.
[58] *Migrant Watch UK, Briefing Paper 5.4: Health 1* (November 2004).

information concerning countries where active recruitment is not supported can be found on the Department of Health website.[59]

7.74 It is possible that ethical issues will become more relevant to recruitment in other sectors. For example, the head of the African Airlines Association, Christian Folly-Kossi alluded to the 'brain drain' of Africa's aviation experts in the aftermath of a Kenya Airways Boeing 737 crash in Cameroon with the loss of 114 lives in May 2007.[60]

7.75 Employment related ethical considerations may also inform purchasing decisions from suppliers based overseas where child labour, minimum wage, equality and health and safety issues may all be relevant. The extent to which organisations can use procurement to influence supplier performance in relation to equality and diversity is dealt with in Chapter 5.

I. Promotion

7.76 Much of what we have written above in relation to recruitment applies equally to promotion. A promotion is simply a way of filling a vacancy with an internal candidate. Again the Codes produced by the former Commissions provide helpful guidance on how an employer should approach promotion. What follows is a composite of that guidance:

- The same selection criteria and procedures should be used for external and internal candidates.
- Rumours or unsubstantiated opinions, particularly of internal candidates should not be taken into account.
- No assumptions should be made about the eligibility of staff based on their current grade, to do so could lead to indirect discrimination.
- Information about all promotion and other development opportunities such as deputising or secondments should be published to all staff.
- Employers should avoid bypassing their recruitment procedures. If an exception genuinely must be made to fill a post quickly, do so on a temporary basis.

7.77 The criteria upon which promotion decisions are based should be tested to ensure they are lawful. For example, where access to training or promotion opportunities is based on length of service there could be indirect discrimination issues on the grounds of age and also gender (where more women than

---

[59] <www.dh.gov.uk>.
[60] <news.bbc.co.uk/2/hi/africa/6646217.stm>, 11 May 2007.

men might have shorter service as a result of taking time away from work to care for children or other dependants).

In *Pratt v Walsall Health Authority*[61] a black charge nurse claimed both direct **7.78** and indirect discrimination when rejected without interview for the post of Senior Nurse Manager. Both claims succeeded. The claim of indirect discrimination was based on the contention that one of the criteria for shortlisting, namely to show evidence of a rapid and vigorous promotion through the ranks, was unjustifiably discriminatory because black applicants had greater difficulties achieving such progress due to the very effects of discrimination.

J. Monitoring

In order for an employer to identify areas of concern where certain groups are **7.79** failing to secure employment or promotion, or for the employer to satisfy itself that its equality and diversity policies are working, it is necessary to monitor each stage of the process. For private sector employers, monitoring is not mandatory. Within the public sector, certain public authorities are covered by the 'specific duty' to monitor certain aspects of employment including monitoring the number of applicants for employment and promotion by reference to the racial groups to which they belong. Monitoring is covered in more detail in Chapter 4.

---

[61] ET Case No 36145/86, ET.

Recruitment and Promotion: In Brief

- An employer that wishes to promote equality and diversity will want to ensure that it attracts a wide pool of candidates for job vacancies and treats them fairly in the recruitment process.

- When advertising a vacancy an employer should take care to ensure that the advert does not demonstrate an intention to discriminate but instead encourages as many candidates as possible to put themselves forward. Best practice suggests that all adverts should contain an 'equality statement' that the employer welcomes applications from all.

- Selection of candidates is best done by more than one trained person marking separately against agreed criteria and then meeting to discuss scores.

- For practical rather than legal reasons an offer of employment should be made as soon as possible after the selection decision has been made to maximise the employer's chances of securing the successful candidate's services. The offer can be made conditional upon obtaining certain things such as confirmation of the right to work in the UK, a medical examination and satisfactory references.

- Employers will commit a criminal offence if they employ someone who cannot legally work in the UK, but can protect themselves against prosecution by checking and photocopying certain documents produced by the employee before s/he starts work.

- Recruiting from the developing world, particularly in the health sector, may create ethical issues that are covered by a Department of Health Code of Practice.

- Much of the above applies equally to promotion as it does to recruitment. A promotion is merely filling a vacancy with an internal candidate.

APPENDIX 7.1

Recruitment Checklist

Pre-recruitment

- Should positive action be considered to target unrepresented groups
- Is the job covered by a GOQ or GOR
- Are there any ethical considerations

Planning

- Draw up a job description
- Draw up a person specification
- Ensure application form has a tear-off monitoring section

Advertising

- Draft job advert to include a suitable equality statement
- Ensure job advert does not give the impression of an intention to discriminate
- Place advert where it is likely to be read by as wide a group of people as possible

↓

Selection

- Ensure more than one person is involved at each stage of the selection process
- Ensure selectors trained in equality and diversity
- Agree marking system in advance and stick to it
- Mark separately—compare scores later
- Any tests should correspond to the job in question
- Take care where proficiency in English might affect test results
- All candidates should take the same test
- When inviting candidate to interview ask about reasonable adjustments
- When inviting candidate to interview ask about relevant religion or belief issues
- Keep interview questions relevant to the job description and person specification
- Do not make stereotypical assumptions

Offer

- Make offer quickly but subject to conditions precedent
- Provide feedback to unsuccessful candidates

Checking

- Check right to work—taking into account relevant Code of Practice
- Medical checks where relevant and not just because a candidate has a disability
- Take up references once selection made

↓

General considerations

- Consider reasonable adjustments for disabled applicants at each stage
- Keep records for at least 12 months
- Monitor the process and adjust if necessary

8

FAMILY-FRIENDLY AND FLEXIBLE WORKING

Many employers have told us why they offer policies to support working parents. The reason is simple: they want to recruit and retain the best people. Far from damaging productivity, supporting working parents has a positive impact on these businesses. [For example] HSBC bank has trebled the number of women returning to work after maternity leave, saving millions on recruitment costs . . . [and] . . . [p]roductivity [at the RAC] has increased by 8 per cent since introducing a policy to allow staff to work their annual hours flexibly. . . .

(EOC[1])

A. Introduction

The promotion of 'family-friendly' initiatives within the workplace has been **8.01** a key plank of 'New Labour' policy. Since coming into power in 1997 the Government has deployed a range of education and awareness-raising campaigns designed to secure a better work-life balance for those with family responsibilities.

An essential part of that policy package has been the development of a complex **8.02** legislative framework which provides extensive and enforceable rights for parents and carers. This legal framework is intended not only to improve the 'real life' lot of those who seek to balance competing responsibilities at home and work—still primarily women—but also to provide them with substantive equality in the workplace. One key initiative has been the right to request flexible working, a right which, while legally limited to parents and carers is increasingly being used by other employees who wish to achieve a better balance between their working lives and their other interests and commitments.

---

[1] *Why Business Needs Working Parents*, <www.eoc.org.uk>.

8.03 Aside from the need for compliance with this legal framework, there is a clear business case for developing a workplace which is truly family-friendly, and flexible, for all employees. An employer who creates such a workplace should benefit from:

- improved staff health, morale and well-being;
- a constantly developing and more productive workforce;
- improved talent, skills and knowledge retention;
- a saving of the costs of replacing and retraining new employees—the costs of which are estimated at £4,000 per leaver;[2] and
- a reduction in the risk of legal claims, including those of sex discrimin-ation—defending such a claim costs an average of £5,000 in legal costs and 13 days in management time.[3]

On a more general societal level, the country simply needs to look after parents and carers at work because the economy needs them.[4]

8.04 Yet many employers still struggle to implement this framework and get the balance right: in 2004, the EOC reported that its helpline received more calls from women facing problems at work because of their pregnancy than on any other subject.[5] Moreover, recent EOC research indicates that around half of the 440,000 women pregnant each year still suffer some form of disadvantage at work on grounds of their pregnancy or maternity leave, or following requests for flexible working upon their return to work; that more than 30,000 women are forced out of their jobs and left without work; and that 23 per cent of mothers who returned to work experienced problems. These difficulties seem to occur because of a lack of knowledge and understanding of maternity rights, a lack of dialogue and planning, a concern about costs and negative attitudes towards pregnancy and maternity.[6]

8.05 In this chapter we guide employers through this legal framework, with a par-ticular focus on the positive steps employers can take not only to avoid unlaw-ful discrimination in the workplace but also to promote family-friendliness, flexibility and fairness for all.

---

[2] *Pregnant and Productive* (EOC, February 2004), p 2.

[3] *Greater Expectations: Final Report of the EOC's Investigation into Discrimination against New and Expectant Mothers in the Workplace* (EOC, June 2005), p 76.

[4] See, for example, *Why Business Needs Working Parents*, <www.eoc.org.uk> and *Britain's Hidden Brain Drain: The EOC's Investigation into Flexible and Part-time Working* (EOC, Septem-ber 2005).

[5] *Pregnant and Productive* (EOC, February 2004), p 1.

[6] *Greater Expectations: Final Report of the EOC's Investigation into Discrimination against New and Expectant Mothers in the Workplace* (EOC, June 2005), pp 5, 9 and 31–45.

B. The Legal Framework: An Overview

The law relating to pregnancy, maternity and family issues is derived from a **8.06** range of domestic and European law sources.

(a) The Sex Discrimination Act 1975

The SDA prohibits direct discrimination, indirect discrimination,[7] victimisa- **8.07** tion[8] and harassment[9] of employees, applicants for employment, contract workers and other groups of working women on grounds of their sex. The SDA prohibits such discrimination with regard to non-contractual terms such as recruitment, promotion, access to benefits (including discretionary bonuses), transfers, training, dismissal and any other detriment.

Discriminatory treatment of a woman in these areas on grounds of her preg- **8.08** nancy or maternity leave is, by definition, sex discrimination. However, a unique feature of this kind of discrimination is, as we noted in Chapter 2, that according to European law no comparator is needed: rather, a simple 'but for' test is applied: 'but for' her pregnancy or maternity leave, would the employee have been treated in this way?[10] This approach means that discrimination on grounds of pregnancy or maternity leave is often referred to as 'automatic' sex discrimination. In reality, this makes for a very wide protection from discrimination for women in these circumstances.

However, the key to understanding, and communicating to other employees, **8.09** why pregnancy and maternity leave issues are treated in this way is also in European law: the ECJ recognises that it is only by providing additional protection to pregnant women, and thereby by removing the disadvantages they would otherwise suffer by pregnancy or maternity leave, that substantive equality in the workplace can be achieved. As the EAT explained in *Fletcher v Blackpool Fylde and Wyre Hospitals NHS Trust*:

> Discrimination in EU law, when considered in the context of sex equality, is defined as meaning either that different rules are applied to men and women in comparable situations, or that the same rule is applied to men and women who are in different situations. . . . As applied in pregnancy and maternity cases, the second limb of this definition means that treating pregnant workers or women on maternity leave in the same way as other employees during the 'protected period' (that is the start of pregnancy through to the end of maternity leave), in circumstances in which they are disadvantaged because of their pregnancy or maternity, is applying the same treatment to different situations

---

[7] SDA, s 1(2).   [8] SDA, s 4.   [9] SDA, s 4A.

[10] For a recent domestic re-statement of the principle, see *Fletcher v Blackpool Fylde and Wyre Hospitals NHS Trust* [2005] IRLR 689, EAT.

and is therefore discrimination. In this way, the law aims to ensure substantive equality for working women, who would otherwise be disadvantaged by their pregnancy.[11]

For this reason the ECJ tends to refer to 'unfavourable' treatment rather than 'less favourable' treatment, stressing that no comparison is necessary.

8.10 The protection from discrimination on grounds of pregnancy or maternity leave applies irrespective of the employee's length of service, hours worked or the extent of her pregnancy, or the size of the employer. Moreover, whether the woman is a permanent or fixed-term employee is also irrelevant. In *Tele Danmark A/S v Handels-og Kontorfunktionaerernes Forbund I Danmark (HK) acting on behalf of Brandt-Nielsen,*[12] for example, the fixed-term contract of a pregnant woman was terminated when she told her employer that she was pregnant. The ECJ held that such a dismissal constituted sex discrimination if it was on ground of pregnancy, notwithstanding that the woman was recruited for a fixed-term period, failed to inform the employer that she was pregnant even though she was aware of this when she was employed, and because of her pregnancy was unable to work during a substantial part of the term of the contract.

8.11 Moreover, the protections apply even if the employer's motive for its treatment of the pregnant employee is benign and perhaps based on a genuine, if but misconceived, view of her welfare needs. This reflects the general principle that the intention of an employer is irrelevant when the Tribunal is deciding whether or not the employer has engaged in unlawful discrimination.[13] This principle was particularly illustrated in the context of pregnancy in *O'Neill v Governors of St Thomas More RCVA Upper School,*[14] where the claimant, an unmarried pregnant teacher working in a Catholic school was dismissed when the school discovered that the father of her child was a Catholic priest. The EAT held that the relevant principles in determining whether treatment is directly discriminatory on the ground of sex do not rely on assessing the subjective mental processes of the employer (namely their intentions, motives, beliefs or subjective purposes): rather, the relevant question is generally 'would the employee have received the same treatment but for her sex?'.[15]

8.12 In order to be causative, pregnancy need not be the only or even main cause of the matter complained of, if it is an 'effective' cause.[16] In the *O'Neill* case, the

---

[11] [2005] IRLR 689, EAT, at para 64.   [12] [2001] IRLR 853, ECJ.
[13] eg *Coleman v Skyrail Oceanic Ltd* [1981] IRLR 398, CA.   [14] [1997] ICR 33, EAT.
[15] *James v Eastleigh Borough Council* [1990] IRLR 288, HL.
[16] *Owen and Briggs v James* [1982] ICR 618, CA; *Nagarajan v London Regional Transport* [2000] 1 AC 501, HL.

EAT concluded that the other factors in the circumstances surrounding the pregnancy relied on by the employers as the 'dominant motive'—namely the paternity of the child, the publicity of that fact and the consequential untenability of the claimant's position as a religious education teacher—were all causally related to her pregnancy, so that it was not possible to say that the ground for her dismissal was anything other than her pregnancy.

The employee is particularly protected from the time the employer is aware that **8.13** she is pregnant until the end of her maternity leave. However, the ECJ held in *Brown v Rentokil*[17] that it is automatic sex discrimination to treat a woman less favourably by taking into account her pregnancy or maternity leave at any time. Further, these protections are not dependent on whether the woman's presence at work during maternity is essential to the proper functioning of the undertaking in which she is employed; and it is no defence to pregnancy-related discrimination that the employer who appointed a pregnant woman would suffer financially for the duration of the pregnancy.[18]

With effect from 1 October 2005, a new section 3A was inserted into the SDA **8.14** to incorporate a specific prohibition of direct discrimination grounds of pregnancy[19] or maternity leave,[20] including the prohibition of less favourable treatment on grounds of pregnancy-related illness.[21] The specific protections in the new section 3A(1)(a) apply for the 'protected period' which begins when the woman becomes pregnant, and ends at the end of her period of Ordinary Maternity Leave ('OML') or Additional Maternity Leave ('AML'), when she returns to work, or two weeks after the end of her pregnancy (for those who, because of their employment status, are not entitled to OML or AML).[22] The specific protections in the new section 3A(1)(b) are not so limited and protect an employee from any less favourable treatment on the ground that she is on maternity leave, about to go on maternity leave, because she has been on maternity leave or because she has sought to exercise her rights in this regard. She would therefore be protected where, for example, her post has changed to her detriment during her absence because a locum or other employee has taken over some of her work, or she was given a different job on her return, to her detriment, because of her absence on maternity leave.

Again it is clear that no comparison with an actual male employee is needed in **8.15** order to make out discrimination: rather, under section 3A(2), the comparison is specified as being between the pregnant woman and the same woman had she not become pregnant. However, in *R (Equal Opportunities Commission) v*

---

[17] [1998] IRLR 445, ECJ.
[18] *Webb v EMO Air Cargo (UK) Ltd* [1994] IRLR 482, ECJ.   [19] SDA, s 3A(1)(a).
[20] SDA, s 3A(1)(b).   [21] SDA, s 3A(3)(b).   [22] SDA, s 3A(3)(a).

Secretary of State for Trade and Industry,[23] the Administrative Court held that section 3A should be recast so as to eliminate the statutory requirement for a comparator, and so the Government is considering whether the legislation in this regard needs to be amended.[24]

8.16 Although there is no specific provision prohibiting indirect discrimination, harassment or victimisation on the grounds of pregnancy or maternity leave, these sorts of discrimination will generally automatically constitute sex discrimination under sections 1(2)(b), 4 and 4A of the SDA. Employers also need to give particular consideration to whether a refusal to permit a female employee to work flexibly might constitute indirect sex discrimination—we consider this issue further towards the end of this chapter, when looking at flexible working generally.

(b) The Equal Pay Act 1970

8.17 The EqPA provides a woman with the right to equality in contractual terms, whether pay or other benefits. 'Pay' is widely defined for these purposes and includes salary and wages, overtime, redundancy pay, contractual and statutory sick pay, maternity pay, compensation for unfair dismissal, contractual bonus payments, and any other payments made directly or indirectly by the employer as a result of the employee's employment.

8.18 Accordingly a pregnant worker can make a claim under the EqPA if she receives lower pay or other contractual terms for a reason related to her pregnancy. In *Alabaster v Barclays Bank plc (No 2)*[25] the Court of Appeal held that in order to give effect to EC law, it was necessary to disapply the requirement in the EqPA to point to an actual male comparator. Therefore where a claim relating to pregnancy or maternity leave is made under the EqPA there is no need for the claimant to show that a male employee was paid more: it is sufficient for her to show that she was treated less favourably and that this was on grounds of pregnancy or maternity leave. However the EqPA does not require employers to pay women on maternity leave full pay.[26]

(c) Additional Provisions Relevant to Pregnancy, Maternity and Family-friendly Working

8.19 In summary:

---

[23] [2007] IRLR 327, QBD (Admin).
[24] DLR consultation paper, p 33, footnote 8.
[25] [2005] IRLR 576, CA.
[26] *Gillespie v Northern Ireland Health and Social Services Board* [1996] IRLR 214, ECJ—see further below.

- The Management of Health and Safety at Work Regulations 1999[27] (the 'MHSWR') and sections 66–70 of the Employment Rights Act 1996 (the 'ERA') make certain health and safety provisions for expectant and new mothers.

- The ERA, the Maternity and Parental Leave etc Regulations 1999[28] (the 'MPLR') and the Paternity and Adoption Leave Regulations 2002[29] (the 'PALR'), all in their variously amended forms, set out the regime of statutory maternity and parental rights for employees, provide for the right to request flexible working, and protect employees from detriment or dismissal for seeking to exercise these rights.

- The Part-time Workers (Prevention of Less Favourable Treatment) Regulations 2000[30] prohibit the less favourable treatment of those who work part-time.

- The Work and Families Act 2006 makes changes to the maternity and adoption leave regime and extends the right to request flexible working to those who care for certain adults in need of care.

In addition: 8.20

- European law—principally the Equal Pay Directive,[31] the Pregnant Workers Directive,[32] the Equal Treatment Directive,[33] the Parental Leave Directive,[34] the Burden of Proof Directive[35] and the Part-Time Workers Directive[36]— may provide greater rights than domestic law.

- Ordinary domestic law employment rights, such as the right to protection from unfair dismissal under the ERA and minimum holiday requirements under the Working Time Regulations 1998,[37] must also be borne in mind. In particular, a dismissal related to pregnancy, maternity or flexible working may well be automatically unfair under the ERA, sections 99, 104 and 104C.

- An employee's contract of employment may make more generous provision in this area than the statutory requirements (such as in relation to pay while on maternity leave, or the length of leave) and if so, this takes precedence over the statutory rights.

---

[27] SI 1999/3242.   [28] SI 1999/3312.   [29] SI 2002/2788.   [30] SI 2000/1551.
[31] Council Directive 75/117/EEC.   [32] Council Directive 92/85/EEC.
[33] Council Directive 76/207/EEC as amended by Council Directive 2002/73/EC.
[34] Council Directive 96/34/EC.   [35] Council Directive 97/80/EC.
[36] Council Directive 97/81/EC as amended by Council Directive 98/23/EC.
[37] SI 1998/1833.

C. Managing Pregnancy and Maternity in the Workplace

(a) Before any Employee Announces a Pregnancy

8.21 As with all the issues we consider in this book, employers should have in place a dedicated policy addressing pregnancy and maternity issues within their workplace. This should mean that the pregnant employee (whether or not she chooses to inform her employer of her pregnancy immediately) and her manager will know from the outset how her pregnancy is likely to be managed in the workplace, and reduce the risk of difficulties arising later on.

8.22 Similarly, proactive training of supervisors in how to manage pregnant employees fairly and effectively is likely to reap benefits once an employee does announce her pregnancy.

8.23 There is a need to carry out a general workplace risk assessment even if the employer is unaware of any pregnant women working there (which we consider further below).

(b) Knowledge or Suspicion that an Employee is Pregnant

8.24 As a general proposition, there will be no discrimination on grounds of pregnancy if the employer is unaware of the woman's pregnancy. This will be a question of fact and normally satisfied by the provision of a sick note that refers to the woman's pregnancy, potentially even where the sick note only refers to a pregnancy-related illness in Latin![38]

8.25 In *Del Monte Foods Ltd v Mundon*,[39] the employee was dismissed for continued absence caused by gastro-enteritis. The day after the dismissal the company discovered that she was pregnant. The EAT held that the dismissal was not automatically unfair because the employers were unaware that the absence was connected to her pregnancy. In *Ramdoolar v Bycity Ltd*,[40] the EAT reiterated the principle established in the *Mundon* case and stressed that an employer was not obliged to undertake enquiries about whether a woman was pregnant, as this itself may be regarded as a detriment.

8.26 However, it was also established in the *Ramdoolar* case that an employer can discriminate against a pregnant woman if the employer merely *suspects* that she is pregnant, without having actual knowledge or belief that she is. The EAT said at paragraph 24 of its judgment that:

---

[38] *Day v T Pickles Farms Ltd* [1999] IRLR 217, EAT, where the sick note referred to 'hyperemesis gravidarum', and the ET concluded that the use of the word 'gravidarum' showed that the condition could only have related to pregnancy, as *Black's Medical Dictionary* made 'quite plain'.
[39] [1980] IRLR 224, EAT.   [40] EAT 0236/04/DM, 2004.

It is conceivable that circumstances might arise in which an employer, detecting the symptoms of pregnancy and fearing the consequences, if the employee is in fact pregnant, but neither knowing nor believing that she is, simply suspecting that she might, dismisses her before his suspicion can be proved right. In such circumstances it may well be that a dismissal would be automatically unfair.

It would also be unlawful to make decisions about a woman's employment **8.27** because the employer *feared* she might become pregnant.

Some of the provisions discussed below—such as the duty to alter a woman's **8.28** working conditions or hours of work, and if this is not possible, to suspend her on full pay, only apply where the employee has notified the employer in writing of her pregnancy or the fact that she has given birth within the last six months, or is breastfeeding.[41]

Recent EOC research indicates that, in fact, the majority (64 per cent) of **8.29** women notify their employer of their pregnancy before the 12-week stage. A third of women do so between 12 and 20 weeks, although two per cent leave it until after 21 weeks.[42]

(c) Once the Employer is Aware that an Employee is Pregnant

There is no statutory obligation on employers to inform employees of their **8.30** rights once they announce they are pregnant. However, in some cases[43] employers have been unable to insist on strict compliance with the law, or have been otherwise criticised by Tribunals, when they have not given their employees guidance on their maternity rights. It is clearly good practice to do so, and it is helpful for employers to produce specific guidance for newly pregnant employees on their rights and responsibilities during pregnancy and maternity. The DTI (now BERR) has produced helpful guides for both employers and employees along these lines.[44]

A key first response to the news of a pregnancy will be the need to carry out an **8.31** employee-specific risk assessment, to ensure that the pregnant employee only does that work which it is safe for her to do. We consider this step further below.

It is also important that once an employer is on notice of an employee's **8.32**

---

[41] MHSWR, reg 18(1).

[42] *Greater Expectations: Final Report of the EOC's Investigation into Discrimination against New and Expectant Mothers in the Workplace* (EOC, June 2005), p 52.

[43] eg *Gray v Smith* [1996] DCLD 30, ET and *Thurisamy v Alma Enterprises Ltd* ET Case No 27627/04, ET.

[44] *Pregnancy and Work: What You Need to Know as an Employer* (DTI, June 2007), <www.dti.gov.uk/files/file34286.pdf>; *Pregnancy and Work: What You Need to Know as an Employee* (DTI, June 2007), <www.dti.gov.uk/files/file34285.pdf>.

pregnancy, negative stereotypical assumptions about women or pregnant workers are avoided. Employers should not, for example, assume or communicate the view that women with young children will no longer be committed to work, that their priorities will change, that they will no longer be able to cope with the demands of their job, that they will want to be given less responsible work, or that they will find that it is not possible to combine a career with childcare. The news of a pregnancy can be an exciting but nerve-wracking time for many women, and so a supportive approach from their employer is particularly important.

8.33 Employers should also consider whether any recently raised issues over the employee may need to be re-assessed in light of her pregnancy. For example, if an employer, while unaware of the pregnancy, has raised issues about the employee's attendance or performance, once the employer is aware that she is pregnant, it may well be contrary to the SDA to continue to treat her less favourably if the attendance or performance issues appear related to her pregnancy or the consequences of it.

8.34 On a practical level, all pregnant women are entitled to reasonable paid time off to attend antenatal care.[45] This can include non-medical care such as parent-craft or relaxation classes. Reasonable allowance should also be made for travelling and waiting time.[46] There is no obligation on the woman to arrange antenatal care outside working hours or to make up the time,[47] and the woman should be paid as though she was still at work.[48] A woman can complain to the Tribunal if she is unreasonably refused time off for antenatal appointments,[49] or has not been paid for any such time off.[50] Any detriment to a woman for taking such time off is likely to be contrary to the SDA and the MPLR, reg 19, as is a dismissal on such grounds. It is also likely to be an automatically unfair dismissal under the ERA, sections 99, 104 or 104C, and potentially also a constructive dismissal if the woman has resigned over the issue.

8.35 Employers will also wish to consider what other arrangements could be made in their workplace to improve the health and well-being of their pregnant employees. If the workplace has a health facility, what can be done to make their services more available to pregnant women? If there is an affiliated gymn or leisure facility, could they offer special classes for pregnant women? In a large workforce, might the employer organise a 'bump club', where all pregnant women get together for lunch once a week?[51]

---

[45] ERA, ss 55–57.   [46] *Dhamrait v United Biscuits Ltd*, ET Case No 10128/83, ET.
[47] *Sajil v Carraro t/a Foubert's Bar*, COIT 1890/34, ET.   [48] ERA, s 56.
[49] ERA, s 57(1)(a).   [50] ERA, s 57(1)(b).
[51] This initiative received positive feedback in *Greater Expectations: Final Report of the EOC's Investigation into Discrimination against New and Expectant Mothers in the Workplace* (EOC, June 2005), p 10.

Employers will also need to begin considering what arrangements will have to **8.36** be made for covering the maternity leave absence. Options may include: recruiting a temporary employee, temporarily promoting an existing employee and recruiting temporary cover for a more junior position, splitting the work up between other staff and/or postponing project work until the employee returns from maternity leave.

(d) Risk Assessments and Suitable Work for Pregnant Women

(i) The Employer's Duties

Employers have duties to protect the health and safety of pregnant women and **8.37** new and breastfeeding mothers derived from the general common law duty of care and the statutory duty under the Health and Safety At Work etc Act 1974. These require that employers provide employees, and others who may be affected by how the workplace is run (such as agency workers), with safe systems of work, a safe place of work, safe plant and equipment and a safe working environment.

The Workplace (Health, Safety and Welfare) Regulations 1992[52] require that **8.38** the employer should provide suitable rest facilities for pregnant women and nursing mothers. These facilities might include a bed or sofa of an appropriate size on which a pregnant or nursing woman can rest, in a quiet area or separate room set aside for this purpose.

A central part of the employer's responsibilities in this area is the obligation to **8.39** carry out appropriate risk assessments under the MHSWR. The Health and Safety Executive has a range of publications which should assist employers in this task, including *New and Expectant Mothers at Work—A Guide for Employers* and *Infection Risks to New and Expectant Mothers in the Workplace—A Guide for Employers.*[53]

(ii) The General Risk Assessment

The first, general, risk assessment must be carried out where there are women of **8.40** childbearing age in the workplace and the work is of a kind which could involve risk, by reason of her condition, to a new or expectant mother or to her baby. A 'new or expectant mother' is an employee who is pregnant, who has given birth within the previous six months, or who is breastfeeding (even if this lasts for longer than six months).[54] In *Day v T Pickles Farms Ltd*[55] the EAT confirmed that the duty to have a risk assessment in place applies irrespective of

---

[52] SI 1992/3004.   [53] These are available from <www.hsebooks.com>.
[54] MHSWR, reg 3(1) and 16(1).   [55] [1999] IRLR 217, EAT.

whether there is actually a new or expectant mother working in the establishment. Mrs Day was a pregnant woman working as an assistant in a sandwich shop. She began to suffer from severe morning sickness which was aggravated by the smell of food cooking and having to handle food in the shop. No assessment had ever been carried out and the EAT held that one should have been in place at the start of Mrs Day's employment at the very latest, as this might have avoided the difficulties she had suffered.

8.41 The general risk assessment should identify all hazards which could pose a health and/or safety risk to new or expectant mothers. The risk could come from any processes, or working conditions, or physical, biological or chemical agents such as those set out in Annexes I and II to the Pregnant Workers Directive. Common risks for pregnant women identified by the Directive and the Health and Safety Executive include:

- Lifting or carrying heavy loads
- Standing or sitting for long periods of time
- Exposure to infectious diseases and lead
- Work-related stress
- Long working hours
- Working alone
- Working at heights
- Having to adopt awkward postures in spaces and workstations
- Cigarette smoke from other employees
- Vibration
- Excessive noise
- Radiation
- Chemical handling
- Extreme temperatures
- Excessive travelling

8.42 Employers should also bear in mind that risks can occur before as well as during pregnancy, and that a pregnant woman is most vulnerable to harm in the early stages of pregnancy when she may not know that she is pregnant. Where an employer has five or more employees, it must record the significant findings of the assessment and note any groups of employees who have been identified as especially at risk.[56] It must then take necessary steps to avoid the risks identified, which may include adapting the work of certain employees, especially as regards the design of workplaces, the choice of equipment and the choice of working and production methods, developing an overall prevention policy

---

[56] MHSWR, reg 3(6).

which covers technology, organisation of work, working conditions, social relationships etc, and giving appropriate instructions to employees.[57] The employer must provide its employees with comprehensible and relevant information on the risks identified and any protective or preventive measures taken.[58]

The general risk assessment should be reviewed whenever there is reason to **8.43** suspect that it is no longer valid or there is a significant change in the matters to which it relates.[59] It should also be reviewed once the employer is informed that a particular employee is pregnant.

(iii) The Specific Risk Assessment

A further, specific risk assessment must be carried out once the employer has **8.44** been informed that a particular employee is pregnant.[60] In practical terms, carrying out this risk assessment is likely to be one of the first things an employer will have to do on being notified of an employee's pregnancy.

Employers may find it helpful to provide pregnant women with a short, self- **8.45** completion questionnaire enabling them to start to identify hazards in their job. This should act as a catalyst to setting the risk assessment process in motion, and would encourage women to participate in the process.[61] Carrying out the risk assessment promptly and properly is also likely to give the employee confidence that her pregnancy will be treated fairly from the outset.

The specific risk assessment should consider any specific health and safety risks **8.46** the pregnant woman may suffer. The following are the consequences of an employee-specific risk assessment:

- if the assessment reveals a risk, the employer must consider whether preventive or protective action can be taken so as to avoid the risk, and if so take that action;

- if the risk cannot be prevented or avoided, the employer must, if it is reasonable to do so, and would avoid such risk, alter the woman's working conditions or hours of work to avoid the risk;[62]

- if no such alteration of her conditions or hours of work is possible, the employer must offer the pregnant woman or new mother alternative work, which is suitable and appropriate for her to do in the circumstances, and

---

[57] MHSWR, reg 4 and Sch 1.   [58] MHSWR, reg 10.
[59] MHSWR, reg 3(3).   [60] MHSWR, reg 16.
[61] *Greater Expectations: Final Report of the EOC's Investigation into Discrimination against New and Expectant Mothers in the Workplace* (EOC, June 2005), p 52.
[62] MHSWR, reg 16(2).

where the terms and conditions are not substantially less favourable than her existing terms and conditions;[63] and

- if no such alternative work is available, as a last resort, she should be suspended on full remuneration at the normal rate (calculated in accordance with the 'week's pay' scheme in the ERA) for as long as is necessary to avoid the risk identified.[64]

8.47 The need to find suitable alternative work was considered in *British Airways v Moore and Botterill*,[65] where pregnant cabin crew, who had been transferred to ground work following a risk assessment, were only paid their basic pay and not their flying allowances. The EAT upheld the Tribunal's findings that given the disparity in pay, the ground work was not suitable alternative work under the ERA, s 67(2).

8.48 The duty to assess risks and review the risk assessment is an ongoing one, and may change throughout a woman's pregnancy: for example, a woman may not develop back pain until the later stages of her pregnancy.

8.49 The same obligations with regard to risk assessments apply to women who have given birth in the last six months and those who are breastfeeding. Annex II to the Pregnant Workers Directive lists risks to which a breastfeeding mother should not be exposed. Guidance from Health and Safety Executive recommends that employers provide breastfeeding employees with a private room, secure, clean refrigerators for storing milk and time off to express milk and breastfeed.

(iv) Risk Assessments, Changes to Working Conditions and Discrimination

8.50 A failure to carry out a risk assessment can itself amount to a detriment entitling the employee to claim sex discrimination, as the EAT made clear in *Hardman v Mallon*.[66] However, in *Madarassy v Nomura*,[67] the Court of Appeal declined to follow the *Hardman* case in circumstances where there was no evidence that the work involved a potential risk to health and safety.

8.51 Moreover, while care must be taken to ensure that a pregnant woman only does those tasks she can safely continue to do, it is important that she does not have her working conditions changed, or responsibilities removed from her, without good reason, as this may itself constitute direct discrimination under the SDA.

---

[63] ERA, s 67.   [64] ERA, ss 69 and 220–229 and MHSWR, reg 16(3).
[65] [2000] IRLR 296, EAT.   [66] [2002] IRLR 516, EAT.
[67] [2007] IRLR 246, CA.

This occurred in *Butler v Chief Constable of Hertfordshire*,[68] where a female **8.52**
police officer's probationary period was suspended as soon as her supervisors
discovered that she was pregnant, and she was given 'undemanding and disappointing' data entry work to do until her baby was born, when again no risk
assessment had been carried out.

Employers must therefore strike a balance between being overly protective in a **8.53**
patronisingly chivalrous way and being so 'light touch' that they neglect their
health and safety responsibilities. Getting the balance right in this area can be
tricky for employers, but ultimately the risk assessment, and not necessarily the
wishes of either the employer or the employee, should define what work can
safely be done during pregnancy.

The SDA, section 51 provides an employer with specific permission to dis- **8.54**
criminate against a woman on certain health and safety grounds relating to
pregnancy and maternity. However, because of the broad overriding obligations
to carry out appropriate risk assessments and avoid discrimination to pregnant
women, section 51 is of limited practical assistance, and only likely to assist the
employer who, for example, wishes to restrict a woman's working arrangements, on the basis of a properly carried out risk assessment, when she does not
agree to the change.

(v) Disputes over Suitable Alternative Work and Suspension of the Pregnant Employee

If an employee is not offered suitable alternative work, she can complain to the **8.55**
Tribunal. If her complaint succeeds, the Tribunal can award compensation for
loss of earnings and injury to feelings.[69] However if an employee unreasonably
refuses suitable alternative work, she will be suspended and forfeit her right to
be paid while suspended.

A breach of the health and safety requirements also leaves an employer vulner- **8.56**
able to proceedings in the civil courts, and prosecution by either the local
environmental health department or the Health and Safety Executive.

(e) Rights During Maternity Leave

The regime for maternity leave and pay can be summarised as follows: **8.57**

• All female employees are entitled to 26 weeks' OML irrespective of their
  hours worked, length of service, and whether they have a permanent or
  temporary contract.

---

[68] ET Case No 1200324/05, ET.   [69] ERA, s 70(4).

- All female employees whose Expected Week of Childbirth ('EWC') is after 1 April 2007 are entitled to AML of a further 26 weeks, which commences the day after the end of OML.[70]

- The earliest maternity leave can start is the beginning of the 11th week before the EWC, unless the baby is born earlier. Otherwise the employee can choose when her leave starts unless she is absent because of her pregnancy in the four weeks before the EWC, in which case the employer has the right to insist that her leave starts the date after her first day of absence. Even if the employer does not exercise this right the period for payment of Statutory Maternity Pay is automatically triggered by such an absence.

- Entitlement to OML and AML depends on the woman giving her employer notice by the end of the 15th week of her pregnancy before the baby is due, or her EWC, and of the date she intends to start her leave, or such notice as is reasonably practicable. An employer must confirm the date the woman's maternity leave will end within 28 days of receiving her notice.

- If a woman has given her employer notice of the date she intends to start her maternity leave, she can subsequently change that date providing she gives her employer at least 28 days' notice before the new date or the original date (whichever is earlier) and the new date is not earlier than the beginning of the 11th week before the EWC, or such notice as is reasonably practicable.

- Where the EWC is on or after 1 April 2007, the employer may make reasonable contact with the employee,[71] in order to enable both parties to keep in touch during maternity leave. An employee may also work for up to ten 'keeping in touch' ('KIT') days during OML or AML without bringing her maternity leave to an end.[72] This work can be consecutive or not, and can include training. Any such work must be by agreement and neither the employer nor the employee can insist on it. Pay for KIT days will be a matter for agreement between the parties but this should probably be full pay, given that the employee is actually working on these days.

- No work, including on KIT days, should take place during the woman's 'compulsory maternity leave' period—this is two weeks immediately after the birth of the baby,[73] or four weeks in the case of factory workers.[74] It is a criminal offence to force a woman to work during this period and the woman is not entitled to be paid for such work.

- KIT days can also be used to consult employees about changes to their work,

---

[70] Those whose EWC was before 1 April 2007 only had this entitlement if they had been employed by the same employer for 26 weeks by the beginning of the 14th week before childbirth.
[71] MPLR, reg 12A(4).   [72] MPLR, reg 12A(1).
[73] MPLR, reg 8.   [74] Public Health Act 1936, s 205 (as amended).

promotion prospects or jobs being advertised, business reorganisations or potential redundancies.

- During OML an employee's terms and conditions of employment (other than the term as to full normal pay) continue. These can include benefits such as health and life insurance, lunch vouchers, mortgage subsidies, participation in share ownership schemes, accrued holiday, health club membership, professional subscriptions, personal use of a company car or mobile telephone and equal access to promotion and other working conditions. An employee is also bound by her obligations under the contract (except the obligation to work).[75]

- During AML an employee continues to be an employee but only some of her terms and conditions apply, such as to the benefit of the employer's obligation to her of trust and confidence, and any terms and conditions of employment relating to her contractual notice period, possibly notice pay, redundancy pay and her employer's disciplinary or grievance procedures. The employee is bound by her implied obligation of good faith to her employer and any terms and conditions of employment relating to notice of the termination of the contract, the disclosure of confidential information, the acceptance of gifts or other benefits and her participation in any other business.[76]

- While the period of AML is taken into account for the purposes of calculating length-of-service-related statutory benefits (such as redundancy pay) it does not have to be counted for the purposes of the woman's seniority and similar contractual rights.[77] However, this is arguably contrary to the ECJ case of *Land Brandenburg v Sass*,[78] and many employers choose to give full credit for AML in order to offer consistent and simplified rights.

- A woman's statutory holiday entitlement under the Working Time Regulations 1998 accrues during OML and AML. The same rules as apply to other employees about when holiday is taken and whether it can be carried over should be applied to women on maternity leave. However, it is arguable that if a woman cannot take her holiday leave during her maternity leave, then it would be discrimination to refuse to allow her to carry it over until the following holiday year, even though there is no provision for this in the Working Time Regulations 1998.[79]

- If a woman wishes to return to work earlier than the end of her OML or

---

[75] ERA, s 71(5) and MPLR, reg 9.   [76] MPLR, reg 17.
[77] MPLR, reg 18A(1)(a)(i).   [78] [2005] IRLR 147, ECJ.
[79] *Merino Gomez v Continental Industries Del Caucho SA* [2004] IRLR 407, ECJ and *Federatie Nederlandse Vakbeweging v Staat Der Nederlanden* [2006] IRLR 561, ECJ.

AML she must give notice (28 days if the EWC was before 1 April 2007 and eight weeks if it was after that date). Otherwise it is assumed that she will return on the date notified by her employer.

- Where a woman has a contractual right relating to maternity leave which is more beneficial than the statutory right, she may take advantage of that, and vice versa, as these are 'composite rights'.[80]

(f) Recruitment, Promotion/Demotion, Transfers, Appraisals and Training

8.58 It will be contrary to the SDA to refuse to consider an applicant for a post, to refuse to appoint her, or to refuse to promote her because she is pregnant, might become pregnant or, potentially, because she has asked to work reduced hours. For example, in *Mahlburg v Land Mecklenburg-Vorpommern*,[81] a pregnant employee was refused a job in a heart surgery clinic because she would not be able to take it up before the end of her maternity leave due to the risk of infection in the operating theatre. The ECJ, making the point that a post was permanent whereas a pregnancy was temporary, held that she had been discriminated against, and that the fact that it would be too expensive for the employer to wait until the women had finished her maternity leave was no defence.

8.59 For these reasons it has been repeatedly held that it is not appropriate to ask questions about pregnancy and childcare responsibilities in interview. For example, in *Woodward v Corus Hotels and Rushton*,[82] the Tribunal held that a hypothetical male comparator employee would not have been asked in interview what arrangements he would make for the care of his child if he had to stay awake overnight on training, as the claimant had been, nor would such a comparator have been told in interview that people with children had left after six weeks in the post.

8.60 Accordingly employers should take practical steps to ensure that questions are not asked at interview about marriage plans, family intentions, pregnancy or childcare issues. Where it is necessary to assess whether personal circumstances will affect performance of the job—if, for example, it involves unsocial hours or extensive travelling—this should be done objectively without detailed reference to family or childcare issues.

8.61 Employers should also consider, when recruiting into new posts, whether they can be done on a part-time or flexible working basis.

8.62 For similar reasons it would clearly be unlawful to demote an employee

---

[80] MPLR, reg 21.   [81] [2000] IRLR 276, ECJ.   [82] ET Case No 1800398/05, ET.

because she announced she was pregnant, as occurred in *Busby v Connect Personnel Ltd*.[83]

It is similarly potentially contrary to the SDA to transfer a woman on grounds **8.63** of her pregnancy or maternity leave. Such a transfer will be unlawful if it is borne out of an unjustified health and safety concern; or out of concerns that the pregnant woman's appearance would not 'look good' with customers (as occurred in *O'Neill v Walthamstow Building Society*[84]).

It is also likely to be unlawful to take account of the consequences of a woman's **8.64** pregnancy or maternity leave, even indirectly, in making these decisions: for example it would be unlawful to refuse to consider a woman for promotion because she had missed certain training courses due to her absence on maternity leave, or because of her disappointing performance in interview, if this was due to her pregnancy. The latter situation arose in *Pearson v Swindells and British Telecommunications Ltd* where the claimant had attended for interview while eight months pregnant and on leave, and did not get the job. The ET[85] held that her absence on maternity leave had led to the first respondent conducting the interview process in a manner that was biased against her, and the EAT[86] upheld this finding.

Women who are pregnant or on maternity leave are still entitled to have **8.65** appraisals of their work, as was made clear by the ECJ in *CNAVTS v Thibault*.[87] In practical terms, if an appraisal is due while the woman is on maternity leave, it is likely to make sense to carry out the appraisal before she goes on leave. Where such appraisals are based on productivity, this should be assessed on the basis of an average over a period which does not include the maternity leave period or any period where the woman's productivity was unusually low because of her pregnancy.

It is likely to be contrary to the SDA to deny a woman access to training **8.66** opportunities on grounds of her pregnancy or maternity leave. In *Tapp v Chief Constable of Suffolk*,[88] for example, a female probationer police officer succeeded in her SDA claim when she was transferred off her training programme.

(g) Pregnancy-related Sickness Absence and Sick Pay

Pregnancy-related sickness can include morning sickness, fatigue, threatened or **8.67** actual miscarriage or any other illness connected with the pregnancy. It will be

---

[83] ET Case No 1101068/05, ET.   [84] ET Case No 27886/89, ET.
[85] [1995] DCLD 25, ET.   [86] EAT1248/94, EAT.   [87] [1998] IRLR 399, ECJ.
[88] ET Case No 1501546/97, ET.

direct discrimination contrary to the SDA to disadvantage a pregnant woman for any pregnancy-related sickness absence prior to her maternity leave, however long—even where a non-pregnant employee with a similar sickness absence record would be disadvantaged.

8.68 This principle was established in *Brown v Rentokil*[89] where the claimant was absent from work for 26 weeks, from almost the beginning of her pregnancy until she went on maternity leave. Her contract provided that an employee who was off sick continuously for 26 weeks would be dismissed and at the end of her 26th week of absence she was so dismissed. The ECJ held that the contractual rule was discriminatory.

8.69 In practical terms, this means that:

- pregnancy-related sickness absence should be recorded as such on an employee's attendance record;
- women should not be disciplined or dismissed for poor attendance due to pregnancy-related sickness absence;
- women should not be denied appraisals or opportunities for promotion because they are absent as a result of pregnancy-related sickness;
- pregnancy-related sickness absence should not be considered when decisions about recruitment, promotion, the payment of bonuses,[90] or redundancy selection are made; and
- employers should take care not to comment adversely on pregnancy-related sickness absences in appraisals, reports or other documents.

8.70 Moreover, as is clear from the *Hoj Pederson* case in the ECJ,[91] a woman off sick with a pregnancy-related illness must be paid the same sick pay as a non-pregnant employee who is off sick for a similar period. Employers will therefore need to make sure that sick pay schemes do not exclude pregnancy-related sickness. However, employers will need to look critically at the level of sick pay being paid, as the EAT made clear in *North Western Health Board v McKenna*[92] that the pay given to pregnant women in these circumstances must not be so low as to 'undermine the objective of protecting pregnant workers'.

---

[89] [1998] IRLR 445, ECJ.
[90] eg *GUS Home Shopping Ltd v Green and McLaughlin* [2001] IRLR 75, EAT.
[91] *Handels-og Kontorfunktionaerernes Forbund I Danmark (acting on behalf of Hoj Pederson) v Faellesforeningen for Fanmarks Brugsforeninger (acting on behalf of Kvickly Skive)* [1999] IRLR 55, ECJ.
[92] [2005] IRLR 895, EAT.

(h) Pay, Pay Rises, Bonuses, Lump Sum Maternity Payments and Pensions

(i) Pay and Pay Rises during Pregnancy

It will be a breach of the EqPA to pay a woman less, or give her fewer benefits, **8.71** because she is pregnant. If, for example, a woman is less productive throughout her pregnancy because of fatigue or morning sickness, she should not be disadvantaged for being less productive in relation to her pay or bonus. A woman must also receive the benefit of any pay rise which she receives at any time prior to her leave.[93]

(ii) Pay and Pay Rises during Maternity Leave

It is not contrary to either the EqPA or the Pregnant Workers Directive to **8.72** refuse to pay a woman her full pay during her maternity leave: in *Gillespie v Northern Ireland Health and Social Services Board,*[94] the ECJ held that women taking maternity leave are in a special position, but one which is not comparable to that of men or women actually at work. Rather, the pay of pregnant women during maternity leave is governed by the Pregnant Workers Directive which simply requires that employers pay an 'adequate allowance'.

In domestic law, the ERA and the MPLR lay down employees' rights to pay **8.73** and other benefits during maternity and other family leave. Currently an employee is entitled to Statutory Maternity Pay ('SMP') where she has 26 weeks' continuous service with the same employer by the end of the qualifying week (the 15th week before the EWC or approximately the 26th week of pregnancy) and has average earnings of at least the lower earnings limit for National Insurance during an eight-week or two-month calculation period ending with the qualifying week. SMP is payable for 39 weeks for women whose EWC is after 1 April 2007,[95] at the rate of 90 per cent of her average earnings for the first six weeks and a flat rate for the remaining weeks. Employers can recover all or most of the SMP they pay.

Many employers do choose to enhance maternity leave by paying full salary **8.74** rather than 90 per cent SMP, possibly for longer than the six-week period, paying half-salary instead of the lower rate of SMP, or making a one-off payment on return. EOC research shows that the more senior the woman is the more likely she is to receive additional maternity pay; and that almost two-thirds of women working in public administration and defence receive additional maternity pay compared to 26 per cent in 'other services' and

---

[93] *Alabaster v Barclays Bank plc (No 2)* [2005] IRLR 576, CA.
[94] [1996] IRLR 214, ECJ.
[95] The previous entitlement was to 26 weeks. It is intended that the period of paid maternity leave will be extended to 52 weeks by 2010.

23 per cent in distribution.[96] Enhancing maternity leave in ways like this is a good way of encouraging a woman to come back to work, which in turn saves the employer the costs of recruitment and retraining a replacement employee.

8.75 If a woman is awarded a pay rise between the start of the calculation period for SMP and the end of her maternity leave, she is entitled to have her SMP re-calculated and receive any extra SMP due.

8.76 If a woman's contractual maternity-related pay provides for such pay to be calculated by reference to her pay at a certain date, then any increase in pay between that date and the end of her maternity leave must be reflected in her contractual maternity-related pay.[97] This would not apply if she was receiving full pay while on maternity leave, provided she had received the benefit of the pay rise in any event.

8.77 There is no entitlement to statutory sick pay during the maternity pay period, and a woman who is unwell during her maternity leave is not entitled to contractual sick pay.[98]

(iii) Pay and Pay Rises on the Employee's Return to Work

8.78 Any pay increase which the woman would have received if she had not been on maternity leave must be paid to her on her return—ie if employees have had a pay rise while she was on leave, she must benefit from it fully when she returns.[99]

(iv) Bonuses

8.79 The law relating to the payment of bonuses to those on maternity leave is complex, and the type of bonus at issue (whether it is contractual or discretionary) will be relevant. Broadly the position is that:

- If the bonus is payable with reference to a period of work the employee has done before going on maternity leave, she should be paid the bonus, even if it is actually paid to her during her maternity leave.

- If a bonus is payable with reference to the period of compulsory maternity leave, when the employee could not work for health and safety reasons, then she should be credited with the bonus in the same way as if she had been working.[100]

---

[96] *Greater Expectations: Final Report of the EOC's Investigation into Discrimination against New and Expectant Mothers in the Workplace* (EOC, June 2005), pp 44–45.

[97] EqPA, ss 1(2)(d), (5A), (5B).

[98] *Todd v Eastern Health and Social Services Board* [1997] IRLR 410, CA (NI).

[99] EqPA, ss 1(2)(f), (5A) and (5B).

[100] *Lewen v Denda* [2000] IRLR 67, ECJ and *Hoyland v Asda Stores Ltd* [2006] IRLR 468, Ct Sess.

- Following the decision of the Court of Session in *Hoyland v Asda Stores Ltd*,[101] where a contractual bonus relates to the period of maternity leave beyond the compulsory maternity leave period (ie OML or AML), it is acceptable to reduce the bonus proportionately to reflect the absence of the employee on OML or AML.

- The position is less clear with regard to discretionary bonuses—in *GUS Home Shopping Ltd v Green and McLaughlin*,[102] the EAT held that the failure to pay a discretionary loyalty bonus to an employee absent due to pregnancy-related sickness and maternity leave was discriminatory, but it is hard to see how this sits with the decision in the *Hoyland* case; and in *Lewen v Denda*,[103] the ECJ appeared to leave open the argument that some bonuses that fell to be paid after the compulsory maternity leave period and during parental leave should be paid in full.

- However, any bonus in respect of the period after the woman returns to work must be paid at the same time as if she had not been on maternity leave.[104]

(v) Lump Sum Maternity Payments and Pensions

It was established in *Abdoulaye v Regie Nationale des Usine Renault*[105] that is not **8.80** discriminatory against men to make a lump sum payment to female workers when they return from maternity leave, and not to men who become fathers.

We consider issues relating to redundancy, pensions and maternity leave further **8.81** in Chapter 13, when considering issues surrounding the ending of employment generally.

(i) Women Returning to Work from Maternity Leave

The rights of women returning to work from maternity leave can be summar- **8.82** ised as follows:

- A woman returning to work after OML is entitled to return to the job in which she was employed before her absence, on the same terms and conditions as if she had not been absent.[106]

- A woman returning to work after AML is entitled to the job in which she was previously employed. If it is not reasonably practicable to allow the woman to return to the same job after AML she must be given another job which is both suitable for her and appropriate for her to do in the circumstances.[107]

---

[101] [2006] IRLR 468, Ct Sess.   [102] [2001] IRLR 75, EAT.
[103] *Lewen v Denda* [2000] IRLR 67, ECJ.   [104] EqPA, ss 1(2)(e), (f), (5A) and (5B).
[105] [1999] IRLR 811, ECJ.   [106] MPLR, regs 18(1), (2) and 18A.
[107] MPLR, regs 18(2) and (4).

- Where a woman is not allowed to return at all, or where she is not given an appropriate job on her return, she will be treated as having been dismissed, and may have a claim for sex discrimination, unfair dismissal and/or automatically unfair dismissal, depending on the reason for the dismissal.

- Where she does return to work but her old job has changed for the worse, she may have a detriment claim under the SDA, or be able to resign and claim constructive dismissal.

- If there has been a transfer of business during a woman's maternity leave, she is entitled to return to her job with the new employer.

- If a woman is made redundant during OML or AML she is entitled to any suitable alternative work with equivalent terms and conditions.

8.83 In *Blundell v Governing Body of St Andrew's Catholic Primary School*[108] the EAT considered the scope of the employee's right to return to 'the job in which she was employed before her absence'. The EAT held that the purpose of the legislation was to 'provide that a returnee comes back to a work situation as near as possible to that she left' and avoid adding to the burdens on mothers with very young children. In considering whether the 'new' job was the same as the 'old' one, it was necessary to consider the nature, capacity and place of the job. Where the employee's role is variable, it is acceptable to have regard to 'the normal range in which variation has previously occurred'. On the facts of this case, the EAT held that the claimant, a teacher, could not insist on coming back to teach the same class, because the school normally required teachers to change classes every two years.

8.84 However, the EAT did hold that the failure of the head teacher to ask the claimant which class she would like to teach in the new school year, in circumstances where teachers who were not on maternity leave, had been asked for their preference, constituted discrimination contrary to the SDA, as by not being asked for her preference, she had 'lost something she might reasonably think of value'. This case therefore also stresses the importance of consulting those on maternity leave about important decisions in the workplace. Such consultation should become easier with the introduction of KIT days (see above).

8.85 However, where an employee is given a different job or the same job with different responsibilities, and this is for a reason related to her absence on maternity leave, this is likely to be sex discrimination, and so this needs to be handled with care.

8.86 It is frequently on her return to work that a woman will wish to change her

---

[108] [2007] IRLR 652, EAT.

working arrangements to work part-time, different hours, work from home, or otherwise work more flexibly in a way that will accommodate her new childcare responsibilities. A refusal to accede to such a request can also raise indirect discrimination issues. As this issue is complex, and affects employees other than those returning from maternity leave, we consider the issue of flexible working separately below.

In practical terms, it can be a daunting experience for anyone returning to work **8.87** after a prolonged absence and loss of confidence and anxiety are common reactions. An employer can assist a woman returning from maternity leave by making her feel welcome on her return, introducing her to new staff, ensuring she is informed of any changes during her absence which affect her work (although this should also have been done via KIT days) and giving her time to settle back into work and regain her confidence.

(j) Pregnancy/Maternity and the Other Discrimination Strands

Employers should also remember that the laws relating to the other discrimin- **8.88** ation strands continue to apply during pregnancy and maternity. Accordingly, employers should ensure that the arrangements made for pregnant women and new mothers are equally favourable to women from all racial groups and to women with disabilities; and recognise and be sympathetic to different cultural and religious practices relating to pregnancy and childbirth.

D. Paternity, Adoption, Parental and Dependants' Leave

(a) Paternity Leave

An employee is entitled to up to two weeks' paternity leave if s/he has been **8.89** continuously employed for at least 26 weeks by the 15th week before the EWC, and is the father of the child or the mother's husband, civil partner or partner (including same sex partner), and has, or expects to have, responsibility for the upbringing of the child. A 'partner' includes a person (other than the mother's relatives) of the same or different sex, who lives with the mother of the child in an 'enduring family relationship'.[109]

Paternity leave can be taken as one or two weeks' consecutive leave, but not odd **8.90** days or as separate weeks.[110] An employee can start paternity leave on the day after the baby is born, or a specified number of days or weeks after the birth, or a pre-determined date after the start of the EWC.[111] It must be completed

---

[109] PALR, regs 2 and 4.   [110] PALR, reg 5(1).   [111] PALR, reg 5(3).

within 56 days of the birth.[112] An employee must give notice to take paternity leave in or before the 15th week before the EWC, stating the EWC, whether s/he is taking one or two weeks' paternity leave, the date s/he intends to start the leave and giving a signed declaration as to the nature of his or her relationship to and responsibility for the child (if requested by the employer). The start date can be changed if appropriate notice is given, including if the baby is born early.[113]

8.91 An employee taking paternity leave is entitled to his or her normal terms and conditions, as if s/he was at work, except remuneration.[114] The employee is also bound by the obligations in his or her contract providing they are not inconsistent with absence on paternity leave. Seniority, pension and other service-related rights continue to accrue throughout the absence.

8.92 Statutory Paternity Pay ('SPP') is payable for up to two weeks provided certain eligibility criteria are met (which are similar to the eligibility criteria for paternity leave and SMP) at a flat rate.

8.93 An employee taking paternity leave is entitled to return to exactly the same job on the same terms and conditions after taking paternity leave[115] (although the provisions vary slightly if the paternity leave is consecutive to other forms of leave).

8.94 As with maternity leave, if an employee has a contractual right to paternity leave and pay that is more favourable than the statutory scheme, s/he cannot take each right separately but is entitled to take whichever right is more favourable.[116]

8.95 An employee must not be subjected to detriment for taking or trying to take paternity leave;[117] employees who are dismissed for doing so will be regarded as unfairly dismissed;[118] and dismissal for any reason which relates to paternity leave is automatically unfair.[119]

8.96 The Work and Families Act 2006 contains powers to introduce a new entitlement to Additional Paternity Leave ('APL') and Additional Statutory Paternity Pay ('ASPP'), which will enable employees to take up to 26 weeks' APL within the first year of the child's life, usually during the second six months. Some of it could be paid if the child's mother has returned to work and has some of her entitlement to SMP or Maternity Allowance left at the time of her return to work. The scheme for APL and APP is unlikely to be introduced before 2009.

---

112 PALR, reg 5(2).   113 PALR, reg 6.   114 PALR, reg 12.
115 PALR, regs 13 and 14.   116 PALR, reg 30(2).
117 ERA, s 47C and PALR, reg 28.   118 PALR, regs 29(1) and (3)(a).
119 PALR, reg 29(5).

(b) Adoption Leave

An employee is entitled to 26 weeks' Ordinary Adoption Leave ('OAL') if s/he **8.97** has been continuously employed for at least 26 weeks by the week in which s/he has been notified of having been matched with a child as an adopter of that child.[120] S/he is also entitled to 26 weeks' Additional Adoption Leave ('AAL') immediately after the OAL period, provided the OAL period was not ended by dismissal or disruption of the adoptive placement.[121] The employee can choose to start her adoption leave on the day of the placement or a fixed date not more than 14 days before the expected date of the placement.[122]

The provisions for notice,[123] changing the start date of leave,[124] the retention of **8.98** terms and conditions of employment,[125] the right to return[126] and the protection from detriment or dismissal are similar to those for OML and AML.[127] There is also now provision for employers to make reasonable contact with those on adoption leave, and for the employee to work for up to ten 'Keeping in Touch' days, as there is for those on maternity leave[128]. Statutory Adoption Pay ('SAP') is also payable for 39 weeks. We consider issues relating to redundancy, pensions and adoption leave further in Chapter 13, when considering issues surrounding the ending of employment generally.

(c) Parental Leave

Each parent who is an employee and has one year's service with the employer is **8.99** entitled to a total of 13 weeks' unpaid parental leave for each child under five, or 18 weeks' leave for a disabled child under 18 who is entitled to disability living allowance, provided s/he has parental responsibility for the child. Parental leave must be taken before the child is five, or within five years of the child being placed for adoption, or, if the child is entitled to disability living allowance, before the child is 18. A default scheme exists where there is no workforce or collective agreement. The default scheme provides that a parent is only entitled to take a maximum of four weeks' parental leave in any one year in relation to the same child. If the default scheme applies, unless the employer agrees, or the child is entitled to disability living allowance, parental leave can only be taken one week at time.[129]

Terms and conditions of employment continue during parental leave as they do **8.100** during AML and AAL, and the position is broadly the same with regard to holidays, pensions and bonuses and the right to return. Any other contractual

---

[120] PALR, reg 15(2).   [121] PALR, reg 20(1).   [122] PALR, reg 16(1).
[123] PALR, reg 17.   [124] PALR, reg 17.   [125] PALR, regs 19 and 21.
[126] ERA, ss 47C and 99 and PALR, regs 28 and 29.   [127] PALR, reg 17.
[128] PALR, reg 21A.   [129] *Rodway v South Central Trains Ltd* [2005] IRLR 583, CA.

matters are subject to agreement between the employer and employee. It is unlawful to subject an employee to detriment or to dismiss him or her for taking parental leave, and so it is advisable, for example, to ensure that employees on parental leave are informed of job opportunities etc, so that they are not disadvantaged on their return. Parental leave is unpaid, although a parent taking time off might be entitled to means-tested benefits.[130]

8.101 With regard to parental leave, employers will therefore have to decide whether to arrange a workforce or collective agreement; what provision if any to make for contractual rights to continue during parental leave; and whether to improve on the statutory scheme in any way, for example, by making parental leave paid.

(d) Dependants' Leave

8.102 An employee can take time off to care for or arrange care for a dependant where the dependant is ill, injured, assaulted, gives birth or dies, where arrangements for the care of a dependant break down or where there is an unexpected incident involving a child at school.[131]

8.103 The entitlement is to a 'reasonable amount of time during the employee's working hours in order to take action which is necessary'.[132] The DTI guidance suggests that in most cases one or two days should be sufficient to deal with the problem, although this will depend on individual circumstances.[133] The length of time off that is reasonable will depend on the nature of the incident that has occurred, the closeness of the relationship between the employee and the dependant, the extent to which anyone else is available to assist, and the number and length of previous absences, as well as the dates when they occurred.[134]

8.104 An employee who claims that s/he has been unreasonably refused dependants' leave may complain to a Tribunal and obtain (i) a declaration that the complaint is well-founded; and (ii) such compensation as is just and equitable.[135] Employees must not be subjected to a detriment for taking dependants' leave. It will be automatically unfair dismissal to dismiss an employee or select him or her for redundancy because s/he sought to or took dependants' leave; it may also be an ordinary unfair dismissal.[136]

---

[130] ERA, ss 76–80 and the MPLR, regs 13–22, Schs 1 and 2.
[131] ERA, ss 57A and 57B.   [132] ERA, s 57A(4).
[133] *Time Off for Dependants: A Guide for Employers and Employees* (DTI, February 2000), p 9.
[134] *Qua v John Ford Morrison Solicitors* [2003] ICR 482, EAT.   [135] ERA, s 57B.
[136] ERA, ss 99 and 104 and MPLR, reg 20.

(e) Discrimination with regard to Paternity, Adoption, Parental or Dependants' Leave

Where an employee has been treated less favourably for a reason which relates **8.105** to paternity, adoption, parental or dependants' leave, s/he may have a direct discrimination claim if s/he can show that an employee of the opposite sex would have been afforded more favourable leave arrangements, and therefore that s/he had been treated less favourably because of sex.

An indirect discrimination claim could lie if male and female employees are **8.106** treated equally with regard to leave but the provision has a disparate impact on women who are more likely to take parental and dependants' leave. For example a rule preventing employees taking time off when a child was sick would potentially be indirectly discriminatory against women who are more likely to need such time off.

E. Flexible Working

(a) The Right to Request Flexible Working

Under section 80F of the ERA, employees who have responsibility for a child **8.107** aged under six, or a disabled child under 18, have the right to request flexible working arrangements. The Government estimates that since 2003, this right has been available to 3.6 million parents of young and disabled children. In April 2007 this right was extended to some 2.5 million employees who care for adults.[137] The purpose of the right is to give employees the opportunity to adopt working arrangements that help them balance their commitments at work with their caring responsibilities.

Employees are only entitled to request a change in their terms and conditions **8.108** of employment if they have been continuously employed by the employer for at least 26 weeks. Employees who wish to request flexible working arrangements in order to care for a child must have, or expect to have, responsibility for the upbringing of a child under the age of six (or, if disabled, 18) either as the mother, father, adopter, guardian, special guardian or foster carer of the child, or the spouse, civil partner or partner of one of these people. From 6 April 2007, an employee who wishes to request flexible working arrangements in order to care for an adult must be, or expect to be, caring for an adult in need of care who is married to, or is the partner or civil partner of, the

---

[137] DLR consultation paper, para 3.5.

employee, or a relative of the employee, or living at the same address as the employee.

8.109 Legally, the right to request flexible working entails the employee making an application to the employer for a change in their terms and conditions of employment which relates to the hours of work they are required to work, the times they are required to work, where (as between the employee's home and the employer's place of business) they are required to work, and/or such other aspect of the employee's terms and conditions as may be specified in Regulations. Under these provisions, employees may make requests for part-time work, compressed hours, flexi-time, home-working, job sharing, teleworking, term-time working, shift working, staggered hours, annualised hours or self-rostering. The change, if agreed, will be a permanent change to the employee's terms and conditions. Neither employee nor employer will have an automatic right to revert to the previous terms and conditions of employment.

(b) The Statutory Procedure

8.110 In order to request flexible working, an employee must make a formal written application for a change to his or her terms and conditions of employment. The application must: state that it is an application for flexible working; specify the change applied for, and the date on which it is proposed the change should become effective; explain what effect, if any, the employee thinks the change will have on the employer and how, in his or her opinion, any such effect may be dealt with; explain how the employee meets the required relationship conditions, and in relation to a request made in order to care for a child, be made before the day on which the child reaches six (or, if disabled, 18). The application must be in writing and be dated by the employee. It must also state whether a previous application has been made to the employer and if so, when.

8.111 An employee cannot make an application within 12 months of having submitted a previous one. From 6 April 2007, this applies irrespective of whether a previous application was made in respect of a different caring responsibility so that, for example, an employee who wishes to make a request to care for an adult would still have to wait 12 months, even if the previous request had been to enable him or her to care for a child.

8.112 Employees who wish to change their working hours should be encouraged to make the application to do so in good time, as it can take several months for an employer to consider an application and make any changes necessary in the workplace such as recruiting a job-share partner or training other staff.

8.113 The law sets out a clear framework for the procedure to be followed by employers when considering a request for flexible working, which we set out at Appendix 8.1.

(c) Flexible Working and Indirect Sex Discrimination

Quite aside from the regime dealing specifically with the right to request flex- **8.114** ible working set out above, employers must also be conscious that it may be unlawful indirect sex discrimination to refuse to accommodate a working mother's request for flexible working. This is because by, for example, requiring all employees to work full-time regular hours, the employer would be applying a provision, criterion or practice which, in reality, had a disparate impact on women, who still tend to require flexibility in working arrangements in order to care for children more than men.

Similarly, statistics from Carers UK show that women are more likely than men **8.115** to be carers in all age groups under 75 years—for example, a quarter of all women aged 50 to 59 compared with about one in six men provide unpaid care. Accordingly, a refusal to allow flexible working for carers of adults may be indirectly discriminatory against women in the same way as a refusal to allow flexible working to those with childcare responsibilities.

We consider a case raising the interaction between flexible working and indirect **8.116** sex discrimination in some detail at Appendix 8.2.

In practical terms, this risk of indirect sex discrimination means that in refusing **8.117** a request for flexible working, an employer will need to ensure that their reasoning for doing so would meet the more stringent evidential test for justification set out in the SDA, rather than simply ensuring that it was for one of the reasons listed in the ERA.

(d) Taking a Positive Approach to Flexible Working

As we have explained above, the statutory right to request flexible working is **8.118** limited to parents and carers. However, many employers have found it works best to extend the right to request flexible working to all employees because:

• To do so is less divisive.

• Flexible working tends to lead to greater productivity and so it makes good business sense to extend this across the workforce.

• Such a policy recognises what the EOC has described as a 'sea-change in what people want and expect from workplaces' whereby the vast majority of employees now believe that '. . . everyone (and not just parents and carers) should be able to balance work and home lives in the way they want. . . .'

• Research from the EOC and the Chartered Institute of Personnel and

Development (the 'CIPD') has shown that flexible working across the work-force has a positive effect on recruitment and staff retention.[138]

We would commend such an approach to employers, as consistent with a positive approach which promotes a better work-life balance across the whole workforce.

8.119   In considering a request for flexible working we would suggest that employers:

- Ask the employee how s/he thinks the work can be reorganised.
- Do not simply assume that the proposal cannot work: there are very few jobs which cannot import some element of flexibility.
- Consider any request carefully and sympathetically.
- Do not automatically accept the views of other managers or of other employees that the job cannot be done flexibly.
- Look creatively at the job requirements to see how the employee's sugges-tions might be accommodated.
- Think of ways in which work can be reorganised with other members of staff or through the recruitment of an extra part-time worker to ensure the work can be carried out.
- Consider job-sharing as an alternative to part-time work if it is crucial that the responsibilities are covered fully during the working week.
- If on balance there remain difficulties with the employee's suggestions, try and reach a consensus or at least a mutual understanding through face-to-face meetings.[139]

8.120   Managers clearly need to be trained in these principles, so that they can deal effectively and fairly with applications for flexible working which they receive. Managers should be encouraged to think and talk in terms of what the job has to achieve (its 'outputs'), rather than how the work of that job has convention-ally been organised. The qualities needed to manage teams flexibly and to think flexibly about working arrangements should become an integral requirement for management roles.

8.121   Moreover, as the EOC has highlighted:

> Flexible working does not always sit easily with traditional 'command and con-trol' techniques of management. It often requires managers to 'let go' of rigid schedules and close supervision, to trust and empower team members to a greater

---

[138] *Britain's Hidden Brain Drain: The EOC's Investigation into Flexible and Part-time Working* (EOC, September 2005) sets out the overall benefits of flexible working. See, in particular, pp 7, 13 and 25.

[139] See also *Ten Practical Tips for Employers* (EOC, June 2007), <www.eoc.org.uk/PDF/ToW_tips_leaflet.pdf>.

degree and to coordinate people working in different locations. This necessitates a greater flexibility of approach from managers, and may involve more thought and effort and forward planning . . .[140]

Equally employees need to be encouraged to make realistic demands, to enter into a mature dialogue and to listen to their managers' concerns. Trade unions and equality representatives can assist with this process. **8.122**

Trial periods of flexible working arrangements can be used to see if the change in working does in fact work sensibly and fairly for both the employer and the employee. **8.123**

Senior managers who work flexibly, and those who speak positively about its benefits, should also act as an incentive for junior employees to consider adopting flexible working models themselves. **8.124**

The organisation should, in the long-term, seek to foster a culture where flexible working is not seen as evidence of insufficient commitment (particularly by peers/colleagues) or seen as detrimental to career progression. **8.125**

Family-friendly and Flexible Working: In Brief

- The Labour Government has been proactive in implementing a range of legal measures to promote family-friendly policies, and flexible working.
- Quite aside from the need for legal compliance with these provisions, promoting a family-friendly and flexible workplace makes sound business sense.
- The Sex Discrimination Act 1975 and Equal Pay Act 1970 provide women with a wide protection from discrimination with regard to pregnancy and maternity leave. This framework covers all aspects of the employment relationship with the expectant or new mother, including recruitment, promotion/demotion, transfers, appraisals and training; pay, pay rises, bonuses and pensions; redundancy and dismissal. Pregnancy-related sickness absence and sick pay also need special consideration.

---

[140] *Britain's Hidden Brain Drain: The EOC's Investigation into Flexible and Part-time Working* (EOC, September 2005), p 30.

- The Management of Health and Safety at Work Regulations 1999 and sections 66 to 70 of the Employment Rights Act 1996 make certain health and safety provisions for expectant and new mothers. Employers are required to ensure that they carry out a general assessment of the risk their workplace poses to expectant and new mothers; and then a specific risk assessment when a female employee indicates that she is pregnant. This can mean that an expectant or new mother's working conditions have to be altered, that she is offered suitable alternative work, or, as a last resort, that she is suspended on full pay until it is safe for her to return.

- All pregnant women are entitled to reasonable paid time off to attend antenatal care.

- Women returning to work from maternity leave are either entitled to return to the same job or another job which is both suitable and appropriate in the circumstances.

- The Maternity and Parental Leave etc Regulations 1999 and the Paternity and Adoption Leave Regulations 2002 set out a regime of paternity, adoption, parental and dependants' leave.

- The Employment Rights Act 1996 established a right for parents to request flexible working. From April 2007, the Work and Families Act 2006 extends this right to request flexible working to those who care for certain adults in need of care.

- There are sound business reasons why employers frequently extend the right to seek flexible working to all employees.

- A refusal to permit flexible working can constitute indirect sex discrimination.

- The Part-time Workers (Prevention of Less Favourable Treatment) Regulations 2000 prohibit the less favourable treatment of those who work part-time.

APPENDIX 8.1

Step-by-step Guide to Considering an Application for Flexible Working

- Once an application for flexible working has been received, an employer must hold a meeting with the employee to discuss the application within 28 days of the date on which the application was made. At this meeting, the employer and employee must consider the request and discuss how it might be accommodated. If the request cannot be accommodated, suitable alternative working arrangements should be considered at the meeting.

- An employer may refuse an application for flexible working where it considers that one or more of the following grounds applies: (i) burden of additional costs; (ii) detrimental effect on ability to meet customer demand; (iii) inability to reorganise work among existing staff; (iv) inability to recruit additional staff; (v) detrimental impact on quality; (vi) insufficiency of work during the periods the employee proposes to work; (vii) planned structural changes; or (viii) such other grounds as may be specified in Regulations.

- An employer must give an employee notice of the decision on the application within 14 days of the date of the meeting. This notice must be in writing and must be signed and dated. If the decision is to approve the application, the notice must state the agreed change and the date from which the change is to take effect.

- If the decision is to refuse the application, the notice must set out the grounds for refusal, contain a sufficient explanation as to why those grounds apply, and set out the appeal procedure.

- An employee is entitled to appeal against the employer's decision by giving notice within 14 days of the date on which the notice of the decision is given. The notice of appeal must be in writing, set out the grounds of appeal and be signed and dated by the employee.

- An employer must hold a meeting with the employee to hear the appeal within 14 days of the date on which the notice of appeal is given by the employee. The employer must then give the employee notice of its decision on appeal within 14 days of the date of the appeal meeting.

- If the employer upholds the appeal, the notice must specify the agreed change and the date on which the change will take effect. If the employer dismisses the appeal, the notice must set out the grounds on which the dismissal is based.

- An employee who applies for flexible working has a right to be accompanied at the meeting to discuss the application. An employee also has a right to be accompanied at an appeal meeting. The companion must be a worker employed by the same employer as the employee making the application, and can be a trade union representative.

- The time limits can be amended in writing, by consent of both the employee and the employer.

- If an employer fails to consider an employee's application for flexible working according to the procedure set out in the Regulations, or the employer's decision to refuse the application on appeal is based on incorrect facts, the employee may bring a claim to the Employment Tribunal. Employees are also protected from detriment or dismissal in exercising the right to request flexible working.

- If the Employment Tribunal considers the employee's complaint is well founded, it shall make a declaration to that effect and may make an order for reconsideration of the application, and make an award of compensation to be paid by the employer to the employee. The Tribunal may award such compensation as it considers just and equitable in all the circumstances, but the amount of compensation will be capped at eight weeks' pay. A week's pay will be subject to a maximum set by the Government and reviewed every year in the same way as statutory redundancy pay.

Flexible Working and Indirect Discrimination: Case Study

Giles v Cornelia Care Homes[141]

Ms Giles worked as a payroll clerk for a company which managed care homes. She was a single parent with a two-year-old son. As she was only able to arrange child care for 16 hours a week her employer agreed that she would only be required to work 16 hours a week. She received monthly timesheets from the manager of each care home, inputted the relevant data using payroll computer software and generated payslips.

In November 2004 Ms Giles's duties were changed in that her employer wanted her to speak to each care home manager on a daily basis and make a note of the relevant hours for each member of staff for each day, rather than receiving monthly timesheets. It was impossible for Ms Giles to do this work within 16 hours a week. For the next seven weeks she did an average of 16 hours a week overtime, most of which she did at home, with her employer's agreement. She worked in a home office that was locked when not in use, on a computer that was password-protected.

In mid-January 2005 Ms Giles was told that her employer wanted her to work full-time in the office. She indicated that for childcare reasons she could not do this. She said that she could work full-time provided she was based partly at home, or she could continue to work 16 hours a week in the office with the remaining hours on a job-share basis. She resigned as her employer said neither of these arrangements was acceptable. Her employer suggested she could work 25 hours a week in the office but that would not accommodate Ms Giles's childcare needs either.

She complained to the Employment Tribunal that she had been indirectly discriminated against on grounds of her sex. The Tribunal upheld her claim, because:

- Ms Giles's employer had applied to her a provision, criterion or practice ('PCP') that she worked full-time or 25 hours a week in the office;

- This PCP would have been to the detriment of a considerably higher proportion of women than men, due to the greater number of women with childcare responsibilities who require flexible working arrangements as a result;

- The employer's arguments seeking to justify this indirect discrimination failed because: (i) the cost to be incurred in permitting Ms Giles to work partly from home were minimal; (ii) despite asserting concerns over the health and safety implications of Ms Giles working from home, her employer had taken no steps to investigate this issue; (iii) she was able to offer sufficient security and protection for confidential information; (iv) her employer's concern that she would be distracted by her childcare responsibilities and therefore at risk of making errors was 'based on wholly outdated stereotypical attitudes'; (v) their concern that she would not be supervised effectively while working at home was 'misplaced' as research indicates that home workers are, in general, more productive than office-based

---

[141] ET Case No 3100720/05, ET.

workers; (vi) her employer had not raised these issues with regard to another female employee who worked from home from time to time; and (vii) Ms Giles had been working from home for at least 16 hours a week for over two months by the time she resigned.

• The Tribunal awarded Ms Giles £19,495.85 in damages including £5,000 in damages for injury to feelings. She was then awarded a further £7,798.34, a 40 per cent uplift in the damages, to reflect the fact that her employer had failed to follow the statutory grievance procedure. She was then awarded a further £2,000 in aggravated damages due to her employer's unjustified attempts to discredit her during the litigation.

9

ATTENDANCE MANAGEMENT

The whole subject [of disability discrimination] presents unique challenges to legislators and to tribunals and courts, as well as to those responsible for the day-to-day operation of the Act in the workplace. Anyone who thinks that there is an easy way of achieving a sensible, workable and fair balance between the different interests of disabled persons, of employers and of able-bodied workers in harmony with the wider public interests in an economically efficient workforce, in access to employment, in equal treatment of workers and in standards of fairness at work, has probably not given much serious thought to the problem.

(Lord Justice Mummery in *Clark v TDG Ltd t/a Novacold*[1])

A. Introduction

This chapter is about managing employees who are absent and unable to work **9.01** on account of a medical condition. Although we have begun the chapter with a quote about disability, we do not wish to give the impression that attendance problems and disability are synonymous: attendance at work is not an issue for many disabled people. However, for some disabled people, regular attendance may be more difficult than for their non-disabled colleagues.

In *Sonia Chacon Navas v Euest Colectividades SA*[2] the ECJ confirmed that Euro- **9.02** pean law did not confer protection against discrimination solely on the grounds of sickness. Whilst disability and sickness are not necessarily one and the same, that does not mean, however, that sickness cannot also amount to a disability.

It is partly because disability rights are relatively recent that the interpreta- **9.03** tion and understanding of those rights is still so obviously evolving. Whilst attendance-related issues may touch the other strands of discrimination, it is in relation to the disability strand that attendance management policies at work have been most under judicial scrutiny in recent years. The majority of this

---

[1] [1999] 2 All ER 977, CA.   [2] [2006] IRLR 706, ECJ.

chapter is therefore devoted to looking at attendance management and disability, although we do mention the way in which attendance might touch the sex, age and race strands at the end of the chapter.

9.04 Attendance management covers two broad areas:

- sick pay; and
- the process of managing the absence.

9.05 In relation to sick pay, areas of dispute have arisen between employers and disabled employees where sick pay has been reduced, notwithstanding that the reduction has been in line with the employer's sick pay rules which apply equally to disabled and non-disabled employees.

9.06 In relation to the process of managing absence, disputes have arisen around the 'trigger points' that lead to certain management actions (such as how many days' absence 'trigger' a back-to-work interview or consideration of whether to give the employee a warning) and whether disability-related absence should be counted towards those trigger points.

9.07 The question of 'reasonable adjustments' is central to these areas of dispute: should reasonable adjustments be made to sick pay or to absence management procedures, on account of disability? If so, what is reasonable? Before coming on to discuss those areas in more detail, we have taken a look at some absence statistics to demonstrate the size of the sickness management issue and have commented on the policy framework used by employers to manage that issue.

B. Sickness Absence Statistics

9.08 The CIPD 2006 national survey of absence management policy and practice contains the following headline information:

- The annual level of absence is 3.5 per cent of working time, which equates to eight days per employee, per year (the lowest level in the last seven years over which the survey has taken place).

- The highest levels of absence are in the public sector, with 9.9 days per employee lost to sickness within the public services generally, 10.5 days within central Government and 11 days within local Government (both central and local Government figures increased slightly from the previous year against an overall downward trend, although the main reasons given for the increase are an improvement in recording and monitoring rather than an increase in absence itself).

- Organisations employing fewer than a hundred employees report absence levels of 2.5 per cent of working time lost (5.7 days per employee per year), compared to 4.8 per cent (10.9 days) for organisations employing 2,000 or more people.

- The lowest levels of absence are in the hotels, restaurants and leisure sector (5.1 days), voluntary services (5.3 days) and media and publishing (5.4 days).

- Regionally, the lowest levels of absence are recorded by organisations based in the south-east of England (3.2 per cent) and London (3 per cent) with the highest in Wales (4.3 per cent).

- The breakdown of absence is generally 60 per cent short-term (seven days or less), 20 per cent medium term (between eight days and four weeks) and 20 per cent long term (four weeks or more); although this varies between size of employer and sector, with, for example, the public sector reporting 25 per cent of absence as being long term.

- The average annual cost per employee of sickness absence is £598 generally and £680 in the public sector (up from £645 the previous year), with the highest private sector costs reported in telecommunications (£1,234) and in the public sector (ironically!) in health services (£778).

- For short-term absences the major causes were: illnesses, colds, flu and stomach bugs followed by back pain and musculo-skeletal injuries (for manual workers); and, minor illnesses followed by stress (for non-manual workers).

- For long-term absences the major causes were: back pain followed by musculo-skeletal injuries (for manual workers); and, stress then acute medical conditions followed by mental ill health (for non-manual workers).

- The number of employers reporting an increase in stress-related absence continued to increase with 46 per cent of employers reporting an increase, compared to 39 per cent the year before.

- Significantly, for our purposes, the respondents to the CIPD survey estimate that 12 per cent of employees (20 per cent in the public sector) on long-term absence are covered by the DDA.

The 2006 CIPD survey is based on replies from 1,083 UK-based HR professionals in organisations employing a total of more than 1.5 million people. **9.09**

C. Contracts, Policies and Procedures

The CIPD survey also found that 90 per cent of respondents have a written **9.10** sickness absence or attendance management policy. This rises to 98 per cent among public services organisations and falls to 87 per cent in the private services sector.

9.11 An employer's absence-related rules are usually a combination of binding contractual terms and non-binding management policy.

9.12 Typically, the contract deals with:

- Any right to sick pay over and above the statutory sick pay scheme (which provides for a minimum payment from the fourth day of sickness for up to 28 weeks). For example, an employer might provide that if an employee is unable to work due to sickness he or she will continue to receive full pay for three months and then half pay for the following three months, after which any payment is discretionary.

- Any obligations placed on the employee to notify sickness absence. For example, the employee might be required to notify the employee that he or she will not be able to work by 10 am on the first day of absence; must complete a self-certification form on return to work explaining why the absence was necessary and (mirroring the statutory sick pay scheme) provide a doctor's certificate covering any absence in excess of seven days.

- Any obligation placed on the employee to attend a medical examination with a doctor appointed by the employer.

9.13 An attendance management policy on the other hand will typically not be a contractual document but rather a set of management procedures providing guidance rather than rights and obligations. Such a policy might deal with:

- Back-to-work interviews.
- An absence monitoring process which triggers a formal procedure once absence reaches a certain level.
- A process for involving medical advice from the employee's doctor or a doctor appointed by the employer.
- A formal disciplinary-style procedure of investigation and hearings for unsatisfactory attendance with the possibility of the employee receiving one of an escalating series of warnings (verbal, written, final written) ending finally in dismissal where the level of absence can no longer be accepted.
- Rights of appeal against management decisions.

9.14 An employer may also adopt a range of additional policies and employee benefits aimed at improving sickness absence such as: attendance bonuses or incentives; taking absence into account in promotion or appraisals; stress counselling and other employee assistance programmes; private health insurance or services; general health promotion, for example, in staff canteen menus, gym membership or assistance in giving up smoking; flexible working arrangements and changes to working patterns or environment.

In equality terms, of course, whether the employer's actions follow from a **9.15** contractual obligation or policy guidance is irrelevant to the question of whether those actions are discriminatory. Employers therefore need to be vigilant that neither the contractual terms they offer nor the policies they follow discriminate, in particular, against disabled employees.

Interestingly, nearly 70 per cent of respondents to the CIPD survey reported **9.16** that their organisation had made changes to how sickness absence is managed in the previous two years. The percentage was highest amongst public services organisations at 82 per cent. Non-profit organisations were least likely to have changed their approach to absence management but 63 per cent of respondents from that sector had made changes. Size was also a factor, with 65 per cent of organisations employing 250 people or fewer having made changes to their absence management policy or practice compared to nearly 80 per cent among employers with 10,000 or more staff.

The situation is therefore similar across all sectors of the economy: the vast **9.17** majority of employers have developed formal policies to guide their management of employee sickness absence and the majority of those policies have been or are being reviewed and amended, mainly in an effort to reduce the amount of sickness absence taken by employees. It is primarily in these efforts to reduce sickness absence, either by more proactive management or by dismissing employees whose absence is deemed unacceptable, that employers risk conflicts with the rights of disabled employees.

D. Disability

(a) The Legal Framework

In Chapter 2 we provided a general overview of the law, including that **9.18** relating to the disability strand. We have decided to include more detail on the disability legislation in this chapter because it is so intertwined with attendance management issues. The legislation is not straightforward. As Lord Justice Sedley put it in *O'Hanlon v Commissioners for HM Revenue & Customs*:

> The DDA in its amended form is not at all easy to follow. This is a particular misfortune in an Act which it ought to be possible for employees and managers to read, understand and implement without legal advice or litigation. It can at least be said with confidence that the Act creates three kinds of discrimination:

(i) direct discrimination 'on the ground of' a person's disability, which is not open to justification (sections 3A(4) and (5));

(ii) disability-related discrimination, which was open to justification (sections 3A(1) and (3)); and

(iii) failure to make reasonable adjustments (sections 4A, 3A(2) and 18B).

In cases where there is no direct discrimination, it will often be useful to take issue (iii) [reasonable adjustments] before issue (ii) [disability-related discrimination].[3]

(i) Reasonable Adjustments

9.19 Under sections 3(A)(2) and 4(A)(1) of the DDA, where a provision, criterion or practice applied by or on behalf of an employer, or any physical feature of premises occupied by the employer, places a disabled person at a substantial disadvantage in comparison with non-disabled persons, the employer has a duty to take such steps as is reasonable, in all the circumstances of the case, to prevent that provision, criterion or practice, or feature, having that effect. If an employer fails to comply with this duty, this will constitute disability discrimination. There is no longer any justification defence to an employer's failure to make reasonable adjustments.

9.20 Section 18B(2) of the DDA provides the following non-exhaustive list of examples of adjustments that might reasonably be made, all of which are potentially relevant to attendance management:

- making adjustments to premises;
- allocating some of the disabled person's duties to another person;
- transferring the disabled person to fill an existing vacancy;
- altering the disabled person's hours of work or training;
- allowing the disabled person to be absent during working or training hours for rehabilitation, assessment or treatment;
- giving, or arranging for, training or mentoring (whether of the disabled person or any other person);
- acquiring or modifying equipment;
- modifying instructions or reference manuals;
- modifying procedures for testing or assessment;
- providing a reader or interpreter;
- providing supervision or other support.

(ii) Disability-related Discrimination

9.21 Disability-related discrimination falls under section 3(A)(1) of the DDA. An employer will discriminate against a disabled person if, for a reason which

---

[3] [2007] IRLR 404, CA.

relates to that person's disability, he treats him or her less favourably than he treats or would treat others to whom that reason does not or would not apply. Disability-related discrimination can be justified, but only where the reason for it is both material to the circumstances of the particular case and substantial.[4]

(iii) Relationship between Disability-related Discrimination and Reasonable Adjustments

Where the employer is under a duty to make a reasonable adjustment but fails **9.22** to comply, the employer cannot justify any disability-related discrimination under section 3A(1)(b) of the DDA unless the treatment would have been justified even if the employer had complied with that duty.[5]

An analysis of the way these concepts interrelate is therefore a three-stage **9.23** process:

- first, is the treatment disability related;
- secondly, is there a duty to make reasonable adjustments and if so, has it been complied with; and
- thirdly, can the disability-related treatment be justified.

This interrelationship between the duty to make reasonable adjustments and **9.24** justification of disability-related treatment lies at the heart of some of the attendance management cases dealt with below.

(b) Problems of Perspective and Expectation

The concept of disability discrimination is still relatively new. Set within the **9.25** framework and experience of equality law, some of the principles of disability discrimination are hard for some managers to understand. For example, treating disabled people more favourably through the provision of reasonable adjustments seems at first to jar with the more familiar concept of equal treatment.

It helps to see reasonable adjustments as taking active steps to produce an **9.26** equality of outcome for the disabled employee rather than equality of treatment, ie assisting the employee to overcome the disability that puts him or her in an unequal position to begin with. Reasonable adjustments are also sometimes referred to as addressing a 'social model of disability' where obstacles to inclusion for the disabled are more about the built environment and policy than individual impairment.

---

[4] DDA, s 3A(3).   [5] DDA, s 3A(6).

9.27 Many employers, unfortunately, still see the provision of reasonable adjustments as 'doing the employee a favour' rather than complying with their legal obligation under section 4A (read with section 18B) of the DDA. Such employers, consciously or subconsciously, see the cost of reasonable adjustments, whether direct (eg provision of equipment) or indirect (eg management time) as a form of tax on their act of charity in employing the disabled employee. Human nature drives such employers to look for gratitude from the disabled employee who has been the beneficiary of this largesse.

9.28 Many disabled employees, on the other hand, understand that the provision of reasonable adjustments is their legal right. As such, they are not naturally disposed to being overly grateful to an employer that is merely complying with its legal obligations.

9.29 This fundamental disjoint between these two opposing perspectives is not helped by the inherently nebulous nature of what constitutes 'reasonable adjustments'. Some employers tend towards a minimalist approach but equally some employees read 'reasonable' as meaning 'anything that I believe will benefit me'. The result can be an acrimonious downward spiral in the relationship between employer and employee:

- the employer provides some reasonable adjustments and expects the employee to be grateful;
- the employee believes that the adjustments do not go far enough and rather than showing gratitude, requests further adjustments;
- the employer perceives the employee as ungrateful and problematic;
- the employee perceives the employer's attitude as hostile and feels (possibly correctly) victimised;
- entrenched positions are taken and the matter becomes litigious.

9.30 Advisers on both sides have a role in preventing this downward spiral. On the employer side of the relationship more training may be necessary for managers, to achieve more of a realisation of legal obligations combined with less of an expectation of gratitude, and a more thorough consideration of reasonable adjustments. On the employee side of the relationship again more training may be necessary and more of an understanding of what constitutes 'reasonable' in the making of adjustments.

(c) **Disabled or Not Disabled—Who Decides?**

9.31 Ultimately, only an Employment Tribunal (or a higher court on appeal) can decide whether an employee is disabled or not. An employer can take medical advice, consult the individual employee and take a view, but this could be challenged through litigation. Of course, there is only likely to be a challenge from the employee if the employer takes a view that he or she is not disabled.

Reasonable Adjustments—A Modern Fable

The following, no doubt apocryphal, anecdote about reasonable adjustments did the rounds not long after the DDA first came into force.

A wheelchair user joined a financial institution based on the top floor of a city tower. From her wheelchair she was unable to reach the top button on the lift to access the office. The employer's facilities management team met to discuss what reasonable adjustments were necessary. They contacted the building managers who brought in the lift engineers. A feasibility study was carried out on lowering the lift buttons and estimates were given to the employer's board of directors. The board were locked in debate over the high cost and likely benefit of the proposed adjustment. It was then discovered that the employee had been quite happily operating the lift for weeks using a short piece of garden cane that she had bought herself!

The moral of the story is that (a) there may be a number of different ways in which an adjustment can be made, and (b) it is usually best practice to consult the employee before making any adjustment decisions.

Epilogue: of course, the story might have played out differently (and perhaps more realistically), had the employee been insistent that nothing short of lowering the lift buttons would have been a reasonable adjustment and had the employer instead offered nothing more than a garden cane!

There are two main problems with the employer taking a view. First, it could **9.32** result in a fairly artificial approach to managing an individual employment problem. This might be the case if, for example, the employer's determination on disability results in potentially different courses of management action: if the employee is deemed to be disabled, reasonable adjustments will be made but if the employee is deemed not to be disabled, the employer will do nothing. Secondly, if the employer erroneously takes the view that the employee is not disabled this may lead to management decisions in respect of the employee that are discriminatory.

It is probably better for the employer to treat all employees with health-related **9.33** issues as being potentially in need of assistance. What type of adjustments might be made would then be determined by the degree of impairment caused by the health issue and the prognosis rather than by the employer becoming distracted by trying to pigeon-hole the employee as 'disabled' or 'not disabled'.

9.34 That said, some employees who are disabled will wish to see from their employers a tangible recognition of their disability status and the rights and obligations that follow on from that status. There are also certain cases of deemed disability (where a person is automatically treated as being disabled), such as: a person who has cancer, HIV infection or multiple sclerosis,[6] a person who was in the register of disabled persons maintained under section 6 of the Disabled Persons (Employment) Act 1944[7] (now repealed); and a person who is certified as blind or partially sighted by a consultant ophthalmologist, or registered with a local authority.[8]

9.35 In practice, employees will most likely fall into three broad categories: (a) those who are obviously disabled as defined by section 1 of the DDA; (b) those who are obviously not disabled, and (c) a group in the middle who may or may not be disabled as defined. By acknowledging the disability status of the first group only, the employer may bring itself into conflict with those in the third group who consider themselves to be disabled. On balance we still think that an employer wishing to promote equality and diversity will be better advised to focus on the provision of reasonable adjustments to all those in need in the first and third groups, and whether all health-related treatment can be justified, rather than becoming distracted by categorising employees according to the precise definition of disability.

9.36 The role of medical evidence in determining the question of disability was considered in *Vicary v British Telecommunications plc*,[9] where the EAT held it is not for a doctor to express an opinion as to what is a normal day-to-day activity; nor is it for a medical expert to tell the tribunal whether the impairments which had been found proven were or were not substantial: rather these are matters for the employment tribunal to assess themselves.

9.37 The question for the employer in a management, rather than litigation, situation is, in any event, different. An employer seeking medical advice on how best to assist an employee should not, in our view, be asking the doctor to advise whether or not in his or her opinion the employee is disabled. Rather, the doctor should be asked to advise on the nature of any impairment and the effect that it has on the employee at work. This would include the employee's ability to carry out his or her duties and what adjustments the doctor might recommend to assist the employee.

---

⁶ DDA, sch 1, para 6A.   ⁷ DDA, sch 1, para 7(1).
⁸ Disability Discrimination (Blind and Partially Sighted Persons) Regulations 2003.
⁹ [1999] IRLR 680, EAT.

Note that these are very different questions from those an employer would **9.38**
ask where it is defending litigation and seeking to argue that the employee is
not disabled. In such circumstances, for example, the question of disability is
determined by the employee's ability to carry out normal day-to-day activities and not his or her duties. Also, in determining whether or not an
employee is disabled as defined, one disregards any measures taken to treat or
correct an impairment[10] (eg medical treatment, prosthesis or other aid) but
such treatment would be relevant to the question of what adjustments might
be needed to assist the employee. Too many employers fall into the trap of
thinking only of the legislative definition of disability and potential litigation
at the expense of seeking practical medical advice in how best to assist an
employee for whom a combination of health and circumstance create
disadvantage.

In gathering medical information, employers will need to comply with the **9.39**
terms of the Access to Medical Reports Act 1988 where a medical report has
been prepared by a medical practitioner who is or has been responsible for the
clinical care of the individual (ie the employee's own GP or consultant but not
a doctor appointed by the employer to carry out a medical assessment). Given
that medical reports will contain 'sensitive personal data' as defined in section
2 of the DPA, the employer will also need to comply with the terms of that
Act, including in particular the data protection principles in Schedule 1,
and with the 'Employment Practices Code' published by the Information
Commissioner.

E. Sick Pay

Prior to the coming into force of the employment sections of the DDA **9.40**
in December 1996, sick pay was largely a straightforward matter of contract.
An employer would choose, in consultation with any recognised trade unions
or employee representatives, to what extent, if at all, it wished to provide a
benefit over and above the statutory sick pay scheme. So long as the benefit
was provided in accordance with any contractual obligation there would be
no contractual issue and so long as it was provided without prejudice to
gender or race, there were no discrimination issues. The introduction of disability rights has, however, resulted in a number of recent claims relating to
sick pay.

---

[10] DDA, sch 1, para 6.

(a) The *Meikle* Case

9.41 *Nottinghamshire County Council v Meikle*[11] addressed the extent of an employer's obligation to continue paying full sick pay to a disabled employee beyond the requirements of the employer's normal policy. Mrs Meikle was employed by the Council as a school teacher. She had deteriorating vision, resulting in loss of sight in one eye and some sight in the other. She made various requests for the school to make adjustments including to her classroom location, the amount of preparation time she was given and that written materials and notices should be enlarged. Few of these steps were taken by the school.

9.42 She eventually took sick leave resulting, on the evidence of the consultant occupational health physician, not only from eye strain but also from the distress caused by the school's delay and general failure to implement reasonable adjustments to enable Mrs Meikle to continue working. Initially, under the Council's sick pay policy she was paid her full salary. However, after a hundred days of absence, that was reduced to half pay.

9.43 Mrs Meikle claimed that the reduction in her sickness benefit to half pay because of her absence from work amounted to two forms of disability discrimination:

- less favourable treatment for a reason related to disability that could not be justified, under what was then section 5(1) of the DDA (now section 3A(1)); and

- an unjustified[12] failure to comply with the duty under what was then section 6 of the DDA (now section 4A) to make reasonable adjustments to prevent her being at a substantial disadvantage compared to those who are not disabled under what was then section 5(2) of the DDA (now section 3A(2)).

9.44 Disability-related treatment: As regards the claim of disability-related treatment the questions were (a) was Mrs Meikle's sick pay reduced for a reason that related to her disability, and (b) if so, did the Council treat her less favourably than they would have treated others to whom that reason would not apply?

9.45 The answer to (a) was that the reason Mrs Meikle's sick pay was reduced was because she was unable to work; and she was unable to work because of her disability. The 'others', ie the appropriate comparators, for the purposes of assessing whether there had been less favourable treatment under (b), were

---

[11] [2004] IRLR 703, CA.
[12] DDA, s 5(2)(b) and s 5(4), which provided a justification defence to a failure to make reasonable adjustments, were repealed by the Disability Discrimination Act 1995 (Amendment) Regulations 2003.

other employees who were able to work (and not non-disabled employees on long-term sick leave who would also have had their sickness benefit reduced to half pay under the policy[13]).

In other words, the answer to the two questions, would have been: (a) Mrs **9.46** Meikle's sick pay was reduced for a reason that related to her disability, and (b) she was treated less favourably than her colleagues who were able to work. In the event, the Council accepted that the treatment was disability related.

Reasonable adjustments: The Court of Appeal found that the cause of Mrs **9.47** Meikle's absence from work was the Council's failure to make reasonable adjustments, and the placing of her on half pay put her at a substantial dis-advantage. A reasonable adjustment would, in the Court's view, have been to maintain sickness benefit at full pay. The fact that the Council reduced her sickness benefit to half pay was therefore a failure to make a reasonable adjustment and an act of discrimination under what was then section 5(2) of the DDA.

Justification: The Tribunal had originally found the disability-related treatment **9.48** justified; seemingly, simply on the basis that the Council had complied with its sick pay policy. However, having found that the Council had neglected to make the reasonable adjustment of maintaining sickness benefit at full pay, what was section 5(5) of the DDA (now section 3A(6)) prevented the treatment being justified.

Notwithstanding obvious sympathy for Mrs Meikle, this decision seemed **9.49** counter-intuitive. It seemed logical that a failure to make the original reason-able adjustments would lead to compensation either under the DDA or in the form of a personal injury claim; and that compensation would include loss of earnings once sick pay was reduced to half pay. But a finding that the later reduction in sick pay was itself a failure to make a reasonable adjustment seemed a step too far. Given the potential cost to employers of this finding it was only a matter of time before a test case was found.

(b) The *Archibald* Case

At around the same time that the Court of Appeal reached its decision in **9.50** *Meikle* the House of Lords were also busy doing their bit to extend our understanding of the meaning of reasonable adjustments. In *Archibald v Fife Council*[14] it was found that the duty extended to transferring an employee to another post at a higher grade or level of pay without a competitive interview

---

[13] *Clark v Novacold* [1999] ICR 951, CA.   [14] [2004] 4 All ER 303, HL.

even though an interview was a requirement of the Council's redeployment policy. Although the *Archibald* case was not about sick pay, it highlighted the point that to the extent that the duty to make reasonable adjustments requires it, the employer is not only permitted but obliged to treat a disabled person more favourably than others.

9.51 At paragraph 47 of the judgment in the *Archibald* case, Baroness Hale recognised that the DDA is indeed different from the SDA and the RRA:

> ... [the DDA] ... does not regard the differences between disabled people and others as irrelevant. It does not expect each to be treated in the same way. It expects reasonable adjustments to be made to cater for the special needs of disabled people. It necessarily entails an element of more favourable treatment. . . .

9.52 It is this legal obligation to treat disabled employees more favourably by actively making reasonable adjustments that employers must never overlook.

(c) Cabinet Office Guidance

9.53 On the back of this developing area of law, on 3 March 2005 the Cabinet Office issued guidance to public sector HR Directors which included the following statement:

> ... absences which were as a result of the individual's disability should be disregarded when considering trigger points for inefficiency action or the entitlement to contractual sick pay. Absences as a result of a condition not relating to the individual's disability should be considered to be counted in the usual way.[15]

9.54 This appeared to suggest that sick leave for disability-related reasons had to be completely disregarded when considering whether or not to warn or dismiss the employee and in relation to contractual sick pay. In other words, the guidance appeared to mean that an employee on long-term sick leave for disability-related reasons would be entitled to full pay and could never be dismissed.

9.55 Following what the Cabinet Office described euphemistically as several departments seeking 'clarification', the following further guidance was circulated on 1 June 2005:

> This is to clarify that departments *should not automatically* disregard any sickness absence related to disability when considering whether inefficiency/unsatisfactory attendance procedures should be put in place or when reducing pay when either full or half pay has been exhausted as a result of absence [emphasis added].[16]

---

[15] HRD Main (05)(16), HRD Small (05)(16), HRD NDPBs (05)(5).
[16] HRDG (Main)(05) 46, HRDG (Small)(05) 46, HRDG (NDPBs)(05) 21.

We mention this guidance partly to illustrate that this is not a straightforward **9.56**
area on which to advise, and partly because there are still occasions when
individual public sector employees and their trade union representatives quote
the original guidance but overlook the further guidance.

(d) The *O'Hanlon* case

The post-*Meikle* test case eventually arrived in the shape of *O'Hanlon v The* **9.57**
Commissioners for HM Revenue and Customs[17] (an EAT decision later effectively
rubber stamped by the Court of Appeal[18]).

Mrs O'Hanlon had been employed by Her Majesty's Revenue and Customs **9.58**
('HMRC') since 1985. She had suffered from clinical depression since 1988,
which was accepted between the parties as amounting to a disability under the
DDA. She took significant periods of absence and, from 1988 to 2002, her total
sickness absence was 365 days, only 45 of which did not relate to her disability.

Under HMRC's sick pay rules, employees were entitled to receive full pay for **9.59**
up to six months' sickness absence in any period of 12 months, and half pay for
a further maximum period of six months. This was subject to an overriding
maximum of 12 months' paid sickness absence in any period of four years.
HMRC's rules then provided that employees may receive the lesser of their
equivalent pension rate of pay, or half pay. The application of the rules meant
that Mrs O'Hanlon was on pension rate for all absences after October 2002.
The HMRC sick pay scheme also provided for a further 40 days' additional sick
absence with full pay. Mrs O'Hanlon applied for this but HMRC would not
grant this on a retrospective basis.

Mrs O'Hanlon brought a claim under the DDA. She claimed that she should **9.60**
have received full pay for all her disability-related sickness absences. She
claimed that she was substantially disadvantaged by the sick pay rules, compared to a non-disabled person, and that HMRC had failed to make any
reasonable adjustments to counter that disadvantage, to enable her to continue
to receive full pay during her absence. She claimed that she had also been
subject to disability-related discrimination, as her absence was related to her
disability, and the failure to continue paying her was not justified. The EAT
decision emphasises the parameters and purpose of the DDA.

Disability-related discrimination: The reason for HMRC's failure to pay Mrs **9.61**
O'Hanlon full pay under its sick pay rules was clearly related to her disability.
The reason Mrs O'Hanlon's sick pay was reduced was because she was unable
to work; and she was unable to work because of her disability.

---

[17] [2006] ICR 1579, EAT.   [18] [2007] IRLR 404, CA.

9.62 Reasonable adjustments: The EAT found that the sick pay rules constituted a provision, criterion or practice potentially placing Mrs O'Hanlon at a disadvantage and a duty to make reasonable adjustments was applicable. However, it held that it would be a 'very rare case indeed' for an employer to be obliged, as a reasonable adjustment, to give more sick pay to a disabled employee than it would otherwise give to a non-disabled employee who in general does not suffer the same disability-related absences.

9.63 The EAT commented that such an obligation would mean that Tribunals would be entering into a form of 'wage fixing for the disabled sick' and would fall foul of the purpose of disability discrimination legislation, which is to assist the disabled to obtain employment and to integrate them into the workforce. The EAT noted that the provisions of section 18B of the DDA, relating to the scope of reasonable adjustments, reinforce this approach. None of the provisions suggest that it will ever be necessary simply to put more money into the wage packet of the disabled—particularly where this might result in a disincentive to return to work. The EAT also stated that the DDA is designed to recognise the dignity of the disabled and to require modifications which will enable the disabled to play a full part in the world of work, not to treat them as an 'object of charity'.

9.64 Justification: As it was found that it was not a reasonable adjustment for HMRC to adjust the sick pay rules, it followed that the disability-related discrimination could be justified. The EAT noted that there were powerful economic reasons for the employer to adopt its sick pay rules. It would have cost a very significant sum to pay full pay to all disabled employees who were absent sick in circumstances where their pay would otherwise be reduced. There was therefore a material and substantial reason for the treatment. The EAT also added that the justification could simply be the fact that the employer considered it appropriate to pay those who attend work and contribute to the operation more than those whose absence prevents that.

(e) **Reconciling the *Meikle* and *O'Hanlon* Cases**

9.65 The Court of Appeal in the *Meikle* case did not find that the payment of full pay was a reasonable adjustment in isolation from the other specific adjustments that, had they been made, would have allowed Mrs Meikle to continue working without any, or such lengthy, absences. As the EAT in the *O'Hanlon* case put it: 'It was never suggested that the adjustment lay simply in granting full pay.' In addition, the EAT in the *O'Hanlon* case seemed slightly bemused that the *Meikle* case had not been argued in a more straightforward way that liability arose because of the failure to make reasonable adjustments and that included the loss of income once her sickness benefit was reduced to half pay.

Reasonable Adjustments and Sick Pay—Conclusions

- It will be a 'very rare case indeed' where an employer is obliged to give more sick pay to a disabled employee than is normally provided for in the employer's sick pay rules (*O'Hanlon v The Commissioners for HM Revenue and Customs*).
- There remains some doubt as to whether the 'very rare case indeed' envisaged by the EAT in the *O'Hanlon* case includes the (not that uncommon) situation in *Nottinghamshire County Council v Meikle* where the employee alleges that sickness absence has resulted from the employer's failure to make reasonable adjustments in the first place.
- In our view the wrong approach was followed in the *Meikle* case. Liability was established under the DDA with a finding that the employer neglected to make reasonable adjustments causing Mrs Meikle to take sick leave. Her resulting loss included loss of income when sickness benefit was changed to half pay. There was no need to deal with sick pay as a reasonable adjustment issue to prevent Mrs Meikle suffering financial loss. Although the reduction in sick pay did put Mrs Meikle at a substantial disadvantage triggering the obligation to make reasonable adjustments, in our view retaining sickness benefit at full pay would not have been a reasonable adjustment for the reasons given in the *O'Hanlon* case.
- Those employers who interpret the *Meikle* case as meaning that sickness benefit should be maintained at full pay as a reasonable adjustment where the employee alleges that the reason for absence results from the employer's failures (but not otherwise) need to proceed with caution. The point is not yet legally certain. In any event, were the employer to take the view that full pay should be maintained, such an adjustment is tantamount to an admission of liability and should not be made without the approval of the employer's insurers and/or legal advisers.

F. Managing Absence

(a) Reasonable Adjustments

Reasonable adjustments are central to attendance management given the **9.66** common overlap between absence and disability. The approach suggested by paragraph 8.16 of the DRC Code 2004 is:

- first consider adjustments that would enable the employee to remain in his or her job if at all possible;
- consult the employee including over future needs where the employee has a progressive condition;
- seek expert advice on the extent of the employee's capabilities and what might be done to change premises or working arrangements—a phased return may be appropriate; and
- if there are no reasonable adjustments that can be made to keep the employee in his or her present job, only then consider redeployment to suitable alternative positions.

9.67 Any adjustments should ideally be made in consultation with the employee, however, as the EAT pointed out in *Cosgrove v Caesar and Howie*,[19] the duty to make reasonable adjustments is not limited to adjustments identified or suggested at the time by the claimant. In the *Cosgrove* case neither the employee nor her doctor put forward suggested reasonable adjustments. However, there were adjustments that the employer could have made but did not consider, such as a change of working hours or location.

9.68 In *Archibald v Fife Council*[20] Ms Archibald's job involved refuse collection, cleaning of public toilets, road sweeping and similar tasks. She had a spinal anaesthetic for a minor surgical procedure, which led to a complication of severe pain over her heels, as a result of which she was unable to walk. Initially, she used a wheelchair and later was only able to walk with the assistance of sticks. The Council obtained medical advice about Ms Archibald's likely prospects of being fit to return to work and steps were taken to explore whether suitable alternative employment might be available in other departments.

9.69 Over a period of months, Ms Archibald unsuccessfully applied for over a hundred alternative posts. She was unable to meet the physical demands of the posts or the environmental constraints in which they were to be performed. The posts for which she applied had a basic salary marginally higher than her own. As a result, in accordance with the Council's redeployment policy, she had to undertake competitive interviews. Eventually, the Council took the view that the redeployment procedure had been exhausted and that she should be dismissed, having regard to the length of her absence and the advice received that she would be unable to return to work as a road sweeper in the foreseeable future.

9.70 The House of Lords found that it would have been a reasonable adjustment not to require Ms Archibald to go through competitive interviews if she

---

[19] [2001] IRLR 653, EAT.   [20] [2004] 4 All ER 303, HL.

could show that she was qualified and suitable for an existing vacancy. In other words, it would have been reasonable to disapply the Council's redeployment policy and appoint Ms Archibald to a position at a slightly higher rate of pay.

Ultimately, an employer needs employees to turn up for work and to ensure **9.71** that dismissal of those who are unable to do so, even for disability-related reasons, can be justified. Such cases are always going to be fact-sensitive and making out the justification defence is likely to involve the type of impact assessment we described above.

There may be times where the employer cannot be expected to wait any longer **9.72** even if there is some prospect of an employee on long-term sick leave returning. In *Home Office v Collins*,[21] for example, the claimant had a 'poor' attendance during the first six months of her employment followed by more than 12 months' absence. There was medical evidence to suggest that she should have been able to return on a part-time basis in three to six months. However, the Tribunal was entitled to conclude that it was reasonable for the employer not to pursue the possibility of a phased return to part-time work until the employee could indicate a definite date for her return to work.

(b) Adjustments, Assessment and Consultation

The theme of this book, to which we keep returning, is the promotion of **9.73** equality and diversity. Assessment and consultation with employees in order to establish what reasonable adjustments might be made to avoid absence or facilitate a return to work are integral to best practice in absence management. There are, however, conflicting authorities in the EAT as to whether they are integral to satisfying the duty to make reasonable adjustments ie whether a failure to assess and consult is in itself discrimination.

On the one hand, in *Mid-Staffordshire General Hospitals NHS Trust v Cam-* **9.74** *bridge*[22] the EAT found that 'a proper assessment of what is required to eliminate a disabled person's disadvantage is a necessary part of the duty [to make reasonable adjustments] since that duty cannot be complied with unless the employer makes a proper assessment of what needs to be done'. The facts of the case were never going to endear the employer to the Tribunal:

- the evidence suggested that the employers had caused or exacerbated Mrs Cambridge's condition, a bowing of the vocal cords and tracheitis, by demolishing a wall in her working area, creating extreme amounts of dust;

---

[21] [2005] EWCA 598, CA.   [22] [2003] IRLR 566, EAT.

- although she was eventually certified fit to return to work for up to two hours per day, management gave no thought to any reasonable adjustments;
- when managers discovered that it would take her at least 12 months to make a full recovery, they decided that unless she could return to full-time working within a reasonable time they would recommend dismissal;
- when Mrs Cambridge discovered this she was extremely distressed and certified unfit to work for just over two weeks;
- on Christmas Eve, whilst off sick, she was sent a recorded delivery package containing a formal notice of a disciplinary hearing;
- although there was a long delay, she was eventually dismissed on the grounds of incapacity due to ill health.

9.75 The Tribunal took the view that the reasonable adjustments wording of what was then section 6 of the DDA (now section 4A) required an employer 'to take such steps as . . . is reasonable . . . to prevent' substantial disadvantage and that this included taking such steps as would enable the employers to decide what steps would be reasonable to prevent Mrs Cambridge from being at such disadvantage. The fact that the employers had failed to 'seek, obtain or act on a full and proper assessment of Mrs Cambridge's position' meant that they had failed to comply with the duty to make reasonable adjustments. The EAT agreed with the Tribunal, finding that the making of an assessment cannot be separated from the duty to make reasonable adjustments 'because it is a necessary precondition to the fulfilment of that duty and therefore part of it'.

9.76 In the opposing camp is *Tarbuck v Sainsbury's Supermarket Ltd*[23] where the EAT found that there was no separate and distinct duty of reasonable adjustment on an employer to consult a disabled employee about what adjustment might be made—describing the *Mid-Staffordshire* case as 'incorrect'. The only question is whether objectively the employer has complied with its obligation or not—what the employer did or did not do, not what the employer considered or discussed. If the employer does make reasonable adjustments then the fact that there was a failure to consult or even complete ignorance of the reasonable adjustment duty[24] is irrelevant.

9.77 In *Tarbuck* the EAT do, however, say that it will always be good practice to consult and that a failure to do so will not allow an employer to argue a lack of knowledge of things that it would have discovered in consultation, as a defence to a complaint that reasonable adjustments have not been made. *Tarbuck* was subsequently followed by the EAT in *NCH Scotland v McHugh*[25] which

---

[23] [2006] IRLR 664, EAT.
[24] *British Gas Services Ltd v McCaull* [2001] IRLR 60, EAT.
[25] UKEATS/0010/06/MT, EAT.

summarised the lines of cases on both sides of the argument and summarised *Tarbuck* as finding that 'the duty is to **make** reasonable adjustments'. Therefore assessment and consultation are not required as an end in themselves but rather as a means for the employer properly to inform itself of what reasonable adjustments it is required to make.

In *Hay v Surrey County Council*[26] Ms Hay was a mobile library manager who **9.78** developed a degenerative knee condition which made it impossible to continue all of her duties, including driving the mobile library and carrying and stacking books. The Council obtained medical advice from a number of doctors which pointed towards moving Ms Hay to a sedentary role but did not carry out a 'formal risk assessment' of the mobile library manager role. The Court of Appeal found that a Tribunal's conclusion that the absence of a risk assessment exercise was fundamental to the case, so 'infected their decision as a whole' that they failed to identify which adjustments ought to have been made by the Council.

It is worth noting at this point, however, that there is a separate and distinct **9.79** obligation on employers under regulation 3 of the Management of Health and Safety at Work Regulations 1999, to carry out suitable and sufficient assessment of the risks to the health and safety of their employees to which they are exposed whilst at work.

In the *Hay* case the Court of Appeal declined the invitation to rule on which of **9.80** the *Mid-Staffordshire* and *Tarbuck* cases was correctly decided, since the parties in *Hay* had themselves both agreed that it was *Tarbuck*. Interestingly, Ms Hay was represented by leading counsel instructed on behalf of the DRC who had intervened in the case. Although there was no issue between the parties on the *Tarbuck* point, Mr Allen QC did indicate that the DRC was concerned about certain aspects of the guidance in *Tarbuck*, which the DRC would like to see clarified. This may well happen in *Spence v Intype Libra Ltd*[27] where leave to appeal to the Court of Appeal on this issue has been granted.

Project Management Institute v Latif[28] is another case in which the DRC were **9.81** involved (again represented by leading counsel), where the parties also agreed that the *Tarbuck* case was correctly decided. This case also dealt with the application of the rules on burden of proof to reasonable adjustments. The EAT very much doubted whether the burden shifts at all in respect of establishing the provision, criterion or practice, or demonstrating substantial disadvantage. These are simply questions of fact for the tribunal to decide after hearing

---

[26] [2007] EWCA Civ 93, CA.   [27] UKEAT/0617/06/JOJ, EAT.   [28] UKEAT/0028/07.

all the evidence, with the onus of proof resting throughout on the claimant. However, the employer is in the best position to say whether any apparently reasonable amendment is in fact reasonable given its own particular circumstances. That is why the burden is reversed once a potentially reasonable amendment has been identified.

Absence, Adjustments, Assessments and Consultation— Conclusions

- The duty to make reasonable adjustments applies to an employer where a provision, criterion or practice or physical feature of the employer's premises places a disabled person at substantial disadvantage (sections 3A(2), 4A and 18B of the DDA).
- The duty is not limited to adjustments identified or suggested by the employee (*Cosgrove v Caesar and Howie*).
- In litigation, it is for the employee to identify what adjustments might have been reasonable. The burden then shifts to the employer to show that such adjustment would not have been reasonable (*Project Management Institute v Latif*).
- A failure by the employer to carry out a risk assessment or consult the employee about reasonable adjustments is not, in itself, a failure to make a reasonable adjustment (*Tarbuck v Sainsbury's Supermarket Ltd*).
- However, an employer that fails to carry out a risk assessment or consult the employee may fail to understand what adjustments could be made to remove substantial disadvantage and assist the employee. Such an employer may only discover later, in Employment Tribunal proceedings, what adjustments the employee thinks would have been reasonable. By that point the employer will have swapped the opportunity to consult the employee about the proposed adjustments for the legal burden of proving that the adjustments proposed would not have been reasonable.

(c) Recording Absence

9.82 Although the DRC Code 2004 does not say, in clear terms, that disability-related sickness absence should be recorded separately from non-disability-related sickness absence, this is mentioned in two of the good practice examples:

- paragraph 2.13: 'a redundancy policy that has sickness absence as a selection criteria is amended to exclude disability-related absence. The sickness absence policy is also changed so that disability-related sickness is recorded separately'; and

- paragraph 5.20: 'a woman with an autoimmune disease has taken several short periods of absence during the year because of the condition. When her employer is taking absences into account as a criterion for selecting people for redundancy, he discounts these periods of disability-related absence.'

Any attempt to record disability-related absence separately from non-disability-related absence is never going to be a precise science. First, there is the issue of who decides whether the employee is disabled and whether or not this is an appropriate exercise in any event (see above). Separately, it may not always be obvious whether a particular absence is disability related. **9.83**

Nevertheless, we do suggest in situations where the employee's attendance is below a level which the employer considers acceptable, that it is appropriate for the employer to enquire whether a particular absence is (a) connected to an underlying health condition or (b) unconnected to any such condition and, where an underlying health condition exists, to record the two categories of absence separately. This will assist the employer, in consultation with the employee and medical advisers, to assess to what extent the underlying health condition impacts upon the employee's attendance. The employer can then make informed decisions about whether adjustments can be made to improve attendance and, were those adjustments to be made, whether the resulting level of attendance is supportable by the employer. **9.84**

However, the provisions of the DDA do not impose an absolute obligation on an employer to refrain from dismissing an employee who is absent wholly or in part on grounds of ill health due to disability. This was made clear, to the extent it needed to be, in *Royal Liverpool Children's NHS Trust v Dunsby*[29] where an Employment Tribunal muddled up the issue of justifying disability-related discrimination and the practice of recording disability-related absence separately from non-disability-related absence. **9.85**

Two of Mrs Dunsby's many absences had been contemporaneously recorded as being on account of 'headaches'. Much later, in the context of litigation, she sought to recategorise them as migraines related to a disability. The Tribunal reasoned that had they originally been categorised as disability-related absence then stage 2 of the Trust's disciplinary procedure would not have been triggered, which in turn would have meant that stage 4 of the procedure, which led to dismissal, would instead have only been stage 3. There was nothing, **9.86**

---

[29] UKEAT/0426/05.

incidentally, in the Trust's procedure to suggest that disability-related absence would be disregarded.

9.87 In dismissing the Tribunal's reasoning in fairly scathing terms, the EAT made it clear that an employer may take into account disability-related absences in operating a sickness absence procedure. Whether by doing so the employer treats the employee less favourably and acts unlawfully will generally depend on whether or not the treatment is justified.

(d) Benchmarking and Trigger Points

9.88 Employers may benchmark their attendance rates against other employers nationally or regionally. For our purposes the most important type of benchmarking occurs where the employer adopts an acceptable level of absence against which to measure the 'performance' of its employees; typically and in line with the CIPD survey report, the average is eight days' absence, per employee, per year. Attendance management procedures are then 'triggered' when attendance reaches or exceeds the eight day 'trigger point'. The promotion of equality and diversity is not about slack management so adopting this type of procedure is entirely compatible with those aims. Where the promotion of equality and diversity is relevant is in how those procedures are adapted, in particular, to deal with disability issues.

9.89 Best practice suggests that an employer should be working with any employee who reaches the trigger point and with medical advisers where appropriate. The first task will be to see whether attendance can be improved. Poor attendance may result from malingering which back-to-work interviews and attendance-related warnings might address. Where there are underlying health issues, reasonable adjustments might be identified which will help improve attendance.

9.90 In some circumstances the types of reasonable adjustment that would assist an employee to improve attendance might have no effect; the employee's health condition may simply result in higher than average levels of absence. For these employees, employers should consider (a) obtaining medical advice as to what level of absence is likely, and, (b) carrying out an assessment on the impact that level of absence will have on the organisation and whether that impact can be mitigated. If the predicted absence can reasonably be accommodated the employer may then want to adjust the trigger point for that employee to a level that will assist the employer and the employee to monitor the employee's absence against that predicted by the medical advice and assessed as capable of being accommodated by the employer.

(e) Disciplinary Procedures

The ACAS Code of Practice 1: Disciplinary and Grievance Procedures (2004) **9.91** contains a number of hints that a standard disciplinary approach to managing conduct and performance at work is perhaps not the best way of dealing with absence from work for genuine health-related reasons:

- paragraph 2: '. . . unsatisfactory performance (or capability) may require different treatment from misconduct . . .';

- paragraphs 37 and 38: 'When dealing with absence from work it is important to determine the reasons why the employee has not been at work. If there is no acceptable reason, the matter should be treated as a conduct issue and dealt with as a disciplinary matter. If the absence is due to genuine (including medically certified) illness, the issue becomes one of capability and the employer should take a sympathetic and considerate approach'; and

- paragraph 58: 'Some organisations may prefer to have separate procedures for dealing with issues of conduct and capability.'

A standard disciplinary procedure, with its formal hearings and verbal, written **9.92** and final written warnings, is not naturally designed to deal with genuine sickness absence, implying as it does, a suggestion of 'fault' or 'guilt' on the part of the employee. An employee with genuine health issues is not guilty of any misconduct. A 'warning' in the sense of 'don't do it again' is meaningless if the employee is powerless to control his or her health.

That said, the use of disciplinary procedures was rated by the respondents to **9.93** the CIPD report as one of the most effective methods of managing short-term absence—suggesting that employees do have a degree of control over minor ailment-related absence. However, the involvement of occupational health professionals and rehabilitation programmes were rated as the most effective approaches to managing long-term absence.

The ACAS Code does not give any detailed guidance on what an attendance **9.94** management policy might contain. We would suggest that any procedure adopted by an employer does not stray too far from the established types of disciplinary procedure envisaged by ACAS. Whilst it would be unwise to scrap the staged 'warning' based approach completely, any 'warning' given should be more advisory rather than penal. In other words, the employer should be explaining that the level of attendance cannot continue with an explanation for why that is the case, for example, the severe operational difficulties caused by the employee's non-attendance or the cost in terms of lost production or temporary staff cover.

9.95 The evidence from the CIPD report suggests that impact assessing employee absence is relatively uncommon and unsophisticated. Less than half of the respondents monitored the cost to their organisations of employee absence and even smaller percentages monitored indirect costs: cost of replacement labour (44 per cent), overtime costs (35 per cent), cost of reduced performance (21 per cent) and administration (9 per cent). We see the monitoring of cost and impact as essential to any employer that has to explain to an employee (or worse an Employment Tribunal) that the level of absence was at a level that the employer could not be expected to accept.

(f) Keeping in Touch

9.96 It is important to absence management that regular contact is kept with an employee who is absent from work on account of sickness. It would help if the process was set out in the absence management procedure. Such contact might include requesting a general update from the employee on their health, encouraging the employee to attend appropriate medical appointments and maintain up-to-date medical certificates and keeping the employee in touch with developments at work. Clearly this needs to be handled sensitively especially if the absence is work related. Over-zealous management could lead to allegations of harassment but a scheduled weekly catch-up phone call is unlikely to lead to any justifiable complaints from the employee.

A Final Thought

It is easy to forget just how recently there was no concept of 'disability rights'. As recently as 1994—the year Tony Blair became leader of the Labour Party, Nelson Mandela was elected as President of South Africa, and Hugh Grant attended Four Weddings and a Funeral—it remained perfectly legal to discriminate against disabled people. By the end of 2006 it was against the law to discriminate against disabled people in virtually every area of life.

(Speech by Bert Massie, DRC Chairman, at the launch of the DRC's 'Disability Agenda', 14th February 2007)

G. Attendance and the Other Discrimination Strands

9.97 We mention briefly below the ways in which attendance management may lead to issues in respect of the strands of discrimination other than disability.

(a) Attendance and Gender

(i) Gender Reassignment

'Gender reassignment' is defined in section 82(1) of the SDA to mean 'a **9.98** process which is undertaken under medical supervision for the purpose of reassigning a person's sex by changing physiological or other characteristics of sex, and includes any part of such a process'. Where an employee is absent from work or from vocational training because he or she is undergoing gender reassignment, in putting in place any arrangements relating to that absence, the employer must ensure that the employee is not treated less favourably than would be the case if the absence was due to:

- sickness or injury; or
- some other cause and, having regard to the circumstances of the case, it is reasonable for him or her to be treated no less favourably.[30]

The legislation does not specify how much absence an employer should reason- **9.99** ably be expected to accommodate. The process of gender assignment can take place over a period of years and may or may not involve surgery. The law merely provides for comparable treatment with other employees who take time off work for other reasons, such as sickness and injury.

(ii) Sickness and Pregnancy

We have considered sickness and pregnancy in Chapter 8. **9.100**

(b) Attendance and Age

There is a risk of discrimination occurring whenever one starts to make **9.101** assumptions generally without examining the particular facts of each individual's case. We in no way wish to suggest that older employees are likely to have more health-related issues at work or poorer attendance records than their younger colleagues. Employers whose decisions in individual cases are based upon such assumptions may well expose themselves to age discrimination claims.

However, as some employees get older they may develop medical conditions **9.102** associated with aging that affect their performance at work or their attendance records. Employers who take action to manage such employees will need to ensure that their actions are consistent with their management of employees in other age groups so as to avoid discriminating on the grounds of age.

---

[30] SDA, s 2A(3).

9.103 There may, in addition, be an overlap between age and disability where the age-related condition fits the DDA definition of a physical or mental impairment that has a substantial, long-term, adverse effect on ability to carry out day-to-day activities.

(c) **Attendance and Race**

9.104 In limited circumstances where conditions are inherited, there might be an overlap between attendance and race. For example, sickle cell anaemia in the UK is most common in people of African and Caribbean descent, cystic fibrosis is most common in those of European descent and Tay-Sachs disease most common in those of Jewish descent. However, provided that attendance management procedures are consistently applied there should be no direct discrimination and any indirect discrimination should be capable of justification.

Attendance Management: In Brief

- The discrimination strand most commonly associated with attendance management is disability. However, attendance problems and disability are not synonymous: attendance at work is not an issue for many disabled people. However, for some disabled people, regular attendance may be more difficult than for their non-disabled colleagues.

- It will be a 'very rare case indeed' where an employer is obliged to give more sick pay to a disabled employee than is normally provided for in the employer's sick pay rules.

- The duty to make reasonable adjustments applies to an employer where a provision, criterion or practice (which includes the elements of an attendance management procedure) or physical feature of the employer's premises places a disabled person at substantial disadvantage.

- A failure by the employer to carry out a risk assessment or consult the employee about reasonable adjustments is not, in itself, a failure to make a reasonable adjustment.

- Ultimately, an employer needs employees to turn up for work and dismissal of those who are unable to do so, even for disability-related reasons, can be justified. However, an employer should ensure that it follows a structured attendance management procedure, obtains medical advice and monitors the cost and impact of the absence before making any decision that the level of absence was at a level that the employer could not be expected to accept.

- In limited circumstances there may be an overlap between attendance and some of the other discrimination strands, such as sickness and pregnancy, absence for gender reassignment, absence for medical conditions related to age and absence for inherited conditions that affect a greater proportion of people from a particular racial group.

10

RELIGIOUS PRACTICE, DRESS CODES AND FREEDOM OF EXPRESSION IN THE WORKPLACE

Another key theme [in 461 cases brought under the RBR] were claims stemming from difficulties over working hours, time off or leave to follow religious practices, promotion or retirement and workplace dress codes . . .

(ACAS[1])

A. Introduction

The interplay between equality and diversity law and human rights principles in the workplace is perhaps strongest in the areas of religious practice, dress codes and freedom of expression. These three areas are interrelated in that they often overlap in practice, and all involve a tension between the employee's right not to be discriminated against on any of the prohibited grounds and their right to respect for their human rights in the workplace (most strikingly if they are public sector employees[2]); and the employer's desire to run their business in efficient ways that are fair to all. In this chapter we explore the law relating to these issues and seek to offer practical ways in which advisers can strike a fair balance between these competing needs. **10.01**

B. Religious Practice

Religious practice can become relevant in the workplace in several ways: employees may wish to work certain days or hours to facilitate the observance **10.02**

---

[1] B Savage, *Sexual Orientation and Religion or Belief Discrimination in the Workplace* (ACAS Research Summary, 2007), as summarised at <www.acas.org.uk/index.aspx?articleid=1258>.
[2] As it is only public sector employees who can bring a free-standing HRA claim for breach of their Convention rights against their employer, as we explain further in Chapter 2.

269

of their religion; they may need absences from work to celebrate festivals or carry out certain rituals; and they may request certain facilities within the workplace to enable them to observe their religion during working hours. There are various ways in which the law provides a framework for addressing and resolving these issues.

(a) The Legal Framework

(i) Religious Practice and the RRA

10.03 Certain religions are particularly common among people of a certain race, and so workplace policies relating to religion can have a disparate impact on those of a certain race, raising a *prima facie* case of indirect race discrimination. This has meant that even before the passage of the RBR (which provide a specific means of enforcing certain religious provision in the workplace, as we discuss below) the RRA was used to challenge policies which were primarily concerned with religious issues but which were indirectly discriminatory on grounds of race. In *Walker v Hussain and others*,[3] for example, 17 Muslim production workers who had been disciplined for taking a day off work to celebrate Eid—one of the most important religious occasions in the Muslim calendar—succeeded in their claim under the RRA on the basis that a rule prohibiting time off during May, June or July indirectly discriminated against Asian workers, and could not be justified.

10.04 Recent research by ACAS concluded that religious discrimination in the workplace remained 'closely aligned' with race discrimination; and that in two-thirds of the 461 cases brought under the RBR between February 2004 and August 2006, race discrimination was also complained of.[4] Employers will therefore still need to be conscious that policies which relate to religious practices may also be indirectly discriminatory on grounds of race.

(ii) Religious Practice and the HRA

10.05 Permitting employees space to practise their religion also raises issues under the HRA, because Article 9(1) protects the right to 'manifest' thought, conscience and religion, and such 'manifestation' of religious belief through worshipping, teaching, practising or otherwise observing religion can require accommodation in the workplace. Interferences with the right to manifest religious belief under Article 9(1) can only be justified under Article 9(2) if they are in accordance with law, and are proportionate and necessary in a democratic society in the interests of national security, public safety, for the economic well-being of

---

[3] [1996] ICR 291, EAT.
[4] B Savage, *Sexual Orientation and Religion or Belief Discrimination in the Workplace* (ACAS Research Summary, 2007), p 3.

the country, for the prevention of disorder or crime, for the protection of health or morals, or for the protection of the rights and freedoms of others.

However, those who have sought to deploy Article 9 in litigation before the **10.06** European Court of Human Rights (and the old European Commission of Human Rights) to generate working hours which coincide with their religious practices have largely been unsuccessful.

In *Ahmad v UK*,[5] for example, a Muslim employee challenged his employer's **10.07** refusal to allow him to attend mosque on a Friday afternoon as a breach of his Article 9 rights. The Commission ruled that his complaint was inadmissible on the basis that he had suffered no interference with his Article 9 rights—he had not disclosed his need for time off during his interview, and during the first six years of his employment he had been employed at such a distance from the mosque that he had been excused attendance at Friday afternoon prayers.

Similarly, in *Stedman v UK*,[6] a Christian employee complained that she had **10.08** been dismissed for refusing to work on Sundays. The Commission, as in the *Ahmad* case, concluded that she had suffered no interference with her Article 9 rights because she had been dismissed for failing to work certain agreed hours, rather than for her religious beliefs, and because she was free to resign and find another job elsewhere which did not require her to work on Sundays.

The domestic courts are, at least at present, and albeit with some apparent **10.09** reluctance, following the line set in the *Ahmad* and *Stedman* cases. In *Copsey v WWB Clays Ltd*,[7] for example, a practising Christian refused to agree to change his hours to work a seven-day shift which would have required him to work some Sundays. He was willing to work Sundays in an emergency, but not on a regular, basis. He argued that this interfered with his Article 9 rights. The Court of Appeal concluded, applying the Strasbourg approach, that Article 9 was not engaged because Mr Copsey could resign and find another job. Lord Justice Mummery in the Court of Appeal was critical of the *Ahmad/Stedman* approach, though, and pointed out that it was 'difficult to square with the supposed fundamental nature of the rights' in the EHCR. He also noted that it had not been argued in respect of the applicants in *Smith and Grady v UK*[8] (the case involving the homosexual service personnel who challenged the ban on gay people serving in the military) that there was no infringement of their Article 8 rights because they were free to resign and find other careers.

There are some signs that this restrictive approach may be changing—in *R* **10.10**

---

[5] (1982) 4 EHRR 126, ECtHR.   [6] (1997) 23 EHRR CD 168, ECtHR.
[7] [2005] IRLR 511, CA.   [8] (2000) 29 EHRR 493, ECtHR.

(Williamson and others) v Secretary of State for Education and Employment,[9] for example, the House of Lords accepted that a belief that physical punishment should be administered in schools was a manifestation of a Christian religious belief, which fell to be justified, even though, as argued by the Secretary of State, the parents could have sought to educate their children in a manner which would permit such physical punishment (by attending schools themselves to discipline their children; disciplining them after school; or educating them at home).

10.11 Employers who refuse to accommodate the religious needs of their employees may therefore find themselves more vulnerable to successful arguments under the HRA in the future than they might be now.

(iii) Religious Practice and the RBR

10.12 Finally, the RBR is proving a reasonably popular means by which employees are seeking to ensure accommodation for their religious practices at work, and an additional measure by which employers need to assess their policies in this area.

10.13 Although the DTI Guidance to the RBR stated that 'religion or belief' did not include the manifestation of or conduct based on or expressing a religion or belief, such as praying at certain times,[10] this would seem an unduly restrictive reading of the RBR. This is because it is not consistent with the general approach to the 'on grounds of' phrase in the equality enactments,[11] and because in *R (Amicus—MSF Section) v Secretary of State for Trade and Industry,*[12] the High Court held that discrimination on grounds of sexual orientation relates 'as much to the manifestation of that orientation in the form of sexual behaviour as it does to sexuality as such'—and this approach applies by analogy to manifestations of religion and belief.

10.14 The key issue as far as direct discrimination in this area is concerned will never-theless be whether an employee has been treated less favourably on grounds of his or her religion than an employee of another religion has or would have been treated. An example of this in operation was *Husain v Bhullar Bros t/a BB Supersave,*[13] where a Muslim shop worker claimed that he had been discrimi-nated against with regard to a refusal to permit him time off work in order to carry out religious rituals at home over three days and nights to honour his dead grandmother. The Tribunal concluded that he had been refused the leave

---

[9] [2005] All ER 1, HL.

[10] *Explanation of the Provisions of the Employment Equality (Sexual Orientation) Regulations 2003 and Employment Equality (Religion or Belief) Regulations 2003* (DTI), para 15.

[11] Which we discuss further in Chapter 2.

[12] [2004] IRLR 430, QBD (Admin), para 119.   [13] ET Case No 1806638/04, ET.

because, for business reasons, there had to be two people on the shop floor at all times, and his absence would have meant there was only one. The Tribunal went on to conclude that a hypothetical employee of another religion, seeking time off at a time when the store was understaffed, would have been treated in the same way, so that his claim failed.

In contrast, a successful working hours case under the RBR was *Khan v NIC Hygiene*,[14] where a Muslim bus cleaner was dismissed after taking extended leave to make a religious pilgrimage to Mecca. His employer alleged that he had used his holiday entitlement and had a further week's unpaid leave without authorisation in order to make the pilgrimage; Mr Khan alleged that he had sought permission from his employer, but when he did not receive a reply his manager said that if he did not hear anything further, he should assume that the leave had been granted. He took the leave and his employer dismissed him for gross misconduct. The Tribunal found that he had been unfairly dismissed and discriminated against on grounds of his religion. **10.15**

The RBR also prohibit indirect religious discrimination. If, therefore, for example, a policy with regard to time off or working hours is applied to all employees, but has a disparate impact on those of a particular religion, and cannot be justified, indirect discrimination will be made out. **10.16**

In *Williams-Drabble v Pathway Care Solutions Ltd*,[15] for example, the Tribunal found that a residential home worker had been indirectly discriminated against by her employer when a shift pattern was permanently altered for all staff and this prevented her from attending church on Sunday. As such the Tribunal found that she was entitled to terminate her contract with the employer because of their unfair conduct and so she succeeded in her claim of constructive dismissal, as well as her claim for indirect discrimination under the RBR, for which she was awarded £4,000 in compensation for injury to feelings. **10.17**

Similarly, in *Fugler v Macmillan-London Hairstudios Ltd*[16] a Jewish hair stylist had wanted to take a Saturday as holiday to celebrate a key religious festival which fell on that day. His employer was reluctant to allow this given that Saturday was the busiest day for customers. The employee succeeded in his indirect religious discrimination claim and was awarded £500 in compensation for injury to feelings. Here the Tribunal felt that the employer should have considered how to rearrange the employee's duties and customers for that particular Saturday. **10.18**

---

[14] ET Case No 1803250/04, ET.   [15] ET Case No 2601718/04, ET.
[16] ET Case No 2205090/04, ET.

(b) What Should Employers Do to Facilitate Religious Practice among their Employees?

10.19 As we have explained above the RRA, the HRA and the RBR in varying degrees impose a legal requirement for employers to make appropriate provision for employees' religious needs in the workplace. However, quite aside from the legal mandate to take action in this area, addressing religious issues sensitively makes for better employee relations generally, and makes good business sense.

10.20 Generally, we would advise employers to assess all their policies with the above principles in mind, to consider whether any established practices may in fact raise issues that would conflict with employees' rights to religious freedom within the workplace.

10.21 Although there is no legal requirement to monitor religion within the workforce, and although employees should not be compelled to provide information about their religion, employers may well find monitoring helpful in order to assess whether their policies and procedures are working in a non-discriminatory way in practice. This can be done either through the general equality monitoring process, or through staff attitude surveys. Either way, employees should be told why such information is being collected and how it will be used.

10.22 We would also make the following more specific suggestions.

(i) Leave and Hours Issues

10.23 Managers should be made aware of the main religions and beliefs together with their customs, needs and festivals. These are set out in Appendix 2 to the very useful ACAS guide to religious issues,[17] which we would commend to employers. However, the scope of both Article 9 and the RBR is wider than the mainstream religions and beliefs listed there, and so managers will need to be aware that valid requests could be made by those of less mainstream faiths.

10.24 Managers should also be fully trained in these issues. Such training should stress, for example, that some religious festivals are aligned to lunar phases and therefore the dates change from year to year; and that for some, the dates do not become clear until quite close to the actual day.

10.25 Employers should seek to have clear and objectively reasonable procedures for handling applications for leave, or for flexible hours, and ensure that all employees are familiar with and follow the procedures. Employees should be required to give as much notice as possible when applying for leave or

---

[17] *Religion or Belief and the Workplace* (ACAS, 2005), available at <www.acas.org.uk/media/pdf/f/l/religion_1.pdf>.

flexible hours, and encouraged to bear in mind that other employees may like to take their leave at the same time. Managers should be encouraged to be as open-minded and flexible as the workplace environment allows.

Employers will need to make sure that any refusals of requests for leave or to work certain hours for religious reasons can be justified in sound business terms. **10.26**

A Request for Flexible Hours for Religious Reasons: Case Study

A school would like its teachers and classroom assistants to work on a Friday afternoon/early evening to provide an after-school drama club for pupils. A Muslim teacher would like to leave early on Fridays during the winter, so as to get home before nightfall, for religious reasons. He is willing to assist with the after-school activities on other days.

If the school is small, there is no other night the drama club can be held, or this teacher is the only one qualified to teach drama, then a refusal of his request is likely to be justified.

However, if the school is large, the drama club could take place after school on another day, or there are other teachers willing to work late on a Friday in lieu of shorter hours on other days, then it would probably not be justified to refuse the teacher's request.

If a large number of staff wish to take time off or work certain hours for religious reasons, employers should discuss this with the employees affected, and with any recognised trade union or other employee representatives, in the hope of balancing the needs of the employees and the needs of the organisation. **10.27**

Employers who operate a holiday system whereby the workplace closes down for specific periods when all staff are required to take their annual leave should consider whether a closure of this sort is justified, as it may prevent certain employees taking annual leave at times of specific religious significance to them. Business needs, such as annual maintenance of the workplace, may be capable of justifying such a closure policy, but employers will need to balance these kinds of issues carefully against the impact such a policy could have on their employees. **10.28**

(ii) Facilities for Prayer, Eating and Washing/Changing

Employers may be asked to make provision in the workplace for facilities such as prayer or quiet rooms because certain religions require their followers to pray at specific times during the day. **10.29**

10.30   Employers will need to ensure that if provision is made for certain religions, the needs of other religions, and those who have no particular religion or belief, are also met in a fair and even-handed way: in the British Airways case we discuss below, for example, Ms Eweida publicly expressed her concern that while Muslims were permitted time off to pray, Christians were not.

10.31   One way of avoiding this sort of issue is for an employer to make available a designated area for all staff for any kind of contemplative thought, rather than a room specifically for religious prayer, or specifically for use by a certain religion. This would ensure that the provision of such a room does not discriminate against those religions that do not need such facilities, or those who do not follow a particular religion. It would also have the benefit of providing a quiet space for those who, for example, have been recently bereaved and wish to mourn quietly during rest periods.

10.32   Employers may also need to consider providing separate storage facilities for certain religious ceremonial objects; or facilities so as to enable those of religions which require them to wash before prayer to do so.

10.33   Employees may need to pray at certain times of day, and so may request absences from the workplace for that purpose. Employers should consider whether such absences can be accommodated within existing employee rest break entitlements (note that employees are entitled to a 20-minute rest period every six hours under the Working Time Regulations 1998); and if not, whether the business needs of the organisation can support such a request.

10.34   Certain religions or beliefs also have specific dietary requirements and so if employees bring food into the workplace, they may need particular facilities— such as for Muslim employees, the ability to ensure that their food is not in contact with pork or anything that may have had contact with pork, like napkins or cloths. Some religions require extended periods of fasting and employers will need to consider how best to support their staff through this period.

10.35   Some religions do not permit their followers to undress or wash in front of others, even those of the same sex, and so organisations where employees have to change their clothing or shower may need to make special arrangements to accommodate staff following those religions.

10.36   The extent to which workplace religious facilities are required will again vary depending on the size of the organisation—broadly, the larger the organisation, the more the law would expect in terms of the accommodation of religious needs.

(iii) Employer Initiatives and Social Events

Employers will also need to consider whether indirect discrimination issues 10.37
might arise from employer initiatives which could conflict with religious beliefs
or practices. Included in this category would be work-organised social events,
which would need to accommodate the fact that certain religions are prohibited
from eating or handling certain food and/or drinking alcohol.

In *Khan v Direct Line Ltd*,[18] for example, a Muslim insurance company employee 10.38
alleged race and religious discrimination after he was offered alcohol as a performance initiative. He and 13 others were awarded the bonus for sales of pet
and household insurance policies. He claimed that the offering of bottles of
wine as a reward put him at a disadvantage compared with his colleagues as the
Muslim faith strictly forbids the drinking of alcohol. However, his claim failed.
The Tribunal was persuaded that a non-Muslim, teetotal employee would have
been treated in the same way as Mr Khan as regards the bonus, and therefore
held that he had failed to show that he had received less favourable treatment
than would have been afforded to such a comparator. Moreover, there was
evidence that a Muslim colleague of Mr Khan's had been able to exchange his
wine for another reward, so that even if he had been treated less favourably he
could not be said to have suffered a detriment, or a disadvantage for the
purposes of his indirect discrimination claim. Although not an issue in his
claim, part of the factual background was that he had been required to pick
prize notifications out of a 'gunk tank' which he was distressed to find had
contained pork sausages. Although the *Khan* case failed on its facts, had there
been no alternative reward available other than the alcohol the outcome for the
employer would probably have been different.

Similarly, employers should also be aware that some religions forbid gambling, 10.39
so staff should not be pressured to take part in raffles or sweepstakes if they do
not wish to.

(iv) Christmas Parties

Whether or not the RBR precludes employers from holding Christmas parties 10.40
became a big news item at the end of 2006—Radio 4 reported the results of a
poll in which 70 per cent of employers said they would not be celebrating
Christmas at work for fear of offending non-Christian staff or customers.[19] This
is the type of issue that the red-top newspapers love to over-simplify. Whilst it

---

[18] ET Case No 1400026/05, ET.
[19] 'Cancelling Christmas is an overreaction', *Personnel Today*, 12 December 2006,
<www.personneltoday.com/Articles/2006/12/12/38500/cancelling-christmas-is-an-
overreaction.html>.

is tempting to say that the issue is simply exaggerated, there are potential legal issues that might arise in relation to employer-organised events that have a religious connection.

10.41 If an employer organises an event linked to a particular religion, for example, a Christian carol service, then those who adhere to different religions may argue that they have suffered a detriment if the employer does not organise a similar event linked to their religion. Any such claim would amount to direct discrimination under the RBR and if detrimental treatment was established, that treatment could not be justified by the employer, for example, on the basis that there were considerably more adherents within the workforce to the religion in respect of which the event in question had been organised.

10.42 'Christmas' parties on the other hand rarely, in practice, have any true connection to the Christian religion. Provided the Christmas party remains nothing more than an end of year celebration, and does not in fact have any religious connotation in practice, there should be no issue under the RBR—which only applies if preferential treatment is afforded to one religion over another. As with any social event though, employers must ensure that there are sufficient food and drink choices available to cater for all religious groups.

10.43 It seems unlikely that there will be a flood of litigation in this area. Most employees will simply not attend events that have a religious connection if they do not adhere to the religion in question. Employers in turn only ever arrange these events as a benefit to staff and to improve staff morale and team working. If employees start to stay away from these events, employers are likely to adapt the events to encourage more employees to attend or put their money to better use.

10.44 Given the overall theme of this book we would argue that holding a range of events which celebrate different religions is a positive step to promoting both equality and diversity. However if budgets or logistics do not permit such a range of activities, then the best way of ensuring fairness is to have only secular events.

(v) Unclear Cases

10.45 Sometimes an issue will arise as to the extent to which the accommodation sought is actually required by the religion in question. In *Devine v Home Office (Immigration and Nationality Directorate)*,[20] for example, the Tribunal concluded that a claim of religious discrimination based on the argument that sympathy with underprivileged asylum seekers and disadvantaged people was a demonstration of the Christian virtue of charity was 'far too vague and ill defined to amount to a case to answer'.

---

[20] ET Case No 2302061/04, ET.

278

This issue also arose in *Husain v Bhullar Bros t/a BB Supersave* where, as we have **10.46** explained above, the complainant sought time off after a family bereavement as part of his Muslim faith. However, the Tribunal, giving a wide interpretation to 'religion' and 'religious belief', held that if a person 'genuinely believes' that his or her faith requires a particular course of action, that is sufficient to make it part of his or her religion. The Tribunal concluded that trying to differentiate between cultural manifestation, traditions and religious observance would lead to 'unnecessary complications and endless debate'.[21]

The net result is that in cases of doubt, an employer is likely to be entitled to ask **10.47** for some proof that the employee genuinely believes the provision sought is required by his or her religion. Consulting Appendix 2 to the ACAS guide referred to above is also likely to assist in determining what a particular religion requires.

C. Dress Codes

Employers frequently wish to regulate the appearance of their employees, so as **10.48** to, for example, present a consistent, professional image to the public, or respect health and safety rules. However, the issue of dress codes has led to a certain amount of litigation under the SDA, RRA and latterly under the RBR—indeed a 2001 Home Office Research Study concluded that dress codes were seen as one of the most obvious areas for religious discrimination, forcing many employers to rethink their policies.[22] Dress codes can also raise a tension with ECHR rights protected by the HRA, namely those under:

- Article 8, the right to privacy, which is underpinned by notions of personal autonomy, human dignity, freedom and 'self-determination'.[23]
- Article 9, the right to freedom of thought, conscience and religion, which includes the right to certain forms of dress that constitute a 'manifestation' of religious faith.
- Article 10, the right of freedom of expression, which can include expression through clothing and appearance.
- Article 14, the right not to be discriminated against in the enjoyment of the other ECHR rights, which could apply if there was a difference in the application of dress codes to different groups.

Interferences with Articles 8, 9 or 10 can only be justified if they are in

---

[21] ET Case No 1806638/04, ET.

[22] *Tackling Religious Discrimination: Practical Implications for Policy Makers and Legislators* (Home Office Research Study 221, February 2001)

[23] *Pretty v UK* (2002) 35 EHRR 1.

accordance with law, necessary in a democratic society and in furtherance of one of the aims stated in Articles 8(2), 9(2) or 10(2).

(a) Dress Codes and the RRA and SDA

10.49   In *Harrods Ltd v Remick; Harrods Ltd v Seeley*[24] two women working at concessions in the Harrods store argued that they had been discriminated against on grounds of race when their approval to work there was withdrawn on the basis that they did not comply with the store dress code—Ms Remick was black, and given no particulars of why she did not comply with the code, but dismissed; Ms Seeley was Asian, and was dismissed when she refused to remove the nose ring she had worn since she was a child. The legal issue in their claim was whether or not they could bring RRA claims against Harrods itself given that they worked for concessions within the store. The Court of Appeal concluded that they could in principle bring such claims.

10.50   The SDA has been used on several occasions by both male and female employees seeking to challenge dress codes which were different as between men and women as discriminatory on grounds of sex:

- In *Schmidt v Austicks Bookshops Ltd*[25] a female employee had been dismissed from a bookstore for refusing to obey the store's rules about clothing. She complained, unsuccessfully, that the store's requirements that she wear a skirt and not wear trousers whilst serving the public and that she wear overalls constituted unlawful discrimination on grounds of sex.

- In *Smith v Safeway Plc*[26] a male supermarket worker had been dismissed because his ponytail grew too long to be kept under his hat. This was contrary to Safeway's rule concerning appearance for male delicatessen staff which specified: 'Tidy hair not below shirt-collar length. No unconventional hairstyles or colouring.' He complained, again unsuccessfully, of sex discrimination on the basis that different lengths of hair were permitted as between men and women.

- In *Jarman v Link Stores Ltd*[27] a male employee succeeded in his complaint of discrimination when he was disciplined for refusing to remove an earring in contravention of the company dress code which allowed female staff to wear them.

- In *Department of Work and Pensions v Thompson*,[28] a male administrative assistant at Jobcentre Plus took issue with the fact that he, but not women working alongside him, had to wear a collar and tie to work, even though he

---

[24] [1998] 1 All ER 52, CA.   [25] [1978] ICR 85, EAT.   [26] [1996] ICR 868, CA.
[27] ET Case No 2505091/03, ET.   [28] [2004] IRLR 348, EAT.

had no direct contact with the public. This was because his employers had introduced a new dress code requiring all staff to dress 'in a professional and businesslike way'. He had been disciplined for refusing to comply with the code and succeeded in his claim of sex discrimination.

The claimants in the two earlier claims failed because the courts broadly held **10.51** that different treatment as between the sexes in this context is not necessarily less favourable treatment for the purposes of the SDA.

In the *Schmidt* case, the EAT held that the 'no trousers' rule for women did **10.52** not constitute less favourable treatment because no comparable rule could have been applied to men. The EAT also held that, insofar as a comparison could be drawn between the sexes, the employers had treated both sexes alike, as both male and female employees were subject to a dress codes, albeit that the terms of that code differed as between the sexes.

The Court of Appeal accepted this reasoning in the *Smith* case, holding that the **10.53** Safeway supermarket chain had not discriminated on grounds of sex because the store had applied equally rigorous dress codes as between male and female employees. The Court of Appeal held that in order to succeed in an SDA claim arising out of a dress codes issue, the employee would need to show not simply that male and female employees were treated differently, but that overall the treatment given to one sex was less favourable than that given to the other. If the Safeway code was looked at 'as a whole', then, said Lord Phillips in the Court of Appeal, neither men nor women were treated less favourably.

However, the two later cases (albeit that the *Jarman* case was only at first **10.54** instance) appear to show the courts taking a more employee-friendly approach.

The claimant in the *Jarman* case succeeded in his claim on the simple basis that **10.55** his employer's dress code did differentiate between men and women in that women could wear earrings but men could not when they were on the shop floor. He was awarded £750 in injury to feelings.

In the *Thompson* case, the EAT concluded that Jobcentre Plus had applied **10.56** an 'overarching requirement for its staff to dress in a professional and business-like way'. The issue then was whether, applying 'contemporary standards of conventional dress-wear, the level of smartness . . . required of all . . . staff could only be achieved for men by requiring them to wear a collar and tie'. Regard was clearly had to the level of smartness that was deemed appropriate for the business environment in question—Jobcentre Plus centres—and the question posed as to whether that level of smartness could be achieved any other way than by restricting the choice of clothing male members of staff had, by requiring them to wear a collar and tie. The EAT concluded that it was not for them to answer this question, and remitted the issue back to the Tribunal.

10.57 What is clear is that Tribunals will apply a close scrutiny to the business justification for a particular dress code advanced by an employer. This has always been the case to some extent, even in non-discrimination cases. In *Catharell v Glynn Nuttall Ltd*,[29] for example, an electrician argued that his dismissal for refusing to cut his hair short was unfair. The Tribunal looked closely at the nature of his work, and the business of his employer, and upheld his unfair dismissal claim because '. . . long hair was not detrimental to the respondent's business or his performance of his duties'.

10.58 However, what is particularly notable about the *Thompson* case is that despite the fact that it was argued as a direct discrimination claim under the SDA and not as an indirect discrimination claim, or under the HRA, the EAT applied something close to a 'proportionality' test – in that it looked to see whether the employer's business need could be met by any less restrictive method than the method applied. The EAT looked very carefully at the particular business needs of Jobcentre Plus and the level of smartness in their employees they required; and sought to balance those needs against the restriction on Mr Thompson's freedom of choice. Had the dress code in question impacted on his appearance outside work (eg if it had precluded him from growing his hair long, or dyeing his hair) then the balance may well have been struck differently. This balancing exercise is derived from the proportionality approach, a concept well entrenched in human rights law. Proportionality would be one threshold (if not the main one) for an employer to meet in order to show that a dress code was a justifiable interference with the rights to privacy, freedom of religion or freedom of expression under, respectively, Articles 8(2), 9(2) or 10(2).

(b) Dress Codes and the HRA

10.59 The Convention rights have also been deployed to challenge dress codes, both before the Strasbourg bodies and domestically, although, again, with limited success.

10.60 In *Kara v UK*,[30] for example, a male trainee administrator was told by his employer, Hackney Council, that he could not wear female clothing to work. He complained that this was in breach of his rights under Articles 8, 10 and 14. The European Commission on Human Rights accepted that his mode of dress was embraced by his Article 8 right to privacy, and that this had been interfered with, but concluded that overall the Council's approach was justified under

---

[29] ET Case No 7935/81, ET.   [30] (1996) 24 EHRR 205, ECtHR.

Article 8(2). This was because the Council had a written dress policy; because it protected the 'rights of others', namely the right of the Council to enhance its public image and facilitate external contacts; and because it was reasonably regarded by the employer as necessary to safeguard their public image and so was proportionate.

Domestically, *R (Begum) v Headteacher and Governors of Denbigh High School*[31] **10.61** was a high profile case brought by a female Muslim pupil who challenged her school's refusal to permit her to wear a jilbab (a long loose robe) to school. She argued that her Islamic faith obliged her to wear the jilbab and that the school was unjustifiably interfering with her Article 9 right to 'manifest' her religion by refusing to allow her to do so. Her claim went all the way to the House of Lords. Although the case was about dress codes in school, the principles it set out are directly relevant to the workplace.

The different members of the House of Lords, although all dismissing the **10.62** claimant's claim, varied in their reasoning. Lord Bingham, Lord Hoffmann and Lord Scott applied the approach set out in the *Ahmad* and *Stedman* cases referred to above to conclude that there was no limitation on the manifestation of her religious beliefs, because she could have chosen to go to another school where she would have been permitted to wear the jilbab. In reaching this conclusion, Lord Bingham observed (at paragraph 23 of the judgment) that the Strasbourg bodies were reluctant to find an interference with the right to manifest religious belief in practice or observance '. . . where a person has voluntarily accepted an employment or role which did not accommodate that practice or observance and there were other means open to the individual to practice or observe their religion without hardship or inconvenience. . . .' In contrast, Lord Nicholls and Baroness Hale held that there had been such a limitation on the pupil's rights, but that this was justified within Article 9(2).

All of the members of the House of Lords looked closely at the extent to which **10.63** the actions of the school affected the claimant, and the evidential basis the school had to justify its policy. It was also noted that the school 'had taken immense pains to devise a uniform policy which respected Muslim beliefs' and that it had done so in an 'inclusive, unthreatening and uncompetitive way'.[32]

In *R (on the application of X) v Headteachers and Governors of Y School*,[33] a **10.64** female pupil sought to establish the right to wear the niqab (the full-face veil) under the HRA, but again failed: Mr Justice Silber held that although the right to wear the niqab had engaged her right to manifest her religion under

---

[31] [2007] 1 AC 100, HL.   [32] Per Lord Bingham at para 34.
[33] (2007) HRLR 20, CA.

Article 9(1), that right had not been infringed, and even if it had been, the decision was objectively justified under Article 9(2).

10.65 The reasoning in the *Begum* and *X* cases was followed in *R (Playfoot) (A child) v Millais School Governing Body*,[34] where it was held that a decision of a school to refuse to permit a pupil to wear a purity ring as an expression of her Christian faith and sign of her belief in celibacy before marriage did not breach Articles 9 or 14.

10.66 Notably, other countries have taken a more strict approach to the issue of the wearing of the veil: in France, Islamic headscarves and other religious symbols are banned from French state schools completely; in Italy a regional court has ruled that crucifixes should be removed from schools; the Netherlands has announced a ban on face-covering Islamic clothing, as have several Belgian municipalities; Singapore has taken a similar approach; and in Turkey head-scarves are banned in civic spaces because they are deemed 'backward looking'. The ban was upheld in *Sahin v Turkey*,[35] where a Turkish medical student at the University of Istanbul challenged the fact that she was denied access to her classes and exams while she was wearing the Islamic headscarf. The European Court of Human Rights accepted that there had been an interference with her right to manifest her religious beliefs, but held that this was justified because of the protection of the rights and freedoms of others and the maintenance of public order, given the importance of the secular state in Turkey, and the fact that the headscarf had taken on 'political significance' in Turkey in recent years. The same ban also covered students with beards.

(c) **Dress Codes and the RBR**

10.67 The RBR also clearly provides a potential remedy for employees who wish to challenge dress codes that impinge on their religious freedom.

10.68 In *Mohmed v West Coast Trains Ltd*, for example, a Muslim employee argued that he had been discriminated against contrary to the RBR after he had been asked to trim his beard, which he wore for religious reasons. The EAT upheld the Tribunal's conclusion to the effect that the reason for his dismissal was not influenced by the issue around his beard.[36]

10.69 In *Ferri v Key Languages Ltd*,[37] a Catholic employee had worn three necklaces during the interview and induction process for a job at a language school—a

---

[34] [2007] EWHC 1698, QBD (Admin).
[35] Application 00044774/98, 10 November 2005, ECtHR.
[36] For a similar decision as first instance, see *Mohmed v West Coast Trains Ltd*, ET Case No 2201814/04, ET.
[37] ET Case No 2302172/04, ET.

small gold crucifix on a gold chain, a small representation of the Virgin Mary on a gold chain and a large, gold-covered cross encrusted with ruby-coloured gems. Her employer felt that these were overtly religious symbols and asked her not to wear the ruby cross with the other two necklaces. Ms Ferri agreed. However, when her working relationship with her employer broke down, Ms Ferri argued that the allegations of her poor performance were really motivated by this initial dispute over the ruby cross. The Tribunal dismissed her claim, accepting the employer's argument that any employee who had performed as poorly as Ms Ferri would have been treated in the same way. However, the Tribunal accepted that in another case, this sort of dispute could well have been 'highly relevant' and 'exactly the type of background evidentiary fact from which it might well have been reasonable to draw adverse inferences against the Respondent'.

(d) The *Azmi* Case

One of the highest profile RBR cases, *Azmi v Kirklees Metropolitan Borough Council*,[38] also involved dress codes. In this case, the Muslim complainant was employed as a bilingual teaching assistant in a predominantly Muslim school, the Headfield Church of England Junior School in Dewsbury, West Yorkshire. She was assisting pupils with maths and English for year-six pupils, aged 11. She was interviewed by a man and wore a black tunic and headscarf. She did not mention during the interview that she would in future have to wear her niqab (full-face veil) on occasions when she was in the company of men. She did not wear the veil on her training day either. However, during her first week of work, she asked the head teacher whether she could only work with female teachers, and said that if she had to work with male teachers she would have to wear the veil.   **10.70**

The head teacher sought the advice of the Council's local education department and in the meantime permitted Ms Azmi to wear the veil to work. The head teacher then monitored Ms Azmi's performance in the classroom and found that pupils could not see her facial expressions and so sought visual clues in order to enable them to understand her; and that Ms Azmi's diction was not as clear or loud as it would have been had she not been wearing the veil.   **10.71**

On that basis the headteacher told Ms Azmi that she could not wear her veil when working directly with children in the classroom. Ms Azmi said that she could not work in accordance with those instructions. In order to try to resolve matters, the council reconsidered its guidelines, and concluded that '. . . the desire to express religious identity does not overcome the primary requirement   **10.72**

---

[38] [2007] IRLR 484, EAT.

for optimal communication between adults and children'. However, the council did ask that there be further monitoring of Ms Azmi's teaching. This took place, this time by her line manager, who reached similar conclusions to the head teacher. Accordingly, Ms Azmi was given a management instruction that she should be unveiled while in school. She was signed off on grounds of stress thereafter and had a lengthy period of absence from work. She then returned for a short period of time and worked only with female teachers without a veil. However, she made it plain that if she had to work with male colleagues she would have to wear the veil and on that basis she was suspended for refusing to obey management instructions.

10.73 Ms Azmi then brought proceedings alleging direct discrimination, indirect discrimination, harassment and victimisation under the RBR. There were clear political overtones to her case, with the then Prime Minister having publicly stated that the veil '. . . is a mark of separation and that's why it makes people from outside the community feel uncomfortable'.[39]

10.74 She failed in her claim before the Employment Tribunal and appealed to the EAT:

• In her direct discrimination claim, she argued that the correct comparator was a Muslim woman who did not cover her face, and that compared to that person, she had been less favourably treated on grounds of her religion. However, the Tribunal did not accept this comparator—rather, it was concluded that the correct comparator was another teacher not of Muslim faith who, for whatever reason, covered their face. Ms Azmi's counsel challenged this before the EAT and argued that it was like comparing her case to that of someone who, for whatever reason, chose to wear a balaclava to teach. However, the EAT upheld the Tribunal's choice of comparator, and on that basis concluded that there was no less favourable treatment. In other words, she had not been directly discriminated against because of her religious belief but because of her restricted ability to communicate with the children. Her suspension and the various acts of less favourable treatment of which she complained did not therefore amount to less favourable treatment.

• In her indirect discrimination claim she argued that she was subject to a provision, criterion or practice deriving from 'the requirement not to wear clothing which covers, or covers a considerable part of, the face and/or mouth and/or the requirement not to wear clothing which interferes unduly with the employee's ability to communicate appropriately with pupils'; that this

---

[39] 'Blair's concerns over veils', 17 October 2006, <news.bbc.co.uk/1/hi/uk_politics/6058672.stm>.

requirement arose out of the school's 'intention to target the veil'; and was not a proportionate means of achieving a legitimate aim. Both the Tribunal and the EAT disagreed and concluded that the school's policy was indeed proportionate and justified. It was borne out of her restricted ability to communicate fully with her pupils, and this requirement was of the utmost importance if the school was to comply with the requirements of the Office for Standards in Education, Children Services and Skills. Complying with this requirement was a legitimate aim for the school, and the method of achieving that aim was proportionate because the instruction was confined to those occasions when she was teaching the children.

• In her harassment and victimisation claims she argued that the school was aware that she had contacted ACAS and her local MP; that she was alleging that her treatment constituted religious discrimination; and that she had been harassed and victimised by the school's treatment of her thereafter, with regard to comments made to her, being sent home, and being asked to return her laptop computer. Ms Azmi lost her harassment claim, but succeeded in her victimisation claim on the basis that there had been a marked change in the way she was dealt with once it was clear that she was raising a complaint, and that this was 'unsatisfactory and insensitive'. She was awarded £1,100 in damages (that comprising £1,000 for injury to feelings and an automatic £100 uplift for the employer's failure to comply with the statutory grievance procedures).

10.75 The EAT in the *Azmi* case did not rule out the possibility that a case involving a restrictive dress code could amount to direct discrimination under the RBR. However, it did not have to rule on the issue and considered Ms Azmi's claim within the context of indirect discrimination.

10.76 A key feature in that claim was the evidence the school had collated to show that the pupils were in fact experiencing difficulties in hearing Ms Azmi because of her veil, and evidence that generally, visual stimulus, provided in this context by looking at human faces is an important part of the way children communicate. The school had also given serious consideration to whether there were other means by which Ms Azmi could have done her job while respecting her religious wishes: they looked at whether she could have been timetabled to work only with female teachers, whether she could have used a screen, whether she could have stood with her back to the teacher and whether she could have used more hand and body gestures. It was apparent that the school had not imposed its ban on her wearing the veil without a detailed assessment exercise. It was the clear and legitimate teaching methodology identified by the school, and its careful assessment of possible alternative ways of working, which led to the Tribunal's finding that the disparate impact of the dress code policy was justifiable.

10.77 On a similar note, in early November 2006 the Chair of the Stoke on Trent Immigration Tribunal had to adjourn its proceedings as he could not fully comprehend Shabnam Mughal, an advocate, because she was wearing a veil which she refused to remove. The Judicial Studies Board's Equal Treatment Advisory Committee examined whether women should be allowed to wear the niqab. It concluded that decisions should be made on a case-by-case basis, and that veils should only be removed where to do otherwise would interfere with the administration of justice.[40] Some commentators have argued that this guidance goes too far, and conflicts with the fundamental principle that British justice should be open and transparent.[41]

10.78 The *Azmi* case should not, however, be taken as authority for the proposition that a blanket ban on veils, or any other kind of religious attire, in the workplace is justified. Rather, each case raising the issue of religious dress at work will have to be assessed on its own facts, as the Judicial Studies Board's guidelines indicate is the approach that will have to be adopted to women wishing to wear the veil in court.

10.79 An employer is likely to find it easier to restrict a particular kind of attire if it can show that the restriction is necessary on grounds of health and safety, security, or, as in Ms Azmi's case, in order to enable the employee to do their job properly. An employer should nevertheless seek to explore with the employee whether there are means by which the employer's objectives could be met in a less restrictive way than a complete ban on the religious freedom sought by the employee. A lot will depend on the nature of the job and the nature of the workplace—Ms Azmi's case may well have been decided differently if her job did not require face-to-face contact, and place a premium on oral communication skills—for example, if she had an internet-based role, or worked in a call centre.

(e) **The *Eweida* Case**

10.80 Similarly press-worthy to the *Azmi* case was the case of the British Airways employee who wished to wear a Christian cross about the size of a five pence piece to work. Nadia Eweida had worn the crucifix over her British Airways uniform for seven years, while working on a check-in desk, without difficulty. British Airways then decided that she could not wear the cross, although their dress code policy would enable their employees to wear the Muslim hijab, or Sikh turban or kara (bangle).

---

[40] 'Muslim veil "allowed in courts"', 24 April 2007, <news.bbc.co.uk/1/hi/england/staffordshire/6588157.stm>.
[41] See eg B Hewson, 'Let Us See Your Face', *Counsel*, June 2007, pp 10–12.

The rationale for the new policy was that the airline did not want any of its **10.81** employees wearing jewellery that was visible over their uniform, whether the jewellery was worn for fashion or for religious purposes. Rather, any such jewellery had to be worn under the clothing and not put on display whilst on duty without the permission of the manager. In other words, this was a policy about visible jewellery and not really about religion: it just so happened that Ms Eweida's religious symbol was in the form of visible jewellery (her cross), whereas the Muslim hijab and Sikh turban, at least, were not. Ms Eweida lost her appeal against the decision refusing to allow her to wear the cross, and declined to accept an alternative, non-uniformed job British Airways had offered her. She was then suspended.

The case again prompted comments at the most senior level: the Archbishop of **10.82** York pointed out that if Ms Eweida's cross was three feet tall, she would have not been able to conceal it under her BA blouse and so would surely have been able to wear it freely;[42] and the Prime Minister himself, in addressing the Confederation of British Industry conference, urged British Airways to get themselves on 'the right side of the line' on the issue, given '. . . [t]here are some battles really, really worth fighting, and there are battles really, really not worth fighting . . .'.[43]

As a result of Ms Eweida's case, British Airways carried out a comprehensive **10.83** review of its uniform policy in consultation with a wide range of religious groups including the Church of England, the Catholic Church and the Muslim Council of Britain. The review concluded that the uniform policy should be amended to allow staff to wear a symbol of faith such as a Christian cross or a Jewish Star of David as a lapel pin, with some flexibility for them to wear a symbol of faith on a chain. Ms Eweida was permitted to wear her cross, and so returned to work wearing her BA scarf as a cravat, as employees are permitted to do, with her cross on view.

However, had Ms Eweida pursued her claim to the Employment Tribunal, she **10.84** would appear to have had good prospects of success in claims of:

• direct discrimination under the RBR—because she had been less favourably treated than employees of other religions who were permitted to wear their religious symbols, and particularly Sikhs who were permitted to wear a religious symbol (the kara bangle) which would at least on occasion have been visible over uniform; and

---

[42] <www.christianconcernforournation.co.uk/Press/20nov6.php>.
[43] A Seager, 'Blair chides British Airways for fighting employees over cross', The Guardian, 28 November 2006.

- indirect discrimination under the RBR—because the apparently neutral 'no visible jewellery' policy had a disparate impact on Christians who often chose a religious symbol (a cross on neck chain) which fell into the category of visible jewellery, and so the policy fell to be justified.

10.85   As to justification in an indirect discrimination claim or under Article 9(2), it would no doubt have been relevant, and potentially damaging to British Airways' case, that:

- other airlines such as Virgin Atlantic did not feel the business need to impose a dress code precluding Christians from wearing visible crosses;
- the potential health and safety risk posed by Ms Eweida wearing her cross in close proximity to the conveyor belts which moved luggage away from her counter did not seem to be the driving force behind British Airways' policy, as it applied to all its 34,000 staff and not simply those who worked on check-in counters;
- the Sikh kara, which employees were permitted to wear, would surely have constituted visible jewellery in the same way as Ms Eweida's cross did; and
- there appeared no basis for saying that the wearing of the cross affected Ms Eweida's performance.

(f) How Should Employers Manage the Dress Codes Issue?

10.86   As with leave issues, having in place clear policies and procedures on dress codes is the best possible start for employers. Clear policies not only have the practical benefit of giving guidance to new and current employees and managers, but the existence of an accessible written policy has a legal benefit: provided the policy is clear, and reasonable, it is likely to be sufficient to meet the 'clear legal basis' limb of any justification defence under Articles 8(2), 9(2) or 10(2) (as is shown by the *Kara* and *Begum* cases, where the written dress codes policies met this test). We have set out a sample dress code policy at Appendix 10.1 to this chapter.

10.87   Policies in relation to dress codes should generally be couched in neutral terms, so as to avoid the impression of targeting a particular item of clothing or particular religion.

10.88   Similarly, training staff in dress code issues is important. Appendix 2 to the ACAS guide, *Religion or Belief and the Workplace*[44] is a good starting point for managers who need to be aware of the clothing requirements of major world religions.

---

[44] Available at <www.acas.org.uk/media/pdf/f/l/religion_1.pdf>.

D. Freedom of Expression

The RBR on their face extend to the protection from discrimination on the **10.89** grounds of religion or 'belief'. This begs the question of how far the RBR extend to the protection of freedom of expression beyond religion, for example, *political* beliefs.

Under the original wording of the RBR, 'philosophical' beliefs were embraced **10.90** by the RBR, but only to the extent that they were 'similar to' religious beliefs. The claimant in *Baggs v Fudge*[45] argued that he had been discriminated against under the RBR when he was not interviewed for a post because he was an active member of the British National Party. The Tribunal held that the BNP is a political party since it has political ends and fields candidates in elections, and is therefore not a 'religion, religious belief or similar philosophical belief' within the meaning of Regulation 2(1) of the RBR.

Similarly, in *Williams v South Central Ltd*,[46] a US citizen, who had been dis- **10.91** missed from his job as a train dispatcher with South Central Ltd, because he refused to comply with an instruction to remove a US flag which he had stitched to his reflective safety jacket, failed in his claim. The Tribunal held that loyalty to one's national flag or to one's native country could not possibly fit within the definition of 'belief' contained in the Regulations, because as defined in the dictionary, a 'belief' is 'persuasion of the truth of anything or opinion or doctrine or recognition of an awakened sense of a higher being controlling power or powers and the morality connected therewith, rights of worship or any system of such belief or worship'.

The definition of 'belief' in the RBR was amended with effect from 30 April **10.92** 2007 so that there is no longer a requirement for a philosophical belief to be 'similar to' a religious one in order to be covered. The Government's position on this amendment was that it was necessary to bring consistency with the definition of belief under Article 9, and that it would therefore embrace a 'world view or life stance'.[47] Even if this is not the Government's intention, it is likely that the amended wording will encourage fresh challenges by employees of the kind brought in *Baggs* and *Williams*, or potentially those who have a firm belief in, for example, ardent animal rights activism, pacifism or vegetarianism.

However, whether or not the RBR cover the expression of political views in the **10.93** workplace, Article 10 of the ECHR certainly does, and this extends both to the

---

[45] ET Case No 1400114/05, ET.   [46] ET Case No 2306989/03, ET.
[47] This was made clear by the comments of Baroness Scotland at *Hansard*, HL Debates col 1109, 13 July 2005.

right to 'hold' opinions, but also the right to 'receive' and 'impart' information and ideas. The right to free expression also embraces the right of employees to, for example, wear badges displaying support for political parties, or display items or circulate material around the workplace expressing support for particular causes.

10.94 Interferences with the right to freedom of expression can only be justified under Article 10(2) if they are in accordance with law, and are proportionate and necessary in a democratic society in the interests of national security, territorial integrity or public safety, for the prevention of disorder or crime, for the protection of health or morals, for the protection of the reputation or rights of others, for preventing the disclosure of information received in confidence, or for maintaining the authority and impartiality of the judiciary.

10.95 Employers will therefore need to assess each situation on its own facts and ensure that, if they wish to restrict employees in such an exercise of their rights to freedom of expression, that same can be justified in accordance with Article 10(2). Similar proportionality considerations would apply to this sort of issue as have arisen in the context of dress codes, as we discuss above.

Religious Practice, Dress Codes and Freedom of Expression in the Workplace: In Brief

- Religious practice can become relevant in the workplace in several ways: employees may wish to work certain days or hours, to facilitate the observance of their religion; they may need absences from work to celebrate festivals or attend ceremonies; and they may request certain facilities within the workplace to enable them to observe their religion during working hours. There are various ways in which the law provides a framework for addressing and resolving these issues.

- The Race Relations Act 1976 (the 'RRA'), the Human Rights Act 1998 (the 'HRA') and the Employment Equality (Religion or Belief) Regulations 2003 (the 'RBR') in varying degrees can require employers to make suitable provision for employees' religious practice in the workplace.

- This might entail allowing employees to work certain hours, or have leave at certain times of year, so as to facilitate them in attending religious festivals or ceremonies; or making particular facilities available in the workplace for prayer, eating and washing/changing.

- Dress codes can also raise tensions under the discrimination statutes and the HRA.

- Auditing policies for potentially discriminatory impact; ensuring that there are clear policies on leave and dress code issues; training staff; and monitoring the workforce will all ensure that employers promote equality in this area.

- There is a sample dress code policy at Appendix 1 to this chapter.

- Employers may also need to adopt clear policies to regulate freedom of political expression in the workplace, as this can raise issues under the RBR and the HRA.

293

Sample Dress Code Policy

FAIRSHIRE COUNTY COUNCIL
DRESS CODE POLICY

General principles

1. Fairshire County Council operates a dress code for all employees. We aim to ensure that everyone looks smart and professional while at work, and wears clothes that are practical and safe for the work they do.

2. It is particularly important that those employees who have regular direct contact with service users or visitors look smart and professional. However, our aim is to ensure that everyone working on Council property, or attending meetings or events elsewhere that are related to Council business, is dressed appropriately.

3. We are proud that the Council has a diverse workforce and we recognise the fact that this means that there are different ways in which people would like to dress at work. This policy seeks to strike a fair balance between the Council's needs and those of our employees.

General minimum standards of dress for office-based staff

4. The majority of the Council's employees are based in offices at Council Hall.

5. The following are our general minimum standards for male office-based employees:
- Clean, pressed, formal trousers (not shorts);
- A clean, pressed shirt;
- Clean, polished shoes in a good state of repair (not trainers);
- Simple and appropriate jewellery;
- Clean, smart hair;
- Clean-shaven or neatly trimmed facial hair; and
- No distracting badges, emblems or logos.

For employees who do have regular contact with service users and visitors, we would add the following minimum standards:
- A clean jacket to match the trousers; and
- An appropriate tie.

6. The following are our general minimum standards for female office-based employees:
- Clean, pressed, formal trousers, skirt or dress;
- A clean, pressed blouse or other suitable top;
- Clean, polished shoes in a good state of repair (not trainers);
- Simple and appropriate jewellery;
- Clean, smart hair; and

- No distracting badges, emblems or logos.

For employees who have regular contact with service users and visitors, we would add the following minimum standards:

- A clean matching jacket or suitably smart twin-set/cardigan type top.

7. For employees who do not have contact with service users and visitors, managers may decide to apply the above minimum standards more flexibly, subject always to employees being appropriately dressed for a professional working environment.

'Dress down' days

8. The Council has developed a system of 'dress down' days for office-based staff on Fridays, and throughout June, July and August. On dress down days we ask that all staff:

- Wear clothes that are clean, tidy and in a good state of repair;
- Do not wear jeans, denims or shorts;
- Do not wear trainers or sportswear;
- Do not wear skimpy or low-cut clothing or those that reveal the shoulders;
- Abide by the requirements in relation to hair and jewellery set out at paragraphs 5–6 above;
- Dress for all meetings with external partners and all events away from Council property in accordance with the general minimum standards set out above; and
- Keep clothing consistent with the general minimum standards set out above in the office to change into at short notice if need be.

Guidance for non-office based employees

9. Employees who are not based in offices will be provided with appropriate overalls and headgear by their line managers. They will also be given particular health and safety rules which must be followed at all times, and guidance about their hair and jewellery insofar as it is affected by health and safety requirements.

10. Generally, though, all non-office based employees should abide by the requirements in relation to hair, jewellery and appropriate professional appearance set out at paragraphs 5 and 6 above.

Dealing with issues under this policy

11. This dress code is for general guidance only, and does not seek to set out an exhaustive or rigid set of rules.

12. If employees have any concerns about how this policy applies to them they should discuss the issue with their line manager.

13. Managers will consider each employee's case on its own basis, and aim to ensure that their response to any particular request is necessary, justifiable and proportionate, and has due regard to religious, cultural and health and safety needs. We ask that managers apply a common sense approach to what is a 'smart and professional' standard within their teams, whilst aiming to maintain consistent standards across the Council's workforce.

14. We also ask employees to adopt a reasonable approach to the policy and comply with our minimum standards at all times, unless they have specific permission to do otherwise from their manager. An unreasonable refusal to comply with this policy may lead to formal disciplinary procedures.

11

HARASSMENT

[The major challenge facing our organisation in tackling bullying is] . . . [t]o change what is seen as acceptable management to an understanding of good people management. Management training is needed not only on how to deal with bullying and harassment, but also on how to treat employees with respect . . .[1]

A. Introduction

Harassment on one of the prohibited grounds is one of the most problematic **11.01** diversity issues in the workplace: it is distressing for employees, difficult for managers to address, and yet, if left unchecked, can have a wide range of damaging and expensive consequences. In this chapter we discuss the nature, extent and effects of harassment in the workplace, set out the relevant legal provisions and consider practical steps employers can take to prevent, identify and respond to allegations of harassment in the most fair and effective way.

B. The Nature, Extent and Effects of Workplace Harassment

(a) The Nature of Workplace Harassment

Harassment can and does take many forms. The following are some examples **11.02** of the sort of behaviour which can individually or cumulatively constitute harassment of an employee:

• Descriptions or name-calling of an employee that refer in a derogatory fashion to their sex, race, disability, religion/belief, sexual orientation or age. This can be in an overt form such as 'goddamn Yank', 'thick Paddy',

---

[1] Quote from one of the 1,190 respondents to the CIPD Managing Conflict at Work survey 2004, cited in *Bullying at Work: Beyond Policies to a Culture of Respect* (CIPD, 2005), p 17.

'typical Irish' or 'black cunt'[2] or more subtle, such as in the case of *Liversidge v Chief Constable of Bedfordshire*,[3] where a female police officer complained that she was described by her colleagues as 'PM', standing for 'Porch Monkey', a derogatory term for black women in southern states of America.

- Comments that reflect a stereotyped approach to a particular group—eg to the effect that 'all Muslims sympathise with Islamic terrorist groups', or that 'all older people are forgetful'.
- Jokes, graffiti, text messages or emails which refer to sex, race, disability, religion/belief, sexual orientation or age, or which have a sexual innuendo.
- Indecent or suggestive remarks, or inappropriate comments or questions about an employee's private or sex life.
- Comments about a woman's biological functions or about a particular religion's practices, or belittling comments about personal appearance or clothing.
- Displays of pin-ups, posters or calendars of naked men or women, the downloading of pornographic images, or the circulation of obscene emails.[4]
- Repeatedly suggesting socialising after work even when it has been made clear that such invitations are unwelcome.
- Physical or sexual assaults or abuse, unwelcome touching, unwanted sexual advances or demands, pestering someone for a relationship, or indecent exposure.[5]
- Ridiculing or demeaning someone, constantly picking on them or humiliating them in front of others, or setting them up to fail.
- Unfairly allocating work to an employee, in particular, unpopular or demeaning tasks.
- Overburdening an employee with excessive work.
- Giving an employee too little meaningful work to do, so that they cannot learn and progress in their role.
- Excluding or isolating an employee.
- Deliberately undermining a competent employee by constantly criticising their work.
- Copying memos or emails that are critical of an employee to others who do not need to be on the circulation list.
- Non-specific and unjustified complaints about an employee's performance

---

[2] As occurred in, respectively, *Ruizo v Tesco Stores and Lea* [1995] DCLD 24, ET; *Macauley v Auto Alloys Foundry Ltd and Taylor* [1994] DCLD 21, ET; and *Belliafantie v British Rail* [1994] DLCD 21, ET.

[3] [2002] ICR 1135, CA.

[4] eg *Moonsar v Fiveways Express Transport Ltd* [2005] IRLR 9, EAT.

[5] eg *Bloomfield v Quadrant Stationery* [1998] DCLD 38, ET.

or popularity in the workplace, such as alleging that they are 'hopeless' or 'do not fit in'.

- Overbearing or excessive supervision or other misuse of power or position.
- Blaming an employee for problems caused by others.
- Spreading malicious rumours about an employee.
- Making threats or comments about job security that have no real basis.
- Preventing an employee from progressing by deliberately obstructing their opportunities for training and promotion.
- Repeated requests that a disabled employee do things which it is known he or she cannot or will struggle to do.

Harassment can occur in person, in writing, by email or text messages. Indeed as technology develops at a rapid pace, employers may find that individuals are subjected to ever changing (and less overt, and therefore harder to identify) forms of harassment—employees may already be being harassed through instant messenger services, web blogs, networking sites such as 'Facebook' or even the internet-based 'Second Life'.[6]

Employers should also be conscious that: **11.03**

- Harassment can occur even if it was only intended 'as a bit of fun', 'harmless banter' or 'innocent flirting'.
- People of both sexes, all races, religions, orientations and ages can be harassed, as can those with a disability.
- Harassment is not always obvious.
- Harassment can happen away from the workplace and still be something for which the employer is liable, given that case law has given an extended meaning to the 'course of employment' concept, which establishes an employer's vicarious liability.[7]
- Harassment does not have to be directed at any one individual, and can be made out by the cumulative creation of a harassing atmosphere which many employees are subjected to.
- Harassment can occur by a single incident, or by an accumulation of events over a lengthy period.
- If left ignored, harassment will rarely simply 'blow over' or sort itself out.

Research has shown that among women, those who are young, new entrants to   **11.04**
the labour market, separated or who have irregular or precarious employment

---

[6] To read more about the types of harassment and the kinds of personality most prone to bullying, see *Bullying at Work: Beyond Policies to a Culture of Respect* (CIPD, 2005), p 13.

[7] See *Chief Constable of Lincolnshire Police v Stubbs* [1999] IRLR 81, EAT, which we discuss further in Chapter 14.

contracts are disproportionately at risk of harassment.[8] In addition, women working in male-dominated environments, women with disabilities, lesbians and women from racial minorities are more vulnerable, as are gay men and young men.[9]

(b) The Extent of Workplace Harassment

11.05 Workplace harassment remains rife, and serious. In March 2007 the DTI First Fair Treatment at Work Survey reported that around 1 million or 3.6 per cent of employees had personally experienced bullying or harassment at work in the last two years; and that around one in ten, or 10.6 per cent of employees, were aware of others in their workplace being bullied or harassed.[10] Across the individual strands:

- In 2005/2006, 14,250 claims were lodged with Employment Tribunals on the grounds of sex discrimination.[11]

- Race and religious discrimination also remains commonplace: in the aftermath of the 7 July 2005 bombing attacks in London, the CRE received a large number of enquiries from employers asking for advice on how to deal with and prevent racial and religious harassment in the workplace;[12] and in May 2007 the CRE reported that it had received over 5,000 complaints of race discrimination in the previous six months, of which 43 per cent related to employment, and many of which related to workplace harassment (as well as to limits to career progression or an inability to secure interviews).[13]

- The DTI First Fair Treatment at Work Survey reported that the incidence of personal unfair treatment, bullying and harassment of disabled employees was very high, at 19.7 per cent of employees compared to 7.6 per cent of those who were not disabled.[14]

- In May 2007, a third of respondents to a TUC Wales survey of lesbian, gay and bisexual workers in Wales reported being subject to harassment in the workplace.[15]

- The DTI First Fair Treatment at Work Survey also noted that 0.8 per cent of

---

[8] *Sexual Harassment: Managers' Questions Answered* (EOC, March 2006), p 5.   [9] ibid.

[10] 'Unfair and unjust? New Findings on Discrimination, Bullying and Sexual Harassment in British Workplaces' (DTI, March 2007), <www.dti.gov.uk/files/file38570.ppt>.

[11] *Sexual harassment in the workplace: a literature review* (EOC, 2007), para 2.4.

[12] <www.cre.gov.uk/gdpract/preventingharassment.html>.

[13] 'Latest CRE Statistics Show Racism is Still Rife in the Workplace', 17 May 2007, <www.cre.gov.uk/default.aspx.locid–0hgnew0uv.Lang-EN.htm>.

[14] 'Unfair and Unjust? New Findings on Discrimination, Bullying and Sexual Harassment in British Workplaces' (DTI, March 2007), <www.dti.gov.uk/files/file38570.ppt>.

[15] 'Union Report Highlights High Levels of Harassment for Lesbian, Gay and Bisexual Workers', 17 May 2007, <www.tuc.org.uk/equality/tuc–13342.f0.cfm.>

employees reported personal unfair treatment on grounds of their age in the last two years.[16]

(c) The Effects of Workplace Harassment

The effects of workplace harassment can also be hugely damaging for both employees and employers.   **11.06**

In 2001 the European Commission's Employment and Social Affairs Committee reported that the effects of harassment on the health of an employee can be 'devastating', and can include stress, nervous tension, headaches/migraines and depression, and psychosomatic illnesses such as stomach ulcers, colitis, thyroid problems, insomnia, high blood pressure and skin diseases. The Committee also pointed out that in most cases victims of harassment take long-term sick leave or even resign from their jobs.[17]   **11.07**

The damaging consequences of unchecked harassment for employers can include: **11.08**

- a reduction in morale among the victims of harassment, those accused of it, their colleagues, and others who witness harassment;
- sickness, absenteeism and resignations;
- consequential negative effects on productivity and economic performance and the actual and hidden costs of replacing staff;
- the payment of legal costs if a harassment claim is brought in the Employment Tribunal or civil courts, whose costs are normally not recoverable in the Employment Tribunal even if the employer successfully defends the claim;
- the payment of potentially high damages if such a claim succeeds;
- the 'hidden costs' of litigation in terms of the internal time spent in mounting a defence to the claim, and the productivity lost by employees having to attend the Tribunal or court to give evidence; and
- damage to the 'brand' which can be generated by adverse publicity of harassment claims.

According to one estimate, bullying costs employers 80 million lost working days and up to £2 billion in lost revenue each year. It also accounts for up to 50 per cent of stress-related workplace illnesses.[18] Recent research by the CIPD indicates that employers receive an average of 3.1 Employment Tribunal claims per year; that on average preparing for each Employment Tribunal takes   **11.09**

---

[16] 'Unfair and Unjust? New Findings on Discrimination, Bullying and Sexual Harassment in British Workplaces' (DTI, March 2007), <www.dti.gov.uk/files/file38570.ppt>.

[17] *Harassment at the Workplace* (Employment and Social Affairs Committee of the European Commission, July 2001, Document Reference 2001/2339).

[18] *Managing Conflict at Work* (CIPD, October 2004), p 15.

15 days of management time, Human Resources time and in-house employment lawyers' time; and that the average annual costs associated with Employment Tribunals comes to almost £20,000 per employer.[19]

11.10 We set out what can happen when serious harassment occurs by way of a case study at Appendix 11.1.

C. The Prohibition of Harassment in the Equality Enactments

(a) The Definition of Harassment

11.11 Harassment in the workplace on grounds of sex, race (other than nationality or colour), married status, gender reassignment, disability, religion or belief, sexual orientation or age is specifically prohibited by the SDA, RRA, DDA, RBR, SOR and AR.

11.12 By section 3A(1) of the RRA:

> A person subjects another to harassment . . . where, on grounds of race or ethnic or national origins, he engages in unwanted conduct which has the purpose or effect of—
>
> (a) violating that other person's dignity, or
> (b) creating an intimidating, hostile, degrading, humiliating or offensive environment for him.
>
> Conduct shall be regarded as having the effect specified in paragraph (a) or (b) . . . only if, having regard to all the circumstances, including in particular the perception of that other person, it should reasonably be considered as having that effect.

This provision in the RRA only applies to harassment on grounds of race or ethnic or national origins and not colour or nationality which is dealt with separately (see below). There are broadly comparable provisions in the employment provisions of the SDA, DDA, RBR, SOR and AR.[20] The definitions of harassment under the SDA apply equally to men and women.[21]

11.13 However, the definition of harassment under the SDA is wider than that in the other statutes in that in addition to unwanted 'conduct',[22] it specifically prohibits 'unwanted verbal, non-verbal or physical conduct of a sexual nature'.[23] The definition also specifically prohibits the less favourable treatment of a woman on grounds that she has rejected or submitted to harassment, compared to the treatment that would have been given to her had she not rejected or submitted to the conduct.[24] This means that a woman cannot be penalised

---

[19] *Managing Conflict at Work* (CIPD, February 2007), pp 23–24 and 32.
[20] SDA, s 4A; DDA, s 3B; RBR, reg 5; SOR, reg 5, and AR, reg 6.   [21] SDA, s 4A(6).
[22] SDA, s 4A(1)(a).   [23] SDA, s 4A(1)(b).   [24] SDA, s 4A(1)(c).

because she rejects the harassing treatment advanced to her (by, for example, the harasser demoting her, ridiculing her, or giving her lower quality work, because she refuses to engage in sexual banter, or rejects his sexual advances), nor can she be treated less favourably because she submits to such conduct (by, for example, the harasser making her promotion contingent on her continued submission to the conduct in question).

There is no specific provision in the other harassment definitions prohibiting **11.14** the less favourable treatment of employees because they have rejected, or sub-mitted to, harassment on grounds of race, disability, religion/belief, sexual orientation or age. However, if the rejection or submission to the treatment in question has occurred in the context of the employee alleging that their rights under the equality enactments have been breached, any consequent less favourable treatment of them may constitute victimisation.

(b) Harassment on the Grounds of Perception and Association

The harassment definition under the SDA is currently more limited than some **11.15** of the other definitions to the extent that harassment is only prohibited on the grounds of the victim's sex or gender reassignment, rather than on grounds of sex or gender reassignment generally. By contrast, the definitions of harassment under the RRA, RBR, SOR and AR refer to harassment simply 'on grounds of' race, religion or belief, etc—this means that harassment is prohibited if, for example, it is based on the victim's perceived religion, orientation etc, or their association with someone else's race, religion etc (such as that of their partner, parent, child or colleague).

This lacuna in the SDA definition was successfully challenged in *R (Equal* **11.16** *Opportunities Commission) v Secretary of State for Trade and Industry*,[25] as a result of which the Government has committed to amending the definition of harassment to make clear that harassment is not limited to conduct caused by the sex of the claimant.[26]

Harassment, as with the other kinds of discrimination, only occurs under the **11.17** DDA if it is related to the victim's disability.[27] The issue of whether or not the law should be extended to prohibit discrimination by reference to association with someone else's disability is currently being considered by the ECJ in the case of *Coleman v Attridge Law*.[28]

---

[25] [2007] IRLR 327, QBD (Admin).
[26] DLR consultation paper, paras 1.24 and 14.6.
[27] DDA, s 18D.   [28] C–303/06, ECJ.

(c) **Comparators and** *Macdonald v Advocate General for Scotland*

11.18 A key feature of all the statutory definitions of harassment is that no comparator is needed—harassment will legally have occurred if the conditions described
in the definitions are found, whether or not it can be shown that the same
treatment would not have been afforded to someone of a different sex, race etc.
However, the complainant would still need to prove that the harassment was
'on grounds of' the prohibited strand of discrimination. In assessing this issue,
it is likely that where the conduct in question is specific to sex, race etc, the
Tribunal will quite easily be able to draw the inference that the conduct was
indeed on grounds of sex or race etc. However, where there is nothing in
the behaviour which itself indicates that it was motivated by sex, race etc (for
example, where it takes the form of criticism for lateness which is targeted at a
female or black employee, when other employees are not criticised for being
late), it is likely that some form of comparison will in practice be needed in
order to show that the behaviour was indeed on the prohibited ground.

11.19 Historically, allegations of harassment were framed as complaints of direct
discrimination. However, since the coming into force of the specific definitions
of harassment the equality enactments now provide that 'detriment' does not
include harassment, thus ensuring that the definitions are mutually exclusive.[29]
This means that the same set of facts cannot generate both a harassment and a
direct discrimination claim. Employees can nevertheless argue that their experience has constituted harassment and direct discrimination in the alternative—
in those cases, the Employment Tribunal should consider first whether harassment under the statutory definition has occurred, and if it finds that it has
not, it should then consider the issue of direct discrimination.

11.20 As harassment on the grounds of nationality or colour is not covered by the
new statutory definition of harassment in the RRA, employees who complain
of this will still need to characterise their claim as one of direct race discrimination.[30] Following the decision of the House of Lords in *Macdonald v Advocate
General for Scotland; Pearce v Mayfield Secondary School Governing Body*,[31] in
such cases it will always be necessary for a harassment complainant to identify a
comparator (albeit that the comparator can be hypothetical) even where the
conduct is specific to race.

11.21 The fact that the new statutory definitions of harassment do not require a
comparator means that older harassment cases decided under the direct discrimination provisions need to be treated with caution, as many no longer

---

[29] SDA, s 82(1); RRA, s 78; DDA, s 18D; RBR, reg 3; SOR, reg 3; and AR, reg 2(2).
[30] RRA, s 1(1)(a).   [31] [2004] 1 All ER 339, HL.

represent good law. In *Stewart v Cleveland Guest (Engineering) Ltd*,[32] for example, a female employee failed in her claim under the SDA arising out of the display by her male co-workers of calendars and other pictures of nude and partially nude women on the grounds that a hypothetical male employee would have been equally offended. Similarly, in *Brumfitt v Ministry of Defence*,[33] a female acting corporal in the RAF Military Police failed to prove sex discrimination by the sexual jokes and comments made by her supervisor during a training course, because the Tribunal found that all those who attended the training course in question had been similarly poorly treated. It is quite likely that these cases would have been decided differently had they been argued under the harassment provisions.

The *Macdonald* case also made clear that for the purposes of the SDA, 'sex' **11.22** means 'gender' and not sexual orientation, so that in a complaint of harassment under the SDA by a homosexual, the appropriate comparator would be a homosexual person of the opposite sex and not a heterosexual person of the same sex. The practical consequences of the *Macdonald* decision in this regard have since been limited by the coming into force of the SOR, specifically outlawing harassment on the grounds of sexual orientation.

Another important consequence of the *Macdonald* case was its overturning of **11.23** the finding in *Burton v de Vere Hotels Ltd*[34] that an employer's failure to take reasonable steps to protect its employees from sexual or racial harassment by third parties was itself discrimination, even where the failure to protect the employees had nothing itself to do with their sex or race. We discuss this principle and the proposals to change the law back to the position in the *Burton* case further in Chapter 14.

(d) 'Unwanted' Conduct

Also common to the new definitions of harassment is that the conduct in **11.24** question was 'unwanted'. This issue had arisen under some of the old cases alleging harassment as direct discrimination in the sense that it was argued that provocation or consent by the alleged victim to the conduct in question meant that they could not have suffered a 'detriment' by it. However, the fact that the employee does not complain about the alleged harassment at the time does not prevent it from having been harassment: in fact Tribunals increasingly recognise how difficult it is for employees to complain about such issues, and that many victims will not complain for fear of the damage it will do to their careers.

---

[32] [1996] ICR 535, EAT.   [33] [2005] IRLR 4, EAT.   [34] [1997] ICR 1, EAT.

11.25   In *Driskel v Peninsular Business Services Ltd*,[35] for example, a female employee complained of sexual harassment when her manager subjected her to sexual 'banter' and comments over a period of many months. The Tribunal rejected her complaint partly on the basis that she had not complained at the time. However, the EAT, in allowing Ms Driskel's appeal, recognised that the absence of a contemporaneous complaint does not necessarily mean that the conduct in question was not in fact 'unwanted'. The EAT also noted that it would have been particularly hard for Ms Driskel to have complained given that she was keen to secure a promotion from the very person she felt was harassing her. Similarly, in *Moonsar v Fiveways Express Transport Ltd*,[36] the EAT held that the fact that a female employee had not complained contemporaneously about the downloading of pornography by her male colleagues did not afford her employers a defence to an SDA claim.

11.26   That said, there have been cases where an employee's conduct has been held to be such that they cannot prove that the alleged harassment was indeed unwanted or unwelcome.

11.27   In *Steele v Optika Ltd*,[37] for example, a female employee complained that a 'strippergram' had been organised for her birthday. The strippergram had handcuffed Ms Steele and undressed to a g-string. He had then thrown her over his shoulder and removed his g-string so that her face was in close contact with his groin. The Tribunal found that Ms Steele had 'entered into the spirit' of the strippergram with 'evident enjoyment', and, when asked at the time whether the incident had caused her embarrassment had said 'not at all . . . I only wish I could have spent more time with him'. On that basis she could not be said to have suffered a detriment. The Tribunal also appeared to have been influenced by the fact that Ms Steele was an 'active and willing participant in sexually explicit banter' with the colleagues who had organised the strippergram.

11.28   Similarly in *Wileman v Minilec Engineering Ltd*[38] and *Snowball v Gardner Merchant Ltd*[39] Tribunals permitted employers to cross-examine complainants as to whether the fact that they had talked freely to colleagues about sexual matters, or worn scanty clothing at work, indicated that the sexual conduct to which they had been subjected was not in fact unwanted.

11.29   However, these decisions and the approach they engender need to be treated with some care. Legally, the new statutory definition of harassment under the SDA specifically recognises that sometimes women 'submit' to harassment, and that this does not necessarily stop it being such. This principle is also

---

[35] [2000] IRLR 151, EAT.   [36] [2005] IRLR 9, EAT.   [37] [1997] DCLD 31, ET.
[38] [1988] IRLR 144, EAT.   [39] [1987] IRLR 397, EAT.

specifically recognised by Article 2 of the European Commission's Code of Practice on Protecting the Dignity of Women and Men at Work.[40] Tribunals may well be less sympathetic now than they would have been historically to the implicit argument that by wearing a short skirt, for example, a woman is inviting harassment and not entitled to complain about any such harassment that occurs. Practically, adopting such an approach in the Tribunal can make employers appear vindictive, and is unlikely to improve relations between an employer and other female employees.

(e) Cumulative and Single-incident Harassment

In assessing whether or not harassment has occurred, it is also necessary for the Tribunal to consider the conduct in question as a whole. This is because harassment often takes the form of a series of incidents which, if analysed individually, might appear petty, but which, when analysed cumulatively, achieve a greater and more sinister significance. **11.30**

This approach was identified in *Reed and Bull Information Systems Ltd v Stedman*[41] where the EAT, citing American case law with approval, warned that Tribunals should not 'carve up the case into a series of specific incidents and try and measure the harm or detriment in relation to each'. This was because in some cases, a blatant act of a sexual nature (such as the deliberate looking up a victim's skirt when she was sitting down) may well make other incidents (such as asking to be shown personal photographs which the victim was looking at whilst at work) take on 'a different colour and significance'. Once unwelcome sexual interest has been shown by a man in a female employee, she may well feel bothered about his attentions which '. . . in a different context, would appear quite unobjectionable'. **11.31**

The need to look at incidents cumulatively was also recognised in *Driskel v Peninsular Business Services Ltd*,[42] where the EAT observed that in hearing the evidence and finding the facts, it is: **11.32**

> . . . desirable . . . [for Tribunals] . . . not to include in this exercise judgments as to the discriminatory significance, if any, of individual incidents—judgment thus far should be limited to the finding of all facts that are prima facie relevant. If ad hoc assessments 'discrimination or no' are made the result is a fragmented and discursive judgment; more importantly, there is the potential . . . for ignoring the impact of the totality of successive incidents, individually trivial.

On the facts of the *Driskel* case the EAT concluded that had the Tribunal

---

[40] This is annexed to the EC Commission Recommendation on the Protection of the Dignity of Men and Women at Work, 92/131/EEC.
[41] [1999] IRLR 299, EAT, paras 25–29.   [42] [2000] IRLR 151, EAT at para 12.

adopted this cumulative approach, it would have concluded that Ms Driskel had indeed been the subject of a campaign of harassment, made up of sexual banter and comments over a period of about three months, sexist comments to the effect that she should wear a 'short skirt and see-through blouse showing plenty of cleavage' if she wanted to succeed in a promotion, and ultimately her dismissal when she refused to return to her old job with the same manager.

11.33 However, case law also recognises that harassment can take the form of a single incident. In *Insitu Cleaning Co Ltd v Heads*,[43] a female employee complained that one of her managers, who was also the son of one of the directors of the company where she worked, said 'Hiya big tits' to her in a meeting. The company had sought to argue that conduct could not be regarded as 'unwanted' if it was a one-off incident because it was only when conduct had been carried out, rejected, and was then repeated, that it could properly be described as 'unwanted'. The EAT commented that this argument was 'specious' and that '. . . if it were correct it would mean that a man was always entitled to argue that every act of harassment was different from the first and that he was testing to see if it was unwanted: in other words it would amount to a licence to harassment'. The EAT held that the question whether any single incident amounted to a detriment was a matter of fact for the tribunal; and the same approach will apply in assessing whether a single incident amounts to the new statutory tort of harassment. The EAT also observed that 'unwanted' is essentially the same as 'unwelcome' or 'uninvited' and that '. . . [n]o-one, other than a person used to indulging in loutish behaviour, could think that the remark made in this case was other than obviously unwanted'.

(f) The Intention of the Harasser

11.34 There is no requirement to prove that the conduct in question was intended to harass the victim. In the *Driskel* case, for example,[44] the employer argued that the comment suggesting Ms Driskel should wear sexually provocative clothing for her interview was 'flippant and not meant to be taken seriously'. The EAT held that it was irrelevant that the harasser had not actually expected Ms Driskel to dress as he had suggested—rather what was relevant was that 'by this remark (flippant or not) he was undermining her dignity as a woman'.

11.35 This common law principle is reflected in the second limb of the statutory definition of harassment set out at paragraph 11.12 above, which provides that—regardless of the intention of the harasser—if the 'effect' of the actions in question is of violating the victim's dignity, or creating an intimidating,

---

[43] [1995] IRLR 4, EAT.
[44] *Driskel v Peninsular Business Services Ltd* [2000] IRLR 151, EAT, at para 14.

hostile, degrading, humiliating or offensive environment for him or her, then the statutory definition of harassment will be made out. However, the conduct in question is only to be regarded as having one of these effects if, having regard to all the circumstances, including in particular the perception of that other person, it should reasonably be considered as having that effect.

That said, if it can be proved that the harasser actually did have the 'purpose' **11.36** by his or her actions of violating the victim's dignity, or creating an intimidating, hostile, degrading, humiliating or offensive environment for him or her, then harassment will have occurred, via the first limb of the statutory definition, regardless of whether the effect on the victim could actually be described in these terms. In reality, though, if there has only been a very limited effect on the victim, this is likely to be reflected in the level of any damages awarded.

Harassment can occur even if it is not directed at the complainant personally. For **11.37** example in *Chin v Post Office*[45] an employee witnessed the name-calling to which a black employee was frequently subjected. Although the remarks were not addressed to the complainant, a tribunal upheld his complaint on the basis that the harassment and abuse of his fellow worker constituted a detriment to him.

(g) Harassment, Direct Discrimination and Victimisation

Employers must also ensure that they do not engage in direct discrimination in **11.38** the manner in which complaints of harassment are investigated; and that employees who have made complaints of harassment are not victimised by, for example, isolation from other employees or the denial of opportunities for overtime, bonuses, training or promotion.

(h) Harassment and 'Multiple' Discrimination

Harassment often occurs at the 'intersection' of one or more of the prohibited **11.39** grounds—for example, a black woman may be harassed because she is black and because she is a woman; or an Asian gay male may be harassed because he is both Asian and gay. This is often referred to as 'multiple' discrimination. Under the current legislative framework such a victim would need to prove their case under each and every of the applicable equality enactments. The inability of the current law to address such 'multiple' harassment in a straightforward way is a limitation of the current legal framework.

The Government recognises that: **11.40**

> . . . [if] a person experiences discrimination, it may sometimes be hard to disentangle which of their protected characteristics is driving the less favourable

---

[45] [1997] DCLD 31, ET.

treatment to which they have been subjected, or whether more than one protected characteristic was involved.[46]

In the Discrimination Law Review consultation process, the Government has called for evidence as to whether these limitations are in practice meaning that claimants are not bringing or losing cases. If such evidence is provided, the Government may legislate to permit fully combined multiple claims to be presented (although they do not at present appear keen to do so).[47]

D. Other Legal Mechanisms Outlawing Harassment

(a) The Protection from Harassment Act 1997

11.41 Harassment may also amount to a breach of the Protection from Harassment Act 1997 (the 'PHA'), section 1. This legislation created a new statutory tort of harassment, providing that a person must not '. . . pursue a course of conduct (a) which amounts to harassment of another, and (b) which he knows or ought to know amounts to harassment of the other'.[48] For the purposes of this definition, the person whose conduct is in question ought to know that it amounts to harassment if '. . . a reasonable person in possession of the same information would think the course of conduct amounted to harassment of the other'.[49] Whether a person ought to have known that his course of conduct amounts to harassment is therefore tested objectively—by reference to what a reasonable person, in possession of the same information, would have thought.

11.42 Although the PHA does not provide a specific definition of harassment, it is made clear that '. . . [r]eferences to harassing a person include alarming the person or causing the person distress',[50] and that 'conduct' includes speech.[51] A 'course of conduct' is only made out if it involves conduct on at least two occasions.[52]

11.43 In *Majrowksi v Guys and St Thomas's NHS Trust*,[53] the House of Lords ruled that an employer could be vicariously liable for a breach of the PHA by an employee where the alleged unlawful conduct occurred in the course of the employee's employment. This is an important judgment in practical terms as it enables employees to bring civil claims under the PHA against employers, and recover compensation in the same. Moreover, there is no 'reasonable steps' defence akin to those in the equality enactments available to an employer faced

---

[46] DLR consultation paper, para 7.31.   [47] DLR consultation paper, paras 7.33–7.34.
[48] PHA, s 1(1).   [49] PHA, s 1(2).   [50] PHA, s 2.   [51] PHA, s 7(4).
[52] PHA, s 7(3).   [53] [2007] 1 AC 224, HL.

with such a claim and the limitation period for a PHA claim is six years rather than the three months under the equality enactments.

However, a claim can only be brought under the PHA if the harassment is said **11.44** to have been committed by either (i) one employee having on at least two occasions pursued a course of conduct amounting to harassment; or (ii) by more than one employee each acting on different occasions in furtherance of some joint design. This principle was established in *Daniels v Metropolitan Police Commissioner*,[54] where a former military policewoman who then joined the Metropolitan Police Service (the 'MPS') complained of 11 instances of acts of harassment under the PHA from October 1994 to May 2002 while serving with the MPS. She alleged that the harassment she had suffered was such that she had suffered a breakdown of her health in the form of depression, ultimately left the police and had not worked since. She claimed that throughout her police service she was the victim of harassment and victimisation and that her employers were negligent in their response to the stress to which she was subjected at her workplace. Although her claim failed on its facts, the judgment made clear that such a claim will not lie where the employee is alleging one-off incidents by different employees, not acting in furtherance of some common plan.

A victim of harassment under the PHA may bring a civil claim for damages, **11.45** and/or a claim for injunctive relief to prevent further harassment.[55] The high profile *Green v DB Group Services (UK) Ltd*[56] case which we discuss at Appendix 11.1 above was a case brought partly under the PHA.

(b) Negligence, the Human Rights Act 1998 and Other Torts

A victim of harassment in the workplace may also bring a claim in negligence **11.46** against the employer for breach of the duty of care owed to him or her as an employee. Such a claim will only succeed, however, where there was a real risk of psychiatric damage which the employer ought reasonably to have foreseen and which they ought properly to have averted.

If the employer is a public authority, an employee may also claim that serious **11.47** harassment has constituted a breach of their rights as protected by Schedule 1 of the HRA, such as those under Article 3 (the right to protection from torture and inhuman or degrading treatment) or Article 8 (the right to respect for private and family life, home and correspondence). In *East African Asians v UK*,[57] for example, the European Commission on Human Rights recognised that

---

[54] [2006] EWHC 1622, HC, at para 9.   [55] PHA, ss 3(1) and (2).
[56] [2006] IRLR 764, HC.   [57] (1973) 3 EHRR 76.

severe race discrimination can, in certain circumstances constitute degrading treatment within Article 3.

11.48 Other torts may also be engaged by harassment, such as the common law tort of harassment,[58] private nuisance[59] and assault and battery.[60]

(c) The Criminal Law

11.49 Serious harassment may also involve criminal offences, such as assault, indecent assault, criminal damage, criminal harassment, intentional harassment and putting a person in fear of violence under the Public Order Act 1986[61] and offences under the Malicious Communications Act 1988[62] and Telecommunications Act 1983.[63]

11.50 There are also specific racially aggravated forms of certain offences, such as assault, criminal damage, and the offences under the Public Order Act 1986 referred to above. These offences are committed where the primary offence (assault, criminal damage etc) 'involves or is motivated by' hostility based on the victim's actual or perceived racial or religious group. If proved, a racially or religiously aggravated offence carries a higher maximum penalty than the basic offence.[64]

11.51 Moreover, in any case where it is shown that the offence was aggravated by the victim's race, religion or belief, disability or sexual orientation, the judge is required to treat that fact as an aggravating factor and to state in court any additional part of the sentence imposed for that factor.[65]

11.52 Powers of arrest can also be attached to civil injunctions including those under the PHA.

11.53 Serious harassment may also form the basis for an application for an Anti-Social Behaviour Order.

---

[58] As considered in *Khorasandjian v Bush* [1993] QB 727, CA.

[59] As considered in *Malone v Laskey* [1907] 2 KB 141, CA.

[60] An unwanted kiss, for example, may constitute a battery—see *R v Chief Constable of Devon and Cornwall ex p CEGB* [1982] QB 458, CA at 471.

[61] Sections 2, 4, 4A and 5.

[62] Section 1 of which sets out the offence of sending a letter with intent to cause distress or anxiety.

[63] Section 43 of which sets out the offences of sending messages by telephone that are grossly offensive, indecent, obscene or menacing or of misusing the telephone to cause anxiety or annoyance.

[64] Crime and Disorder Act 1988, ss 28–32, as amended by the Anti-terrorism Crime and Security Act 2001.

[65] Criminal Justice Act 2003, ss 145–146.

E. Employer's Liability for Harassment

Harassment is one area where questions of the employer's liability frequently **11.54** arise, because (i) an employer may seek to argue that the alleged harassment took place outside the course of the alleged harasser's employment, such that the employer cannot be vicariously liable for any proven harassment; and/or (ii) an employer may seek to invoke the statutory defence under the equality enactments that it took such steps as were 'reasonably practicable' to prevent the harassment taking place.[66] We consider these concepts in further detail in Chapter 14 when looking at litigation issues generally.

F. Preventing and Investigating Harassment

(a) Anti-harassment Policies

We think that the introduction of a clear, consistent and easily understood **11.55** policy dedicated to harassment issues is the best possible starting point for an employer seeking to promote an anti-harassment strategy. An effective anti-harassment policy should:

- include a statement of commitment to eradicating harassment from senior management within the organisation;
- include an acknowledgment that harassment and bullying are problems for the organisation;
- give a clear definition of harassment, so as to make clear what is and what is not acceptable behaviour within the workplace;
- provide examples of what could constitute harassment, including less 'obvious' examples of harassing behaviour;
- make clear that the policy will apply on the organisation's premises, and away from work if the context is work-related (such as a training day, conference or work social event);
- stress that a 'zero tolerance' approach will be adopted to harassment, so that (i) all complaints of harassment will be taken seriously; and (ii) all proven harassment will be dealt with firmly, including where necessary as a disciplinary offence;
- include reference to protection from victimisation;
- set out the steps the organisation will take towards preventing harassment;
- set out the responsibilities of supervisors and managers;
- provide a clear and confidential procedure for resolving a complaint of

---

[66] SDA, s 41(3); RRA, s 32(3); DDA, s 58(5); RBR, 22(3); SOR, reg 22(3) and AR, reg 25(3).

harassment, which should include both informal as well as formal routes, and timescales for action;

- ensure that employees are made aware that complaints will be dealt with as fairly, confidentially and sensitively as possible;
- include arrangements for supporting the victims of harassment, and those accused of harassment;
- include arrangements for support to managers or those otherwise involved in investigating allegations of harassment;
- include information as to how the policy is to be implemented, reviewed and monitored;
- have input from relevant employee representatives at the drafting stage; and
- be well publicised, through the organisation's staff handbooks, induction packs, intranet, posters, notice boards and other means of communication, and by providing all existing and new employees with their own copy of the policy, so that all employees are familiar with it and understand why it has been adopted, how it works, how it affects them and who they can approach to make a complaint.

(b) Training

11.56 Training is an essential stage in any anti-harassment strategy. To be most effective in this area we would advise employers to:

- ensure that all staff, supervisors and managers are thoroughly trained in the anti-harassment policy and their responsibilities under it;
- make training on harassment issues a key component of all induction courses;
- ensure that training includes defining unacceptable behaviour, how to get bullies to recognise and change that behaviour, and in counselling victims and perpetrators;
- ensure that those who will have responsibility for investigating allegations of harassment are specifically trained in that skill, so as to handle complaints sensitively and in accordance with the policy, and to ensure that they are not tempted simply to dismiss allegations on the basis that there is a 'personality clash', or because they fear the alleged harasser's position within the organisation may be at risk;
- ensure that there is diversity among those trained to hear complaints of harassment, given that some such complaints can raise sensitive issues, which employees may only wish to discuss with investigators of the same sex, race, religion/belief etc; and
- ensure that training is regularly updated, and that refresher training is

regularly given, particularly in light of the frequent pace of legal change in this area.

As well as training in the use of grievance and/or disciplinary procedures, many **11.57** employers choose to offer training to line managers and/or human resources professionals in conflict management/resolution skills. A smaller number of employers—around 30 per cent—train their employees in mediation skills. However, there is some evidence that employers who provide mediation training receive fewer employment tribunal claims than those who do not.[67] We consider mediation further at paragraph 11.102 below.

(c) Creating an Anti-harassment Culture

It is an essential part of any effective anti-harassment strategy that managers **11.58** and supervisors set a good example. Indeed recent CIPD research shows that 52 per cent of employers identified either 'line manager behaviour' or 'top team behaviour' in 'building a culture that doesn't support bullying/harassment' as the most effective success factor in tackling harassment at work.[68]

In practical terms, it is essential that managers and supervisors: **11.59**

- do not themselves engage in any harassing behaviour;
- treat all employees with respect;
- identify and promote positive as well as identify negative behaviour;
- take immediate appropriate action when any complaints of harassment are made, so as not to appear to condone such behaviour;
- do not tolerate or encourage a working atmosphere where abusive 'banter' becomes commonplace (just because no employee has complained does not mean that no employee feels harassed); and
- indicate, generally, by their actions how seriously harassment is viewed by the organisation.

However, it is increasingly recognised that in order to eradicate harassment, **11.60** employers must go further than simply regulating the actions of their managers and supervisors: rather efforts must be made to build a positive culture within the working environment which of itself acts as a control mechanism, preventing harassment from occurring. The title of a recent CIPD report—*Bullying at Work: Beyond Policies to a Culture of Respect*[69]—embodies this approach, and identifies the following elements as essential to building an anti-harassment culture in the workplace:

---

[67] *Managing Conflict at Work* (CIPD, February 2007), pp 3, 15–17.
[68] *Managing Conflict at Work* (CIPD, October 2004), p 19.   [69] (CIPD, 2005).

- creating an atmosphere in which the organisation and its leaders have a clear vision and sense of what a culture of dignity and respect would be like in practice;
- establishing and integrating a continuous assessment and improvement approach that is built on the shared belief that change does not happen by chance, but is made to happen;
- developing monitoring tools that measure qualitative and quantitative improvements in the culture of the organisation; and
- identifying the necessary tools and approaches required for maintaining the momentum of dignity at work.[70]

11.61 In addition, the general culture of the workplace can also have an effect on the incidence of harassment. The CIPD has observed that:

> Bullies aren't monsters that exist in a vacuum. . . . Organisational cultures can create and sustain 'institutionalised bullying' behaviours in a variety of ways. These can include autocratic management styles, overloading individuals with work, having a 'blame' culture, tolerating or even promoting aggressive behaviour and not training people in identifying, challenging and changing bullying behaviours. In fact, if bullying is supported by an organisational culture, behaving like a bully can be seen as a way to improve your career prospects.[71]

11.62 Employers may therefore find that fostering a general culture which avoids these elements itself forms an essential part of an anti-harassment strategy, as harassment and bullying are less likely to develop in such an environment.

(d) Identifying Harassment

11.63 There are a range of ways in which an employer can identify that harassment may have occurred.

11.64 In many cases, harassment will be identified by an employer because an employee makes a specific complaint that he or she has been the victim of harassment. This may take the form of a verbal complaint, an internal memo, an official grievance, or comments made in an appraisal.

11.65 Sometimes an employee other than the victim, or a trade union representative, will make a complaint on the victim's behalf via one of the above methods.

11.66 However, making a complaint of harassment is not easy and it is often appropriate for employers to establish routes that facilitate this process. This might be an employee hotline, or a system of internal but independent bullying advisers and supporters who are able to listen to employees experiencing

---

[70] *Bullying at Work: Beyond Policies to a Culture of Respect* (CIPD, 2005), p 17.
[71] *Managing Conflict at Work* (CIPD, October 2004), p 20.

personal difficulties with their manager or colleagues. In such schemes, the role of the buddy/listener is to provide confidential information on the policies and procedures and to help the troubled employee identify the most appropriate action for their circumstances, which may or may not include raising the complaint formally. Buddies or listeners should be specially trained in the skills needed for this role.

In addition to direct complaints of harassment, it is also important for employ-   **11.67**
ers to be live to indirect means by which harassment can be identified—such as from persistent rumours, anonymous comments, comments made in exit interviews by departing staff, rising levels of absence in a certain department or team (which could indicate a problem with a particular manager or team leader), or via workplace surveys such as stress audits or general satisfaction surveys.

(e) Investigating Allegations of Harassment

Once a possible case of harassment has been identified, the employer's policy   **11.68**
should set out clear procedures for investigating the allegation, so that managers know what to do immediately.

(f) Key Principles of any Investigation

The EOC has suggested that all such procedures should be carried out 'con-   **11.69**
fidentially, compassionately and without delay',[72] and we would agree that these principles represent the key principles of any harassment investigation:

* Confidentiality is an important safeguard for the victims of alleged harassment, and for those accused of having carried it out. Confidentiality can, in
  theory at least, be achieved by not revealing the names of any parties to the
  wider workforce, and by keeping the paperwork relating to the complaint in
  a locked drawer or cabinet. If confidentiality is not practicable, perhaps if a
  complaint of harassment is made in a small team, the parties concerned
  should be advised not to communicate between themselves, directly or
  indirectly, about the complaint.

* Compassion is vital to ensuring that victims feel able to talk frankly, and
  without fear of censure. Consistent with a 'zero tolerance' approach, victims
  should not be made to feel, even inadvertently, that they are being 'over-
  sensitive'. Equally, from the perspective of both the complainant and those
  accused of harassment, and the wider workforce, the investigation must be
  seen to be fairly and objectively carried out, and those investigating the

---

[72] *Sexual Harassment: Managers' Questions Answered* (EOC, March 2006), Annex 2.

allegations must be keen to avoid any perception that they have 'taken sides' or prejudged the outcome.

- Promptness is a further important safeguard for both victims and those accused, as it is in no-one's interests for investigations to 'hang over' those involved for a lengthy period of time, particularly if they continue to work together. Moreover, speeding up an investigative process can have real practical outcomes—Fife Council, for example, found that when they combined their harassment and grievance policies and procedures into one 'fair treatment at work' policy, and cut the time investigating complaints from an average of 165 days to 25 days, this significantly reduced the number of people off sick as a result of the old drawn-out process.[73]

(g) Stage 1: A Preliminary Discussion with the Complainant

11.70 This would be a typical first step in any harassment investigation. During such a discussion, the employer should seek to establish the extent and seriousness of the allegation the employee is making: was the incident complained of repeated with this employee, or have similar issues occurred with the same alleged harasser and other employees?

11.71 The employer should also use this opportunity to establish what the employee would like to happen.

11.72 The employee may not wish any action to be taken other than for the complaint to be noted. At that stage it may be sensible to provide them with diary sheets, to enable them to keep records of any dates and times of further incidents, any witnesses etc, in case in the future they decide they would like the matter investigated further. They would also be well advised to keep copies of any emails, memos or notes which they feel evidence the harassment in question.

11.73 However, it is ultimately an employer's decision whether to investigate the allegations made, even if the complainant does not support such a process. An employer may decide to proceed against the complainant's wishes if the complaint made is particularly serious, or appears to involve a repeat harasser, so that the employer feels such action is necessary in light of the duty of care to the alleged victim and other employees. Such action also has the benefit of clearing the harasser's name if in fact the complaint turns out to be unsubstantiated. However, in taking such a course an employer must bear in mind that this may cause serious distress to the complainant, diminish their confidence and that of

---

[73] *Managing Conflict at Work* (CIPD, February 2007), pp 3, 21.

other employees in the anti-harassment process and particularly the confidentiality of it, and ultimately mean that other employees are less willing to make complaints of harassment.

(h) Stage 2: Informal Resolution

It is normally appropriate to include an informal stage in a harassment investi- **11.74** gation process, which involves an attempt to resolve the issue between the parties quickly and by consent.

Informal resolution may well be possible where, for example, the alleged har- **11.75** asser admits the alleged behaviour but is genuinely unaware that this is unwelcome or inappropriate. In those circumstances, the employee should have the impact of their behaviour explained to them; be advised that their behaviour contravenes the organisation's harassment policy; be reminded of the standard of behaviour expected of all employees; be asked to stop their behaviour; be advised of the consequences of continuing with the behaviour; and be told that the discussion was informal and confidential but that the situation will continue to be monitored. A manager, person from Human Resources, or trade union representative could carry out this meeting. The victim may or may not wish to be present.

Such an informal route may not, however, be appropriate where the harassment **11.76** alleged is very serious; where the alleged victim is very distressed and/or does not wish the informal route to be followed; where the alleged offender is in a position of trust and responsibility; where the choice of an informal procedure may send the wrong message to other staff about the seriousness the allegation has been afforded; where the informal procedure does not have the capacity to deter a recurrence of the harassment; or where the harassment, if repeated, could be very damaging.

An informal stage can take the form of mediation, which we consider further at **11.77** paragraph 11.102 below.

(i) Stage 3: A Formal Investigation

After an informal stage has proved unsuccessful, or is not appropriate, it is **11.78** normally appropriate for the investigation to become more formalised. As with any such issue it is important to follow a process that is fair to both parties. We set out the key features of a fair investigation into a harassment allegation at Appendix 11.2 to this chapter.

Under the Employment Act 2002, standard internal systems for dealing **11.79** with dismissal, disciplinary and grievance issues were introduced. These are mandatory across all employers, irrespective of their size. These steps require a minimum 'three-step' procedure, involving a statement (setting out in writing the action or grievance), a meeting between the parties, and a right to appeal. We would regard this sort of process as the very minimum that any employer should follow, and suggest that the fuller process we have set out in Appendix 11.2 is much more likely to be effective in the difficult area of harassment in particular. Consideration is currently being given, in any event, to abolishing the statutory procedures.[74]

11.80 Employers may also find it helpful to ensure that the language used throughout such an investigative process is positive, and focuses on resolving the issue rather than establishing blame. West Midlands Police, for example, carried out a lengthy process of revising their grievance procedure shortly before the statutory dispute resolution procedures came into force. They consulted over eight months with the Police Federation, the Police Superintendents' Association, trade unions, the Black and Asian Police Association and the Rainbow Forum which represents gay and lesbian staff and transsexuals. One of the changes they implemented was to rename the process the 'Resolution Process'.[75]

(j) Separating the Parties during an Investigation

11.81 While the investigation is ongoing employers will understandably be concerned about ongoing difficulties between the complainant and the alleged harasser. Limiting contact between the parties will minimise the danger of any alleged harassment being repeated, and of anyone involved being victimised or retaliated against. Separation of the parties should have the effect of defusing the situation and enabling the investigation to be carried out in a less pressurised environment.

11.82 Often the most appropriate course is to move the alleged harasser. However, this should not be to a post which is likely to be viewed as an internal promotion, as this could have the effect of appearing to condone the alleged harassment.

11.83 Moreover, if the harassment alleged is serious, it may be more appropriate to suspend the alleged harasser rather than to move him or her into a fresh working environment where the harassment could be repeated. Such suspension should generally be on full pay, unless the contract of employment provides for suspension in such circumstances with no or reduced pay. However,

---

[74] *Resolving Disputes in the Workplace—A Consultation* (DTI, March 2007) and the Employment Simplification Bill, which featured in the Government's draft legislative programme in July 2007.
[75] *Managing Conflict at Work* (CIPD, February 2007), p 9.

this should be the exception rather than the norm as suspension with no or reduced pay can itself amount to a disciplinary sanction at a stage when the outcome is still unknown, which would clearly be unfair. For the same reason, employees should not be required to use periods of leave while they are suspended. Generally, periods of suspension, whether paid or otherwise, should be kept as short as possible as lengthy periods of suspension may mean that the employee becomes disengaged from his or her work and skills.

In many cases it may be tempting to move the complainant if he or she is in the more junior position and therefore easier to relocate elsewhere. However, the complainant should really only be transferred from their post, or encouraged to transfer, if they ask for such a move, as otherwise such a move could easily be characterised as victimisation of the complainant for seeking to exercise their rights. It is also not likely to promote an atmosphere in which other employees feel confident that they too could raise complaints should the need arise, without suffering adverse consequences. **11.84**

Another option other than a formal transfer of either party might be to arrange for one or both to work from home, or from another location. **11.85**

If the complainant is absent on sick leave, employers should still consider the need to separate him or her from the alleged harasser—as otherwise, the employee may not feel that there is an 'open door' to returning to a working environment in which he or she feels supported and safe. **11.86**

(k) The Duty to the Alleged Harasser

Employers do need to bear in mind their duty to the alleged perpetrator in harassment cases and the imperative to avoid what might be seen as a 'witch-hunt'. To take such a course is perhaps all the more tempting given that a 'zero tolerance' approach to harassment should be adopted—but that does not mean 'zero fairness' to the alleged perpetrator. **11.87**

The dangers of getting the balance wrong were well illustrated by *Scott v Commissioners of Inland Revenue*.[76] In this case a female employee, Ms Fitch, complained that she had been sexually harassed by Mr Scott. The Employment Tribunal found that his employers had, without investigation, taken it more seriously than any reasonable person would have done. Mr Scott's denials were ignored and his employers settled the claim brought against it by Ms Fitch for £5,000. The employers also publicised the settlement amongst its staff at a time when Mr Scott was going through an internal appeal process. From mid-1999 **11.88**

---

[76] [2004] IRLR 713, CA.

onwards he suffered increasing stress and clinical depression. His employers failed to address his concerns and finally retired him on medical grounds despite a letter from his GP indicating that it was what he perceived as unfair treatment of him which was making him unwell. The Employment Tribunal found that Mr Scott had been unfairly and wrongfully dismissed, and discriminated against on grounds of both sex and disability. Moreover, his dismissal amounted to victimisation on the grounds that he had protested about the unfairness of his treatment. The EAT and Court of Appeal upheld the award of £15,000 for injury to feelings and £5,000 aggravated damages, but remitted the additional award of £15,000 for psychiatric damage back to the Tribunal for further consideration as to Mr Scott's prognosis.

(l) Involving Additional Agencies

11.89   In serious cases of harassment, employers may need to consider contacting the police. If the police do become involved they may ask employers to postpone their own investigation pending the completion of their criminal enquiries. However, this should be resisted by the employer wherever possible as it is likely to cause massive delays in resolving the internal process, to the detriment of all concerned. Even if the employer does defer to the police investigation, it is likely that whatever the outcome of that investigation, the employer will still need to conduct an internal investigation for its own employment purposes.

11.90   It is also important to bear in mind that a decision by the police and/or Crown Prosecution Service not to charge or prosecute the alleged harasser is only of limited relevance—such decisions are taken based on the likelihood of proving a case to the criminal standard of beyond reasonable doubt, and can be influenced by a public interest test, neither of which considerations apply in civil employment cases (the test under the equality enactments and the one employers should generally apply is the lower civil standard, of the balance of probabilities; and there is no public interest 'defence' to harassment). Accordingly, the fact that no criminal charges are laid does not mean that employers should not take allegations of harassment arising out of the same facts seriously, or that the harassment did not in fact occur.

11.91   In serious cases of harassment, employers may also need to consider involving health care professionals to assist one of the parties.

(m) Resignation or Withdrawal of One of the Parties

11.92   If either of the parties involved resigns during the process, the employer will need to clarify whether they will continue to cooperate. However, an employer should still seek to complete the investigation, with or without such cooperation, rather than leave the issues permanently unresolved.

If the complainant decides to withdraw his or her complaint during the process, again the employer will need to decide whether or not to continue. The employer should also consider carefully why the complainant may have had a change of heart, and recognise that this does not necessarily mean that the allegations did not have merit. Again it may well be appropriate for the employer to continue the investigation to its conclusion in any event, given the ongoing obligation to eradicate harassment in the workplace. **11.93**

(n) Sanctions and Other Post-investigation Action

If an allegation of harassment is partially or completely upheld, employers will need to ensure that effective action is taken against the harasser, potentially by the use of an appropriate disciplinary sanction. **11.94**

In deciding on the appropriate sanction, employers should, consistent with general employment law principles, consider all the circumstances of the case, but in particular, issues such as: **11.95**

- the severity of the proven harassment;
- the employee's disciplinary and general work record;
- whether the procedure suggests an appropriate penalty for the nature of harassment found;
- the explanation offered by the employee, and any other circumstances he or she relies on; and
- the actions taken in other comparable cases.

Sanctions may include compulsory counselling or training, informal written warnings, transfer, demotion, loss of pay, or in the most serious cases, dismissal. Any employer contemplating dismissal must also ensure that there has been compliance with the three-step statutory procedure relating to dismissal.

In addition to imposing an appropriate sanction, employers will need to consider whether the complainant wishes to continue working with the harasser (assuming the sanction is not dismissal), and if s/he does not, make arrangement so that there will be no further contact between the two if this is possible. Ideally, this should be by transferring the harasser. It should only be achieved by moving the complainant if s/he does not object to such a move and is not disadvantaged by it. If neither party can be moved, efforts will be needed to manage their reintegration back into their old team. **11.96**

Employers will also need to ensure that the harassment has actually stopped, particularly if the parties continue to work together; and take steps to ensure **11.97** the complainant is not victimised for having made the complaint, and check regularly on their welfare in this regard. Employers should also note that even if a complaint is not upheld, others may consider that there was 'no smoke without fire' or that the complainant is a 'troublemaker'. They should take steps to address any such issues as soon as they arise.

11.98 If an allegation of harassment is not upheld or the evidence is inconclusive, the employer may decide to offer voluntary transfers to one or both parties. Mediation (which we consider further below) may also assist if the harasser and victim have to continue working together even though an allegation has been upheld. It may also be of benefit to those who have given evidence on behalf of either party, or other colleagues or team members who have been disrupted by the investigation. Team-building strategies or further training to reaffirm the organisation's commitment to eradicating harassment may also assist in this regard.

11.99 If an allegation of harassment is not only not upheld but found to have been made on malicious grounds (ie that the complainant was deliberately dishonest rather than just emotional and confused), an employer may need to consider invoking the disciplinary process against the employee who made the allegation. This avenue needs to be considered carefully, because, invoked improperly it could be grossly unfair to the complainant (because not every complaint that is not upheld will necessarily have been made maliciously) and could be perceived as, or in fact amount to, victimisation of the complainant for making their complaint. Conversely, in cases where it is plain that the complaint was made maliciously, this sort of action can be an appropriate means of showing how seriously the organisation regards harassment, including making knowingly false allegations of harassment, and can assist in improving the relationship with the falsely accused harasser.

(o) Counselling and Other Support Mechanisms

11.100 Counselling can play an important role in both large and small organisations. Some organisations train internal staff to become counsellors; others contract with a specialist counselling provider. Counselling can provide a confidential avenue for complaints of harassment to be raised in the first place; can support the alleged victims and the alleged harassers through the process; and can also perform a valuable function once the investigation is over and the parties need to reintegrate into the workplace.

11.101 It can also be helpful to set up other support mechanisms for those involved in a harassment process, such as by facilitating them in having access to a mentor/ buddy, welfare officer or occupational health worker. Those investigating allegations of harassment may need additional support from the human resources department or other managers.

(p) Mediation

Mediation is, essentially, a voluntary process that supports existing procedures. **11.102** It is an informal approach by a third party to try and resolve a dispute. The neutral third party works with the individuals involved to help them understand each other's point of view and reach an agreed solution to their problems. If a solution cannot be achieved, the third party may make recommendations for consideration by the individuals involved. Providing a forum for mediation can lead to early resolution of harassment complaints, but can be valuable at any stage in the process, including in rehabilitating the parties back into the workforce.

West Midlands Police, for example, found that in the first two years their **11.103** mediation scheme was operative, they had more than 40 referrals to the scheme, well over half of which resulted in a successful outcome, and that the scheme resulted in at least three employment tribunal claims being withdrawn. The organisation has 17 accredited volunteer mediators selected from a range of levels within the organisation. Each potential mediator's manager had to confirm that s/he had the necessary skills and attributes to act as mediator, and that they could be released at short notice to carry out their mediation duties. All were interviewed by Human Resources and the successful applicants trained over five days in the necessary mediation skills.[77]

However, the use of mediation nationally remains fairly low—with only one in **11.104** four organisations using internal mediations, and around a fifth using external mediation services (such as ACAS). Public sector and larger employers are much more likely to use mediation services.[78]

(q) Monitoring

Whatever the outcome of a harassment investigation, employers may also find **11.105** it helpful to obtain feedback from those involved as to their experiences of the process, with a view to informing the process in future, and amending it if need be.

Employers should also, as a rolling process, monitor the effectiveness of their **11.106** anti-harassment strategy. Evaluating the effectiveness of the policy, and changing it if necessary, means that employers have the opportunity to learn from

---

[77] *Managing Conflict at Work* (CIPD, February 2007), p 18.
[78] *Managing Conflict at Work* (CIPD, February 2007), p 17.

mistakes, respond to change, and keep the policy as a relevant part of the organisation's culture. It also means that tackling harassment at work remains a dynamic, evolving process, rather than a static, entrenched one.

11.107 In practical terms, evaluation of an anti-harassment policy can involve:

- keeping and reviewing statistics on the number of complaints of harassment made; the nature of those complaints;
- analysing from the data which if any of the prohibited grounds are engaged by the complaints; whether the procedures set down in the policy were followed with regard to investigating the complaints; and the outcome of those complaints; and
- evaluating relevant comments made through informal employee feedback and in employee attitude surveys, training feedback, appraisal discussions, return-to-work interviews and exit interviews.

11.108 We deal with monitoring generally in more detail in Chapter 4.

11.109 Research shows that evaluation does have practical benefits: following evaluation, 37 per cent of employers change how they communicate their policy; 32 per cent improve their training; 30 per cent change the policy itself; and 20 per cent introduce training.[79]

Harassment: In Brief

- Harassment in the workplace takes many forms and is widespread: recent DTI figures reported that around 1 million or 3.6 per cent of employees had personally experienced bullying or harassment at work in the last two years; and that around one in ten, or 10.6 per cent of employees, were aware of others in their workplace being bullied or harassed.

- If unchecked, harassment can have serious consequences for the health and well-being of the victim. It can also have damaging consequences for employers: one estimate is that bullying costs employers 80 million lost working days and up to £2 billion in lost revenue each year. It also accounts for up to 50 per cent of stress-related workplace illnesses.

---

[79] *Managing Conflict at Work* (CIPD, October 2004), p 17.

- Harassment on grounds of sex, gender reassignment, race or ethnic origins, disability, religion or belief, or age is now specifically prohibited by the equality enactments. Harassment is broadly defined as unwanted conduct which has the purpose or effect of violating the victim's dignity or creating an intimidating, hostile, degrading, humiliating or offensive environment for him or her.

- The Protection from Harassment Act 1997 and other provisions in the civil and criminal law also prohibit harassment.

- Employers will be liable for all harassment carried out by their employees in the course of their employment unless they successfully deploy the specific defence under the equality enactments, that they took such steps as were 'reasonably practicable' to prevent the harassment taking place.

- An employer can best combat harassment in the workplace by:
  - Developing a thorough anti-harassment policy;
  - Implementing an effective, appropriate training programme;
  - By example from managers and supervisors creating a culture where harassment is not tolerated;
  - Being live to the indirect ways in which harassment can be identified, including setting up measures to facilitate employees in making complaints, such as helplines and buddy/mentoring schemes;
  - Establishing a clear, staged process for investigating an allegation of discrimination, which is carried out confidentially, compassionately and without delay, and which is fair to both the alleged victim and the alleged harasser;
  - Having a clear approach to sanctions and other appropriate action once an investigation is concluded;
  - Ensuring access to counselling and other support mechanisms for those involved in a harassment investigation;
  - Facilitating the use of mediation where appropriate; and
  - Having clear systems for monitoring the effectiveness of its anti-harassment strategy.

APPENDIX 11.1

What Can Happen When Harassment Occurs: Case Study

Helen Green worked as a company secretary assistant. She was subjected to two separate campaigns of bullying and harassment by, respectively, a group of four women who worked in her department and her male assistant. She complained about both issues to her manager and the Human Resources Department but no effective action was taken. She went on holiday and on her return felt unable to walk through the company's front door. She was admitted to hospital suffering from a major depressive disorder. She returned to work for a short period of time but then had a relapse and never returned. She was dismissed from her employment two years later when her psychiatrist confirmed that she would never be able to return to a role within the company.

Ms Green brought proceedings claiming damages for personal injury in negligence and under the Protection from Harassment Act 1997. She alleged that her employer was vicariously liable for the actions of those who had harassed her, and that her employer was also negligent in failing to take any or any adequate steps to protect her from the harassment.

The High Court upheld Ms Green's claim and awarded her damages of just over £800,000.[80] In his judgment Mr Justice Owen observed that:

- A reasonable employer would have intervened as soon as he became aware of the problem;

- Ms Green's managers 'simply failed to take any or any adequate steps to address it' and 'collectively closed their eyes to what was going on, no doubt in the hope that the problem would go away';

- Had her managers intervened as they ought to have done, there were obvious steps that could have been taken to stop the bullying. It ought to have been made clear that such behaviour was unacceptable. The perpetrators should have been warned that if they persisted in the bullying disciplinary action would follow. If necessary, the perpetrators could have been moved to a different location or to a different department. By whatever means, the bullying 'could and should have been stopped'; and

- The harassment, when 'pursued relentlessly on a daily basis', had given rise to a foreseeable risk of psychiatric injury, especially where, as in Ms Green's case, the employer was aware of the employee's greater vulnerability to psychiatric injury.

Although Ms Green did not allege harassment under any of the equality enactments, there is no reason to believe that her case would have been decided any differently, nor the level of compensation awarded to her been any lower, had she done so.

---

[80] *Green v DB Group Services (UK) Ltd* [2006] IRLR 764, HC.

APPENDIX 11.2

Key Features of a Fair Investigation into a Harassment Allegation

The following features should ensure that an investigation into a harassment allegation is conducted fairly:

Submission of the complaint and immediate steps by the employer

- The complainant submits a formal written grievance or other document setting out their complaints of harassment in detail. Having the grievance in writing is practically beneficial, as it enables all involved to know the exact nature of the allegations. From the employee's perspective, making the grievance written is also a pre-requisite of the statutory grievance procedure.
- The individual accused is fully aware of the allegations made.
- The individual accused and the complainant are aware of whether the investigation is being treated as a disciplinary investigation, and if so, what the alleged disciplinary offence is and the type of disciplinary action that could result, and by whom.
- Clear 'terms of reference' have been set at the outset of the investigation, which state precisely what the complaint is about; the alleged incident(s) and when they are said to have taken place; who is said to have witnessed what; from whom statements will be taken; who is the investigating manager/team; how the process will be managed and in what time frame; and the conduct and venue of the meetings.
- All parties are aware of the process to be followed and how the investigation will be conducted.
- All parties are aware of independent and confidential support systems in place which they can use.

The carrying out of the investigation

- The investigation is carried out by managers or other senior individuals who have been trained in and have a good understanding of discrimination issues, who are not involved in the allegations in any way, and who are likely to be seen by those involved as having sufficient credibility, impartiality and integrity.
- The fact-finding process is resolved quickly, and has clear and achievable stages and timescales, as to which the EOC suggests: (i) within three to five working days, witness statements from those involved and any witnesses are obtained; (ii) within a further three to five working days, separate meetings are held with the complainant, the alleged harasser, and any witnesses, to establish the facts; and (iii) within a short period thereafter, further meetings are held to obtain such additional information as has proved necessary, or to clarify points arising from earlier interviews.[81]

---

[81] *Sexual Harassment: Guidance for Managers and Supervisors* (EOC, April 2006), at p 10.

- The process allows individuals to be accompanied by an employee representative or colleague.

- Meetings with the complainant are rearranged as appropriate to accommodate the complainant's wishes, as required by the statutory grievance procedure at a minimum.

- The person carrying out the investigation keeps written records of all meetings.

The taking of evidence

- All meetings are held in an appropriate venue—if the parties or witnesses prefer this not to be at work, it should nevertheless be appropriate to the serious matter in hand, and enable the person to speak freely about sensitive matters.

- Parties and witnesses are allowed to give their accounts freely; words are not put into their mouths nor are they asked 'leading' questions; they are also given the opportunity to check over the investigator's notes of their meetings and/or their witness statements and sign the same as a true record of their evidence.

- Any reluctance of the parties or witnesses to speak is also noted by the investigator, as this can be relevant to the overall assessment of the merits of the complaint. If absolutely necessary, statements are taken from witnesses anonymously, but only as a last resort.

Counter-allegations

- If counter-allegations are made, which are about matters unrelated to the terms of reference, these are addressed via a separate procedure and do not detract from the investigation of the original complaint.

Confidentiality

- Steps are taken to preserve confidentiality in that all those involved have impressed upon them the need for absolute confidentiality; witnesses are only given such information as is necessary to enable them to give their accounts; paperwork is kept securely; rumours and speculation among other colleagues are dealt with firmly; appropriate and fair information is given to those who may be affected by the absence of one of their colleagues (through suspension or a transfer, pending the conclusion of the investigation); and all concerned have made clear to them that a breach of confidentiality could result in disciplinary action.

The conclusion of the process

- At the end of the process, the investigator evaluates the information obtained, and completes a written report, outlining the allegations, the evidence, and the facts found (to the balance of probabilities standard, not that of beyond reasonable doubt), in a style consistent with earlier reports.[82]

- The report gives clear conclusions as to whether it accepts or rejects some or all of the allegations, or whether it is unable to come to any conclusions.

---

[82] For further guidance on the steps in evaluating the evidence and deciding the outcome, see *Sexual Harassment: Managers' Questions Answered* (EOC, March 2006), pp 16–19.

- The findings of the report are then communicated separately to the parties involved, in writing, and at a meeting if necessary.
- The entire process is completed promptly—the EOC suggests an overall timescale for the entire process of 20 days;[83] and

Appeals

- Provision is made for an appeals process, and any such appeal is heard by an independent, and if possible, more senior manager. If no such person is available within the organisation, an external person may be nominated to hear the appeal.

---

[83] *Sexual Harassment: Managers' Questions Answered* (EOC, March 2006), p 10.

12

HANDLING REQUESTS FOR INFORMATION AND GRIEVANCES

To have a grievance is to have a purpose in life.

(Alan Coren, *The Sanity Inspector*)

A. Introduction

The 'Handling Customer Complaints' section of a particular international **12.01** restaurant chain's employee manual suggests that only one in ten diners complain if they are dissatisfied with their meal or the service they have received: the other nine pay their bill and never return. A complaint is therefore seen by that company as an opportunity to rescue a failing relationship. Translating that principle to the employment context, an employee grievance represents an opportunity to resolve an issue that might otherwise result in morale and staff retention problems or, in extreme cases, stress and sickness and ultimately litigation.

Of course, not every grievance has merit. Many employers have experience of **12.02** the employee whose grievance has become a 'purpose in life'—for whom no amount of management time can produce a satisfactory result. Labyrinthine grievance procedures, with multiple levels of appeal and stages dealt with by panels rather than individual managers, might appear to be appropriate safeguards for employers on paper but in practice, can hamper a swift resolution of an issue, particularly in the hands of a recalcitrant employee.

The objective of any grievance procedure is to encourage employees to raise **12.03** grievances if they are dissatisfied and to provide an effective system for dealing with those grievances. That system will need to incorporate safeguards such as allowing the employee to be accompanied to certain hearings by a colleague or trade union representative[1] and an appeal against any determination. Outside of these safeguards, successful resolution of grievances is probably more likely the simpler the grievance procedure.

12.04 A hearing that requires a panel will typically be more difficult to arrange quickly than one that requires a single manager. An employee with an outstanding grievance in relation to which an ET deadline is about to expire may be forced to submit a claim to protect his or her position whilst the grievance slowly proceeds through the internal procedure.

12.05 Many disputes in the workplace should be capable of being managed and resolved without the need to resort to litigation. Central to such management and resolution is often an employee's request for information. The law provides an ever increasing number of ways for an employee to access information from an employer that might be relevant to the grievance. Employers are often unaware that such requests are legal rights and that there are sanctions for non-compliance.

12.06 We therefore begin this chapter by looking at the ways in which an employee can access information, before moving on to look at handling the grievances themselves. We also examine the statutory grievance procedure, which can be initiated at any stage of the employment relationship including after the employment has terminated, and may therefore precede or follow a request for information.

B. Employee Requests for Information

(a) General Approach

12.07 Employers often respond in different ways to employee requests for information: some employers ignore such requests and others endeavour to provide only a bare minimum response. However, in the context of avoiding litigation, a request for information may represent an opportunity to provide information that will resolve a dispute. Best practice would therefore be to focus on responding positively to a request for information in an effort to achieve the early resolution of a dispute.

12.08 This section outlines the key ways in which an employee can obtain information from an employer, together with the legal consequences of non-compliance.

---

[1] Employment Relations Act 1999, s 10 and s 13(5).

(b) Discrimination Questionnaires

A questionnaire procedure exists under all strands of discrimination law includ-   **12.09**
ing a separate procedure for equal pay cases. The general purpose of the questionnaire procedure is to enable a person who considers that s/he may have
been discriminated against or subjected to harassment (generally referred to as
'the person aggrieved'[2] or 'the complainant'[3]) to question the actions of the
employer. The answers given by the employer will then assist the employee and
his or her advisers in taking an informed view of whether there is an appropriate explanation for the employer's act or omission or whether there is an issue
to take forward.

Questionnaires are admissible as evidence in Tribunal proceedings. This is a   **12.10**
disadvantage to the employer that provides an evasive or equivocal response.
Equally, it is an advantage to the employer that provides an appropriate and
comprehensive response but is nevertheless sued by the employee.

Questionnaires do exert a significant amount of pressure on employers to   **12.11**
respond fully and within the requisite time frame. Responding to questionnaires is often time consuming: paperwork needs to be collated and reviewed,
management input will be required and work will be needed to produce
appropriate responses. It helps, however, to look at this work as front-loading
the work that would otherwise be done in preparing a Tribunal defence with
the added advantage that such proceedings could be avoided if the response
provides a full and appropriate explanation. Even where the employee is not
satisfied with the response and still brings a Tribunal claim, the answers given
to a questionnaire will often help focus the dispute on the key issues of
disagreement.

The questionnaire procedure is reasonably consistent across the different   **12.12**
strands of discrimination law. The form of the questionnaire under each strand
is prescribed in orders or regulations.[4] However, it is important to note that an
employee or claimant is not restricted to using the prescribed form of questionnaire. Employers are required to respond to questions whether or not they are
made in accordance with the corresponding order or regulation: in *Dattani v
Chief Constable of West Mercia Police*,[5] it was held that the relevant provision

---

[2] SDA, s 74; RRA, s 65; DDA, s 56; RBR, reg 33; SOR, reg 33; AR, reg 41.
[3] EqPA, s 7B.
[4] Sex Discrimination (Questions and Replies) Order 1975/2048, Schedules 1 and 2; Race
Relations (Questions and Replies) Order 1977/842, Schedules 1 and 2; Disability Discrimination
(Questions and Replies) Order 2004/1168, Schedules 1 and 2; RBR, Schedules 2 and 3; SOR,
Schedules 2 and 3; AR, Schedules 3 and 4; Equal Pay (Questions and Replies) Order 2003/722,
Schedules 1 and 2.
[5] [2005] IRLR 327.

under the RRA which provides for the Tribunal to draw an inference of discrimination from a failure to reply or an evasive or equivocal reply to questions from a person aggrieved (section 65(1)), covers replies given to questions whether or not they are presented in the form prescribed for statutory discrimination questionnaires. The logic for this was that a respondent asked a direct question in writing by an aggrieved person who failed to respond, or does so evasively, ought to be treated in the same way irrespective of whether the question has been asked under the statutory procedure.

12.13 Questions are only admissible in evidence if they are submitted within the statutory time frame. That time frame depends on whether or not a complaint has been presented to the Tribunal. Where Tribunal procedures have not yet commenced, a questionnaire will be admissible if it is served on an employer within three months of the date of the act complained of, or within six months where the time limit for presentation of claims has been extended to six months because of a statutory grievance procedure or statutory disciplinary and dismissal procedure.[6]

12.14 Where a complaint has been presented to a Tribunal, the questionnaire will be admissible if it is served on the employer within 21 days (or 28 days under the DDA[7]) beginning with the day on which the complaint was presented, or within a later period specified by a direction of the Tribunal.[8]

12.15 Equal pay questionnaires are admissible if served on the employer at any time before a complaint is presented to a Tribunal. Where a complaint has been presented to a Tribunal a questionnaire is admissible if served on the employer either within 21 days after presentation of the complaint or any longer period specified by the Tribunal.[9]

12.16 Under most strands of discrimination legislation, if a respondent deliberately or without reasonable excuse omits to reply within eight weeks, or if the reply is evasive or equivocal, the Tribunal may draw any inference that it considers just and equitable to draw, including an inference that the employer did discriminate.[10]

---

[6] Sex Discrimination (Questions and Replies) Order 1975/2048, art 5; Race Relations (Questions and Replies) Order 1977/842, art 5; Disability Discrimination (Questions and Replies) Order 2004/1168, art 4; RBR, reg 33(4); SOR, reg 33(4); NB AR, reg 41(4) does not deal with the statutory dismissal and grievance procedures.

[7] Disability Discrimination (Questions and Replies) Order 2004/1168, art 4(b).

[8] Sex Discrimination (Question and Replies) Order 1975/2048, art 5(b); Race Relations (Questions and Replies) Order 1977/842, art 5(b); RBR, reg 33(4)(b); SOR, reg 33(4)(b); AR, reg 41(4)(b).

[9] Equal Pay (Questions and Replies) Order 2003/722, arts 2 and 3.

[10] SDA, s 74(2A); DDA, s 56(3)(b); RBR, reg 33(2)(b); SOR, reg 33(2)(b); AR, reg 41(2)(b).

However, where the discrimination alleged is on the grounds of colour or **12.17** nationality (due to anomalies arising between domestic and European legislation) the employer must reply within a 'reasonable time', rather than the usual eight weeks (which applies if the questionnaire relates to discrimination on the grounds of race, ethnic or national origins, or harassment).[11]

Since discrimination on the grounds of colour, nationality, and race, ethnic or **12.18** national origins often overlap, and because the questions may not specify which grounds are being invoked, best practice would be to respond to a questionnaire within the standard eight-week timeframe, to avoid any adverse inference being drawn by the Tribunal.

(c) Data Subject Access Requests

(i) The Employee's Rights under the DPA

Over recent years, a subject access request has become one of the most popular **12.19** ways of obtaining information from an employer, particularly when disputes arise. Many employers try to minimise the information they produce in response to a subject access request, automatically adopting a 'defensive' stance to the request. However, employers are equally able to use the request as an opportunity to attempt to resolve the dispute at an early stage.

In essence, an individual is entitled to make a subject access request to find out **12.20** what information a data controller holds about them. This right originates from the Data Protection Directive[12] which was implemented in the UK by the DPA.

A detailed discussion of the DPA falls outside the scope of this book although **12.21** further information is included in Chapter 4. For present purposes, it is important to note that the DPA covers documents held on computer and potentially covers personnel files and other manual records. Employers must ensure that the personal data they keep on job applicants, employees and former employees, complies with the data protection principles, and must provide such individuals with access to their personal data following a subject access request.

In order to be covered by the DPA, data must be 'personal'. *Durant v Financial* **12.22** *Services Authority*[13] concluded that this means that such data is either 'biographical in a significant sense' or has the individual as its focus. Anonymous data is not covered unless the employer has (or is likely to have) other information to identify the individual. Personal data includes facts, opinions and intentions (eg 'poor performer', 'promotion unlikely', or 'useless').

---

[11] RRA, s 65(2)(b).   [12] 19/46 EC.
[13] [2003] EWCA Civ 1746, (2004), The Times, 2 January, CA.

12.23 Data processed automatically (eg by computer) or held manually in a 'relevant filing system' is covered. The *Durant* case also clarified what amounts to a 'relevant filing system': it concluded that a relevant filing system is a manual filing system of sufficient sophistication to provide the same or similar ready accessibility as a computerised filing system.

12.24 According to the Information Commissioner:

> . . . a filing system containing files about individuals, or topics about individuals, where the content of each file is structured purely in chronological order will not be a relevant filing system as the files are not appropriately structured/indexed/ divided or referenced to allow the retrieval of personal data without leafing through the file. Personnel files and other manual files using individuals' names or unique identifiers as the file names, which are sub-divided/indexed to allow retrieval of personal data without a manual search (such as, sickness, absence, contact details etc), are likely to be held in a 'relevant filing system' for the purposes of the DPA. However, following the *Durant* judgment it is likely that very few manual files will be covered by the provisions of the DPA.[14]

12.25 Notwithstanding both the Court of Appeal's and the Information Commissioner's extremely narrow interpretation of 'relevant filing system', any refusal by an employer to allow an employee access to his or her personnel records is likely to create an immediate suspicion that the employer has something to hide. We suggest that best practice would be for the employer to comply with a request even where the DPA does not strictly apply, unless the request was clearly frivolous or vexatious.

12.26 A data subject (an employee for these purposes) who makes a subject access request is entitled:

- to be informed by a data controller (an employer for these purposes) whether personal data of which that employee is the data subject are being processed by or on behalf of that employer; and
- if that is the case, to be given a description of: (i) the personal data of which that employee is the data subject; (ii) the purposes for which the data are being or are to be processed; and (iii) the recipient, or classes of recipients, to whom they are or may be disclosed.[15]

12.27 The employee is also entitled to have communicated to him in an intelligible form the personal data of which the individual is the data subject and any information available to the employer as to the source of those data. Where the processing by automatic means was for the purposes of evaluating matters such

---

[14] *The Durant Case and its Impact on the Interpretation of the Data Protection Act 1998*, <www.ico.gov.uk>.

[15] DPA, s 7(1).

as performance at work, credit worthiness, reliability or conduct, and has constituted or is likely to constitute the sole basis for any decision significantly affecting him or her, the employee is also entitled to be informed by the employer of the logic involved in that decision-taking.[16]

(ii) How to Respond to a Subject Access Request

An employer is not obliged to supply any information in response to a request **12.28** unless it has received a request in writing. An employer is also entitled to request a fee of up to £10. If an employer reasonably requests further information in order to satisfy itself as to the identity of the individual making the request and to locate the information sought, the employer does not have to comply with the request unless he is provided with that further information.[17] There is unlikely to be an issue about identity where the employee remains employed by the employer, but it is good practice to check that the request is from the employee.

An employer must comply with a subject access request promptly and in any **12.29** event within 40 calendar days of the receipt of the request or, if later, within 40 calendar days of receipt of both the £10 fee and the information required to confirm the identity of the individual and the location of the information sought.[18]

If an employer has previously complied with a subject access request, it is not **12.30** obliged to comply with a subsequent identical or similar request by the same individual unless a reasonable interval has elapsed between compliance with the previous request and the current one.[19] To determine whether there has been a reasonable interval, regard will be had to the nature of the data, the purpose for which the data are processed and the frequency with which the data are altered.

When responding to a subject access request, an employer should supply to the **12.31** employee a copy of the information constituting the personal data to the employee in permanent form, unless the supply of a copy is not possible or would involve disproportionate effort.[20] If any of the information is expressed in terms which are not intelligible without explanation, the copy must be accompanied by an explanation of those terms.

The information should be supplied by reference to the data in existence at the **12.32** time when the request is received, except that account may be taken of any amendments or deletion made between that time and the time when the

---

[16] DPA, s 7(1)(d). [17] DPA, s 7(3). [18] DPA, s 7(8), s 7(10).
[19] DPA, s 8(3). [20] DPA, s 8(2).

information is supplied, irrespective of the request (ie the amendment or deletion would have happened in any event).[21] This, in effect, prevents the employer destroying the information to avoid having to disclose it.

(iii) Third Parties

12.33 An employer must take care if responding to a subject access request would result in the disclosure of information relating to another individual (a third party). Where an employer cannot comply with a request without disclosing information relating to a third party who can be identified from that information, it does not have to comply with the request unless that third party has consented to the disclosure of the information to the employee, or it is reasonable in all the circumstances to comply with the request without the consent of the other individual.[22] The main guiding principle is for the employer in these circumstances to try and disclose as much of the information as can be disclosed without disclosing the identity of the third party.[23] This may be achieved, for example, by redacting or deleting the relevant names or other identifying particulars.

12.34 To establish whether it is reasonable in all the circumstances to disclose information without consent of the third party, regard should be had to:

- any duty of confidentiality owed to the third party;
- any steps taken with a view to seek the consent of the third party;
- whether the third party is capable of giving consent; and
- any express refusal of consent by the third party.[24]

12.35 If an employer considers that it cannot comply with a subject access request without disclosing information relating to a third party, the 40 day calendar period in which the employer must supply the data can be extended.[25] However, data which do not identify the third party should be supplied, as outlined above, within 40 days.

(iv) Exemptions

12.36 Some categories of data are exempt from the obligation to comply with a subject access request including:

- confidential references given by the employer for employment, educational or training purposes. However, a subject access request must be complied with in relation to a reference received by the employer;
- personal data processed for the purposes of management forecasting or man-

---

[21] DPA, s 8(6). [22] DPA, s 7(4). [23] DPA, s 7(5). [24] DPA, s 7(6).
[25] DPA, s 7(4) and 7(8).

agement planning, to the extent that complying with a subject access request would be likely to prejudice the conduct of the business;

- personal data consisting of records of the intention of the employer in relation to any negotiations with the data subject to the extent that complying with a subject access request would be likely to prejudice those negotiations; and
- personal data subject to legal privilege.[26]

(v) Failure to Comply

If an employer breaches the subject access request rules, an individual may make a statutory request to the Information Commissioner to determine whether or not it is likely that the request has been carried out lawfully. An individual may also apply to court and seek an order for compliance.[27] The court has power to inspect relevant information but, unless it finds in the individual's favour, it cannot require the information to be disclosed to the individual.[28] **12.37**

A claim for damages can also be brought against the employer. An employee can also claim for distress.[29] It is, however, a defence for an employer to prove that he had taken such care as in all the circumstances was reasonably required to comply with the subject access rules. **12.38**

If the data are inaccurate, the court may order a data controller to rectify, block, erase or destroy those data and any other personal data in respect of which he is the data controller and which contain an expression of opinion that appears to the court to be based on the inaccurate data.[30] **12.39**

(vi) Best Practice

As outlined above, although subject access requests may often seem onerous to employers (particularly, where large amounts of data are held by the employer), it is best practice to ensure such requests are addressed promptly. Whilst penalties may apply where there is a failure to comply with the request, any such failure may have wider ramifications, especially where Tribunal litigation ensues. **12.40**

(d) Freedom of Information Act 2000

The Freedom of Information Act 2000 ('FOIA') is a wide-ranging piece of legislation offering any individual the right to access information of any type, whether electronic or in hard copy, held by any UK public authority. Job applicants, employees and former employees of public authorities, can use **12.41**

---

[26] DPA, sch 7.   [27] DPA, s 7(9).   [28] DPA, s 15(2).   [29] DPA, s 13.
[30] DPA, s 13.

FOIA as a quick and simple way of obtaining information that might assist their grievance.

12.42 FOIA applies to 'public authorities' which are defined in a series of generic categories. These cover:

- Government departments;
- Parliament and the devolved Assemblies in Wales and Northern Ireland;
- the armed forces;
- local Government;
- the NHS;
- schools and universities; and
- the police.

12.43 The rules also apply to 'publicly-owned' companies, that is, companies wholly owned by the Crown or by another public authority.

12.44 The list of potential requests for information under FOIA is as wide as the operational remit of every Government Department, local authority and quango in the country. However, whilst the right of access under FOIA is wide, it is not unlimited and requests are subject to a number of potential exemptions (as outlined further below). If an exemption applies, the public authority may be able to refuse the request.

12.45 On receipt of a request an authority must confirm or deny whether it holds the information requested and, if it does hold the information, communicate it to the applicant. Both the duty to confirm or deny and the duty to communicate must be fulfilled within 20 working days. FOIA also imposes a duty on public authorities to advise and assist applicants. All public authorities must also maintain a Publication Scheme setting out the categories or classes of information routinely made available to the general public.

12.46 There are very few requirements under FOIA about the way requests have to be made. They must be:

- in writing (emails are acceptable);
- state the applicant's name and correspondence address; and
- describe the information requested.

12.47 Requests must also be legible and capable of use for subsequent reference. Public authorities may, where reasonable, ask for clarification to help identify or locate information. Regulations govern fees which authorities may charge for requests, but only for the cost of things such as photocopying and postage. Authorities are not entitled to charge simply for processing the request itself.

There are two types of exemption under FOIA: absolute exemptions and qualified exemptions. The absolute exemptions apply to all information which falls within any of the categories listed. The categories cover things such as security and the confidential information of third parties. It also covers information accessible to the applicant by other means, Parliamentary privilege, personal information where the applicant is the subject of the information and information provided in confidence. **12.48**

The qualified exemptions only apply where information falls within the scope of one of the categories and where the public interest allows. Examples of qualified exemptions include information intended for future publication, commercial and sensitive information and defence. **12.49**

When applying the public interest test, authorities must weigh the public interest in disclosing information with the public interest in withholding it. If, and only if, the public interest in withholding outweighs the public interest in disclosing, then the authority can rely on the exemptions. Some of the qualified exemptions are subject to an additional prejudice test. This means that, in certain circumstances, public authorities have to ask whether disclosure of the information and/or the duties to confirm or deny would cause prejudice to the particular interest which is the subject of the exemption. **12.50**

If a public authority refuses a request because an exemption applies, it must tell the applicant which exemption it is relying on and why. It must also notify the applicant of its procedures for dealing with the complaints about the way requests are handled and the applicant's right to apply to the Information Commissioner for an assessment of whether the request was dealt with correctly. **12.51**

The Information Commissioner has been given a wide range of powers to police the FOIA, which can be enforced through the courts if necessary. The FOIA also creates two criminal offences. These relate to the deliberate destruction or concealment of records with the intention of preventing disclosure and the intentional obstruction of a person in the execution of a warrant issued under the FOIA. **12.52**

Where an information request is made by an individual for personal information about himself, the public authority will be exempt from having to comply with the request under section 40(1) of the FOIA. The effect of this exemption is to disapply the FOIA and by implication give precedence to the subject access request provisions of the DPA. For our purposes this would apply to employees of public authorities requesting information about themselves from their employers. **12.53**

12.54 That does not mean, however, that the FOIA is irrelevant in the employment context. It could be used, for example, to obtain the type of statistical or background information one typically sees in discrimination questionnaires either from the public authority employer or from any public authority if the information might be of assistance in an employment dispute. The advantages to an employee of a FOIA request over a discrimination questionnaire are a faster turn around time (twenty working days under the FOIA to eight weeks for a questionnaire response) and the backing of the enforcement regime of the Information Commissioner if a response is not forthcoming.

(e) Part-time Working

12.55 Part-time Workers (Prevention of Less Favourable Treatment) Regulations 2000[31] came into force on 1 July 2000, implementing the EC Council Directive 97/81 EC. In essence, the Regulations are designed to ensure that part-time workers are not treated less favourably than comparable full-time workers.

12.56 The Regulations apply to all workers, not just employees and the Regulations apply to men as well as women. Most importantly, for present purposes, under the Regulations, part-time workers are entitled in certain cases to a written explanation for the treatment they have received.

12.57 A worker who considers that his or her employer may have treated him or her less favourably on the grounds of his or her part-time status has the right to request a written statement giving particulars of the reasons for the treatment. He or she is entitled to receive a statement from his or her employer within 21 days of the request under regulation 6(1).

12.58 A written statement is admissible in evidence in any subsequent proceedings under the Regulations. If the employer deliberately and without reasonable excuse omits to provide a written statement, or the written statement is evasive or equivocal, it is open to the Tribunal under regulation 6(3) to infer that the worker has been discriminated against on the ground of part-time status.

12.59 It should be noted that the right to receive a written statement under the Regulations does not apply when the employee is complaining of dismissal and is entitled to a written statement of the reasons for his or her dismissal under the Employment Rights Act 1996.

---

[31] SI 2000/1551.

(f) National Minimum Wage

Whilst the National Minimum Wage Act 1998 (the 'NMWA') is not directly relevant to equality, it provides protection to those in low paid employment, many of whom are economic migrants. The NMWA provides workers with an additional way to gather information from their employers—and, as outlined throughout this section, an additional way for employers to resolve a dispute without proceeding to litigation. **12.60**

The National Minimum Wage (the 'NMW') was introduced by the NMWA, and provides workers with the right to a specified minimum hourly rate of pay (currently £5.35[32]). **12.61**

Employers are required to keep records in relation to their workers' hours and the payments made to them, sufficient to establish that their workers have been paid at least the NMW. The records must be in a form which enables them to be produced in a single document.[33] **12.62**

If a worker has reasonable grounds to believe that he or she is being or has been remunerated for any pay reference period at a rate which is less than the NMW, he or she can give notice (a 'production notice') to the employer to request the production of the relevant records relating to the periods listed in the notice.[34] The employer must give the worker reasonable notice of the time and place at which the records will be produced, which must be: **12.63**

- the worker's place of work;
- any other place at which it is reasonable, in all the circumstances, for the worker to attend and inspect the relevant records; or
- such other place as may be agreed between the worker and the employer.

An employer must produce the records within 14 days of the notice or at such later time as may be agreed between the worker and employer. The worker is entitled to make a copy of the records. **12.64**

A worker can also complain to the Tribunal if the employer fails to comply with a request for information in respect of a pay period.[35] If the claim is successful, the Tribunal can make a declaration to that effect and order the employer to pay the worker an award of 80 times the relevant NMW. This award is a fixed amount. Where an employee has been consistently under-paid the NMW he might serve a string of production notices going back over the period of his employment, one for each pay reference period. If the **12.65**

---

[32] See <www.dti.gov.uk/employment/pay/national-minimum-wage/index.html>.
[33] National Minimum Wage Regulations 1999 (SI 1999/584), regs 38(1) and (2).
[34] NMWA, s 10.   [35] NMWA, s 11.

employer neglects to respond, the employer could be faced with a string of awards.

(g) Written Reasons for Dismissal

12.66 The final example of legislation that provides opportunities to employees to obtain pre-action disclosure of information is a request for written reasons for dismissal. Where the employee had more than one year's service at the effective date of termination, s/he can request written reasons for dismissal and the employer must respond within 14 days.[36] An unreasonable failure to respond will risk a Tribunal award of two weeks' pay if the employee subsequently brings an unfair dismissal claim.[37]

12.67 An employee is entitled to written reasons for dismissal without having to make a request and irrespective of length of service when dismissed:

- while pregnant;[38]
- after childbirth but during OML or AML;[39] or
- during OAL or AAL.[40]

C. Grievance Procedures

12.68 Most employers have grievance procedures and most grievance procedures are based upon or at least reflect the guidance in the ACAS Code of Practice,[41] most recently updated in 2004 to take account of the statutory dismissal and grievance procedures. It is, at the very least, a requirement[42] that the employer includes in a statement of particulars of employment, given to an employee within two months of the employee starting work, details of:

- a person to whom the employee can apply for the purpose of seeking redress of any grievance relating to his or her employment;
- the manner in which any such application should be made; and
- any further steps relating to such application or a cross-referral to another document containing that information.

12.69 The purpose of a grievance procedure is to resolve a dispute internally without the need to take a dispute to litigation. Some employers tend to see grievance procedures as applying only to employees who have 'complaints' or 'demands' when a more positive frame of mind might see 'concerns' or 'issues' in need of

---

[36] ERA, s 92.   [37] ERA, s 93.   [38] ERA, s 92(4)(a).   [39] ERA, s 92(4)(b).
[40] ERA, s 92(4A).
[41] ACAS Code of Practice 1: Disciplinary & Grievance Procedures (2004).
[42] ERA, s 3(1)(b)(ii) and (c).

resolution. Either way, the employer should at least adhere to both the statutory grievance procedure and its own procedures when attempting to resolve the grievance.

(a) Statutory Grievance Procedure

The Employment Act 2002 (Dispute Resolution) Regulations 2004[43] came into force on 10 October 2004 and determine when the statutory procedures introduced by the Employment Act 2002 apply. Whilst the original aim of the Regulations was to promote dispute resolution in the workplace so that fewer cases ended up in Tribunal, the Regulations have instead created a whole new body of procedure-related case law and mostly confused rather than simplified grievance processes. Following a review of the procedures[44] it seems likely that they will be repealed if not in their entirety, at least in part.

12.70

At the time of writing, however, the Regulations remain in their current form, imposing mandatory disciplinary and grievance procedures on all employers and employees. Schedule 2, Part 2 of the Employment Act 2002 sets out the two statutory minimum grievance procedures: the 'standard procedure' and the 'modified procedure.' Broadly, the standard procedure is to be used for most grievances including complaints of discrimination, whereas the modified procedure is to be used after employment has ended and then only by agreement.

12.71

The standard procedure is a three-step process of written grievance, face-to-face meeting and face-to-face appeal:[45]

12.72

- *Step 1*: the employee must set out the grievance in writing and send the statement or a copy of it to the employer;

- *Step 2*: the employer must invite the employee to a meeting to discuss the grievance. That meeting must not take place unless the employee has informed the employer of the basis for the grievance and the employer has had an opportunity to consider its response. The employee must take all reasonable steps to attend the meeting. After the meeting, the employer must inform the employee of its decision and notify the employee of the right to appeal;

---

[43] SI 2004/752.

[44] The DTI published an independent review of employment dispute resolution in March 2007 calling for the complete repeal of the statutory dispute resolution procedures. The review, led by Michael Gibbons, made a number of recommendations, in response to which a consultation paper was issued by the DTI, *Resolving Disputes in the Workplace—A Consultation* (DTI, March 2007).

[45] Employment Act 2002, Schedule 2, Part 2, Chapter 1.

- *Step 3*: if the employee is dissatisfied with the decision and wishes to appeal, the employee must inform the employer. The employer must then invite the employee to attend a further meeting which the employee must take all reasonable steps to attend. After the appeal meeting the employer must inform the employee of its final decision.

12.73 The modified grievance procedure applies only after termination of employment. The employer should not have been aware of the grievance before the employment ceased, or, if it was aware, the statutory grievance procedure should not have been commenced or completed before the last day of employment. Both parties must also have agreed in writing to apply the modified procedure.[46]

12.74 The modified procedure has two steps:

- *Step 1*: the employee gives to the employer written notice of the grievance and the basis for it; and
- *Step 2*: the employer sets out the response in writing and sends a copy to the employee.[47]

12.75 The Employment Act 2002 and the Employment Act (Dispute Resolution) Regulations 2004 modify the time limits for submitting a Tribunal claim. Whilst the provisions are reasonably complex (and outside the scope of this book), the basic principle is that an employee should submit a written grievance within what would otherwise have been the normal time limit for bringing a claim (usually three months), and the time limit for bringing the claim is then extended by a further three months (the aim being to provide the parties with extra time to carry out the grievance procedure).

12.76 Generally, a Tribunal claim will be inadmissible if it arises out of a grievance to which the statutory grievance procedure applies and the employee either has not sent a written statement of grievance (under either statutory procedure) or has sent a written grievance but waited fewer than twenty-eight days before submitting the Tribunal claim.[48]

12.77 The Regulations do not provide an employee or employer with a free-standing statutory right to sue each other for failure to comply with the procedures. However, a dismissal in breach of the procedures by the employer will be automatically unfair, and adjustments can be made by a Tribunal to any compensation awarded to reflect a breach by either the employee or employer.

---

[46] Employment Act (Dispute Resolution) Regulations 2004, reg 6(3).
[47] Employment Act 2002, Sch 2, Ch 2.   [48] Employment Act 2002, s 32(1)–(3).

(b) ACAS Code of Practice

The ACAS Code of Practice 1: Disciplinary and Grievance Procedures (2004) **12.78**
contains good practice guidance on dealing with grievances. The guidance
covers but expands upon the statutory minimum grievance procedures and
makes a number of specific suggestions. Broadly, it suggests that grievance
procedures should be simple and recorded in writing; that grievances should be
dealt with informally by line managers where possible; that grievances should
be dealt with in a timely fashion; that an employee should be offered an appeal
when dissatisfied with a decision and that records should be kept of the nature
of the grievance, the employer's response and any action taken.

Where grievances cover more than one employee the Code suggests that it may **12.79**
be appropriate to seek to resolve the dispute with any recognised trade union. It
also notes that complaints about discrimination, bullying and harassment are
sensitive issues which in larger organisations may merit their own separate
procedures. In particular, any procedure dealing with complaints about discrimination, bullying and harassment will need to anticipate that the alleged
perpetrator might be the employee's line manager who would otherwise be the
person with whom a grievance is raised. We consider the handling of harassment grievances in some detail in Chapter 11 when discussing harassment
generally.

(c) Right to be Accompanied

The employee has a right to be accompanied to a grievance meeting by a **12.80**
colleague or trade union official[49] (even where the employer does not recognise
a trade union). This right applies only to grievances which concern the performance of a duty by an employer in relation to a worker.[50] This prevents the
employee, for example, using the grievance procedure and the right to be
accompanied as part of a demand for a pay increase—since in most cases the
employer will not be under a duty to give the employee a pay rise. In practice most employers allow employees to be accompanied for most types of
grievance.

Text explaining the rules on companions in grievance meetings from section **12.81**
10 of the Employment Relations Act 1999 is included at Appendix 12.1.
This could be inserted into any letter inviting the employee to a grievance
meeting.

---

[49] Employment Relations Act 1999, s 10.   [50] Employment Relations Act 1999, s 13(5).

Handling Grievances: In Brief

• A grievance is an opportunity to resolve an employment dispute that might otherwise result in workplace morale issues or, ultimately, litigation.

• A variety of statutes offer to employees an opportunity to obtain from their employers information that might assist them in pursuit of their grievances.

• Employers are often unaware of these statutory rules and the sanctions that apply if they ignore the requests, delay in responding or respond with equivocal or evasive answers.

• Employees can obtain information, for example: through discrimination questions for each of the strands plus equal pay; data subject access requests; freedom of information requests; requests in respect of part-time working and the national minimum wage and requests for written reasons for dismissal.

• Employees and employers should ensure that they follow the statutory minimum grievance procedures or there are potential consequences in any subsequent litigation.

• Whether the parties are following the statutory minimum procedure or an employer's own procedure based on the ACAS Code of Practice, employees often have a right to be accompanied to grievance meetings and appeals.

APPENDIX 12.1

Summary for Employee of Rules relating to Companions in Grievance Meetings

You may bring a companion with you to the hearing. This is your choice. You do not have to bring a companion. If you would like to bring a companion then the following rules apply.

1. Your companion must be:
   (a) chosen by you; and
   (b) be an employee of the Company or a trade union official.
2. The Company will permit your companion to:
   (a) address the hearing in order to:
      (i) put your case; and
      (ii) sum up that case;
   (b) confer with you during the hearing.
3. Your companion is not permitted to:
   (a) answer questions on your behalf;
   (b) address the hearing if you indicate at the hearing that you do not wish your companion to do so; or
   (c) prevent the Company from explaining its case or prevent any other person at the hearing from making his or her contribution to it.
4. Where necessary, the Company will allow your companion time away from his or her duties in order to accompany you to the hearing.
5. If your companion is not available at the time proposed by the Company for the hearing you should notify the Company as soon as possible. You may propose an alternative time for the hearing provided that your proposal is reasonable and within a period of five working days beginning with the first working day after the day proposed by the Company.

13

ENDING EMPLOYMENT

Don't cry because it's over. Smile because it happened.

(Dr Seuss, American writer and cartoonist)

A. Introduction

There are a range of good reasons why an employer may wish to terminate an **13.01** employee's employment: lack of capability, misconduct, redundancy, because continuing the relationship would breach a statutory requirement, retirement, or some other substantial reason. Yet the ending of the employment relationship can be one of the most stressful and upsetting experiences for employees to face. We cannot promise that, by following the suggestions we make in this chapter, an employee whose contract is terminated will depart on good terms. However, what we can do is guide the employer through the termination process, so as to ensure that it fully takes on board equality and diversity issues, thereby reducing the risk of carrying out a discriminatory dismissal. In particular, we deal at some length in this chapter with the new law relating to retirement and age discrimination. We also discuss the discrimination issues arising from the giving of references and the operation of occupational pension schemes.

B. The Equality Enactments and the Right not to be Unfairly Dismissed

The equality enactments all specifically prohibit dismissals on the protected **13.02** grounds.[1] It is therefore unlawful to dismiss someone on grounds of their sex, pregnancy/maternity leave, married status or gender reassignment, or on

---

[1] SDA, s 6(2)(b); RRA, s 4(2)(c); DDA, s 4(2)(c); SOR reg 6(2)(d); RBR reg 6(2)(d) and AR reg 7(2)(d).

grounds of race, disability, sexual orientation, religion or belief or age (subject to the exception relating to retirement which we consider further below).

13.03 A dismissal can be directly or indirectly discriminatory; can constitute an act of victimisation or harassment; and under the DDA can constitute disability-related discrimination. There is some confusion in the case law as to whether a dismissal can also itself constitute a failure to make a reasonable adjustment under the DDA, or whether it is the failure to take the steps that would prevent the dismissal (such as changing the disabled person's tasks, or transferring them to an existing vacancy): *Clark v TDG Ltd t/a Novacold*[2] suggested that it was possible to characterise a dismissal as a failure to make a reasonable adjustment, but *Archibald v Fife Council*[3] seemed to assume not. In any event, a disability-related dismissal cannot be justified if there has been a failure to comply with a reasonable adjustment duty, unless the dismissal would have been justified had the duty been complied with.[4]

13.04 Section 94 of the ERA contains the right not to be unfairly dismissed. Under section 98 of the ERA, in order to show that a dismissal was fair, an employer must show first that the principal reason for the dismissal falls within the category of reasons listed in the ERA as potentially fair, namely capability or qualifications,[5] conduct,[6] redundancy,[7] a breach of statutory requirements (illegality),[8] retirement[9] or some other substantial reason justifying dismissal.[10] The employer must then show that in all the circumstances it acted reasonably in treating that reason as a sufficient ground for dismissing the employee.[11]

13.05 Although the statutory tests and frameworks are different, a dismissal which is discriminatory under the equality enactments will almost always also be unfair under the ERA, because in those circumstances, it cannot be said that the employer acted reasonably in treating the reason as a sufficient reason for dismissing the employee under the ERA, section 98(4).[12]

13.06 Frequently, an employee who claims that s/he has been subjected to a discriminatory dismissal will bring a claim under the equality enactments in tandem with one of unfair dismissal under the ERA. Although there is an overlap between the two types of claims, there are some key practical and tactical differences:

- Certain groups of workers are excluded from bringing a claim of unfair dismissal, and so can only challenge a discriminatory dismissal under the

---

[2] [1999] 2 All ER 977, CA.   [3] [2004] 4 All ER 303, HL.   [4] DDA, s 3A(4).
[5] ERA, s 98(2)(a).   [6] ERA, s 98(2)(b).   [7] ERA, s 98(2)(c).
[8] ERA, s 98(2)(d).   [9] ERA, s 98(2)(ba).   [10] ERA, s 95(1)(a).
[11] ERA, s 98(4).
[12] *Clarke v Eley (IMI) Kynoch Ltd* [1982] IRLR 482, EAT; *HJ Heinz Co Ltd v Kenrick* [2000] ICR 491, EAT.

equality enactments. Included in this group are those who are not employees (such as the self-employed, many casual workers and those such as police officers who are office holders and not employees)[13] and those who have less than one year's service[14] (unless, in some cases, they can show that their dismissal was automatically unfair[15]).

- The questionnaire process is only available under the equality enactments and not the ERA;

- Compensation for unfair dismissal under the ERA includes a 'basic award' equivalent to the statutory payment for redundancy,[16] which is not available under the equality enactments;

- Compensation for unfair dismissal under the ERA usually also includes an award (normally of around £300) to reflect the loss of the employee's statutory rights, in that s/he will have to work for a further year with a new employer to secure the protection from unfair dismissal again, whereas no such award is available under the equality enactments (and indeed is not necessary, as there is no qualifying period for bringing a discrimination claim against a new employer);

- Compensation under the equality enactments will normally include an amount for injury to feelings which is not available in a claim for unfair dismissal under the ERA;

- Compensation for unfair dismissal under the ERA is subjected to a statutory 'cap',[17] currently set at £60,600 for dismissals after 1 February 2007,[18] whereas compensation for discrimination under the equality enactments is unlimited;

- If there is a finding of unfair dismissal, the employee has the right to claim reinstatement or re-engagement in order to return to his or her job.[19] There is no express right to do so under the equality enactments (although it is arguable that power to make recommendations includes the power to recommend reinstatement or re-engagement as the discretion to make recommendations is 'extremely wide'[20]); and

---

[13] This is because the right not to be unfairly dismissed in the ERA, s 94 only applies to employees.

[14] ERA, s 108(1).   [15] ERA, s 108(3).   [16] ERA, ss 119–122.

[17] ERA, s 124.

[18] The Employment Rights (Increase of Limits) Order 2006 (2006/3045). It generally increases annually.

[19] ERA, ss 113–117.

[20] *Chief Constable of West Yorkshire v Vento (No 2)* [2003] IRLR 102, CA.

- The provisions for the recoupment of social security benefits[21] only apply in unfair dismissal claims and not to those under the equality enactments.

13.07 The ERA defines a dismissal as including:

- the termination of the contract by the employer, with or without notice;[22]
- a failure to renew a limited term contract under the same contract;[23] and
- a constructive dismissal, where the employee resigns after a breach of the employment contract by the employer.[24]

13.08 A constructive dismissal will only have occurred if the employee can show that the breach of the contract by the employer was sufficiently serious to justify their resignation, or was the last in a series of incidents which justifies their resignation; and that s/he has not delayed too long in terminating the contract in response to the employer's breach, because s/he may otherwise be deemed to have waived the breach and agreed to vary the contract.[25]

13.09 Although the equality enactments do not define dismissal, the types of dismissal embraced by the ERA would all potentially generate claims of discriminatory dismissal under the equality enactments. Constructive dismissals can occur in the equality context where, for example, an employee resigns after:

- A period of sexual or racial harassment, as occurred in *Whitehead v Brighton Marine Palace and Pier Co Ltd*,[26] where the claimant, who was gay, succeeded in showing harassment and constructive dismissal on grounds of his sexual orientation after his manager was overheard referring to him as a 'chutney ferret';
- The employer's refusal to permit the employee to change his or her working arrangements in a discriminatory fashion, as occurred in *London Underground v Edwards (No 2)*,[27] where a single parent who resigned after her employer imposed new rostering arrangements requiring her to start work at 4.45 am and to work Sundays succeeded in showing indirect sex discrimination, and a discriminatory constructive dismissal;
- The repeated refusal of the employer to make reasonable adjustments for the employee's disability, as occurred in *Archibald v Fife Council*;[28]
- The discriminatory refusal of the employer to promote the employee, or afford them equal access to benefits, as occurred in *Bower v Schroder Securities*,[29] where a female equities analyst resigned after she was paid a bonus that

---

[21] See *Harvey on Industrial Relations and Employment Law* at para 2703 *et seq.*
[22] ERA, s 95(1)(a).   [23] ERA, s 95(1)(b).   [24] ERA, s 95(1)(c).
[25] *Western Excavating v Sharpe* [1978] QB 761, CA; *Malik v BCCI* [1998] AC 20, HL.
[26] ET Case No 3102595/04, ET.   [27] [1999] ICR 494, CA.
[28] [2004] 4 All ER 303, HL.   [29] [2001] DCLD 48, ET.

was substantially lower than that given to her male colleagues, and succeeded in claims of both sex discrimination and constructive dismissal; or

- The employee has been given an unlawful instruction to discriminate, as occurred in *Weathersfield v Sargent*[30] where a white woman who resigned after she refused an instruction to discriminate against black clients succeeded in showing unfair constructive dismissal.

C. Dismissals Relating to Capability, Qualifications or Conduct

(a) Capability or Qualifications

In order to be potentially fair as a 'capability or qualifications' dismissal, the reason for dismissal must relate to the capability or qualification of the employee to perform work of the kind that s/he is employed by the employer to do.[31] The 'capability' of the employee for these purposes means capability assessed by reference to their skill, aptitude, health or any other physical or mental quality. 'Qualifications' means any degree, diploma or other academic, technical or professional qualification relevant to the position held.[32] **13.10**

The most common situations which fall into this category are: **13.11**

- where the employer considers that the employee is, or has become, incompetent to do the job in question; and
- where the employee is unable to do the job because of sickness and/or sickness absences.

Dismissals for incompetence need to be considered in the context of all the equality enactments. The employer needs to ask, carefully, why it is believed that the employee is not competent, to ensure that there has been no influence of any of the protected grounds. The questions that may need to be asked before making such a dismissal on this basis are: **13.12**

- Is the employer confident that it could offer clear and compelling evidence before an ET as to why it was genuinely believed that the employee was incompetent for the post?
- Can the employer be satisfied that those assessing the employee's competence have done so untainted by sex, race or any of the other grounds? For example, is the employer confident that there has been no history of complaints of discrimination made by this employee against his or her managers, which may mean that additional scrutiny should be applied to the allegations now

---

[30] [1999] ICR 425, CA.   [31] ERA, s 98(3)(a).   [32] ERA, s 98(3)(b).

made by the managers about the employee's competence? Or is there a possibility that the mangers are less tolerant of the failings of the employee than they would be of other employees of, for example, a different sex or race?

- Can the employer be satisfied that even if the employee has been underperforming, there is no discrimination-related reason for this? Might the allegations of incompetence, for example, relate to the fact that the employee has been suffering harassment on one of the protected grounds?

- Similarly, if the employee is disabled, might the employee's perceived incompetence be linked with their disability? Can the employer be satisfied that the obligations of the DDA have been fully met and, for example, all reasonable adjustments made to assist the employee's competence? By dismissing the employee, is the employer vulnerable to a claim of direct discrimination on grounds of disability, or is the employer capable of justifying any claim of disability-related discrimination?

- If there has been absenteeism, might there be a reason for this related to one of the protected grounds? For example, is the employee a single mother with difficulties over childcare? Does the employee have a disability which leads to their absenteeism? Was the absenteeism caused by the employee taking extended leave to visit employees abroad, as occurred in *Khan v NIC Hygiene*?[33] If any of these reasons apply, can the employer nevertheless be satisfied that dismissal is not directly discriminatory, or if it may be indirectly discriminatory, that it can be justified?

- Has the view of competence been reached as a result of an aptitude test? If so, is the employer satisfied that the test was conducted fairly to all participants, and did not contain aspects which could cause a disparate impact on a particular group and so potentially be indirectly discriminatory? In *Mallidi v Post Office*,[34] for example, an Indian casual worker who had been dismissed because she failed an aptitude test was found to have been unlawfully discriminated against on grounds of her race, because there was evidence that three white comparators had been given contracts without the need to pass such aptitude tests.

13.13 Dismissals for perceived poor capability related to sickness or sickness absence need to be considered in the context of all the equality enactments, but particularly the DDA (which we discuss further in Chapter 9 when considering attendance management issues generally) and the protection from pregnancy- and maternity-related discrimination under the SDA (which we discuss further in Chapter 8, when looking at pregnancy and maternity issues more widely).

---

[33] ET Case No 1803250/04, ET. See further para 10.15.   [34] [2001] DCLD 47, ET.

For all capability- and qualifications-related dismissals, the employer must **13.14** ensure that a fair procedure is followed. This would include a careful appraisal of the employee's performance; a discussion with the employee of the concerns so highlighted; a reasonable opportunity for the employee to improve; and a specific warning to the employee that dismissal may result from a failure to improve. Such procedures must be adopted fairly across all the equality strands so that, for example, an employee from one protected group cannot complain under the equality enactments that but for his or her sex, race etc, s/he would have been subjected to a more generous procedure for assessing capability or qualifications for the job.

(b) Misconduct

Conduct is another potentially fair reason for a dismissal under the ERA.[35] **13.15** Common examples of misconduct justifying dismissal are breaches of the organisation's disciplinary rules, absenteeism, criminal offences and poor time-keeping.

Similar considerations apply in deciding whether to dismiss an employee for **13.16** alleged misconduct as for incompetence:

* Is the employer confident that it could offer clear evidence to an ET as to why it was genuinely believed that the employee had committed the act of misconduct (that being the test, not whether the employee actually had committed the act of misconduct[36])?

* Can the employer be satisfied that the misconduct of which the employee is accused would have generated consideration of dismissal in others from a different sex, racial group etc?

* Might there be an equality-related reason for the misconduct? For example, if an employee has shouted at his or her manager and used inappropriate behaviour, might the reason for this have been that s/he is disabled and was in great pain at the time? If so, might a warning rather than dismissal be an appropriate sanction, as a reasonable adjustment under the DDA?[37]

* Has a fair procedure for assessing the alleged misconduct been applied? Is this the same procedure that would have been applied to persons of a different sex, racial group etc?

---

[35] ERA, s 98(2)(b).   [36] *British Home Stores Ltd v Burchell* [1980] ICR 303, EAT.
[37] DRC Code 2004, para 8.26.

D. Dismissals Relating to Redundancy

13.17 Redundancy is a potentially fair reason for dismissal.[38] For a dismissal on grounds of redundancy to be fair under the ERA, the employer must show that a redundancy situation exists—for example, that the workforce is being reduced for business reasons, or that there is no longer a need for an employee to perform that role—and that the procedure for selecting employees for redundancy was fair.[39]

13.18 Employers are legally obliged to offer, where it exists, suitable alternative employment and to allow the employee a trial period in the new job of at least four weeks. Unreasonable refusal to accept such employment will result in the loss of redundancy pay.[40]

13.19 It is possible for an employee to challenge the employer's determination of whether a redundancy situation exists, but Tribunals will be slow to disturb the employer's assessment of this. Most claims of unfair dismissal in redundancy cases allege that the selection of the employee for redundancy was unfair and/or that the process followed was flawed.

13.20 If the employee's selection for redundancy or the manner in which the process was applied to them was tainted by sex, race etc, s/he can bring a claim under the relevant equality enactments as well as under the ERA. In order to show that a dismissal for redundancy was not discriminatory, employers will need to show that the criteria were objectively justified, fairly applied to the employee in question and that the process was otherwise fair.

13.21 Direct discrimination could occur in a redundancy case where, for example, a black employee is selected for redundancy despite the fact that a white employee better matches the previously chosen selection criteria. In *Moonsar v Fiveways Express Transport Ltd*,[41] for example, a data entry clerk was found to have been unfairly dismissed when she was selected for redundancy ahead of a white employee who had shorter service.

13.22 More common is perhaps the risk of indirect discrimination occurring because the redundancy selection criteria have a disparate impact on a certain group and cannot be justified. For example:

- If part-time workers are made redundant before full-time workers, or fixed-term employees before permanent ones, this is likely to have an adverse impact on women as more women than men work part-time and on a non-permanent basis, and will therefore constitute unlawful sex discrimination in

[38] ERA, s 98(2)(c).   [39] ERA, s 105.   [40] ERA, s 141.
[41] [2005] IRLR 9, EAT.

the absence of justification by the employer. In *Allonby v Accrington and Rossendale College*,[42] for example, the Court of Appeal accepted that a college which made all its hourly paid part-time lecturers redundant was held *prima facie* to have indirectly discriminated (subject to the issue of justification), because two-thirds of this group were women compared to a third of men; and men were more heavily represented in the group of full-time salaried lecturers not made redundant.[43] Such an approach may also be discriminatory under the Part-time Workers (Prevention of Less Favourable Treatment) Regulations 2000[44] and the Fixed-Term Employees (Prevention of Less Favourable Treatment) Regulations 2002.[45]

- Using 'flexibility' as a redundancy selection criterion may be indirectly discriminatory against employees with a disability[46] (who may not be able to be as flexible as others due to their disability) or women (who are more likely to have childcare responsibilities such that they prefer fixed hours).

- Use of long-term sickness absence in redundancy selection criteria may amount to disability-related discrimination which would be unlawful in the absence of justification by the employer. Moreover, absence owing to illness resulting from pregnancy or childbirth cannot be taken into account when computing absence periods with a view to dismissal.[47]

- Use of training in redundancy selection criteria may indirectly discriminate against women who have missed such training opportunities due to absences on maternity leave.

- The use of 'last in, first out' as a redundancy selection criterion may be indirectly discriminatory on grounds of sex (because women tend to have shorter service histories than men), race (if recent efforts have been made to diversify a previously homogenous workforce using the positive action provisions under the RRA) or age (as younger people are more likely to be the 'last in'). The EAT suggested, *obiter*, in *Clarke v Eley (IMI) Kynock Ltd*[48] that 'last in, first out' was likely to be justifiable, because it had for many years been regarded as the most commonly agreed selection criterion for redundancy, but that case pre-dates the AR and therefore needs to be treated with some caution.

The duty to make reasonable adjustments for a disabled employee would also apply to a redundancy process, if it puts the disabled employee at a substantial disadvantage compared to non-disabled employees. **13.23**

---

[42] [2001] IRLR 364, CA.

[43] For further examples of this principle in operation see *Clarke v Eley (IMI) Kynock Ltd* [1982] IRLR 482, EAT and *Whiffen v Milham Ford Girls School* [2001] IRLR 468, EAT.

[44] SI 2000/1306.   [45] SI 2002/2034.   [46] DRC Code 2004, para 8.25.

[47] *Brown v Rentokil* [1998] IRLR 445, ECJ.   [48] [1982] IRLR 482, EAT.

13.24 Employers contemplating redundancies must also pay particular attention to employees on maternity or adoption leave, because:

- employees on maternity or adoption leave have the right to be consulted about potential redundancies or business reorganisations in the same way as other employees;

- a failure so to consult an employee on maternity or adoption leave can be unlawful—in *Visa International Services v Paul*,[49] for example, the claimant won her complaint of sex discrimination and constructive dismissal after she resigned having not been informed, while on maternity leave, of the creation of two new posts in her department, even though the ET found that she had no prospects of obtaining the posts;

- where an employee is made redundant during maternity or adoption leave, s/he is entitled to be offered any available suitable alternative vacancy with the employer, the employer's successor or an associated employer.[50] The new contract must take effect immediately after the previous contract; the work must be suitable in relation to the employee and appropriate for the employee to do in the circumstances; and the terms and conditions must not be substantially less favourable; and

- failure to offer the employee such a vacancy, where it exists, will make the dismissal automatically unfair under the ERA, section 99 if the reason or principal reason for the dismissal is redundancy.[51]

E. Dismissal Due to Compliance with Statutory Requirements

13.25 It is potentially fair to dismiss someone because s/he cannot continue to work in the position held without contravening a duty or restriction imposed by an enactment.[52] Even if this condition is met, a dismissal may be unfair if some reasonable modification could have been made to the employee's job so as to have accommodated the prohibition. Such a modification could involve alteration to the method of doing the work, or the offer of alternative employment.

F. Dismissal for Retirement

(a) The Default Retirement Age of 65

13.26 After lengthy consultation prior to the introduction of the AR, the Government fixed 65 as a default retirement age. Regulation 30 of the AR therefore

---

[49] [2004] IRLR 42, EAT.   [50] MPLR, regs 10(1) and 20; PALR regs 23 and 29.
[51] MPLR, reg 20(1)(b); PALR reg 29(1)(b).   [52] ERA, s 98(2)(d).

now provides that dismissal for reason of retirement of a person aged 65 or over will not constitute age discrimination.

Although this provision effectively gives statutory approval to the less favour-**13.27** able treatment of the over 65s, the Government's view is that the default retirement age is within the exemption in Article 6(1) of the Employment Directive,[53] on the grounds that it meets a legitimate social policy aim, namely meeting the concerns of employers in relation to workforce planning and avoiding an adverse impact on the provision of occupational pensions and other work-related benefits. The DTI Notes on the AR[54] explain this further:

> 100. What is meant by workforce planning in this context can be summarised as including the following:
>
> - workforce planning means that a retirement age is a target age against which employers can plan their work and employees can plan their careers and retirement;
> - for employers, being able to rely on a set retirement age allows the recruitment, training and development of employees, and the planning of wage structures and occupational pensions, against a known attrition profile. This is indirectly recognised in the Directive itself, where Article 6.1(c) lists as a justifiable difference of treatment: 'the fixing of a maximum age for recruitment which is based on the training requirements of the post in question or the need for a reasonable period of employment before retirement'. While other events may give rise to employees leaving the workforce, the age of retirement is nevertheless a significant element in employers' workforce planning;
> - for both employers and employees, being able to rely on a set retirement age avoids the blocking of jobs (and often the more senior jobs) from younger workers;
> - for employees, knowing there is a set retirement age means they cannot be certain that they will be in work after that time. This will encourage employees to save now and make provision for their retirement, and avoid them putting off career and pension planning on the assumption that they will be able to continue working indefinitely. This ties in with the Government's policy of encouraging employees to save more for retirement.
>
> 101. The need to avoid an adverse impact on the provision of occupational pensions and other work-related benefits stems from concern that if all employers only had the option of individually objectively justified retirement ages, this could risk adverse consequences for occupational pension schemes and other work-related benefits. Some employers would instead simply reduce or remove benefits to offset the cost of providing them to all employees, including those over 65.

However, there are arguments that the justification test is not in fact met, and **13.28** that to introduce a default retirement age when previously there was none in domestic law contravenes Article 8(2) of the Employment Directive, which

---

[53] Council Directive 2000/78/EC.
[54] Available at <www.dti.gov.uk/files/file27136.pdf> ('AR Notes').

prohibits Member States from using the Directive as a basis for reducing the legal protection previously available.

13.29 The introduction of the default retirement age was challenged by the National Council in Ageing (which operates under the names Age Concern and Heyday) in *R (The Incorporated Trustees of the National Council on Ageing) v Secretary of State for Trade and Industry* in December 2006, and the parties have agreed that the question of whether the AR comply with the Employment Directive by effectively introducing a mandatory retirement age of 65 will be referred to the ECJ. Cases raising the issue will be stayed pending the outcome. However, in a similar case from Spain, the Advocate General decided in February 2007 that a mandatory retirement age of 65 could be justified.[55] The ECJ's ruling in that case is also awaited. The Government has already committed to reviewing the decision to have a default retirement age in 2011, to assess whether it is still necessary, and if not, to abolish it.[56]

13.30 The default retirement age, the retirement exception from age discrimination protection and the detailed new procedures for retirement dismissal (which we discuss further below) only apply to employees as defined by section 230 of the ERA, civil servants and relevant members of staff of the houses of parliament. Accordingly the retirement exception does not apply to police officers, office holders, barristers/advocates or partners within a firm, in relation to whom an age-related retirement scheme would constitute unlawful discrimination unless it can be justified under regulation 3 of the AR.

(b) Retirement Procedure under the AR

13.31 The AR set out a procedure for retirement dismissal. If the procedure is not followed, the employer may be precluded from showing that retirement was a, or the, reason for the dismissal. We have summarised the procedure at Appendix 13.1 to this chapter.

(c) Retirement and Unfair Dismissal

13.32 The AR effected amendments to the ERA to add 'retirement of the employee' as a potentially fair reason for dismissal (ERA, section 98(2)(ba)), and set out a range of situations addressing the interaction between retirement dismissal and unfair dismissal (ERA, sections 98ZA–98ZH). The latter sections describe fifteen different scenarios, distinguishing between those in which:

---

[55] *Palacios de la Villa v Cortefiel Servicios SA*, C–411/05 (2007) Pens LR 109, ECJ (AG).
[56] *Equality and Diversity: Coming of Age: Consultation on the draft Employment Equality (Age) Regulations 2006* (DTI, 2005), <www.dti.gov.uk/files/file16397.pdf>, at section 6.4.

- retirement is the only reason for the dismissal;
- retirement is not the, or a, reason for dismissal; and
- the ET must determine whether retirement is the reason for the dismissal.

Whether retirement is the, or a, reason for the dismissal is to be determined **13.33** solely by sections 98ZA–98ZF. The statutory dispute resolution procedures do not apply. Where the reason or the principal reason for the dismissal is retirement, the fairness or unfairness of the dismissal is to be determined in accordance with the new section 98ZG.

The net result is that: **13.34**

- When the reason, or principal reason, for the dismissal is retirement, and the statutory procedures are followed, the employee will not be able to challenge the dismissal as unfair. The dismissal will only be unfair if the employer has failed to comply with the notification obligation, or the duty to consider a request not to retire or an appeal.[57] This effectively means that for those over 65 who are dismissed for retirement, the only test for whether their dismissal was fair is a procedural one.
- If the reason for dismissal is not retirement, the employee can challenge the dismissal under the AR.
- If an employer relies on an employee's 'normal retirement age' below aged 65 to dismiss, then the dismissal will constitute age discrimination unless the decision to dismiss can be objectively justified by the employer.
- Whether or not the reason for dismissal is retirement, the dismissed employee will still be able to complain that the dismissal was discriminatory under one of the other strands if and where applicable.

The AR effected several other consequential amendments to the unfair dismissal **13.35** provisions in the ERA to:

- remove the upper age limit for bringing claims of unfair dismissal;[58]
- remove the requirement to reduce the amount of the basic award for every month employed after the employee's 64th birthday;[59]
- remove, for the purposes of calculating the period of continuous employment, the exclusion of any period of employment before the 18th birthday;[60]
- remove, for cases where the employee or companion is dismissed in connection with a request not to be retired, the qualifying period for unfair dismissal;[61] and

---

[57] ie the duties under, respectively, the AR, Sch 6, paras 2, 6, 7 and 8.
[58] Thereby deleting the ERA, s 109.   [59] Thereby deleting the ERA, s 119(4) and (5).
[60] Thereby deleting the ERA s 211(2).   [61] Thereby amending the ERA, s 108.

- insert a provision to the effect that where an ET upholds a complaint under section 98ZG that a 'retirement' dismissal was unfair, and makes an order for reinstatement or re-engagement, the ET must also award compensation of four weeks' pay, unless this would result in injustice to the employer.[62]

13.36 Comparable amendments were made with regard to redundancy payments.[63]

G. Dismissal for 'Some Other Substantial Reason'

13.37 If the dismissal does not fall into any of the above categories it may still be fair if it is for 'some other substantial reason of a kind such as to justify the dismissal of the employee holding the position which the employer held'[64] ('SOSR'). If the reason does not fall into one of the above categories, or SOSR, then the employer will not be able to show that the dismissal was fair.

13.38 The ERA provides no further definition of the situations when SOSR will apply, but provided the reason is substantial and not whimsical, it is capable of falling under this heading. Most of the fair dismissals under the SOSR heading have arisen because the employer is taking action to protect its business interests by, for example, reorganising, preventing the divulgence of confidential information to a competitor, or restricting the opportunity for his employees to resign and set up in competition to him. These changes generally necessitate the employee accepting a change in the terms and conditions of his or her employment, and it is his or her refusal to accept this change that brings about his or her dismissal (either actual or constructive).

13.39 SOSR has also been successfully invoked in cases involving temporary engagements, personality differences, dismissal at the request of third parties, the imprisonment of the employee, or other situations where there has been a breakdown in the relationship of trust and confidence.

13.40 Under all the equality enactments it can be lawful to dismiss an employee if a GOQ or GOR applies,[65] although this does not apply to the sex strand under the SDA, other than in relation to gender reassignment.[66] We discuss these concepts further in Chapter 6, as they tend to arise in practice more at the recruitment stage. A dismissal which was not discriminatory under the equality enactments because of the correct use of a GOQ or GOR would be likely to be fair under the SOSR heading of the ERA.

---

[62] Thereby amending the ERA, s 112. [63] Thereby deleting the ERA, ss 156 and 158.
[64] ERA, s 98(1)(b).
[65] SDA, s 7A; RRA, ss 4A and 5; SOR, reg 7; RBR, reg 7 and AR, reg 8.
[66] This is because the SDA, s 7(1), permitting the use of sex as a GOQ in certain circumstances, does not extend to dismissals under s 6(2)(b).

H. Automatically Unfair Dismissals

There are a range of dismissals which are deemed to be automatically unfair, set **13.41** out at sections 98B and 99 to 105 of the ERA, several of which touch on equality and diversity issues, namely dismissals:

- in connection with pregnancy;
- for reasons related to parental leave or time off for family reasons; and
- because the employee has asserted a statutory right, such as the right to time off for antenatal care.

A dismissal will also be regarded as unfair under section 98A of the ERA if the **13.42** employer has failed to comply with one of the statutory dispute resolution procedures.

I. Monitoring Dismissals

It is good practice for an employer to monitor all dismissals by gender, racial **13.43** group, etc, and then use the data to see if there are any significant disparities between different groups. If so, the employer should seek to establish whether there are any common themes in the relevant policies, procedures or practices that might have contributed to the statistical skew, and make changes to remedy this accordingly. We consider monitoring, and in particular the monitoring requirements of the public sector race equality duty, in further detail in Chapter 4.

J. References

It has long been established[67] that the giver of a reference owes a duty of care to **13.44** the recipient of the reference. Consequently, employers owe a duty to other employers to whom they give a reference for one of their ex-employees. However, employers began to become particularly reluctant to provide reference material beyond minimal information about job title and dates of employment, after the decision in *Spring v Guardian Royal Exchange*.[68] The House of Lords in the *Spring* case implied a duty of care on the former employer in respect of its ex-employee and subject of the reference.

Moreover, all the equality enactments now require that employers do not dis- **13.45** criminate against former employees with regard to events closely connected

---

[67] *Hedley Byrne v Heller* [1964] AC 465, HL.   [68] [1995] 2 AC 296, HL.

with the employment relationship, which would include actions with regard to the giving of references.[69]

13.46 An additional complicating feature in the giving of references, where the ex-employee has made allegations or otherwise done a 'protected act' under the equality enactments, is the risk that the employer's actions with regard to the reference (either by not providing one, or by providing a poor one) will be construed as victimisation.

13.47 The victimisation issue arose in *Chief Constable of West Yorkshire Police v Khan*.[70] The claimant, Sergeant Khan, complained of race discrimination when he was refused promotion over a number of years because of assessments made by his managers. The promotion assessment identified weaknesses in the claimant that were regarded as making him unsuitable for promotion to a more senior post. While the claimant was awaiting the hearing of his complaint before the ET he applied for a post with another force. Any reference that his old police force would have given him would inevitably have been based on the promotion assessments which Sergeant Khan alleged were discriminatory. The force took advice and decided not to provide a reference because of the outstanding ET case. The Chief Constable therefore replied to the request for a reference by indicating that there was an outstanding claim by Sergeant Khan, and that he would make no further comment for fear of prejudicing his defence to those proceedings.

13.48 Sergeant Khan then commenced further proceedings, alleging that the failure to give him a reference constituted victimisation. The Chief Constable successfully defended the claim on the basis of his evidence that he would have refused to provide a reference to any person who had brought proceedings against him where the accuracy of the reference was going to be the subject matter of the proceedings, whether or not they were brought under the RRA.

13.49 In the *Khan* case, the focus of the House of Lords appeared to be on whether the employer had acted honestly and reasonably. However, the decision in the *Khan* case needs to be reassessed in light of the more recent case of *St Helens Metropolitan Borough Council v Derbyshire*,[71] where the House of Lords held that when deciding whether a person has been victimised the ET should focus on the 'detriment' allegedly suffered by that person, rather than the honesty and reasonableness of the employer's actions.

13.50 It may well therefore be that the safest options for employers is to have a policy of providing no references or only minimal information, a policy which is

---

[69] SDA, s 20A; RRA, s 27A; DDA, s 16A; RBR, reg 21; SOR, reg 21 and AR, reg 24.
[70] [2001] 4 All ER 834, HL.   [71] [2007] ICR 841, HL.

consistently applied in all cases. It is, however, a sad state of affairs where an employee who has worked hard and provided good service is denied a correspondingly effusive reference because the employer takes the view, not that it should make sure it provides accurate references supported by objective evidence, but that it should provide no references at all or only the very basic information.

K. Occupational Pension Schemes

(a) Pension Schemes and Age Discrimination

The most obvious equality issue which occupational pension schemes raise is the interaction between the use of age-related criteria and the prohibition on age discrimination.   **13.51**

However, the Employment Directive[72] recognises that age is a key factor in occupational pension schemes. Article 6(2) of the Directive permits Member States to exclude from the prohibition of age discrimination certain age-related criteria used in occupational pension schemes, provided that no sex discrimination results.   **13.52**

The AR prohibit age discrimination in admission to occupational pension schemes and in the treatment of members or prospective members.[73] They also provide that every occupational pension scheme is to be treated as including a 'non-discrimination' rule, that is, a requirement that the trustees and managers of the scheme must not do anything that is unlawful under regulation 11.[74]   **13.53**

However, Schedule 2, Part 2 of the AR goes on to list the rules, practices, actions and decisions that are exempt from the prohibition of discrimination even though they rely directly or indirectly on age criteria. The Government's view[75] is that many of these rules, practices, actions and decisions are objectively justified under the Directive, or fall within the exemption in Article 6(2) referred to above. Further provision with regard to pension schemes is made by the Employment Equality (Age) (Amendment No 2) Regulations 2006.[76]   **13.54**

In September 2006 the trade union Unison brought judicial review proceedings of the Government's decision, following the introduction of the AR, to abolish the '85 year rule' from local Government pension schemes, the rules of which are statutory, on the grounds that it was age discriminatory and costly. The rule had previously allowed members of the scheme to retire early with full benefits   **13.55**

---

[72] Council Directive 2000/78/EC.   [73] AR, reg 11.   [74] AR, Sch 2, Part 1, para 2.
[75] AR Notes, para 191.   [76] SI 2006/2931, as amended.

if the sum of their age and their number of years' service was 85 or more. This was clearly a benefit which tended to favour older workers and those with long service. Unison's application for judicial review of the decision to abolish the provision failed, partly because the Government could have removed the rule on a policy basis in any event, given the costs considerations, and partly because the Administrative Court concluded that the Government was right to regard the provision as potentially discriminatory on grounds of age (even though, under the AR, an employer could have invoked the service and benefits exemption in the Employment Directive to seek to defend any such claim).[77]

(b) Pension Schemes and Discrimination on Grounds of Sex

13.56 EC law recognises that 'pay' for the purposes of the principle of equal pay in Article 141 of the EC Treaty applies to most aspects of occupational pension schemes, including access to an occupational pension scheme, pensionable ages, contributions made by the employer and employee, transitional provisions and survivors' benefits. This means that:

- There must be no discrimination, direct or indirect, in access to pension schemes. An exclusion of women, or a category of women (such as those who are married) will therefore breach Article 141; and any less favourable treatment of part-time workers, where this is indirectly discriminatory and cannot be objectively justified, will also be unlawful.[78]

- Equal pension benefits under occupational pension schemes must be paid to men and women at the same age.[79]

- The employer's contributions to the scheme must be equal for men and women.[80]

- Restricting the payment of survivors' benefits to just widows, or just widowers, will be discriminatory.[81]

- Where there is a transfer between pension schemes, for example, on a change of job, the second scheme must increase benefits to eliminate the effect of any previous discrimination,[82] and if there are insufficient funds to do this, the scheme should do everything possible to ensure that there is equality.

- Where the pensionable age for women is raised to that which applies to men,

---

[77] *R (Unison) v First Secretary of State* [2006] IRLR 926, QBD (Admin).
[78] *Bilka-Kaufhaus GmBH v Weber von Hartz* [1986] ECR 1607, ECJ; *Vroege v NCIV Institut voor Volkshuisvesting BV* [1994] ECR I–4541, ECJ.
[79] *Barber v GRE Assurance* [1991] 1 QB 344, ECJ.
[80] *Worringham and Humphreys v Lloyds Bank* [1981] 2 All ER 434, ECJ.
[81] *Razzouk and Beydoun v European Commission* [1984] ECR 1509, ECJ.
[82] *Coloroll Pension Trustees Ltd v Russell* [1993] ECR I–4389, ECJ.

the employer cannot take steps to limit the consequences of this change for women, as any such transitional arrangements would discriminate against men,[83] in other words, equalisation for men and women for the period prior to the change must be effected by way of 'levelling up'.

However, the obligation to ensure equal treatment in relation to benefits for members and for survivors does not apply to benefits in respect of service before 17 May 1990, as the ECJ held in *Barber v GRE Assurance*[84] that those involved in the provision of pensions had been entitled, prior to that date (the date of the ECJ's decision), to consider that Article 141 did not extend to occupational pension schemes. **13.57**

Moreover, actuarial factors are an exception to the equal treatment rule. In pension schemes, actuarial assumptions about the life expectancy of men and women are used to assess the level of contributions that are necessary to fund the scheme. Since women live, on average, longer than men, employers must make higher contributions for female members than male members in order to achieve equal annual retirement benefits in a salary-related scheme. Such higher contributions do not provide male scheme members with grounds for a valid claim. In a money purchase scheme the same fund value will, on conversion to an annuity with an insurer, provide a higher annual pension for a man than for a woman. Provided the pension paid varies between men and women due to actuarial calculations in the determination of benefits, this is permitted. **13.58**

The Pensions Act 1995 and the Occupational Pension Scheme (Equal Treatment) Regulations 1995[85] sought to bring domestic law into line with EC law following the *Barber* case. **13.59**

(c) Pension Rights During Maternity and Family Leave

Under the Social Security Act 1989, Schedule 5, paras 5 and 6 an employee on paid maternity leave (whether OML or AML) is entitled to the same pension contributions from her employer as when she was working and receiving normal pay. In addition while she is on paid maternity leave the woman must be treated for all purposes (except her liability to pay contributions) as though she was in work and receiving full pay. These provisions apply to final salary and money purchase schemes, whether or not the woman returns to work at the end of the OML or AML, and whether or not she is in receipt of statutory or contractual maternity pay. **13.60**

There are similar provisions under the Social Security Act 1989 for adoption **13.61**

---

[83] *Van den Akker v Stickting Shell Pensioenfunds* [1994] ECR I–4527, ECJ.
[84] [1991] 1 QB 344, ECJ.   [85] SI 1995/3185.

leave, paternity leave and other paid family leave,[86] which mean that the employer must continue paying pension contributions during any part of *paid* leave.

(d) Pension Schemes and Discrimination on Grounds of Disability, Sexual Orientation and Religion or Belief

13.62 The DDA makes no distinction between employers' obligations of non-discrimination and reasonable adjustment between occupational pension schemes and other employment provisions. The only differences relate to the manner in which pension claims are litigated in the ET in that:

- where the complaint is against the trustees or managers of the pension scheme, the employer is treated as a party to the proceedings, and is entitled to appear at the hearing and make representations, because the employer may be required to fund any award made against the trustees or managers;[87] and

- where the complaint is brought by a non-member of the scheme and relates to the terms on which people become members of the scheme, or the terms on which members are treated, the ET may make a declaration that the complainant has the right to be admitted to the scheme or to membership without discrimination in respect of a specified period. However, in these circumstances, the only compensation which the ET may award is for injury to feelings.[88]

13.63 By section 4G of the DDA a 'non-discrimination' rule is deemed to be included in every occupational pension scheme. This rule requires that the scheme's trustees and managers do not discriminate against current or prospective members and imposes on them a duty to make reasonable adjustments. The rule prevails over all other rules of the scheme and trustees and managers are given the power to make alterations to the scheme in order to make it comply with the rule. The non-discrimination rule only applies to rights accrued and benefits payable for periods of service after 1 October 2004, and to all communications about rights and benefits, irrespective of the time period to which those rights and benefits relate.

13.64 Schedule 1A to the SOR and Schedule 1A to the RBR provide for similar non-discrimination clauses to be inserted into occupational pension schemes with regard to sexual orientation and religion or belief.

13.65 In addition, following the Civil Partnership Act 2004, regulation 25 of the SOR, which previously protected workplace benefits linked to marriage, was

---

[86] Social Security Act 1989, Sch 5, Part 1, paras 5A, 5B and 6.   [87] DDA, s 4I.
[88] DDA, s 4J.

amended to provide for the equal treatment of those who are married and those who are in civil partnerships. This is most likely to apply in relation to the availability of lump sums and pensions to a surviving partner on death of the scheme member. Discrimination on the grounds of status is still permitted between those in marriages or civil partnerships as a single category and, on the other hand, those in relationships without such legal status.

Ending Employment: In Brief

- A dismissal occurs where the employer terminates the employee's contract or fails to renew a fixed-term contract. It also occurs where the employee resigns in response to a major breach of contract by the employer. This situation is called a 'constructive' dismissal.

- It is unlawful under the equality enactments to dismiss someone on grounds of their sex, pregnancy/maternity leave, married status or gender reassignment, or on grounds of race, disability, sexual orientation, religion or belief or age (subject to the exception relating to retirement).

- In addition, the Employment Rights Act 1996 (the 'ERA') makes extensive provision to protect employees from being unfairly dismissed. There are a range of situations where a dismissal is rendered automatically unfair under these provisions, several of which touch on equality and diversity issues.

- A dismissal is potentially fair under the ERA if it relates to capability or qualifications, conduct, redundancy, statutory requirements, retirement or some other substantial reason justifying dismissal.

- Employers need to ensure that dismissals related to capability or qualifications, conduct or redundancy are not in themselves acts of discrimination contrary to the equality enactments.

- The Employment Equality (Age) Regulations 2006 (the 'AR') make extensive new provision for dismissal on grounds of retirement. They fix a default retirement age of 65 beyond which, where the reason for dismissal is retirement, employees can only challenge their dismissal as unfair on the basis that the employer has not followed the proper retirement procedure.

- It is good practice for an employer to monitor all dismissals by gender, racial group, etc, and seek to establish from the data so obtained whether there are any worrying trends across the different groups.

- The law relating to references, including the risk of vicitimisation claims, has led many employers to take a cautious approach to giving references.

- There are various provisions within the AR and the Employment Equality (Age) (Amendment No 2) Regulations 2006 which regulate the interaction between age discrimination and occupational pension schemes.

- There are similar provisions to ensure that occupational pension schemes do not discriminate on grounds of sex, disability, sexual orientation and religion or belief.

- There are also provisions relating to the preservation of pension rights during maternity and family leave.

- Following the Civil Partnership Act 2004, occupational pension scheme benefits must be extended to married people and those in civil partnerships in the same way.

APPENDIX 13.1

Step-by-Step Guide to Retirement Dismissal under the AR

Notification by the employer

- An employer who seeks to retire an employee must notify the employee in writing of the employee's right to request not to retire, and the date the employer intends the employee to retire (the 'IDR' or Intended Date of Retirement). This notification must be no more than 12 and not less than six months before the IDR.[89] An employee can complain to the ET if an employer fails to comply with this notification requirement.[90]

- If the employer fails to notify the employee six months before the IDR, the employer has a continuing duty to notify the employee of the right to request not to retire and the IDR until 14 days before the date of termination.[91]

The employee's right to request not to retire

- The employee then has the right to request not to retire on the IDR. If the employer's notification was not less than six months before the IDR, then the employee's request not to retire must be given to the employer not less than three months, but not more than six months, before the IDR. If the employer fails to notify the employee at least six months before the IDR, then the employee's right to request not to retire continues until s/he retires. If no notification of the IDR has been received from the employer but the employee has reasonable grounds to believe that the employer intends to retire him or her on a certain date, the employee must identify that date and request not to retire on that date.[92]

- The employee's request not to retire on the IDR must state whether s/he wants to continue working indefinitely, for a stated period or until a fixed date. A request must be made in writing and must state that it is made under the AR, Schedule 6, paragraph 5. Only one request may be made in relation to one IDR. There is no requirement for the employee to set out the reasons why s/he wishes to continue working but there is no restriction on doing so, and in practice employees are likely to seek to support such requests with evidence as to their capacity to continue working for the employer.[93]

The employer's duty to consider the employee's request

- The employer is then obliged to consider the employee's request not to retire.[94]

- The employer must also meet the employee to discuss the request within a 'reasonable period' of receiving it. However, the employer is not required to hold a meeting if the employee's request is accepted or if it is not reasonably practicable to do so within

---

[89] AR, Sch 6, para 2.   [90] AR, Sch 6, para 11.   [91] AR, Sch 6, para 4.
[92] AR, Sch 6, para 5.   [93] AR, Sch 6, para 5.   [94] AR, Sch 6, para 5.

a reasonable period, and the employer considers any representations made by the employee.[95]

- If the employee exercises the right to request not to retire then s/he cannot be retired until at least one day after the employer gives the employee notice of the decision regarding the request, even if the employment contract would otherwise have terminated earlier.[96]

Notification of the employer's decision

- The employer must notify the employee of the decision as soon as reasonably practicable after the meeting or after considering the employee's representations. This notice must be in writing and dated.[97]
- If the employee's request is accepted and the decision is that the employee's employment will continue indefinitely, or until a specified future date, then the notice must state that fact.[98] The contract of employment should also be amended to show either that the contract will continue indefinitely, or the new agreed retirement date, and any other agreed changes.
- If the request is refused, the notice must confirm that the employer wishes to retire the employee earlier than that requested by the employee. The notice must also inform the employee of the right to appeal.[99] The employer is not required to give reasons for the decision.

Appeals

- The employee has the right to appeal against a refusal of a request not to retire, or a decision to retire the employee earlier than s/he requested. Notification of the intention to appeal must be given in writing, 'as soon as is practicable' after the date of the employer's notice setting out the decision. The notice of appeal may be given after the dismissal has taken place. The employer has a duty to consider the appeal in the same way as the employer is obliged to consider the original request in that there is also a requirement to hold a meeting, and give written notice of the decision on the appeal.[100]

The employee's right to be accompanied

- If the employee so requests, s/he has the right to be accompanied at any meeting to discuss the request or appeal, by a colleague or trade union representative. If the employee's chosen companion is not available at the time proposed for the meeting, the employer must postpone the meeting to a time proposed by the employee convenient for all parties not later than seven days after the meeting date proposed by the employer.[101]
- The employee can complain to the ET if the employer does not, or threatens not to, allow him or her to be accompanied. Both the employee and their companion can complain to the ET if they suffer any detriment as a result of their request to attend such a meeting, and any dismissal on that basis will be automatically unfair.[102]

---

[95] AR, Sch 6, para 7(1)–(5).
[96] AR, Sch 6, para 10.   [97] AR, Sch 6, para 7(6) and 7(8).   [98] AR, Sch 6, para 7(7)(a).
[99] AR, Sch 6, para 7(7)(b).   [100] AR, Sch 6, para 8.   [101] AR, Sch 6, para 7(9).
[102] AR, Sch 6, paras 12 and 13 and ERA, section 105.

14

MANAGING LITIGATION

Trials by the adversarial contest must in time go the way of the ancient trial by battle and blood . . .

(Warren E. Burger, Chief Justice of the United States, 1969–1986)

A. Introduction

The intention of this book is to encourage employers to take a proactive and **14.01** positive approach to equality and diversity issues, so that decisions can be made throughout the employment process which strike the correct balance between the employer's needs and those of their employees. We hope that one consequence of such an approach is that the risk of litigation is avoided, or at least minimised. However, we recognise the reality that in some cases, and sometimes despite the best efforts of both employers and their employees, equality and diversity issues do end in litigation, and that this can be a hugely distressing, damaging and expensive experience for all concerned. In this, the last substantive chapter of this book, we therefore try and give practical advice to employers about how best to manage litigation when it occurs.

B. Pre-action Processes, Questionnaires, Commencing and Responding to a Claim

Nearly all equality and diversity disputes in the workplace which end in litiga- **14.02** tion will arise as claims before the ET, under the SDA, RRA, DDA, RBR, SBR, AR or EqPA. However, related cases for breach of contract, in negligence or under the PHA (such as *Green v DB Group Services (UK) Ltd*[1] which we discuss in Chapter 11) may be started in the County Court or High Court depending

---

[1] [2006] IRLR 764, HC.

on the predicted value of the claim; free-standing claims under the HRA on behalf of public sector employees (which we explain at paragraphs 2.107 to 2.108 above) are brought in the County Court; and public law claims (such as a challenge to secondary employment legislation, or an allegation that a public body has failed to comply with one of its equality duties) are brought in the Administrative Court (part of the High Court) by judicial review.

14.03 There are now processes in place to ensure that in both the Tribunal and civil courts systems, employers should have had some prior notice of a claim, and opportunity to respond to/resolve it, before legal proceedings are formally commenced. In the ET, the pre-action process consists of the statutory grievance procedure requiring employees to have lodged a written grievance with their employer before issuing a claim in the ET; and (to some extent) the statutory disciplinary and dismissal procedures which employers must follow. In the County and High Courts, there are a range of formal pre-action protocols under the Civil Procedure Rules (the 'CPR') which require all parties to submit a pre-action letter to the defendant setting out their claim, and giving the defendant time to respond before proceedings are issued. In cases where no pre-action protocol applies, the CPR expects the parties to act reasonably in exchanging information and documents relevant to the claim and in generally trying to avoid starting proceedings.[2]

14.04 The serving of a questionnaire under one of the equality enactments may also, in practice, provide a clear hint to an employer that proceedings are being considered. The questionnaire will normally contain the employee's account of the factual background, with a question to the employer as to whether that account is accepted. The employee is then entitled to ask a range of questions relevant to their allegation of discrimination, which can include requests for statistical information as to the breakdown of the workforce, or other background material such as the training records of those alleged to have acted in a discriminatory way. The questionnaire process may also be used to request copies of relevant documents. Employers should answer such questionnaires within an eight-week period.[3] The questions and answers are admissible in evidence. If an employer deliberately and without reasonable excuse fails to reply within the eight-week period or is evasive or equivocal in replying, the ET may draw any inference from that fact that it thinks is just and equitable, including the inference that the employer has committed an act of

---

[2] CPR Practice Direction (Protocols) (1999), para 4.
[3] SDA, s 74(2)(a); RRA, s 65(2)(a); DDA, s 56(3)(a); SOR, reg 33(2)(a); RBR, reg 33(2)(a); and AR, reg 41(2)(a).

discrimination.[4] We deal with the answering of questionnaires more fully in Chapter 12, when looking at requests for information generally.

Formal notification of a claim will normally occur by the employer being served **14.05** with a copy of the claim form that has been issued in the ET (known as an 'ET1') or relevant civil court. The ET1 form requires the employee to set out his or her grounds of complaint;[5] and in the civil court system there is a similar requirement to do so either by Particulars of Claim (in the County/High Court) or as part of the standard judicial review claim form (in the Administrative Court).[6]

If formal notification of a claim is received this will normally mean that it has **14.06** not been possible to resolve matters at the pre-action stage. The formal issuing of proceedings may nevertheless provide employers with a fresh incentive to look again at whether matters can be resolved, rather than having both parties incur the costs and distress of litigation.

However, if matters cannot be resolved at this stage, then the employer must **14.07** immediately take steps to prepare and file its response to the claim, within the relatively tight time limits set by the procedural rules: 28 days for a response in the ET[7] (known as an 'ET3'), or 14 days for a Defence in the County or High Court[8] and 21 days for an Acknowledgement of Service and Summary Grounds in the Administrative Court.[9] Applications to extend these time limits can be made to the tribunal or court, but there are draconian default penalties for an employer who fails to comply with these deadlines, which can preclude the employer from further participation in the proceedings.

The employer will wish to use the procedural step of filing its response to set **14.08** out its factual and legal case as fully and persuasively as possible. In practical terms, because of the importance often later attached to these 'statements of case', many organisations will, if they have not already, delegate this task and future handling of the case to their internal or external legal advisers.

C. Time Limits

A common issue that will often arise at the outset of proceedings, and form part **14.09** of the employer's defence, is whether or not the claim has been issued in time.

---

[4] SDA, s 74(2)(b); RRA, s 65(2)(b); DDA, s 56(3)(b); RBR, reg 33(2)(b); SOR, reg 33(2)(b); and AR, reg 41(2)(b).
[5] ET Rules, r 1.
[6] CPR, Parts 7 and 8 (for general civil claims) and 54 (for judicial review).
[7] ET Rules, r 4.
[8] CPR, Parts 9 and 15 (for general civil claims) and 54 (for judicial review).
[9] CPR, Part 54.8.

(a) SDA, RRA, DDA, RBR, SOR and AR Claims

14.10 For the majority of claims under the equality enactments in the employment sphere the time limit is short: 'within' three months of the act complained of,[10] which means three months less one day. Thus if the alleged act of discrimination occurs on 3 March, the ET1 must be received by the ET by midnight on 2 June. This is subject to any extension of time created by the use of the statutory dispute resolution procedures.[11] A six-month time limit is applicable to claims brought by members of the armed forces who must use an internal process before commencing ET proceedings, and to any claims brought by the EHRC in relation to discriminatory advertisements or instructions to discriminate.

14.11 Where the inclusion of a term in a contract renders the making of the contract an unlawful act, that act shall be treated as extending throughout the duration of the contract.[12] Accordingly, time does not run until the end of the contract or where the term is varied to remove the discrimination.

14.12 Where an act extends over a period it is to be treated as being 'done' at the end of that period.[13] In interpreting these 'continuing act' provisions it is necessary to distinguish between a continuing course of discrimination (which *is* a 'continuing act') and one act with continuing consequences (which is not). Although this distinction is not always easy to draw, the following relevant principles can be extracted from the case law:

- there will be an act extending over a period where an employer operates a discriminatory regime, rule or practice in accordance with which decisions are taken from time to time. In such cases, time begins to run from the end of the policy or the claimant's employment. For example, in *Barclays Bank Plc v Kapur and other*,[14] the House of Lords held that the effect of an allegedly racially discriminatory pension scheme continued throughout the claimants' employment. The claim therefore had to be brought within three months of the end of the claimant's service, not three months from the date on which the decision was taken to apply the pension scheme to the claimants;

---

[10] SDA, s 76(1)(a); RRA, s 68(1)(a); DDA, Sch 3, para 3(1); RBR, reg 34(1)(a); SOR, reg 34(1)(a); and AR, reg 42(1).

[11] Note, though, that these procedures may well soon be abolished—see *Resolving Disputes in the Workplace—A Consultation* (DTI, March 2007) and the Employment Simplification Bill, which featured in the Government's draft legislative programme in July 2007.

[12] SDA, s 76(6)(a); RRA, s 68(7)(a); DDA, Sch 3, para 3(3)(a); RBR, reg 34(4)(a); SOR, reg 34(4)(a); and AR, reg 42(4)(a).

[13] SDA, s 76(6)(b); RRA, s 68(7)(b); DDA, Sch 3, para 3(3)(b); RBR, reg 34(4)(b); SOR, reg 34(4)(b); and AR, reg 42(4)(b).

[14] [1991] IRLR 136, HL.

- however, tribunals should be cautious about applying the concepts of 'policy, rule, practice, scheme or regime' too literally, particularly in cases where the claimant is alleging a continuing act consisting of numerous incidents occurring over a lengthy period. This was the reasoning of the Court of Appeal in *Hendricks v Commissioner of Police for the Metropolis*,[15] where a distinction was drawn for these purposes between events that were linked and events that were unconnected or isolated. If the events were linked, and amounted to evidence of a 'continuing discriminatory state of affairs' then this would constitute a continuing act for these purpose. On the facts of the *Hendricks* case, the Court of Appeal upheld the ET's finding that it had jurisdiction to hear complaints of sex and race discrimination made by the claimant police officer, spanning an 11 year period, and citing over a hundred incidents involving some 50 officers; and

- where the complaint of discrimination arises out of repeated requests (for example, to work flexibly, or for promotion), which are reconsidered by the employer on each occasion, time runs from the date on which the last request was refused. This does not, however, apply if the employer does not reconsider the request but merely refers back to and confirms the earlier decision.[16]

If the complaint is lodged outside the three-month period, the ET has a discretion to extend time if it considers it 'just and equitable' to do so.[17] This discretion to extend time is wider than that applicable to claims under the ERA, and in fact is as wide as the discretion given to the civil courts by section 33 of the Limitation Act 1980 to decide whether to extend time in personal injury claims. The court must consider the prejudice to each party which would be caused as a result of the grant or refusal of an extension, and have regard to all the circumstances, and in particular: **14.13**

- the length of and reasons for the delay, including where relevant the health of the employee;
- the extent to which the cogency of the evidence is likely to be affected by the delay;
- the extent to which the employer has cooperated with any requests for information;
- how quickly the employee acted once s/he knew of the facts giving rise to the claim;

---

[15] [2003] IRLR 96, CA.   [16] *Cast v Croydon College* [1998] IRLR 318, CA.
[17] SDA, s 76(5); RRA, s 68(6); DDA, Sch 3, para 3(2); RBR, reg 34(3); SOR, reg 34(3); and AR, reg 42(3).

- the steps taken by the employee to take appropriate advice once s/he knew of the possibility of bringing a claim; and
- the merits of the case, to the extent that the ET may wish to 'form some fairly rough idea as to whether it is a strong complaint or a weak complaint', but not to hear the complaint as it would do at a full hearing.[18]

14.14 Historically, it was common for employers on being presented with a discrimination claim which appeared to raise a time limit issue immediately to seek a preliminary hearing on the issue, with a view to having the claim struck out if it was indeed held to be out of time. Determining time limits issues in this way has become less popular in recent years with ETs, who increasingly recognise the need to hear all the evidence before deciding on time limits, and that such a summary determination of the time limits issue often does not in fact lead to a saving of time and costs. This is especially the case where what is alleged is a continuing act of discrimination and/or there is an application to extend time on just and equitable grounds (which arguments are normally run by claimants in the alternative). It is therefore generally only in cases where there is a clear 'one off' act which may be out of time that ETs are willing to order preliminary hearings on time limits issues.

(b) Claims under the ERA, MPLR and Part-time Workers Regulations 2000

14.15 Claims relating to time-off rights, flexible working, paternity leave and adoption leave under the ERA, and those under the MPLR and Part-time Workers Regulations 2000, must also be brought within three months less one day, unless time is extended on the basis that it was not 'reasonably practicable' to have lodged the claim within this time limit. This is a much stricter test than the 'just and equitable' discretion under the equality enactments described above.

(c) EqPA Claims

14.16 EqPA claims must generally be brought within six months of the termination of the relevant contract of employment,[19] except where there are a series of contracts which constitute a stable employment relationship, in which case time runs from the end of the last contract.[20]

(d) HRA Claims

14.17 For HRA claims the time limit is one year from the date on which the act complained of took place, or such longer period as the court or tribunal

---

[18] *Hutchinson v Westward Television* [1977] IRLR 69, EAT and *British Coal Corporation v Keeble* [1997] IRLR 336, EAT.
[19] EqPA, s 2(4).   [20] *Preston v Wolverhampton Healthcare NHS Trust* [2001] AC 455, HL.

considers equitable having regard to all the circumstances.[21] Again, the court has a broad discretion as to the factors to be taken into account in deciding whether to extend time under this provision.[22] This time limit is subject to any rule imposing a stricter time limit in relation to the procedure in question.

(e) Other Civil Claims

Civil claims, including for breach of contract, negligence and under the PHA, **14.18** must generally be brought within six years[23] unless they allege personal injury as a result of negligence, nuisance or other breach of duty, in which case the limitation period is three years.[24] There are specific provisions under which time can be extended if the claimant did not have knowledge of the relevant facts causing the injury in question,[25] as well as a more general discretion to extend time.[26]

(f) Judicial Review Claims

The judicial review time limit is 'promptly, and in any event not later than **14.19** three months after the grounds to make the claim first arose'.[27] Because of the words 'promptly, and in any event' in this provision, practitioners cannot assume that the time limit is in fact three months. Again the court has some discretion in this regard, but generally the time limits are interpreted much more strictly in judicial review cases than in claims under the equality enactments or other branches of the civil law.

D. Employer's Liability

(a) Liability for the Acts of Employees

Another issue that will frequently arise at the outset of proceedings is whether **14.20** or not the employer is willing to accept that it is liable for any discrimination by one of its employees. There are two elements to this issue—the issue of vicarious liability and that of the statutory 'reasonable steps' defence under the equality enactments.

---

[21] HRA, s 7(5).
[22] *Weir v Secretary of State for Transport and Another* [2005] UKHRR 154, HC and *Cameron and others v Network Rail Infrastructure Ltd* [2007] 1 WLR 163, QBD.
[23] Limitation Act 1980, s 2.   [24] Limitation Act 1980, s 11.
[25] Limitation Act 1980, s 11(4)(b).   [26] Limitation Act 1980, s 33.
[27] CPR, Part 54.5(1).

(i) Vicarious Liability

14.21   The equality enactments specifically,[28] and the civil law generally, import a concept of vicarious liability to the effect that the employer will generally be liable for all acts carried out by employees 'in the course of employment', whether or not they are done with the employer's knowledge or approval.

14.22   The leading case on this issue under the equality enactments is *Jones v Tower Boot Co Ltd*.[29] There, the complainant, at 16-year-old boy, had been subjected to horrific physical and verbal abuse, including employees burning him with a hot screwdriver, whipping him on the legs with a welt, throwing bolts at him and trying to put his arm in a lasting machine. The Court of Appeal held[30] that the purpose of the vicarious liability provisions in the equality enactments was:

> . . . to deter racial and sexual harassment in the workplace through a widening of the net of responsibility beyond the guilty employees themselves by making all employers additionally liable for such harassment, and then supplying them with the reasonable steps defence . . . which will exonerate the conscientious employer who has used his best endeavour to prevent such harassment, and will encourage all employers who have not yet undertaken such endeavour to take the steps necessary to make the same defence available in their own workplace . . .

It therefore followed that the employer was liable for the acts of the complainant's fellow employees, however horrific the things they had done, as they had been carried out in the course of their employment.

14.23   Because this concept of 'in the course of employment' is widely defined, it can embrace discrimination which occurs during a rest break, on a work outing, while attending a work course or during other business trips. In the *Jones* case the Court of Appeal recognised[31] that discrimination cases raise an infinite variety of circumstances, and that in each case it will be for the court or tribunal to resolve whether vicarious liability applies, having regard to the broad test set down in that case.

14.24   In *Chief Constable of Lincolnshire Police v Stubbs*,[32] for example, a female police officer complained of inappropriate sexual behaviour that had occurred in pubs—on one occasion when she and her colleagues had gone to the pub immediately after their tour of duty, and on another when they had attended an organised leaving party. The ET held that:

---

[28] SDA, s 41(1); RRA, s 32(1); DDA, s 58(1); RBR, reg 22(1); SOR, reg 22(1); and AR, reg 25(1).
[29] [1997] 2 All ER 406, CA.   [30] At p 415 of its judgment.
[31] At p 416 of its judgment.   [32] [1999] ICR 547, EAT.

... these incidents were connected to work and the workplace. They would not have happened but for the applicant's work. Work-related social functions are an extension of employment and we can see no reason to restrict the course of employment to purely what goes on in the workplace.

The EAT agreed, but recognised that the position would have been different had the harassment occurred during a chance meeting at the pub.[33]

It is also clear that employers can be vicariously liable for the acts of all their employees, and not just those of managerial or supervisory staff.[34]   **14.25**

The common law has now given a similarly wide meaning to this concept. In *Lister and Others v Hesley Hall Ltd*,[35] the House of Lords had to consider whether the defendant company which managed a school could be liable for sexual abuse perpetrated by the warden of one of the boarding houses. Their Lordships held that vicarious liability did lie, because of the '. . . relative closeness of the connection between the nature of the employment and the particular tort . . .'.   **14.26**

In discrimination cases, and particularly those alleging serious harassment, an employer may therefore seek to argue that the alleged discrimination took place outside the course of the alleged discriminator's employment, so as to escape liability. The prospects of succeeding in such an argument are now limited in light of the *Jones* and *Lister* cases and vicarious liability is only likely to be avoided where on the facts it can be said that there really was no connection between the alleged harassment and the employment. A recent such example was *N v Chief Constable of Merseyside*,[36] where it was held that a chief constable was not liable for the rape and indecent assaults perpetrated by an off-duty police officer, as he had genuinely been on a 'frolic of his own'.   **14.27**

(ii) The 'Reasonable Steps' Defence

The equality enactments (but not the common law) provide an employer with a defence that it took such steps as were 'reasonably practicable' to prevent the discrimination taking place.[37] It follows that the defence is concerned with what steps the employer took *before* the alleged discrimination took place. The defence is commonly referred to as the 'statutory defence' or the 'reasonable steps' defence.   **14.28**

In determining whether an employer has taken such reasonably practicable steps, the Tribunal will first look at what the employer did do; and then ask   **14.29**

---

[33] Paragraphs 44–46.   [34] *De Souza v Automobile Association* [1986] ICR 514, CA.
[35] [2002] 1 AC 215, HL.   [36] [2006] EWHC 3041, QBD.
[37] SDA, s 41(3); RRA, s 32(3); DDA, s 58(5); RBR, reg 22(3); SOR, reg 22(3); and AR, reg 25(3).

whether there are any other steps that it could have taken that were reasonably practicable. Regard can be had to whether or not the steps were likely to have prevented the discrimination or harassment (as that in itself determines whether they are regarded as *reasonably* practicable) although whether or not the steps would have been successful is not determinative.[38] The EAT summarised the Tribunal's approach in this way in *Caspersz v Ministry of Defence* at paras 9 to 10 of its judgment:

> . . . measures are to be judged as to their reasonable practicability not by whether they have been effective: by definition, that will not have occurred because otherwise there would be no act of discrimination calling for a defence.

> The steps which are to be assessed against the touchstone of reasonable practicability must be calculated . . . to prevent the employee from doing that act or act of that description.

> What must be assessed is whether putting oneself into the shoes of the employer prior to the acts which are complained about, and looking from that perspective at the possibility such acts might subsequently occur, the steps are reasonably practicable. That involves at that stage considering what effect those steps might have . . .[39]

14.30 The size of the employer will also be a relevant consideration, so that the larger the employer the greater the expectation that it will properly implement and observe an equal opportunities policy.

14.31 However, the mere existence of equality and diversity policies and schemes will not make out the reasonably practicable steps defence, as the ET made clear in *A v Civil Aviation Authority*.[40] Rather, it is necessary:

> . . . to ensure not only that an adequate policy with regard to sex discrimination is in place but also that it is understood, implemented and observed throughout the workplace.

On the facts of the *A* case, the ET concluded that the employers had not made out the 'reasonable steps' defence: although they had had in place a comprehensive equal opportunities policy which referred to sexual harassment as 'wholly unacceptable', there had been no training of managers with regard to sexual harassment issues, nor other steps which might have alerted managers and employees alike to the situations and conduct which could give rise to harassment.

---

[38] *Canniffe v East Riding of Yorkshire Council* [2000] IRLR 555, EAT and *Croft v Royal Mail Group plc* [2003] ICR 1425, CA.

[39] EAT, 0599/05, EAT at para 10.   [40] [1996] DCLD 27, ET.

In *Casperz v Ministry of Defence*[41] the EAT reiterated that the mere existence **14.32** of policies is likely to be insufficient in making out the 'reasonable steps' defence.

It is hard to be prescriptive as to what will or will not make out the defence, but **14.33** we would certainly hope that approaching equality and diversity issues in the proactive way we have described in this book will give employers a head start in doing so.

(iii) Practical Considerations regarding Vicarious Liability and the 'Reasonable Steps' Defence

If the employer succeeds in showing that the acts in question did not occur in **14.34** the course of employment, then neither the employer nor the employee will be liable as the acts will have effectively fallen outside the scope of the employment provisions of the equality enactments. However, if the acts in question are found to have been carried out in the course of employment, but the employer succeeds in making out the 'reasonable steps' defence, then the individual employee will be personally liable because s/he is deemed to have aided the discrimination of their employer.[42]

An employer does need to consider carefully whether to deny vicarious liability **14.35** or to invoke the reasonable steps defence. Invoking the reasonable steps defence has the potential benefit of indicating a 'zero tolerance' approach to allegations of discrimination, and may be appropriate where, for example, an employer's internal disciplinary process has already concluded that the allegations are well founded and that the discrimination occurred despite all appropriate steps by the employer. However, invoking the defence, or denying vicarious liability, where there has been no such conclusion may be highly damaging, particularly if the alleged discriminator remains in employment and therefore feels s/he has been 'hung out to dry' and left with no support when the case against them remains unproven, and indeed may never be.

The risk of the reasonable steps defence succeeding also raises practical issues **14.36** for claimants, who will have to consider joining the individual employee as a named respondent from the outset to avoid being in a situation where they have no appropriate respondent left in the proceedings. Proceeding against individual respondents is generally less satisfactory from a claimant's perspective as there are normally greater risks that an individual respondent will be

---

[41] EAT, 0599/05, EAT at para 10.
[42] SDA, s 42(2); RRA, s 33(2); DDA, s 57(2); RBR, reg 23(2); SOR, reg 23(2); and AR, reg 26(2).

unable to meet any financial award made against them than there are with an employer. Alternatively, the claimant may decide to bring proceedings in negligence/assault/battery or under the PHA as appropriate, because although the vicarious liability concepts are aligned there is no reasonable steps defence available in these types of claim.

(b) Liability for the Acts of Third Parties

14.37 In *Macdonald v Advocate General for Scotland; Pearce v Mayfield Secondary School Governing Body*,[43] the House of Lords overturned the finding in *Burton v de Vere Hotels Ltd*[44] that an employer's failure to take reasonable steps to protect its employees from sexual or racial discrimination by third parties was itself discrimination, even where the failure to protect the employees had nothing itself to do with their sex or race. Accordingly, at present, employers can only be liable for discrimination perpetrated by third parties if it can be shown that their failure to protect their employees from such discrimination was itself motivated by a prohibited ground.

14.38 However, the Government has recently indicated that, since the judgment in *R (Equal Opportunities Commission) v Secretary of State for Trade and Industry*,[45] it proposes to amend the law in this area, to make clear that an employer can be held liable for harassment if it fails to take action to protect an employee in the workplace where it is aware that s/he is being subjected to persistent acts of harassment on grounds of sex by a customer or client. The Government may also extend this provision to the other strands in the Single Equality Bill.[51]

(c) Liability for Aiding Discrimination

14.39 The equality enactments all provide that a person who knowingly aids another to do an act of discrimination is treated as himself doing the act in question.[47] Therefore a person who knowingly aids another to discriminate will be liable for that act. A person aids another person for these purposes if s/he helps, cooperates or collaborates with the other person to discriminate, and is aware that that is what the other person is doing—aiding for these purposes (unlike discrimination itself) cannot be unconscious.[48]

---

[43] [2004] 1 All ER 339, HL.   [44] [1997] ICR 1, EAT.
[45] [2007] IRLR 327, QBD (Admin).   [46] DLR consultation paper, para 14.30.
[47] SDA, s 41(2); RRA, s 32(2); DDA, s 58(2); RBR, reg 22(2); SOR, reg 22(2); and AR, reg 25(2).
[48] *Anyanwu v South Bank Student Union* [2001] IRLR 305, HL and *Sinclair Roche and Temperley v Heard (No 1)* [2004] IRLR 763, EAT.

(d) Liability for the Acts of an Agent

The equality enactments all provide that a principal is liable for the discriminatory acts of their agents.[49] Such a relationship generally arises where one person, the principal, consents to another person, the agent, acting on his or her behalf. Where a principal has given such authority to an agent (whether express or implied, and whether given before or after the event) the principal and the agent will both be liable for any discriminatory acts carried out by the agent.

14.40

E. The Overriding Objective and the General Approach to Procedure

The Employment Tribunals Rules of Procedure[50] (the 'ET Rules') and the CPR share the same overriding objective, which is to deal with all cases 'justly'. Dealing with a case justly includes, so far as is practicable:

14.41

- ensuring the parties are on an equal footing;
- saving expense;
- dealing with the case in ways which are proportionate to the complexity or importance of the issues; and
- ensuring that it is dealt with expeditiously and fairly.

The 'overriding objective' seeks to incorporate into domestic law the concept of 'equality of arms' to be derived from the right to a fair hearing entrenched in Article 6 of the ECHR, which we discuss in more detail at paragraph 2.98 above.

14.42

The ET has evolved from what was historically known as the Industrial Tribunal. Like its predecessor, the ET is meant to adopt a procedure which is informal and accessible to litigants in person. The ET Rules reflects this in that:

14.43

> . . . The chairman or tribunal shall seek to avoid formality in his or its proceedings and shall not be bound by any enactment or rule of law relating to the admissibility of evidence in proceedings before the courts. . . .

> The chairman or tribunal (as the case may be) shall make such enquiries of persons appearing before him or it and of witnesses as he or it considers appropriate and shall otherwise conduct the hearing in such manner as he or it considers most appropriate for the clarification of the issues and generally for the just handling of the proceedings. . . .[51]

---

[49] SDA, s 42(3); RRA, s 33(3); DDA, s 57(3); RBR, reg 23(3); SOR, reg 23(3); and AR, reg 26(3).

[50] These are scheduled to the Employment Tribunals (Constitution and Rules of Procedure) Regulations 2004 (SI 2004/1871).

[51] ET Rules, r 14(2) and (3).

14.44 However, despite this stated aspiration towards informality, the reality is that ET procedure is becoming increasingly formalised and technical, especially in discrimination cases which are among the most complex and high-value claims in the ET system.

14.45 It often surprises people that an employment dispute with a discrimination element can easily take two weeks to hear in the ET, with counsel instructed on both sides, and a fully reasoned judgment, whereas a criminal trial in which the defendant's liberty is at stake can be concluded in a matter of days, by the jury simply uttering the word 'guilty'.

14.46 On a similar note, we have always thought it surprising that most ET buildings contain separate waiting areas for the employee and employer representatives and witnesses, presumably to not risk any difficulties if the opposing camps meet 'face to face' outside the hearing, when no such provision is made in the criminal or other civil courts (unless a party is appearing from custody). We would have thought that such a system of insisting that the parties remain separate before the actual hearing starts makes the proceedings appear more formal rather than less! It is also a physical endorsement of the gulf between the parties which could be particularly unhelpful where the employment relationship is ongoing.

F. Preparation for the Hearing

(a) Procedural Steps

14.47 The steps that will frequently take place between the initiation and response to the claim and the full hearing in the ET can be summarised as follows:

- Applications to amend the claim form by either changing the legal basis of the claim, adding a new claim, or adding a new party, and applications to amend the employer's response.[52] Amendments are generally more easily allowed where the facts are already set out in the claim form and all the amendment does is 're-label' those facts. Amendments which add an entirely new claim will be subject to the rules on time limits. Generally, though, the test the ET will apply is whether or not hardship or injustice would be caused to either party by granting or withholding the application to amend.[53]

---

[52] ET Rules, r 10(2)(q) and (r).

[53] *Selkent Bus Co Ltd v Moore* [1996] ICR 836, EAT and *Ali v Office of National Statistics* [2005] IRLR 210, CA.

- Requests for further information to amplify the employee's claim or employer's response, and responses to such requests.[54]

- Requests for written answers, and responses thereto.[55]

- The disclosure of documents between the parties, and applications for disclosure of specific documents if disclosure cannot be done by consent.[56] The main criterion on which disclosure is ordered is whether or not the document is relevant to an issue in the case. Confidentiality alone is not a bar to disclosure,[57] and in certain cases the ET will order the disclosure of statistical evidence.[58]

- An application to consolidate the claim with one or more other claims which raise similar issues of fact or law, so that they can be heard together.[59] Such a course is often sensible in the interests of saving time and costs, and reducing the risk of inconsistent decisions. Consolidation often happens in discrimination cases where, for example, an initial complaint of discrimination is followed by a further complaint of victimisation.

- The obtaining of medical evidence in respect of a claim under the DDA, or to support a claim for personal injury and/or injury to feelings. ETs nowadays tend to prefer to have joint experts instructed to determine such issues, but in some cases the ET will give the parties permission to instruct their own experts provided a sensible procedure is followed.[60]

- A pre-hearing review[61] to determine a discrete legal or factual point, the determination of which will ultimately assist in narrowing the issues and/or saving costs. Such hearings can be sensible where a 'knock-out' issue needs to be determined between the parties, such as what the appropriate 'pool' for comparison in an indirect discrimination claim is, or whether the claimant is disabled for the purposes of the DDA.

- The setting out of the claimant's financial losses in a schedule of loss, and a response by the employer.

- An application that the ET hears the issues of liability and remedy separately,[62] which will often be appropriate in the interests of saving time and cost where there are complex issues on remedy, particularly those calling for expert evidence (because if the issues are separated, and the claimant fails on liability, there would be no need for a hearing on remedy at all).

---

[54] ET Rules, r 10(2)(b).   [55] ET Rules, r 10(2)(f).   [56] ET Rules, r 10(2)(d).
[57] *Science Research Council v Nassé* [1980] AC 1028, HL.
[58] *West Midlands Passenger Transport Executive v Singh* [1988] IRLR 186, CA.
[59] ET Rules, r 10(2)(j).
[60] ET Rules, r 10(2)(t) and *De Keyser v Wilson* [2001] IRLR 324, EAT.
[61] ET Rules, r 18.   [62] ET Rules, r 10(2)(i).

- The obtaining by both parties of witness statements on issues of liability.[63] From an employer's perspective this usually means obtaining statements of fact from all those involved in the alleged acts of discrimination.

- The obtaining by both parties of evidence as to remedy. From an employer's perspective, as well as medical evidence to challenge any claim of personal injury and/or injury to feelings (see above), this is likely to include evidence as to the job market to show that the claimant has not in fact mitigated his or her loss, as the law requires them to do. This can be in a straightforward form such as copies of advertisements for jobs it is alleged that the claimant could have obtained; or in serious cases, expert evidence as to the claimant's occupational prospects. Expert actuarial evidence can also be needed to calculate any pension losses suffered by the claimant. Again such occupational or actuarial evidence can be obtained through the instruction of a joint expert.

- The preparation of bundles of the documents for use at the hearing, which should generally be in chronological or other logical order—conventionally the statements of case and any questionnaires and responses, followed by the contemporaneous documentation addressing the allegations of discrimination and then the relevant policies and procedures of the employer.

- A request for a witness order that a reluctant witness attend to give evidence.[64]

- A request for a restricted reporting order (which is only available on the grounds that the case involves allegations of sexual misconduct, or is a DDA claim where evidence of a personal nature is likely to be heard[65]), or for the proceedings to be heard in private.[66]

- Near to the hearing, the preparation of chronologies, lists of people involved in the case (still sometimes referred to as the *dramatis personae*), running orders of witnesses and skeleton arguments.

14.48 Directions setting out timetables for compliance with the above steps are normally set in the ET at Case Management Discussions.[67] A party is also free to apply for an order that the other party comply with a particular direction.[68] Non-compliance with an order can result in costs penalties or the party's case being struck out.[69]

14.49 There are similar steps in County and general High Court proceedings, as set out in the CPR, with some relatively minor differences, such as that directions are set at Case Management Conferences, not Discussions!

---

[63] ET Rules, r 10(2)(s).   [64] ET Rules, r 10(2)(c).   [65] ET Rules, r 50.
[66] ET Rules, r 16.   [67] ET Rules, r 17.   [68] ET Rules, r 11.
[69] ET Rules, r 13.

CPR Part 54 provides a specific procedure for judicial review proceedings, the extent of which is outside the scope of this work. One key difference between the interlocutory stages in judicial review claims and those in the ET or general civil courts is that there is a requirement for the claimant to obtain permission before they can proceed with their claim. The issue of permission is normally determined initially on the papers, and if declined, the claimant has the right to renew their application at an oral hearing.   **14.50**

(b) The Evidential Burden on Employers

Throughout this book we have hopefully conveyed the need for consistency and transparency in decision-making at all stages of the employment process, so that issues are resolved by objective reference to clearly defined policies, and the rationales for decisions are thoroughly documented. We regard such an approach as good practice and genuinely likely to lead to a better quality of decision-making. However, in practical terms the keeping of such records is essential to the presentation of a good case before the ET or civil courts. In discrimination cases, in particular, recent case law considering the statutory regime for the shift in the burden of proof has stressed the need for employers to make all appropriate disclosure, and call all relevant witnesses, in order to discharge the burden of proof.   **14.51**

In *Igen and others v Wong and others*,[70] the Court of Appeal gave the following guidance on the burden of proof issue: **14.52**

(1) Pursuant to s.63A of the SDA, it is for the claimant who complains of sex discrimination to prove on the balance of probabilities facts from which the tribunal could conclude, in the absence of an adequate explanation, that the respondent has committed an act of discrimination against the claimant which is unlawful by virtue of Part II or which by virtue of s. 41 or s. 42 of the SDA is to be treated as having been committed against the claimant. These are referred to below as 'such facts'.

(2) If the claimant does not prove such facts he or she will fail.

(3) It is important to bear in mind in deciding whether the claimant has proved such facts that it is unusual to find direct evidence of sex discrimination. Few employers would be prepared to admit such discrimination, even to themselves. In some cases the discrimination will not be an intention but merely based on the assumption that 'he or she would not have fitted in'.

(4) In deciding whether the claimant has proved such facts, it is important to remember that the outcome at this stage of the analysis by the tribunal will therefore usually depend on what inferences it is proper to draw from the primary facts found by the tribunal.

---

[70] [2005] 3 All ER 812, CA.

(5) It is important to note the word 'could' in s.63A(2). At this stage the tribunal does not have to reach a definitive determination that such facts would lead it to the conclusion that there was an act of unlawful discrimination. At this stage a tribunal is looking at the primary facts before it to see what inferences of secondary fact could be drawn from them.

(6) In considering what inferences or conclusions can be drawn from the primary facts, the tribunal must assume that there is no adequate explanation for those facts.

(7) These inferences can include, in appropriate cases, any inferences that it is just and equitable to draw in accordance with s.74(2)(b) of the SDA from an evasive or equivocal reply to a questionnaire or any other questions that fall within s.74(2) of the SDA.

(8) Likewise, the tribunal must decide whether any provision of any relevant code of practice is relevant and if so, take it into account in determining, such facts pursuant to s.56A(10) of the SDA. This means that inferences may also be drawn from any failure to comply with any relevant code of practice.

(9) Where the claimant has proved facts from which conclusions could be drawn that the respondent has treated the claimant less favourably on the ground of sex, then the burden of proof moves to the respondent.

(10) It is then for the respondent to prove that he did not commit, or as the case may be, is not to be treated as having committed, that act.

(11) To discharge that burden it is necessary for the respondent to prove, on the balance of probabilities, that the treatment was in no sense whatsoever on the grounds of sex, since 'no discrimination whatsoever' is compatible with the Burden of Proof Directive.

(12) That requires a tribunal to assess not merely whether the respondent has proved an explanation for the facts from which such inferences can be drawn, but further that it is adequate to discharge the burden of proof on the balance of probabilities that sex was not a ground for the treatment in question.

(13) Since the facts necessary to prove an explanation would normally be in the possession of the respondent, a tribunal would normally expect cogent evidence to discharge that burden of proof. In particular, the tribunal will need to examine carefully explanations for failure to deal with the questionnaire procedure and/or code of practice.

In *Madarassy v Nomura International plc*[71] the Court of Appeal approved its earlier guidance in the *Igen* case, and confirmed that in deciding whether the burden of proof is shifted the tribunal is entitled to look at evidence advanced by the employer as to the reason for any less favourable treatment.

14.53 Employers should therefore note that the Court of Appeal recognised that since the facts necessary to prove an explanation would normally be in the possession of the respondent, a tribunal would normally expect 'cogent evidence' from

---

[71] [2007] IRLR 246, CA.

employers to discharge the burden of proving that there was 'no discrimination whatsoever' in the treatment in question. In particular, the tribunal will need to examine carefully explanations for failure to deal with the questionnaire procedure and/or code of practice.

The Tribunal is also entitled to have regard to any acts of discrimination **14.54** occurring before and after the act complained of; any discriminatory comments made; and any statistical evidence showing relevant imbalances in the workforce (as between, for example, men and women, or white and black employees): *West Midlands Passenger Transport Executive v Singh*[72] discussed the use of such statistics.

In *Dresdner Kleinwort Wasserstein Ltd v Adebayo*[73] the EAT held that the shift- **14.55** ing of the burden to respondents meant that tribunals are entitled to expect employers to call evidence which is sufficient to discharge the burden of proving that the explanation advanced was non-discriminatory and that it was the real reason for what occurred. This means that in cases where the burden does shift, a failure to follow recommendations in relevant codes of practice, or a failure to call as witnesses those who were involved in the events and decisions about which complaint is made, will all properly assume 'a greater significance' than they may have done historically.

In *EB v BA*[74] the Court of Appeal considered the claim of a management con- **14.56** sultant that, following her gender reassignment, she had been discriminated against in the allocation of work, and then unfairly selected for redundancy. The Court held that in light of the primary facts she had proved, the burden of proof shifted to her employer to show why she had only worked on three projects out of what appeared to be over 200 projects after her transition. The Court held that the employer could only have discharged that burden by providing a detailed analysis of the projects and proposals to which she was not allocated.

It is also relevant to note at this stage that where there is no evidence as to the **14.57** treatment of an actual comparator whose position is wholly akin to the claimant's, and the ET therefore has to construct a picture of how a hypothetical comparator would have been treated in comparable surrounding circumstances, it is acceptable for the tribunal to consider how non-identical, but not wholly dissimilar cases were treated.[75] Employers may therefore wish to offer evidence of such cases in their defence.

---

[72] [1988] 2 All ER 873, CA.   [73] [2005] IRLR 514, EAT.
[74] [2006] IRLR 471, CA.
[75] *Chief Constable of West Yorkshire v Vento* [2001] IRLR 124, EAT.

14.58 The quality of evidence advanced by an employer is perhaps particularly important in an indirect discrimination claim where justification is in issue. In *Hardy's and Hansons plc v Lax*[76] the Court of Appeal made clear that in assessing the evidence advanced by an employer on the justification issue, the ET will apply a critical approach, going beyond an assessment of whether the employer's view was within the band of reasonable responses:

> . . . [t]he principle of proportionality requires the tribunal to take into account the reasonable needs of the business. But it has to make its own judgment, upon a fair and detailed analysis of the working practices and business considerations involved, as to whether the proposal is reasonably necessary. I reject the . . . submission . . . that, when reaching its conclusion, the employment tribunal needs to consider only whether or not it is satisfied that the employer's views are within the range of views reasonable in the particular circumstances . . .

> . . . The statute requires the employment tribunal to make judgments upon systems of work, their feasibility or otherwise, the practical problems which may or may not arise from job sharing in a particular business, and the economic impact, in a competitive world, which the restrictions impose upon the employer's freedom of action. The effect of the judgment of the employment tribunal may be profound both for the business and for the employees involved. This is an appraisal requiring considerable skill and insight. As this court has recognised in *Allonby* and in *Cadman*, a critical evaluation is required and is required to be demonstrated in the reasoning of the tribunal. . . .

14.59 An employer should therefore bear in mind these legal principles in preparing its evidence for the hearing of any discrimination case.

G. The Hearing

14.60 The full hearing of an ET discrimination claim normally takes place before a Chair and two wing members, one conventionally with 'employee experience' and one from the 'employer side'. Under the Tribunals, Courts and Enforcement Act 2007 which received Royal Assent in July 2007, ET Chairs will become 'Employment Judges'. Presently, Regional Chairs frequently try and ensure that those who chair discrimination cases have particular experience to qualify them to do so, as it is recognised that they are among the most demanding cases Tribunal Chairs hear.

14.61 The hearing normally proceeds in public, and in the following order:

- Discussion between the Chair and the representatives as to the issues to be decided by the Tribunal and/or opening by the claimant's representative.

---

[76] [2005] IRLR 726, CA, at paras 32–33.

- Evidence of the claimant and any witnesses s/he wishes to call, with references to documents in the bundle as appropriate.
- Evidence of the Respondent and any witnesses it wishes to call, with references to documents in the bundle as appropriate.
- Closing submissions by both parties' representatives.
- The giving of the judgment by the Tribunal, which in cases lasting more than a day or so is often reserved to a future date, and then given in writing with written reasons.

Witnesses are generally examined-in-chief by their own representative, then **14.62** cross-examined by the other party's representative, then asked questions by the Chair and wing members, and then re-examined by their own representative.

Tribunals vary in how the evidence-in-chief is elicited from witnesses. Gener- **14.63** ally the statement of the witness stands as their evidence-in-chief and they either read out the statement to the Tribunal, or the Tribunal retires and reads the statement. If the latter course is adopted, and the statement taken as 'read', then the witness's representative is permitted to ask only such questions as are necessary for amplification or clarification of the witness statement.

If a witness does not attend to give live evidence but the party on whose behalf **14.64** they have given a statement asks the ET to read their evidence, the ET will generally do so but afford less weight to it given that the other party has not had the opportunity to test the evidence through cross-examination of the witness.

The procedure is broadly the same in trials in the County and High Courts, **14.65** save that the usual practice is to take witness statements entirely as 'read'.

Witnesses will need to be well prepared for giving their evidence in order to do **14.66** justice to their account and therefore the claimant or respondent's case. They should be fully familiar with the contents of their witness statement and any document to which they are likely to be referred in evidence. Witnesses may find giving evidence a stressful and distressing experience and so are likely to require additional support from their employer or union at this time.

Again the procedure for judicial review hearings is markedly different to those **14.67** in the ET or general civil courts, in that although witness statements and expert reports are frequently served by the parties the makers of those statements or reports are rarely called to give live evidence.

H. Remedies, Damages, Costs and Appeals

In giving its judgment the ET will indicate what it is ordering by way of **14.68** remedy.

14.69 In cases under the equality enactments the available remedies are:

- an order declaring the rights of the complainant and the respondent;
- an order requiring the respondent to pay to the complainant compensation; and/or
- a recommendation that the respondent take within a specified period action appearing to the Tribunal to be practicable for the purpose of obviating or reducing the adverse effect on the complainant of the acts of discrimination to which the complaint relates.[77]

14.70 Compensation in discrimination claims is normally awarded under the following heads:

- Past losses, such as loss of earnings, benefits and pension, less any earnings received.
- Future losses, such as loss of earnings, benefits and pension.
- Disadvantage on the labour market.[78]
- Injury to feelings.
- Personal injury.[79]
- Aggravated damages.
- Exemplary damages.
- Interest on past financial loss and injury to feelings.[80]

14.71 Injury to feelings awards are calculated in accordance with the guidance in *Vento v Chief Constable of Yorkshire*,[81] where the Court of Appeal indicated that awards for injury to feelings should be considered in three bands:

- The top band would normally be between £15,000 and £25,000 for the most serious cases, such as where there had been a lengthy campaign of discriminatory harassment on the grounds of sex or race. Only in the most exceptional case would an award exceed £25,000.
- The middle band would be between £5,000 and £15,000 and was to be used for serious cases which did not merit an award in the highest band.
- Awards of between £500 and £5,000 would be appropriate for less serious cases, such as where the act of discrimination was an isolated or one-off occurrence.

14.72 Aggravated damages are awarded where the complainant's sense of injury resulting from the manner of the discrimination is justifiably heightened by the

---

[77] SDA, s 65; RRA, s 56; DDA, s 17A; SOR, reg 30; RBR, reg 30; and AR, reg 38.

[78] *Smith v Manchester Corporation* (1974) 17 KIR 1, 118 Sol Jo 597, EAT.

[79] *Sheriff v Klyne Tugs (Lowestoft) Ltd* [1999] IRLR 481, CA.

[80] The Employment Tribunals (Interest on Awards in Discrimination Cases) Regulations 1996 (SI 1996/2803).

[81] [2003] IRLR 102, CA.

manner in which or motive for which the respondent acted as s/he did,[82] or where the conduct was high-handed, malicious, insulting or oppressive,[83] including the conduct of the litigation.[84]

Exemplary damages are intended to punish the perpetrator rather than to compensate the victim, and will only be awarded where the compensation otherwise available is inadequate to punish the wrongdoer. The ruling of the House of Lords in *Kuddus v Chief Constable of Leicestershire*,[85] as interpreted by the EAT in *Virgo Fidelis Senior School v Boyle*,[86] makes clear that such awards are available in discrimination cases. **14.73**

There is no express power under the equality enactments to order reinstate-ment or re-engagement but if the dismissal is also unfair, reinstatement or re-engagement can be ordered under the ERA. It is also arguable that the power to make recommendations includes the power to recommend reinstatement or re-engagement as the discretion to make recommendations is 'extremely wide'.[87] **14.74**

In a successful EqPA claim the ET will declare that an equality clause is to be read into the worker's contract with the effect that its terms are amended not to be less favourable than those of her comparator. The ET may also make an order for payment of up to six years' arrears of remuneration. **14.75**

An employer who has not complied with either of the statutory dispute reso-lution procedures runs the risk of any award being increased by between ten and 50 per cent unless there are exceptional circumstances which would make the ten per cent adjustment unjust or inequitable.[88] A recent high-profile example of this principle in operation was *Azmi v Kirklees Metropolitan Borough Council*[89] (the case involving the teaching assistant who wished to wear a veil to work, which we discuss in some detail in Chapter 10). The claimant succeeded in showing victimisation and was awarded £1,100 in damages, comprising of £1,000 for injury to feelings and an automatic £100 uplift for the employer's failure to comply with the statutory dispute resolution procedures. **14.76**

There is a limited costs regime applicable in the ET in that costs orders are generally only available if a party has behaved 'vexatiously, abusively, dis-ruptively or otherwise unreasonably' or the proceedings have been 'mis-conceived'.[90] However, in *Scott v Commissioners of Inland Revenue*[91] (which **14.77**

---

[82] *Broome v Cassell* [1972] AC 1027, HL.
[83] *Alexander v Home Office* [1988] 1 WLR 968, CA.
[84] *Armitage v Johnson* [1997] IRLR 163, EAT.
[85] [2002] 2 AC 122, HL.   [86] [2004] IRLR 268, EAT.
[87] *Chief Constable of West Yorkshire v Vento (No 2)* [2003] IRLR 102, CA.
[88] Employment Act 2002, s 31(3).   [89] [2007] IRLR 484, EAT.
[90] ET Rules, r 40.   [91] [2004] IRLR 713, CA.

we discuss further in Chapter 11 on harassment), the Court of Appeal warned employers that they do face a costs risk if they spitefully or unfairly use the Employment Tribunal process to pursue an unjust accusation that led to the act of discrimination in the first place. Such conduct also leaves an employer vulnerable to an award of aggravated damages being made against them.

14.78 Remedy in the County or High Court normally consists of an award of damages, or sometimes non-financial relief such as an injunction. In judicial review proceedings what is normally sought is an order quashing the respondent's actions and/or an order compelling them to remedy it. The costs regime in the County, High and Administrative Courts is more liberal and generally follows a 'loser pays' rule.

14.79 An unsuccessful party before the ET may appeal to the EAT on a point of law,[92] within 42 days from the date on which extended written reasons were sent to the parties. The civil court appeals regime is set out in CPR Part 52.

14.80 EAT cases and those on appeal in the civil courts are normally determined by written and oral legal submissions by the parties' representatives. There is normally no need to call witnesses live because the jurisdiction of the appellate courts is generally limited to determining whether the Tribunal or court of first instance erred in law, rather than whether it erred in its conclusions of fact on the evidence.

I. Alternative Dispute Resolution

14.81 Alternative Dispute Resolution ('ADR') is the collective term used to describe the various ways by which parties can settle civil disputes, without the need for a formal court or ET hearing, with the assistance of an independent third party.

14.82 There has been a much greater push towards ADR in recent years, because the following benefits it brings are increasingly recognised:

- Successful ADR is likely to save costs, particularly in ET cases where even the successful party can only recover costs in limited circumstances (see paragraph 14.77 above).
- It is likely to save substantial time that would otherwise be spent in preparing for attending an ET hearing.
- Successful ADR completed early on in the process can allow both sides to move on from the dispute in a way which may prevent the employment relationship from being damaged or irretrievably damaged.

---

[92] Employment Tribunals Act 1996, s 21.

- ADR can prevent both parties from becoming too entrenched in their own position as it reopens a dialogue to discussing and perhaps settling the dispute.
- Successful ADR saves both parties the stress of going through the ET process.
- ADR is confidential and so removes or reduces the risk of adverse publicity consequent upon a public ET hearing.

ACAS has in fact been offering ADR conciliation services to the ET system for many years. It is an independent statutory body governed by a Council consisting of the ACAS Chair and employer, trade union and independent members. Its aim is to improve organisations and working life through better employment relations. It does so by providing information, advice, training and a range of services working with employers and employees to prevent or resolve problems and improve performance. Recent figures indicate that ACAS saves the UK economy approximately £25 million each year through its services.[93] **14.83**

A key part of ACAS's role is its duty to conciliate in ET cases, and all ET claims are sent to ACAS.[94] Any discussions with ACAS are privileged and may not be used in evidence in the Tribunal. ACAS's website, <www.acas.org.uk>, provides a considerable amount of information about the services it provides. If ACAS does negotiate an agreement between the parties, the ACAS officer will draw up a binding agreement referred to as a COT3. **14.84**

In late June 2007, ACAS announced that it would begin offering its services in the EAT, particularly in cases where the parties' employment relationship is ongoing, where a case could be referred back to the ET if successful, or appeals relating to monetary awards.[95] **14.85**

In Northern Ireland, the Labour Relations Agency performs a similar role to that of ACAS. **14.86**

The possibility of a Judicial Mediation ('JM') scheme operating in ET cases is also being considered. In a JM, an ET chair (who will not ultimately hear the case at trial if the mediation fails) acts as mediator. JM will only take place if certain fundamental conditions are agreed by each party: **14.87**

- each party understands that it can withdraw from the JM at any time;
- the person attending must have the authority to make any decisions regarding settlement (ie the employer must provide a manager of sufficient

---

[93] 'ACAS widens its conciliation service to tribunal appeal cases', 29 June 2007; <www.acas.org.uk/index.asp?articleid=1302>.
[94] ET Rules, r 21.
[95] 'ACAS widens its conciliation service to tribunal appeal cases', 29 June 2007.

seniority to commit to a settlement proposal without having to refer it back to anyone else); and

- the content of the JM is confidential and cannot be used in a subsequent hearing if a settlement is not agreed.

14.88 A pilot scheme was started on 31 July 2006 for a period of 12 months in the Birmingham, London Central and Newcastle Employment Tribunals to measure the effect of JM on certain types of claims. The pilot scheme was limited to claims where the employment relationship was ongoing. Predominantly, the scheme focused on discrimination claims, specifically those under the SDA, RRA and DDA, although EqPA claims were also included in the Newcastle Employment Tribunals.

14.89 It will be interesting to see whether the pilot is successful, and leads to the rolling out of a JM scheme to all the ETs in the country. Indeed the Government is generally consulting as to how ADR might better be used in employment-related discrimination disputes.[96]

14.90 It is, of course, open to the parties to seek to resolve a claim between themselves at any stage without the involvement of any third party. If the parties do reach such an agreement, a compromise agreement is drawn up. Such an agreement will only be valid if:

- it is in writing;
- it relates to a specific complaint;
- the employee has received independent legal advice from a qualified lawyer or independent adviser who is insured to give such advice;
- the agreement identifies the adviser; and
- it states that the conditions regulating compromise agreements are satisfied.[97]

14.91 The CPR encourages the parties to seek settlement wherever they can, and some County Courts operate 'in-house' mediation schemes.

14.92 There are several commercial organisations offering the services of mediators, such as the Centre for Effective Dispute Resolution ('CEDR').

J. Litigation and Victimisation

14.93 Employers involved in litigation against current or former employees need constantly to be live to the risk of engaging in action which could be construed

---

[96] *Resolving Disputes in the Workplace: A Consultation* (DTI, March 2007).
[97] ERA, s 203; SDA, s 77; RRA, s 72; DDA, s 9; RBR, Sch 4, s 1; SOR, Sch 4, s 1; and AR, Sch 5, para 1.

as victimisation under the equality enactments, namely less favourable treatment of the claimant because they have done the 'protected act' of:

- bringing proceedings for discrimination;
- giving evidence or information in connection with discrimination proceedings (including those brought by others);
- alleging that the discriminator or any other person has done an act of discrimination (for example, by lodging an internal grievance or questionnaire alleging discrimination); or
- issuing a questionnaire, bringing proceedings, or giving evidence on behalf of someone who has.[98]

We discuss the elements of a victimisation claim in further detail at paragraphs **14.94** 2.80 to 2.84 above. For present purposes the recent case of *St Helens Metropolitan Borough Council v Derbyshire*[99] illustrates the risks for employers, and the key legal principles.

In the *St Helens* case, the employer had sought to head off EqPA claims by **14.95** sending letters to the claimants pointing out that they might be responsible for the loss of their colleagues' jobs if they won their claims, and sending similar letters to their colleagues. The House of Lords held that while employers are entitled to take reasonable steps to seek to settle claims, the employer's actions in this case crossed the line of acceptable behaviour and amounted to victimisation of the claimants. This was because the letters had led to the claimants experiencing indirect pressure, fear of 'public odium', or the reproaches of colleagues, which was just as likely to deter them from enforcing their claims as a direct threat would have been.

The House of Lords stressed that when deciding whether a person had been **14.96** victimised the court should focus on the 'detriment' allegedly suffered by that person, rather than whether the employer had acted honestly and reasonably (the test that had been suggested in *Chief Constable of West Yorkshire Police v Khan*[100]), albeit that in many cases the outcome will be the same.

In his judgment, Lord Hope counselled employers to ensure that they avoid **14.97** doing anything that might make a reasonable employee feel that s/he is being unduly pressurised to concede his or her claim. He stressed that an employer must have 'sensitivity to the wider effects of what he plans to do' as this will be 'crucial to the exercise of an informed judgment as to what is reasonable'.[101] Baroness Hale was more strident in her warning to employers. In expressing the

---

[98] SDA, s 5(1)(a); RRA, s 2(1)(a); RBR, reg 4; SOR, reg 4; and AR, para 4.
[99] [2007] ICR 841, HL.   [100] [2001] 4 All ER 834, HL.
[101] Per Lord Hope, para 27.

view that the *Ste Helens* case was a 'classic case of blaming the victims', she stressed that '. . . the victims of long-standing and deep-seated injustice should not be made to feel guilty if they pursue their claims for justice'. She urged employers to resist the temptation to do so, even where such claims inevitably had financial and other adverse consequences for a workforce.[102]

Managing litigation: In Brief

- We hope that many of the suggestions we have made in this book will lead to the risk of litigation being avoided or reduced. However, in some cases litigation is inevitable.

- Most discrimination cases are started in the Employment Tribunal ('ET') although some sorts of claims are brought in the County Court, High Court or Administrative Court.

- There are various pre-action processes which seek to ensure that disputes are resolved without the need for litigation.

- However, if they fail, an employer is normally put on formal notice of a claim by being served with a copy of the relevant claim form. The employer must then file a response within a short period of time.

- A three-month time limit applies to most discrimination claims but there are various ways in which the time limit can be extended.

- Generally an employer will be liable for all the acts of its employees if these were committed during the course of the employee's employment.

- The equality enactments provide an additional defence for an employer, namely that it took such steps as were 'reasonably practicable' to prevent the discrimination taking place.

- At present an employer cannot be liable for discrimination committed against its employees by third parties but the law is likely to change in this respect.

- A person who knowingly aids another to discriminate will also be liable for the discrimination.

---

[102] Per Baroness Hale, para 30.

- A principal is liable for any discrimination carried out by his or her agent.
- The ET is intended to be informal in its processes, but increasingly in reality it is becoming more like the general civil courts.
- There are various procedural steps to be taken between the commencing of a claim and a full hearing, including the disclosure of documents, the exchanging of witness statements, the obtaining of medical evidence, and other interlocutory steps.
- Recent case law has stressed that in discrimination cases it is particularly important for employers to advance clear and cogent evidence for their actions, in order to discharge the burden of proving that there has been no discrimination.
- The main remedies available in the ET are a declaration of discrimination, compensation or a recommendation for future action by the employer.
- Alternative Dispute Resolution ('ADR') is becoming increasingly popular in all the civil courts. ACAS have long provided conciliation services in ET cases. Judicial Mediation is currently being tested in a pilot scheme.
- Employers engaged in litigation must be conscious of the need not to engage in any act that might be considered victimisation of the claimant.

15

THE EQUALITY AND HUMAN RIGHTS COMMISSION AND A SINGLE EQUALITY ACT: THE FUTURE?

I look forward confidently to the day when all who work for a living will be one with no thought to their separateness as Negroes, Jews, Italians or any other distinctions. This will be the day when we bring into full realization the American dream—a dream yet unfulfilled. A dream of equality of opportunity, of privilege and property widely distributed; a dream of a land where men will not take necessities from the many to give luxuries to the few; a dream of a land where men will not argue that the color of a man's skin determines the content of his character; a dream of a nation where all our gifts and resources are held not for ourselves alone, but as instruments of service for the rest of humanity; the dream of a country where every man will respect the dignity and worth of the human personality.

(Dr Martin Luther King, Jr, in a speech to the AFL–CIO[1] Convention, 1961)

A. Introduction

As this book goes to print, the British discrimination law landscape continues **15.01** to be in a state of flux: the EHRC, formerly known as the CEHR, is beginning its role; and promise of a Single Equality Act, which would provide a more accessible and consistent source of discrimination legislation, appears closer than ever. In this chapter we consider these developments and offer our thoughts on the road ahead.

B. The EHRC

Established by section 1 of the EA this new body corporate takes on the work of **15.02**

---

[1] The AFL–CIO is the American Federation of Labor–Congress of Industrial Organizations, a voluntary federation of 66 unions in the United States.

the dissolved[2] former commissions (the CRE, EOC and DRC) with additional responsibilities in relation to the three newer strands of discrimination (sexual orientation, religion or belief and age) and human rights.

(a) Setting Up the EHRC

15.03 A significant part of the pressure for the establishment of the EHRC came from the introduction into domestic law of the prohibition of discrimination on grounds of sexual orientation, religion or belief and age (via the SOR, RBR and AR) in the wake of the Employment Directive.[3] While the Directive does not in terms require the establishment of statutory commissions along the lines of the EOC, CRE and DRC, the lack of any such bodies to deal with discrimination on grounds of sexual orientation, religion or belief and age created an appearance of unfairness and pressure for reform.

15.04 The Government was confronted with a choice between creating three new commissions, assigning the new grounds to the former commissions' remits (sexual orientation with sex, for example, religion and belief with race and age with disability) or amalgamating the commissions. It chose the last of these options.

15.05 The Government was also facing pressure to establish a human rights commission from those who had been the original architects of the Human Rights Act 1998, and who saw the setting up of such a commission as an essential component of a three-pronged system for the protection of human rights in this country, together with the passing of the Act itself and the establishment of the Parliamentary Joint Committee on Human Rights. To that extent, the setting up of a commission was seen as 'unfinished business'. However, the creation of a commission solely concerned with human rights (as the term is generally understood in the UK) ultimately became unlikely, and those agitating for one accepted the Government's proposal to add human rights to the remit of the proposed equality commission on the basis that, put simply, part of a commission was better than no commission at all.

15.06 The proposal for a single commission was put forward by the Government in its *Towards Equality and Diversity; Making it Happen* consultation in October 2002, followed by its White Paper, *Fairness for All: A New Commission for Equality and Human Rights* in March 2004.

15.07 The EOC and DRC both expressed concerns about the proposals for the Commission—in particular the 'light touch' emphasis of the White Paper, the

---

[2] The power to dissolve the former Commissions is in the Equality Act 2006, s 36.
[3] Council Directive 2000/78/EC.

adequacy of resources intended to be made available to the EHRC, the absence of any commitment to harmonised equality legislation and the apparent narrowing of the commissions' powers to conduct formal investigations and to support litigation. The CRE was even more trenchant in its criticism, and rejected the proposed commission outright, stating that it was 'less a single champion enforcing strong legislation, and more a hopeful chorus of voices, which [*Fairness For All*] speculates can be made to sing in tune'.[4]

Amendments made between the White Paper and the publication of the Equal-   **15.08**
ity Bill in 2004 resulted in a change of heart on the part of the CRE, which in June 2005 declared that it welcomed the Equality Bill. These amendments included the delay until April 2009 of the CRE's incorporation into the EHRC (albeit that this was later brought forward—see paragraph 15.19 below). The EA received Royal Assent on 16 February 2006.

(b) Constitution of the EHRC

(i) Commissioners

Although the EHRC is independent of Government, it is not completely   **15.09**
beyond the influence of Government. For a start, the Commissioners, of which there can be between ten and 15,[5] are appointed by the Secretary of State. In appointing a Commissioner the Secretary of State must think that the individual has experience or knowledge of one or more of the six strands of discrimination or human rights or is suitable for appointment for some other special reason.[6] The Secretary of State must also have regard when making appointments to the desirability of the Commissioners together having experience and knowledge relating, in particular, to all six strands of discrimination and human rights.[7]

Broadly therefore, there are seven subject areas (the six strands and human   **15.10**
rights) and up to 15 Commissioners. Looking at this rather simplistically, dividing one number into the other, this means that there is scope for appointing approximately two Commissioners for each subject area. If the Secretary of State appoints outside of this balance, he or she could be accused of placing more emphasis on one subject area over another and the EHRC could lose the confidence of those with an interest in any subject area perceived as being of lower priority. Even if the balance of Commissioners is symmetrically maintained, there remains scope, given that they are relatively few in number, for Commissioners to be absent from meetings and for meetings therefore to be

---

[4] *Fairness for All: A New Commission for Equality and Human Rights, A Response* (CRE, August 2004).
[5] EA, Sch 1, para 1(1).   [6] EA, Sch 1, para 2(1)(a).   [7] EA, Sch 1, para 2(1)(b).

deprived of the benefit of the experience and knowledge of a particular subject area.

15.11 The Secretary of State also needs to ensure that the Commission includes:

- a Commissioner who is (or has been) disabled;
- a Commissioner appointed with the consent of Scottish Ministers, who knows about conditions in Scotland; and
- a Commissioner appointed with the consent of the National Assembly for Wales, who knows about conditions in Wales.[8]

15.12 Commissioners must be appointed for a fixed term of not less than two years, nor more than five.[9] Commissioners can be reappointed on expiry of their term of office. Commissioners can resign early by notice given to the Secretary of State[10] and the Secretary of State can dismiss a Commissioner who is, in his or her opinion, unable, unfit or unwilling to perform his or her functions.[11]

15.13 The Secretary of State shall appoint one of the Commissioners as Chair and another as Deputy Chair.[12] Anachronistically, and notwithstanding section 6 of the Interpretation Act 1978, the EA refers to the appointment of a Chair*man* and Deputy Chair*man*!

15.14 The Chair's role is to preside over meetings of the Commission, perform such functions as may be specified in his or her appointment and any other functions assigned to him or her by the Commission.[13] The Deputy's role is to act for the Chair when he or she is unavailable and perform such functions as are specified in the terms of his or her appointment and such functions as the Chair may delegate or assign to him or her.[14]

(ii) Appointment of First Chair

15.15 On 8 September 2006 Ruth Kelly, Secretary of State for Communities and Local Government, announced the appointment of Trevor Phillips, then Chair of the CRE, as the Chair of the new Commission for Equality and Human Rights. In announcing the appointment, Ruth Kelly said:

> Trevor Phillips is the best man [sic!] for the job. He has a proven track record, a wealth of experience and is prepared to tackle the difficult and controversial issues head on. This will be a valuable asset right across the whole equalities.

15.16 Mr Phillips's appointment was not, however, universally welcomed. There were

---

[8] EA, Sch 1, para 2(3).   [9] EA, Sch 1, para 3(2).   [10] EA, Sch 1, para 3(4).
[11] EA, Sch 1, para 3(5).   [12] EA, Sch 1, para 4(1).   [13] EA, Sch 1, para 4(2).
[14] EA, Sch 1, para 4(3).

some who felt that his three years as Chair of the CRE had not been successful and that his public statements in the media about, for example, the 'death of multiculturalism', had led to an unfortunate shift in the discrimination debate from a fight against racism and a positive acknowledgement of diversity, to a criticism of the individual for failing to integrate. For example, Black Information Link reported a leak of his appointment on 1 September 2006, beginning its article 'New Labour's Trevor Phillips has been appointed chairman of the Commission for Equality and Human Rights, to the dismay of anti-racism campaigners.'

The appointment was made in accordance with the Office for the Commissioner for Public Appointments Code of Practice. In accordance with that Code all appointments are made on merit and political activity plays no part in the selection process. However, in accordance with the original Nolan recommendations, there is a requirement for an appointee's political activity to be made public. Trevor Phillips confirmed that he had 'obtained office as a member of the London Assembly representing the Labour Party'.   **15.17**

His appointment was therefore controversial, because he was Chair of the CRE moving to the EHRC (which needed to be sensitive to competing demands of all of the strands plus human rights), because of his track record, and because of his political affinity.   **15.18**

The appointment did, however, pave the way to the CRE being brought into the EHRC at an earlier stage. Originally the CRE had negotiated a later entry to the EHRC than the EOC or DRC, with its entry delayed until April 2009. With Trevor Phillips's appointment, the CRE quickly changed its position and joined the EHRC from October 2007 at the same time as the EOC and DRC.   **15.19**

(iii) Appointment of First Commissioners

On 5 December 2006 a number of further appointments were announced. Those appointed Commissioners were: **15.20**

- EHRC Deputy Chair—Baroness Margaret Prosser of Battersea OBE, who has 20 years' experience as a senior trade union official with the Transport and General Workers Union, and who was TUC President in 1995/1996 and an EOC Commissioner from 1985 to 1992.

- Kay Allen—a diversity specialist with over 16 years' direct experience in diversity management, who in January 2000 was appointed as a DRC Commissioner.

- Dame Jane Campbell DBE—an independent health and social care policy adviser, who is Chair of the Office for Disability Issues (ODI) Independent

Living Review Expert Panel, and was a DRC Commissioner from its inception in 2000.

- Kay Carberry—who was appointed Assistant General Secretary of the TUC in January 2003, having previously been the first head of the TUC's Equal Rights Department, and an EOC Commissioner from 1999.

- Baroness Greengross OBE—Director General of Age Concern England from 1987 until 2000, and now their Vice President, who until 2000 was also joint Chair of the Age Concern Institute of Gerontology at Kings College, London and Secretary General of Eurolink Age.

- Francesca Klug—Professorial Research Fellow at the Centre for the Study of Human Rights at the London School of Economics.

- Ziauddin Sardar—writer, broadcaster and academic who has written extensively about issues of human rights, equality and community.

- Ben Summerskill—Chief Executive of Stonewall from March 2003, who from 2004 was a member of the steering group appointed by the Secretary of State to support establishment of the EHRC.

- Dr Neil Wooding—the first equality adviser to be appointed in Wales, who during the course of his career successfully established the NHS Centre for Equality and Human Rights. He is also currently the Equal Opportunities Commissioner for Wales, the Co-Chair of Stonewall Cymru, a Trustee of the National Aids Trust and a Non-Executive Director of South East Wales Race Equality Council.

15.21 On the same day, Ruth Kelly also announced the appointment of three 'Transition Commissioners'—one from each of the existing equality commissions—whose role was to support the Chair and Commissioners through their knowledge and experience of equality and diversity issues. The Transition Commissioners were Jeannie Drake (EOC), Kay Hampton (CRE) and Bert Massie (DRC).

15.22 On 29 March 2007, Morag Alexander was appointed as the Scotland Commissioner.[15] She was appointed the first Convener (Chair) of the Scottish Social Services Council in 2001. She was also director of the Equal Opportunities Commission, Scotland from 1992 to 2001.

(iv) Procedure

15.23 Subject to the terms of Schedule 1 of the Equality Act 2006, it is for the EHRC to regulate its own proceedings.[16] It is for the EHRC, acting through at least five Commissioners, to determine the quorum for its meetings.[17]

---

[15] EA, Sch 1, para 2(3)(b).   [16] EA, Sch 1, para 5.   [17] EA, Sch 1, para 6.

(v) Staff

The Commission shall appoint a Chief Executive and may appoint other staff.[18] In the case of the Chief Executive the appointment requires the consent of the Secretary of State.[19] The Chief Executive is a Commissioner ex officio[20] but cannot also be appointed Chair or Deputy Chair of the EHRC.[21] Dr Nicola Brewer was appointed the EHRC's first Chief Executive in December 2006. She took up her appointment on the 5 March 2007. Prior to joining the EHRC, she was Director General (Europe) at the Foreign and Commonwealth Office. As far as other staff are concerned, their number and their terms and conditions must be consistent with arrangements determined by the EHRC and approved by the Secretary of State.[22] **15.24**

(vi) Investigating Commissioners

The EHRC may, with the consent of the Secretary of State, appoint 'Investigating Commissioners'[23] to carry out an inquiry (EA, section 16), carry out an investigation (section 20), give an unlawful act notice (section 21) or enter into an agreement (section 23). Notwithstanding their title, such individuals are not actually EHRC Commissioners. **15.25**

(vii) Committees

The EHRC may establish both advisory and decision-making committees.[24] Advisory committees advise either the EHRC generally or an Investigating Commissioner and may comprise Commissioners, staff and other non-Commissioners. Decision-making committees can again be comprised of Commissioners, staff and other non-Commissioners. The EHRC may delegate functions to a decision-making committee.[25] **15.26**

The EA requires the EHRC to establish at least three decision-making committees: **15.27**

- the Scotland Committee;[26]
- the Wales Committee;[27] and
- the Disability Committee.[28]

One of the main functions of the Scotland and Wales Committees is to advise the EHRC about the exercise of its functions in so far as they affect Scotland and Wales respectively.[29] Before exercising a function which in the EHRC's **15.28**

---

[18] EA, Sch 1, para 7. [19] EA, Sch 1, para 7(2). [20] EA, Sch 1, para 1(2).
[21] EA, Sch 1, para 4(6). [22] EA, Sch 1, para 7(3). [23] EA, Sch 1, para 9.
[24] EA, Sch 1, paras 11 and 12. [25] EA, Sch 1, para 15(1).
[26] EA, Sch 1, para 16(1). [27] EA, Sch 1, para 24(1). [28] EA, Sch 1, para 49(1).
[29] EA, Sch 1, paras 19 and 27.

opinion is likely to affect persons in Scotland or Wales, the EHRC must consult the relevant Committee.[30]

15.29 The only strand which Parliament decided should definitely have its own committee is disability. A number of functions, so far as they relate to disability, are specifically delegated to the Disability Committee,[31] such as giving advice and information, issuing codes of practice and offering legal assistance. At least half of its members, who may be between seven and nine in number, must be people who have, or have had, a disability.[32] The Chair of the Committee must be, or have been, disabled.[33] The Committee is given a broad remit to advise the EHRC about the exercise of its functions in so far as they affect disabled people, including in particular in so far as they relate to Part 2 of the DDA (the employment provisions).[34]

15.30 The life of the Disability Committee may, however, be finite. Paragraphs 57 to 63 of Schedule 1 to the EA make provision for a five-year review of the activities of the Disability Committee leading to a report which, in particular, recommends for how long the Committee should continue in existence. The implication of these paragraphs read together is that the current differential treatment afforded to disability is not something which Parliament wanted to see continuing indefinitely

(c) The EHRC's Role

15.31 In carrying out its functions, the EHRC's general duty is to encourage and support the development of a society in which:

- people's ability to achieve their potential is not limited by prejudice or discrimination;
- there is respect for and protection of each individual's human rights;
- there is respect for the dignity and worth of each individual;
- each individual has an equal opportunity to participate in society; and
- there is mutual respect between groups based on understanding and valuing of diversity and on shared respect for equality and human rights.[35]

15.32 These are the outcomes for society that the EHRC is required to work towards: they are the EHRC's 'mission statement'. Whatever concerns there may be as to how such 'outcomes' could ever be realistically measured, it should be recognised that this fundamental duty represents the rationale of the EHRC as

---

[30] EA, Sch 1, paras 20 and 28.   [31] EA, Sch 1, para 52.
[32] EA, Sch 1, paras 50(1)(a) and (b).   [33] EA, Sch 1, para 50(1)(c).
[34] EA, Sch 1, para 54.   [35] EA, s 3.

combining work in equality, human rights and good relations between groups within society.

There is a clear division in the EA between the 'equality and diversity' duties (section 8) and the 'human rights' duties (section 9), but the positive preamble in section 3 illustrates in a pragmatic sense the academic recognition that working towards equality and working towards the eradication of breaches of human rights is often (albeit not always) one and the same thing. **15.33**

(d) The EHRC's Strategic Plan

The EHRC must produce a strategic plan showing: **15.34**

- what it will do;
- when it will do it; and
- what or how it will prioritise.[36]

Before preparing this strategic plan the EHRC must consult persons who have knowledge or experience relevant to the EHRC's functions as the EHRC thinks appropriate[37] and such other persons as the EHRC thinks appropriate.[38] It must also issue a general invitation to make representations. That general invitation must be issued in such a way that it is, in the EHRC's opinion, likely to be brought to the attention of as large a class of people who may wish to make representations as is reasonably practicable.[39] In carrying out the consultation and receiving representations, the EHRC is obliged to take account of any representations made.[40] **15.35**

The EHRC must review, and if it thinks appropriate revise, its strategic plan at least once in every three-year period. The first period begins with completion of the plan and then each subsequent period begins with the completion of a review.[41] The same obligations to consult and invite representations as apply before preparing the strategic plan also apply before reviewing the plan.[42] **15.36**

The legislation therefore ties the EHRC to a considerable amount of consultation and consideration of feedback in the drafting and amending of its strategic plan. Although this is not consultation 'with a view to seeking agreement' the requirement to 'take account of any representations made' elevates this exercise above 'inform, listen, ignore'. The architects of the strategic plan will, however, need to draft in sufficient flexibility to enable the EHRC to react appropriately to sudden changes in priority. A strategic plan, for example, drafted on 10 September 2001 would have no doubt needed swift amendment a day **15.37**

---

[36] EA, s 4. [37] EA, s 5(a). [38] EA, s 5(b). [39] EA, s 5(c).
[40] EA, s 5(d). [41] EA, s 4(2). [42] EA, s 5.

later when the World Trade Centre in New York was destroyed and the need for a strong lead on the protection from discrimination on grounds of religion and ethnicity became more immediately relevant.

(e) The EHRC's Duties

15.38 Sections 8 to 12 of the EA set out the EHRC's duties.

(i) Equality and Diversity

15.39 Section 8(1) requires the EHRC to use its powers to:

> (a) promote understanding of the importance of equality and diversity;
> (b) encourage good practice in relation to equality and diversity;
> (c) promote equality of opportunity;
> (d) promote awareness and understanding of rights under the equality enactments;
> (e) enforce the equality enactments;
> (f) work towards the elimination of unlawful discrimination; and
> (g) work towards the elimination of unlawful harassment.

15.40 Each limb of section 8(1) other than (d) and (e) applies more broadly than to the 'equality enactments' as defined in section 33(1) to cover, for example, the RRA, the SDA and the DDA.

15.41 Section 8(2) contains the first legal definition of 'diversity' being 'the fact that individuals are different' with 'equality' defined as 'equality between individuals'.

15.42 Recognising the unique nature of the disability strand, in promoting equality of opportunity between disabled persons and others, the EHRC may, in particular, promote the favourable treatment of disabled persons.[43]

(ii) Human Rights

15.43 The EHRC's duties in respect of human rights are to:

> (a) promote understanding of the importance of human rights;
> (b) encourage good practice in relation to human rights;
> (c) promote awareness, understanding and protection of human rights; and
> (d) encourage public authorities to comply with section 6 of the HRA (which prohibits them from acting in a way which is incompatible with the Convention rights).[44]

15.44 The final human rights duty above applies only to public authorities but the others apply equally to the private and voluntary sectors. The EHRC will, for example, also be able to provide encouragement to the private and voluntary

---

[43] EA, s 8(3).   [44] EA, s 9(1).

sectors and so could, for example, provide guidance to private employers as to how to respect freedom of expression in the workplace.

'Human rights' are defined[45] as meaning the Convention rights within the **15.45** meaning given by section 1 of the Human Rights Act 1998 and 'other human rights'. It is therefore clear that, where 'other human rights' instruments—such as the Convention on the Elimination of All Forms of Discrimination Against Women (CEDAW), the Convention on the Elimination of All Forms of Racial Discrimination (CERD), and the various texts propounded in the employment context by the International Labour Organization—afford more extensive discrimination protection than Article 14, they must be considered by the Commission.

Although the reference to 'other human rights' gives the EHRC a broader **15.46** remit, the EHRC must have particular regard to the importance of exercising its powers in relation to the Convention rights.[46] The EHRC must also take account of relevant human rights when fulfilling its duties under sections 8 (equality and diversity described above) and 10 (groups described below).

(iii) Groups

The EHRC must also exercise its powers to: **15.47**

    (a) promote understanding of the importance of good relations between members of different groups and between members of groups and others;

    (b) encourage good practice in relation to relations between members of different groups and between members of groups and others;

    (c) work towards the elimination of prejudice against, hatred of and hostility towards members of groups; and

    (d) work towards enabling members of groups to participate in society.[47]

The obligation to 'promote' an understanding of the importance of good **15.48** relations between members of different groups and between members of groups and others goes well beyond the requirement to disseminate information about the same. The UN Paris Principles on National Institutions for the Protection and Promotion of Human Rights[48] dictates that 'promotion' is the primary competence required of national human rights commissions, and the equality and diversity element of the EHRC has clearly benefited from that requirement. It is envisaged that the EHRC will develop 'a databank of good practice case studies' and 'sector specific toolkits' to tackle areas of particular challenge for equality and human rights.[49]

---

    [45] EA, s 9(2).   [46] EA, s 9(3).   [47] EA, s 10.
    [48] UN Doc. A/RES/48/143 (20 December 1993).
    [49] *Fairness for All: A New Commission for Equality and Human Rights* (Women and Equality Unit, May 2004), paras 7.51 and 7.54.

15.49 The concept of a 'group' is defined as being a group or class of persons who share a common attribute in respect of age; disability; gender; proposed, commenced or completed reassignment of gender; race; religion or belief or sexual orientation.[50] This definition includes subgroups who share common attributes.[51] Such subgroups might include for example, 'disabled women' or 'gay Muslims'. There is no requirement that a particular group or subgroup needs to be organised into a lobby or be recognisable as a community—there simply needs to be a class of persons who share a particular attribute or attributes.

15.50 The wording of the statute suggests that the definition of a group extends only to two common attributes: 'a common attribute' to define a group (section 10(2)) and 'a common attribute' to define a smaller group within that group (section 10(3)). There seems little logic in stopping at two attributes other than that the subgroups would inevitably get smaller the more attributes are applied, for example: gay, disabled, Muslim men or young, black, Christian women.

15.51 The EHRC should have particular regard to the need to exercise its powers in relation to groups defined by reference to race, religion or belief.[52] This provision is a legacy of the work done by local racial equality councils, previously supported by the CRE.

15.52 In carrying out its group-related duties, the EHRC may promote or encourage the favourable treatment of disabled people.[53]

(iv) Monitoring the Law

15.53 The EHRC is required to monitor the effectiveness of the equality and human rights legislation. It may in addition advise central Government on the effectiveness of that legislation and recommend the amendment, repeal, consolidation or replication of any of that legislation.[54] It may also advise central Government, Scottish Ministers and the Welsh Assembly about the effect of any legislation and about the likely effect of a proposed change in the law.[55] It is likely that in the exercise of this duty the EHRC will place a key role in the development of any Single Equality Act which we discuss further below.

(v) Monitoring Progress

15.54 Section 12 of the EA introduced legal definitions to two concepts that had long been part of the vocabulary of those working in the area of equality and diversity:

- 'outcomes'—meaning results at which to aim for the purpose of encouraging

---

[50] EA, s 10(2). [51] EA, s 10(3). [52] EA, s 10(4).
[53] EA, s 10(5). [54] EA, s 11. [55] EA, ss 11(2)(c) and (d).

and supporting the development a society described in the EHRC's general duty at section 3;[56] and

- 'indicators'—meaning factors by reference to which progress towards those results may be measured.[57]

The EHRC is obliged by section 12 to identify, from time to time, changes in **15.55** society that have occurred or are expected to occur and are relevant to the section 3 general duty and 'outcomes' and 'indicators'. In identifying those outcomes and indictors the EHRC must carry out the same consultation and general invitation to make representations exercise as required by section 5 when preparing or reviewing its strategic plan (discussed above).[58]

The EHRC is then required, from time to time, to monitor progress towards **15.56** each outcome by reference to any relevant identified indicator[59] and to publish a progress report within three years of section 12 coming into force[60] and then within each period of three years beginning with the date on which the previous report was published.[61]

(f) The EHRC's General Powers

Sections 13 to 19 of the EA set out the general powers the EHRC has, in order **15.57** to meet its duties.

(i) Information

The EHRC has the power, either alone or in partnership with others, to publish **15.58** or otherwise disseminate ideas and information, undertake research, provide education or training and give advice or guidance (other than advice or guidance in relation to preparing documents for use in legal proceedings).[62] We hope that the EHRC is as successful in this regard as its predecessor commissions were—a recent Public Interest Research Unit report concluded that the former commissions '. . . have performed an important role in: commissioning research, providing information and guidance to the public and organisations; and helping to keep discrimination and equality issues on the political agenda'.[63]

(ii) Codes of Practice

The EHRC assumed the powers of the former Commissions to issue codes **15.59** of practice in relation to the sex, race and disability strands and was given

---

[56] EA, s 12(1)(b).   [57] EA, s 12(1)(c).   [58] EA, s 12(2).   [59] EA, s 12(c).
[60] At the time of going to print no commencement date had been appointed.
[61] EA, s 12(4).   [62] EA, s 13.
[63] 'Teeth and Their Use—The Enforcement Action by the Three Equality Commissions' (Public Interest Research Unit, 2006, <www.piru.org.uk>), reported in 'Equality Bodies Failing to Enforce Discrimination Law', EOR (October 2006) 157, pp 2–3 ('PIRU article').

additional power to issue codes of practice in relation to sexual orientation, religion or belief and age.[64] The aims of these codes of practice are to ensure compliance with the legislation and promote equality of opportunity.[65] As with the codes of practice issued by the former commissions, a breach of any code issued by the EHRC will not of itself render a person liable to criminal or civil proceedings, but shall be admissible in evidence in criminal or civil proceedings, and shall be taken into account by a court or tribunal in any case in which it appears to the court or tribunal to be relevant.[66]

15.60 Before issuing a code of practice the EHRC is obliged to publish proposals and consult such persons as it thinks appropriate.[67] This is a rather less onerous exercise in engaging with interested parties than those envisaged for the preparation or review of the EHRC's strategic plan (under section 5) or identifying outcomes and indicators (under section 12).

(iii) Inquiries

15.61 Under section 13 the EHRC has the power to conduct an inquiry into any matter relating to its duties under sections 8, 9 and 10. Such inquiries are precluded from considering whether or not any person has committed an unlawful act,[68] and the reports of these inquiries may not allege that anyone has done so.[69] There is provision, if a draft report contains other comments of an adverse nature which relate (whether expressly or by necessary implication) to a specified or identifiable person, for that person to be given a chance to make representations on the draft, and for the EHRC to consider any representations made.[70]

15.62 Although it is clear that these inquiries are intended to be inquisitorial rather than adversarial, we hope that this power will be used widely and effectively by the EHRC. The Explanatory Notes to the Equality Bill indicated, in a promising fashion, that such inquiries could be 'thematic' (for example, into the causes of unequal outcomes) or 'sectoral' (looking at inequality in, for example, the uptake of health screening services or at the employment of disabled people in particular sectors, for instance, eg the retail sector). Reference was also made to the ability of such investigations to relate to one or more named parties, but the efficacy of this now seems limited by the provisions precluding investigation into or comment on whether any named party has committed an unlawful act.

15.63 We will be particularly interested to see the role that the EHRC plays in this regard on the issue of 'intersectional' or 'multiple' discrimination—that being discrimination which crosses the various strands. The current domestic law structure has real conceptual limitations, because it fails to recognise this very

---

[64] EA, s 14.   [65] EA, s 14(2).   [66] EA, s 15(4).
[67] EA, s 14(6).   [68] EA, s 16(2)(a).   [69] EA, s 16(3)(a).   [70] EA, s 16(5).

real concept—for example, a black gay woman who complains of discrimination may not know, or be able to prove, that any less favourable treatment to which she has been subjected was on grounds of her race, orientation or gender, or a combination of all three elements, yet under the current statutory regime she would need to prove (or her employer disprove) each element separately. The Department for Trade and Industry has acknowledged that '. . . [a]s individuals, our identities are diverse, complex and multi-layered. People don't see themselves as solely a woman, or black or gay and neither should our equality organisations'.[71] Research by the Ontario Human Rights Commission has indicated that just under half of all its cases concern multiple discrimination[72] and, if a similar pattern is present in the UK, the existence of a commission capable of providing a response to intersectional or multiple discrimination is crucial.

It is therefore crucial that the EHRC develops a role in understanding and combating such intersectional or multiple discrimination. We therefore welcome the fact that in addition to sector-specific inquiries, the EHRC will have competence to examine issues cutting across different equality strands and human rights. This is all the more pressing given that the Government, as far as its Discrimination Law Review consultation paper is concerned, is not currently persuaded that it should extend the law to make multiple discrimination actionable in itself[73] (see further below). **15.64**

(iv) Grants, Partnership with Human Rights Organisations, and Work with Regard to Particular Groups

The EHRC has power to make financial grants to any other person in pursuance of its duties under sections 8 to 10,[74] and—in pursuance of its duties under section 9—to cooperate with persons interested in human rights within the United Kingdom or elsewhere.[75] These powers may lead to the provision of financial assistance to bodies within the UK working on discrete local issues relating to equality and discrimination issues; and to partnership between the EHRC and other bodies in the world whose remit embraces equality and diversity law.[76] **15.65**

---

[71] DTI press release, 29 October 2003.

[72] See G Moon, 'Multiple Discrimination and the EHRC: a Strategy for Success', JUSTICE Bulletin, Autumn 2005, p 5.

[73] DLR consultation paper, paras 7.33–7.34.

[74] EA, s 16. [75] EA, s 17.

[76] There is much to be learned, for example, from the way in which the Canadian discrimination jurisprudence has developed, as discussed in G Moon, 'From Equal Treatment to Appropriate Treatment: What Lessons Can Canadian Equality Law on Dignity and on Reasonable Accommodation Teach the United Kingdom?' EHRLR (2006) 6, pp 695–721.

15.66 The EHRC also has the power to make, cooperate with or assist in arrangements for the monitoring of kinds of crime affecting certain groups; designed to prevent or reduce crime within or affecting certain groups; and for activities (whether social, recreational, sporting, civic, educational or otherwise) designed to involve members of groups.[77] These sorts of activities, although not directly related to the employment sphere, seek to work towards the sort of substantive societal equality which should ultimately lead to an improvement in workplace conditions in this regard.

(g) The EHRC's Enforcement Powers

15.67 Sections 20 to 32 of the EA set out the EHRC's enforcement powers.

(i) Investigations

15.68 Although the EHRC is precluded in its general investigative power under section 16 from enquiring into or commenting on whether any person has committed an unlawful act, that power is specifically provided for in section 20. This enables the EHRC to investigate whether any person has committed an unlawful act,[78] has complied with a requirement imposed by an unlawful act notice under section 21, or has complied with an undertaking given under section 23.[79] The investigative power is triggered if, but only if, the EHRC suspects that the person concerned may have committed an unlawful act,[80] namely a breach of the equality enactments. That suspicion may, but does not have to, arise as a result of a section 16 inquiry.[81] Again there is provision to permit those criticised in a draft report to comment on the same and a requirement that the EHRC take those representations into account.[82] Schedule 2 to the EA makes further provision for the carrying out of investigations under section 20.

15.69 The section 20 power is similar to the powers held by the former commissions to conduct formal investigations into individuals or organisations. However, the same Public Interest Research Unit report that was so complimentary of the former commissions' ability to disseminate information (see above) was highly critical of the lack of use they made of their enforcement powers, particularly in the latter years of their existence. The CRE, for example, had carried out 25 formal investigations in the first half of the 1980s, but just three from 2000 to 2005—a decrease of 800 per cent. As at July 2006 the CRE had no formal

---

[77] EA, s 19.
[78] This is defined as an act contrary to the equality enactments, other than the general duties therein—EA, s 34.
[79] EA, s 20(1).   [80] EA, s 20(2).   [81] EA, s 20(3).   [82] EA, s 20(4).

investigations ongoing, leading the author of the report to comment that '. . . the [CRE] is set to continue until 2009 [as it then was], but it appears to have already begun packing away its enforcement powers. It needs to remember that it has a statutory duty to enforce the equality enactments . . .'[83]

(ii) Unlawful Act Notices, Action Plans, Agreements and Applications to Court

If during the course of a section 20 investigation, the EHRC is satisfied that a **15.70** person has committed an unlawful act, then the EHRC may serve an unlawful act notice on that person.[84] The notice must specify the unlawful act and the provision of the equality enactments by virtue of which the act is unlawful.[85] It may also require the person to whom the notice is given to prepare an action plan for the purpose of avoiding repetition or continuation of the unlawful act; and/or recommend action to be taken by the person for that purpose.[86]

Section 22 makes further provisions for the preparation of action plans. The **15.71** unlawful act notice will specify a period of time by which the recipient must provide a draft action plan.[87]

If the recipient does not provide an action plan the EHRC may apply to a **15.72** County Court for an order that they do so.[88]

If such an action plan is provided, the EHRC must either approve the draft **15.73** action plan, or give the person a notice which states that the draft is not adequate, requires the person to give the Commission a revised draft by a specified time, and may make recommendations about the content of the revised draft.[89] The EHRC can apply to a County Court for an order requiring a person who has given the Commission a revised draft plan to prepare and give to the Commission a further revised draft plan by a time specified in the order and in accordance with any directions about the plan's content specified in the order.[90] In the absence of the EHRC issuing a notice in response to a draft action plan, or applying to the County Court in this way, or if the Court declines to make the order sought by the EHRC under section 21(6)(b), the action plan will come into force within six weeks of the draft or revised draft being provided to the EHRC.[91]

There is provision for the variation of action plans by agreement between the **15.74** EHRC and the person who prepared it.[92]

Finally, the EHRC has the power to apply to a County Court at any time **15.75**

---

[83] PIRU article, p 2.   [84] EA, s 21(1).   [85] EA, s 21(2).
[86] EA, s 21(4).   [87] EA, s 22(2).   [88] EA, s 22(6)(a).
[89] EA, s 22(3).   [90] EA, s 22(6)(b).   [91] EA, s 22(5)(a).   [92] EA, s 22(7).

within five years of the coming into force of the action plan for an order requiring the person to act in accordance with the action plan or to take specified action for a similar purpose.[93]

15.76 It is a summary offence, punishable with a fine not exceeding level 5 on the standard scale, to refuse to comply with any County Court orders obtained under section 21(6) without reasonable excuse.[94]

15.77 There is a right of appeal, within six weeks, against the issuing of an unlawful act notice, on the grounds either that the unlawful act has not been committed, or that any requirement for the preparation of an action plan under section 21(4)(a) is unreasonable.[95] In cases alleging acts contrary to the equality enactments, such an appeal is to the Employment Tribunal,[96] and the Tribunal has a full range of powers to affirm, annul or vary a notice or requirement, and to make an order for costs or expenses.[97]

15.78 The EHRC has the power, if it thinks a person has committed an unlawful act, to enter into an agreement with that person under which:

• the person undertakes not to commit an unlawful act of a specified kind, and to take, or refrain from taking, other specified action (which may include the preparation of a plan for the purpose of avoiding an unlawful act); and
• the EHRC undertakes not to proceed against the person under section 20 or 21 in respect of any unlawful act of the kind specified in the agreement.[98]

An agreement under section 23 may be entered into whether or not the person is or has been the subject of an investigation under section 20; may include incidental or supplemental provision (which may include provision for termination in specified circumstances), and may be varied or terminated by agreement of the parties.[99] The DRC previously made only three such agreements in exercise of its similar power between 2000 and 2005.[100]

15.79 If the EHRC thinks that a person is likely to commit an unlawful act, it has the power to apply in England and Wales to a County Court for an injunction restraining the person from committing the act, or in Scotland to the Sheriff for an interdict, prohibiting the person from committing the act.[101] Similarly, if the EHRC thinks that a person has failed to comply, or is likely not to comply, with an undertaking under a section 23 agreement, it may apply to the County Court or Sheriff for an order that they do so, or take such other action as the Court or the Sheriff may specify.[102]

---

[93] EA, s 22(6)(c).   [94] EA, s 22(9).   [95] EA, s 22(5).   [96] EA, s 22(7)(a).
[97] EA, s 22(6).   [98] EA, s 23(1).   [99] EA, s 23(4).   [100] PIRU article, p 3.
[101] EA, s 24(1).   [102] EA, ss 24(2) and (3).

These enforcement powers are similar to those held by the former commissions, **15.80** which, again the Public Interest Research Unit report notes were startlingly underused: one only 'non-discrimination notice' was served across the three former commissions (by the CRE, on the London Borough of Hackney, in 2000) and between them the three former commissions applied for only one injunction to prevent persistent discrimination (by the EOC, against Lidl UK GmbH). The report goes on to say that even a brief search of the EAT judgments identified a considerable number of repeat discriminators, whose practices may well have been challenged by the effective uses of injunctions, had the former commissions chosen to use their powers in this regard.

The former commissions appear to have justified their lack of use of their **15.81** enforcement powers on the basis that strong enforcement action is counterproductive or otherwise damaging. Although the Government has expressed the view that it expects the occasions on which the EHRC will use these enforcement powers to be 'rare', the challenge for the EHRC will surely be to assess— perhaps through commissioned research—whether or not the stance taken by the former commissions with regard to enforcement was correct, and to determine the approaches that are most likely to be effective in reducing discrimination and to enable it to achieve its duties.[103]

(iii) Application to Restrain Unlawful Advertising and Instructions or Pressure to Discriminate

Like the former commissions, the EHRC has exclusive power[104] to bring pro- **15.82** ceedings for the various provisions in the equality enactments which outlaw discriminatory advertisements, and giving instructions to or placing pressure on another person to discriminate.[105] In employment cases, the EHRC must bring any such proceedings in the ET,[106] which will then decide whether the allegation is correct.[107] Any such applications must be made within six months of the last date on which the alleged unlawful act occurred, or with the permission of the Tribunal.[108]

The EHRC can also make applications in England and Wales to the County **15.83** Court for an injunction, or in Scotland to the Sheriff for an interdict, to restrain discriminatory advertisements or instructions or pressure to discriminate. An application can be made if a Tribunal has already concluded that this has occurred, or if the EHRC thinks it has, and if the EHRC concludes that if unrestrained the action will happen again.[109] Any such applications must be

---

[103] PIRU article, p 3.   [104] EA, s 25(2).

[105] In the employment sphere, these provisions are SDA, ss 38–40; RRA, ss 29–31; and DDA, ss 16B–C.

[106] EA, s 25(3)(a).   [107] EA, s 25(4).   [108] EA, s 26(1).   [109] EA, s 25(5).

made within five years of the last date on which the alleged unlawful act occurred, or with the permission of the Court.[110]

15.84 The former commissions also had these powers, but again the Public Interest Research Unit report notes but they never used the powers at all.[111] It also therefore remains to be seen whether the EHRC will take a different approach to the former commissions and actually use the powers they have, to seek to prevent the damage that can be done by discriminatory advertising and instructions or pressure to discriminate.

(iv) Conciliation and Legal Assistance

15.85 While the EHRC has the power to make arrangements for the provision of conciliation services for disputes relating to the equality enactments, this does not extend to the employment sphere.[112] However, ACAS conciliate employment disputes.

15.86 The EHRC may assist an individual who is or may become party to legal proceedings if the proceedings relate or may relate (wholly or partly) to a provision of the equality enactments, and the individual alleges that he has been the victim of behaviour contrary to a provision of the equality enactments.[113] This may entail the provision of legal advice, legal representation, facilities for the settlement of a dispute, and any other form of assistance.[114] There is then provision for the EHRC's legal costs to be recouped from any costs awarded to the complainant.[115]

15.87 Concerns have been expressed that, although this provision is potentially wider than that initially proposed (see above), it still weakens the rights of individuals seeking legal assistance. In particular, the EHRC, unlike the EOC and CRE, is not required to consider all such applications for assistance. The former commissions did assist a number of individuals in taking discrimination cases to the Employment Tribunal or County Court. Some were supported as far as the European Court of Justice and were instrumental in bringing about changes in the law.[116] The extent to which the EHRC will support individual litigants in discrimination cases remains unclear, but the wide wording of section 28(1) certainly permits such action.

(v) Judicial Review and Other Legal Proceedings

15.88 The EHRC has capacity to institute or intervene in legal proceedings, whether for judicial review or otherwise, if it appears that the proceedings are relevant to

---

[110] EA, s 26(3).   [111] PIRU article, p 2.   [112] EA, s 27(1)–(3).
[113] EA, s 28(1).   [114] EA, s 28(4).   [115] EA, s 29.   [116] PIRU article, p 2.

a matter in connection with which the EHRC has a function.[117] The former commissions did use their powers to intervene in certain strategically important cases—for example, the EOC intervened in *St Helens MBC v Derbyshire*,[118] the recent case alleging victimisation of several equal pay claimants—and it is likely that the EHRC will do so too.

(vi) Public Sector Duties: Assessment and Compliance

The EHRC has the power to assess the extent to which or the manner in which **15.89** a person has complied with the general duties set out under the SDA, RRA and DDA which we discussed in Chapter 3.[119] If the EHRC has concerns that a person has failed to comply with such a duty it may serve a compliance notice on that person,[120] and in default of compliance with that notice, may apply for a court order requiring such compliance.[121] In employment cases the relevant court to which such an application is made is, in England and Wales, the High Court, and in Scotland, the Court of Session.[122] The EHRC has exclusive jurisdiction to enforce the equality duties in this way.[123]

The race equality duty is the most long-standing of the equality duties, it **15.90** having come into force on 2 April 2001. The CRE has intervened in one judicial review[124] involving an alleged breach of the general duty and issued four compliance notices relating to the specific duties.[125]

As the body with sole responsibility for monitoring compliance with the equality **15.91** duties in practice, we think it essential that the EHRC takes an active role in this, by exercising the powers it has been given under sections 32 and 33.

C. Ongoing Equality Law Reform and the Single Equality Act

As will have become apparent, the current Equality Act, despite its name, did **15.92** not in fact involve a thorough overhaul of the UK's maze of discrimination provisions and the replacement of that maze with a consistent, uniform code: if anything, the Equality Act adds to its complexity.

However, in August 2004 the Government declared that a review of equality **15.93** and discrimination legislation to create a Single Equality Act would be one of the first tasks of the EHRC. The Labour Party's 2005 Manifesto reiterated a commitment to a Single Equality Act and in February 2005 the Government

---

[117] EA, s 30(1).   [118] [2007] ICR 841, HL.   [119] EA, s 31(1).
[120] EA, s 32(2).   [121] EA, s 32(8).   [122] EA, s 32(11).   [123] EA, s 32(9).
[124] *R (on the application of Diana Elias v Secretary of State for Defence and Commission for Racial Equality (Intervenor))* [2005] IRLR 788, CA.
[125] PIRU article, p 3.

announced the creation of the Equalities Review and the Discrimination Law Review.

15.94 The Equalities Review was tasked to:

- investigate the social, economic, cultural and other factors that limit or deny people the opportunity to make the best of their abilities;
- provide an understanding of the long-term and underlying causes of disadvantage that need to be addressed by public policy;
- make practical recommendations on key policy priorities for: the Government and public sector; employers and trade unions; civic society and the voluntary sector; and
- inform both the modernisation of equality legislation, towards a Single Equality Act; and the development of the new EHRC.

15.95 The final report of the Equalities Review was published on 28 February 2007.[126] The Foreword to the report concludes:

> There is no doubt that we have done better than many other countries. Britain has more advanced and effective equality legislation than most other states; our current equality Commissions . . . and the forthcoming EHRC . . . represent an institutional framework to combat discrimination that is unrivalled in Europe.
>
> But as we show in this Report, we are far from eliminating disadvantage. Inequality still scars our society. Yes, everyone has the vote, but on present trends even when the great-great-grandchildren of today's legislators at Westminster cast their votes, they will not enjoy the sight of a Parliament with equal numbers of men and women, or substantial numbers of ethnic minority MPs.
>
> Yes, progress is being made to remove barriers to participation by disabled people, but on current trends it is unlikely that the employment disadvantage they face will ever be overcome. And yes, there is a far wider recognition of the diversity of identities which enrich our society, yet bullying and hate crime against lesbians and gay men, and conflict arising from differences of religion, belief and culture still stand high on the public agenda.
>
> And despite our successes, some kinds of inequality remain at levels that can only be described as intolerable, particularly in education and employment. These are fundamental to the life chances of every person. What is more, our research shows that new economic and social trends—globalisation, for example—will either freeze those inequality gaps or widen them during this century.
>
> In short, when it comes to creating a fairer, more equal society, we have made substantial progress and continue to do so. But that progress is fragile and uneven. In too many areas we have stopped the clock; in some it is starting to turn backwards . . . .

---

[126] *Fairness and Freedom: The Final Report of the Equalities Review* (Communities and Local Government publications, 2007), <www.theequalitiesreview.org.uk>.

Chapter 5 of the report set out a ten-step plan for achieving greater equality: **15.96**

  1: Defining equality
  2: Building a consensus on equality
  3: Measuring progress towards equality
  4: Transparency about progress
  5: Targeted action on persistent inequalities
  6: A simpler legal framework
  7: More accountability for delivering equality
  8: Using public procurement and commissioning positively
  9: Enabling and supporting organisations in all sectors
  10: A more sophisticated enforcement regime.

Under point 6, the report opined that it is essential that a Single Equality Act be **15.97**
developed, that 'focuses on a simpler, more coherent framework; and facilitates
action to help groups as well as individuals'.

The Discrimination Law Review was charged with reviewing the effectiveness of **15.98**
existing equality legislation with a view to making recommendations for clearer
and more streamlined equality law. It saw the following as key to its work:

- A consideration of the fundamental principles of discrimination legislation
  and its underlying concepts and a comparative analysis of the different
  models for discrimination legislation.
- An investigation of different approaches to enforcing discrimination law so
  that a spectrum of enforcement options can be considered.
- An understanding of the evidence of the practical impact of legislation—
  both within the UK and abroad—in tackling inequality and promoting
  equality of opportunity.
- An investigation of new models for encouraging and incentivising
  compliance.
- Consideration of the opportunities for creating a simpler, fairer and more
  streamlined legislative framework in a Single Equality Act.

The Review saw its anticipated product as '. . . a series of proposals for a
coherent, modern, outcome-focused framework for this area of the law with a
view to bringing forward a Single Equality Bill'.[127]

In June 2007 the Review team published its proposals in *Discrimination Law* **15.99**
Review: A Framework for Fairness: Proposals for a Single Equality Bill for Great
Britain[128] (the 'DLR consultation paper').

The DLR consultation paper is broadly to be welcomed, for its overarching **15.100**

---

[127] <www.womenandequalityunit.gov.uk/dlr/terms_of_ref.htm>.
[128] Department for Communities and Local Government, June 2007.

recognition that the current discrimination law framework is now unworkably disparate and complex and in need of reform. The paper accepts that:

> ... [t]here is widespread agreement that everyone who needs to understand discrimination law will benefit from having it in a Single Equality Act which simplifies the law as far as this can be done ... [and] as far as possible our discrimination law should be set out in one piece of legislation (a Single Equality Act) supplemented by clear, practical, common sense guidance and codes of practice.[129]

The Government seems firm, then, in honouring its manifesto commitment to introducing a Single Equality Bill, and for that the consultation should be greeted with open arms by practitioners.

15.101 Several parts of the DLR consultation paper address the harmonisation of discrimination law outside the employment context. However, the following proposals do affect employment practitioners and are, we believe, good news in terms of improving the clarity and accessibility of the law:

- The recognition that the EHRC should have 'primary responsibility' for issuing guidance and codes of practice to support businesses and other organisations in meeting the requirements of discrimination law.[130]
- The retention of the requirement for a comparator in direct discrimination claims.[131]
- The extension of the protection against discrimination on the basis of association, and indirect discrimination, to the gender reassignment strand.[132]
- The harmonisation of the definition of indirect discrimination so that, for example, the same definition would apply to race discrimination based on colour or nationality as is used in relation to the other racial grounds.[133]
- The adoption of a single objective justification test for all indirect discrimination provisions, and for direct discrimination on grounds of age.[134]
- The removal of the requirement for a comparator in victimisation claims.[135]
- The harmonisation of the specific circumstances where discrimination is lawful (in national security cases, to preserve statutory authority etc).[136]
- The commitment to amending the definition of sexual harassment to make clear that harassment is not limited to conduct caused by the sex of the claimant.[137]
- The commitment to amending the law to make clear that an employer can be held liable for harassment if it fails to take action to protect an employee

---

[129] At pp 12 and 26.   [130] Paragraphs 1.2 and 1.5–1.8.
[131] Paragraphs 1.3(a) and 1.9–1.16.   [132] Paragraphs 1.3(c), 1.19–1.25 and 1.35.
[133] Paragraphs 1.3(i) and 1.60–1.62.   [134] Paragraphs 1.3(f) and 1.40–1.45.
[135] Paragraphs 1.3(i) and 1.60–1.62.   [136] Paragraphs 1.4(d) and 1.71–1.76.
[137] Paragraphs 1.24 and 14.6.

in the workplace where it is aware that s/he is being subjected to persistent acts of harassment on grounds of sex by a customer of client.[138]

However, we feel that the consultation paper misses several opportunities to truly harmonise the law and make it properly fair and accessible. For example: **15.102**

- The Government does not propose to extend the prohibition on perceived discrimination to transsexual people.[139] We find the rationale for this hard to accept: is it not equally as wrong for an employer to refuse to give a man a pay rise because of a mistaken belief that he was a transsexual, as it is for the employer to refuse a pay rise to a man who actually was a transsexual?

- The Government does not propose to extend the prohibition on 'association' discrimination to the age strand, and will only extend this prohibition to the disability strand if the ECJ ruling in *Coleman v Attridge Law*[140] compels it.[141] Again we struggle to see the basis for this: surely it is equally pernicious to discriminate against a woman because she has a much younger husband, or a disabled child, as to discriminate against her because of her own age, or disability?

If the intention of the Government is truly to harmonise the law so as to remove lacunae in the protection of individuals, and provide consistency and certainty for employers, then we would hope that it is persuaded during the consultation process to extend the reach of the Single Equality Bill into these two areas.

We have already considered the DLR consultation paper's proposals with regard to the public sector duties, procurement and Genuine Occupational Requirements and 'balancing measures' and discrimination litigation[142] in Chapters 3, 5, 6 and 14 respectively, and will be interested to see how these proposals pan out during the consultation process. **15.103**

D. Conclusion

Whether or not the EHRC will fulfil its promise of an integrated, coordinated approach to equality and diversity or whether it will be a self-loathing, toothless seven-headed hydra remains to be seen. Certainly there are concerns that an integrated approach to equality may prove elusive as strands compete for attention and funds: 'We'll see equalities in the Big Brother house—each trying to **15.104**

---

[138] Paragraph 14.30.   [139] Paragraph 1.24.   [140] C–303/06, ECJ.
[141] Paragraphs 1.22 and 1.25.   [142] Paragraphs 1.4 and 1.64–1.70 and Chapters 4–6.

grab a fair share of power and resources for political influence and budgets.'[143] As we have explained above there are also concerns about the enforcement powers given to the EHRC.

15.105   Ultimately the success of the EHRC is likely to depend on issues such as resources, leadership, the expertise of those who staff it, and the extent of the political will to enable it to effect the changes hoped for. The EHRC's annual budget will be £70 million, which is 43 per cent more than the combined budgets of the former commissions, although the EHRC will have responsibility for double the number of strands plus human rights.

15.106   The findings of the Equalities Review make it clear that there is still much to be done if we are to create a society that is indeed free and fair for all. As the Review concluded, crucial to the achievement of that aim is a transparent and workable legal framework enabling both individuals and organisations to be able to access the law with ease.

15.107   We believe that a truly consistent, harmonised and workable Single Equality Bill would be an important first step in setting in place such a framework, and to the realisation of the lofty ideals inherent in Martin Luther King Jr's famous dream.

---

[143] Lee Jasper, Mayor of London's Director of Equalities and Policing, *The Voice*, 11 September 2006.

The Future: In Brief

- From October 2007, the Equality and Human Rights Commission (the 'EHRC') replaced the Equal Opportunities Commission, the Commission for Racial Equality and the Disability Rights Commission.

- The EHRC has a wide range of duties and powers across all the discrimination strands and human rights issues.

- The EHRC has many of the enforcement powers held by the former Commissions. There are concerns, based on the practice of the former Commissions, about how frequently these powers will be used, and about whether these powers are the most effective means of securing real equality and diversity.

- The EHRC was established by the Equality Act 2006. This also introduced into legislation for the first time the concepts of 'diversity', 'outcomes' and 'indicators'.

- The EHRC is given an important new power to promote understanding of the importance of good relations between different 'groups' which means a class of persons defined by reference to one or two common attributes such as 'gay and Muslim' or 'young and disabled'.

- In 2007 the Equalities Review reported that there remains widespread inequality in Britain in a range of spheres. The Review concluded that a clearer and more accessible legal framework is essential in trying to remedy this inequality.

- The Discrimination Law Review was charged with carrying out a fundamental overhaul of British discrimination law. In June 2007 it published its proposals for a Single Equality Bill, as promised in the 2005 Labour Party manifesto, which it is hoped will ultimately replace the current patchwork of 'strand-specific' legislation.

INDEX

435